T0355496

Internationalizing
"International Communication"

Joseph Turow

SERIES EDITOR

Broadcasting, Voice, and Accountability: A Public Interest
Approach to Policy, Law, and Regulation
*Steve Buckley, Kreszentia Duer, Toby Mendel, and Seán Ó Siochrú,
with Monroe E. Price and Marc Raboy*

Owning the Olympics: Narratives of the New China
Monroe E. Price and Daniel Dayan, editors

The Hyperlinked Society: Questioning Connections in the Digital Age
Joseph Turow and Lokman Tsui, editors

When Media Are New: Understanding the Dynamics of
New Media Adoption and Use
John Carey and Martin C. J. Elton

Making News at *The New York Times*
Nikki Usher

The Media Welfare State: Nordic Media in the Digital Era
Trine Syvertsen, Gunn Enli, Ole J. Mjøs, and Hallvard Moe

Internationalizing "International Communication"
Chin-Chuan Lee, editor

Imagining the Global: Transnational Media and
Popular Culture Beyond East and West
Fabienne Darling-Wolf

DIGITALCULTUREBOOKS, an imprint of the University of Michigan Press,
is dedicated to publishing work in new media studies and the emerging
field of digital humanities.

Internationalizing "International Communication"

CHIN-CHUAN LEE, EDITOR

UNIVERSITY OF MICHIGAN PRESS · ANN ARBOR

Published in the United States of America by the
University of Michigan Press
Printed and bound by CPI Group (UK) Ltd, Croydon, CR0 4YY

2018 2017 2016 2015   4 3 2 1

A CIP catalog record for this book is available from the British Library.

DOI: ttp://dx.doi.org/10.3998/nmw.12748916.0001.001

Library of Congress Cataloging-in-Publication Data

Internationalizing "international communication" / Chin-Chuan Lee, editor.
      pages cm. — (The new media world)
        Includes bibliographical references and index.
      ISBN 978-0-472-07244-6 (hardcover : alk. paper) — ISBN 978-0-472-
05244-8 (pbk. : alk. paper) — ISBN 978-0-472-12078-9 (ebook)
        1. Communication, International. I. Li, Jinquan,
1946– editor.
      P96.I5I55   2014
      302.2—dc23
                                                        2014024947

Contents

1. International Communication Research:
   Critical Reflections and a New Point of Departure   1
   Chin-Chuan Lee

2. Window Shopping: On Internationalizing
   "International Communication"   29
   Elihu Katz

3. Beyond Lazarsfeld: International Communication
   Research and Its Production of Knowledge   41
   Tsan-Kuo Chang

4. Beyond Modernization and the Four Theories
   of the Press   66
   Jan Servaes

5. Professional Models in Journalism: Between
   Homogenization and Diversity   90
   Paolo Mancini

6. Conditions of Capital: Global Media in Local Contexts   109
   Michael Curtin

7. The Enduring Strength of Hollywood:
   The "Imperial Adventure" Genre and *Avatar*   134
   Jaap van Ginneken

8. Resurrecting the Imperial Dimension
   in International Communication   156
   Colin Sparks

9. De-Westernization and Cosmopolitan Media Studies 178
   Silvio Waisbord

10. Local Experiences, Cosmopolitan Theories:
    On Cultural Relevance in International
    Communication Research   201
    Chin-Chuan Lee

11. Theorizing Media Production as a
    Quasi-Autonomous Field: A Reassessment of
    China News Studies   225
    Judy Polumbaum

12. Translation, Communication, and
    East-West Understanding   244
    Zhang Longxi

13. Public Spheres, Fields, Networks: Western
    Concepts for a De-Westernizing World?   258
    Rodney Benson

14. Cosmopolitanism and International Communication:
    Understanding Civil Society Actors   281
    Peter Dahlgren

15. Postcolonial Visual Culture: Arguments from India 302
    Arvind Rajagopal

    Contributors   319

    Index   325

CHAPTER ONE

International Communication Research

Critical Reflections and a New Point of Departure

Chin-Chuan Lee

Various attempts (Curran & Park, 2000; Thussu, 2009; Wang, 2011) have been made in recent years to "de-Westernize" or "internationalize" media studies. What justifies another volume seeking to "internationalize" what is purported to be the most "internationalized" subfield in the whole gamut of media and communication studies? In short, it is because international communication as a field of inquiry actually is not very "internationalized." But why should we fix our horizon on "international" instead of, say, "intercultural" communication, or the even trendier "global" communication? First, it should be acknowledged that nation-states remain central to any theories and practice of the contemporary world order, and that international communication is always (but not completely) intermixed with intercultural communication. Second, international processes obviously are increasingly globalized. However, we wish to emphasize a double-bind fact: if democracy is to survive in the post-communist world, as Alain Touraine (1997) maintains, it must "somehow protect the power of the nation-state at the same time as it limits that power," for only the state "has sufficient means to counterbalance the global corporate wielders of money and information."

Perusing three major handbooks as signposts immediately discloses that international communication has led a relatively marginal existence in the pantheon of media and communication studies. The more generous treatment was given in what was legitimately claimed to be the most comprehensive anthology, *Handbook of Communication* (1973), which ran over 1,000 pages under the eminent editorship of Ithiel de sola Pool and Wilbur Schramm. Six out of 31 chapters (approximately one-fifth), all written by political scientists, addressed in whole or in part selected issues of international communication. All the topics nonetheless concentrated on vital Cold War concerns of the United States: international propaganda, Third World modernization, communication systems in primitive societies, and Communist/totalitarian communication systems. There was a sequel after a lapse of 14 years, the *Handbook of Communication Science*, edited by Charles Berger and Steven Chaffee (1987). Amid its self-congratulatory claim to the self-sufficient status of "communication science," this volume turned cripplingly inward-looking. Showing little welcoming gesture to social scientists from other sister disciplines, it devoted only one chapter to cross-cultural comparisons, and none to substantive issues of international communication. An updated *Handbook of Communication Science*, edited by Berger, Roloff, and Roskos-Ewaldsen (2010), devoted only one token chapter out of 29 to "intercultural communication." What comes to mind is local TV news practice in the United States of covering "the world in a minute."

Surely international matters deserve more time, space, and concerted attention. Why have they been so neglected in our field? Asserting the hard-nosed presumption that "science" is of universal applicability, those defining the field through these influential anthologies did not seem to believe that cross-cultural, national, or systemic differences should matter. The world amounted, ontologically and epistemologically, to America writ large. This prevailing stream of (un)consciousness was widely shared among most members of the U.S. social science community for decades, following on Lerner's conviction (1958) that the entire developing world was emulating the American model in a linear progression to modernization. Moreover, well into the 1980s, even as scholars of communication sought to define their realm as one of overweening importance, the field's vision seemed to be narrowing. Even a cursory glance at the table of contents of the three defining volumes shows an inexorable move toward the process of what Geertz (1963) calls "involution," characterized by greater self-absorption, isolationism, internal development, and parochialism— and this in spite of the vast and rapid march of globalizing processes "out there." Under the pretense of science (more aptly, scientism), the succeeding generations of editors have embraced a far narrower horizon of global landscape than their mentors.

At long last, however, the critique of Cold War perspectives that accompanied political ferment of the 1960s and 1970s, the progress of critical cultural approaches to inquiry in the 1980s and 1990s, and above all the growing participation of international scholars in international communication inquiry have generated a search for new directions. We hope this book can contribute to this movement.

Why Internationalizing "International Communication"?

In this introductory chapter I shall refer to the "West" as a generic term to make first-stroke comparisons with the "non-West," bearing in mind that the West is larger than the United States and both "the West" and "the non-West" are internally full of notable variations and conflicts.[1] In other words, we are at this point more interested in understanding the "between variances" than the "within variances." Yet media studies remain, to borrow from Jeremy Tunstall (1977), largely "American" or Anglo-American, and the erosion of this dominance has been glacial. As a field of inquiry born out of the U.S. context of the 1950s, international communication still addresses the world largely through the prism of middle-class America, and the narrow agenda that prevailed for so long—focusing on Cold War propaganda, Third World development, political campaigns, and consumer persuasion—continues to exert its influence through the topics, methods, questions, and very vocabularies of our studies. As Colin Sparks sums up in his chapter, "Lasswell, Lippmann and Bernays in the first generation, and Lerner and Schramm in the second, were all deeply concerned with the ways in which states used the resources of propaganda both to secure internal consent and to undermine the support available to their enemies."

If we were to follow C. Wright Mills's (1959) call for the "sociological imagination," we should stand firm to reject any attempts to balkanize media studies into domestic and international turfs, because in principle all significant questions should be situated in the cross-nexus of comparative (world) and temporal (historical) contexts. But that is not how the academic division of labor or the bureaucratic ethos usually operate. In reality, international communication has been taken as a conceptual extension or empirical application of U.S. communication. Furthermore, it has provided territory for scholarly colonization: as early as six decades ago, Lazarsfeld (1952–53) foresaw that "the domestic area will not have many opportunities" in the years to come and postulated that international research could be a fertile land to "open up new and exciting subjects for investigation."

Rather than taking advantage of the widened window of opportunity to produce "local knowledge" (Geertz, 1983) of general relevance and also in a comparative light, international communication more often than not has acted as an overseas testing station of U.S. or, secondarily, European worldviews.

Moreover, aside from fixating on a narrow range of conceptual problems, mainstream scholarship in our field has long promoted a positivistic methodology that in its extreme form has especially detrimental implications for international communication studies. Hard-core positivists assume that specificities can and should be subsumed into generality, but they seem comfortable with the fact that the supposed "generality" tends to be grounded in a specific U.S. cultural soil or European setting. The "West" is being generalized if not universalized, while the "exceptions" and outliers are explained away and cross-cultural meanings homogenized to the extent of defying the rigor of comparative logic. For many, systemic differences do not seem to be pertinent in the way of impinging on conceptualization or, for that matter, on the relationships between concepts and their empirical referents (Smelser, 1976). Nor is there room for any serious discourse about the crossing of cultural boundaries.

Worse yet, much of the non-West has been socialized to adopt truncated versions of Pax Americana's notion of international communication. U.S.-cum-international communication is taken for granted by way of the hegemonic process, with an army of non-Western disciples eagerly promoting, embracing, and reproducing the generalized model and wisdom from their Western tutors. The popularity of "diffusion of innovation" (Rogers, 2003), which comprised streams of overseas projects trying to copy or replicate models born in the specific settings of Iowa, Ohio, or New York, was celebrated as a seminal cross-cultural achievement.

How much has the situation been improved? Invited just recently to offer comments on papers presented by Asian PhD students at a research symposium, I asked the audience to judge whether we were witnessing a colored, colonized, Asian map of U.S. research trajectories. "Where is, for example, Korea—or Singapore—in scripting the scholarly agendas?" I asked. "Is there a real place to account for cultural flow and interaction?" Stunned to hear my remarks, most students did not seem to possess the kind of cultural awareness needed to feel anything was wrong with lifting a page from the U.S. research directory, asking the same set of technical (even trivial) questions, adopting the same conceptual frameworks, and imitating the same research techniques down to minute details. What could be faulted, they must have wondered, given that their vaunted display of sophisticated skills was, after all, coached by advanced Western authorities? And this is hardly an isolated encounter.

There is no reason to reject a concept or theory out of hand simply on account of its cultural origin, but it surely is unwise to buy into any theory without reflecting on its built-in premises and limitations. It is one thing to import or apply certain Western models as a critical choice because some problems are appropriate for more generalized lenses. It is quite another to unquestioningly accept a whole set of specific worldviews, problematics, and core agendas to serve a field boldly called "*international* communication." At stake is the "subject position" of academic and cultural inquirers: Who get to ask what kind of questions? Why shouldn't we treasure the right to ask original questions that are most important to us instead of submitting indigenous data or evidence only to further fuel the Western-cum-universal theories? This is a case of academic hegemony par excellence that naturalizes the process of ideological transfer and practical emulation. Hegemony in the Gramscian sense is never equal or simply coerced, but based in part on acts of mutual consent and willing collaboration between the intellectual patron and client, resulting in ideological conditioning in such a way that the fact of domination is unrecognized, accepted, or taken for granted. Hegemony rules unabated unless its fundamental and often hidden assumptions are openly exposed and questioned.

If the trajectory is depressing, the past also yields lessons that can further our attempts to promote wiser, more enlightened, and more cosmopolitan approaches to scholarship. We believe that the imperative of academic autonomy must be founded on active, open, and mutually respectful interaction with cultural currents of thought and interests from other traditions. Symbolizing a critical moment of cultural awakening, this volume intends to do just that and, further, to present alternative and critical discourses about the study of international communication. It is time to develop a more complex and integrated framework of multiculturalism and globalism as a new point of departure. All our contributors have long been immersed in rich intercultural or diasporic experiences, which Stuart Hall depicts as being "familiar strangers" between cultures who "know both places intimately" but are "not wholly of either place" (Chen, 1996, p. 490). Represented in this volume are a group of distinguished scholars from different generations and from an array of diverse cultural backgrounds—Argentinian, Italian, Dutch, American, British, Swedish, Belgian, Israeli, Indian, and Chinese—who have either received advanced training in the

West or affiliated with major Western universities during various periods of their careers. Such "in-between" cross-cultural experiences form an essential part of intellectual biography and capital for them to traverse multiple borders and to dialectically negotiate and synthesize the insider's perspectives with the outsider's perspectives (Merton, 1972), thereby enabling them to emerge from critical reflections with refreshing views on where the field has come from and whither it goes.

Origin and Paradigm Shift

From the outset, international communication research has been affiliated with power and the nation-state, and most particularly with U.S. foreign policy interests and objectives. Setting the tone was Harold Lasswell (1927) in an early work on propaganda technique during World War I. Some 15 years later, social scientists were called on to advise the Office of War Information of the U.S. government in fighting Nazi propaganda during World War II, a war that paved the way for the rise of the United States to world hegemony. No sooner had the world war ended than the Cold War ensued, lasting for half a century. In this ideologically polarized world, in which the United States perceived itself as "a righter of wrongs around the world, in pursuit of tyranny, in defense of freedom no matter the place or cost" (Said, 1993, p. 5), propaganda concerns loomed ever larger.

In retrospect, however, the neo-imperial impetus driving U.S. communication studies was not the only dynamic. The field actually was developing in different institutional settings for different purposes, taking two parallel yet rather separate trajectories. One stream of academic pedigree could be traced back to the University of Chicago in the 1930s and 1940s, where urban sociologists (such as Robert Park and Herbert Blumer) under the influence of pragmatism (John Dewey) and symbolic interactionism (George Herbert Mead) pursued their fascination with the integrative role of the media in the building of community amid large-scale social transformation produced by industrialization, urbanization, and immigration. The preeminence of Chicago sociology in U.S. studies of mass communication was replaced in the 1950s by the structural-functionalist school of sociology and social psychology led by Robert K. Merton and Paul Lazarsfeld at Columbia University. At this juncture, domestic communication research came to acquire another character, tenet, and direction as the Columbia researchers turned their primary attention to investigating how the media instrumentally altered voter intention or consumer behavior. Overall they were collectively frustrated to discover, time and again, that the media did not live up to the theorized expectation of swaying the public's attitudes and behaviors, but only served to reinforce their existing predispositions. As a result, Bernard Berelson (1959), a member of the Columbia group, was on the verge of announcing a funeral for communication research. The transition from Chicago's to Columbia's emphasis (Czitrom, 1982, pp. 91–146; Hardt, 1992, pp. 31–122) has far-reaching implications that provide a domestic counterpoint to the international focus of this essay.

In contrast, coming from a different set of political and intellectual concerns, post–World War II international communication research came to revolve around a circle of MIT political sociologists who were decidedly cold warriors: Ithiel de sola Pool, Daniel Lerner, and Lucian W. Pye. When Columbia researchers lamented, on the *domestic* front, the media's "null effects" in the 1960s, the MIT scholars did just the opposite: they enthusiastically promoted, albeit abroad, an image of omnipotent media capable of shaping *international* propaganda and stimulating Third World development. As an interesting chapter in the sociology of knowledge, how do we account for these diametrically opposing views of media power between the Columbia and MIT schools of thought? Was the discrepancy caused by different ecological conditions of propaganda—for example, what Lazarsfeld and Merton (1971) referred to as monopolization, canalization, and supplementation of mass communication—at home and abroad? To what extent did this gap arise from differing notions of media power? The Columbia group was intent on capturing the manifest, micro-level attitude and behavior change exerted by the media on individuals or groups in the *short* run. Conversely, the MIT group displayed supreme confidence in advocating the cumulative role of the media in cultivating macro-level ideological consciousness and triggering social transformation in the *long* haul. Still, how can Columbia's narrowly conceived empirical findings in the U.S. setting be reconciled with MIT's broadly speculative advocacy in the thick of the Cold War?

The MIT-based international communication research was primarily informed by modernization theory, as conceived by American social scientists with the active encouragement of the U.S. government. Such an approach gained popularity alongside the post-war ascendancy of American political, military, and commercial expansion in the world (Tipps, 1973). Initiated at Columbia and finished at MIT, Lerner's *The Passing of Traditional Society* (1958) was generally considered the key baseline work in the area of international development communication. Lerner insisted that

Western countries were simply holding up a mirror for what the developing world aspired to become on the road to modernization, setting out the vision of the universal relevance of Western experiences. Pye (1963) followed suit, editing an important volume on the role of communication in facilitating political development, while Pool (1973) and his students invested enormous energy in the study of the Communist media systems of China and the Soviet Union. For want of quality empirical studies in the international realm, Wilbur Schramm (1964) started with Lerner's thesis and extrapolated from the Columbia group's hodge-podge findings to offer policy advice to an international audience; his UNESCO-sponsored *Mass Media and National Development* was greeted by many Third World planners as something of a development "bible."

Through the 1960s and 1970s, from Stanford and later the East-West Center, Schramm fostered cross-institutional collaboration between two coasts across the continent, working closely with MIT's Lerner, Pye, and Pool on "development communication" (Pye, 1963; Lerner & Schramm, 1967; Pool & Schramm, 1973; Schramm & Lerner, 1976). As the next generation of scholars began to elaborate on modernization theory, one variant that emerged preeminent was diffusion of innovations. Synthesizing the tradition of news diffusion studies with their origin in New York and that of agricultural diffusion studies from the farm belt of Iowa, Rogers (2003) elevated the diffusion model to international status by transplanting it to various overseas outposts. In the field of international communication, this thesis provoked by far the largest number of empirical studies abroad in replication of its U.S. origins. Looking back, it may be said that modernization theory (especially the versions of Lerner, Schramm, and Rogers) owed its popularity during the heyday of East-West conflict in part to the illusory charm it offered the elite in poor Third World countries—the promise of simplistic solutions to tough problems. In his chapter Jan Servaes, among others, has criticized modernization theory for (a) a lack of empirical support; (b) behavioristic and positivistic biases; (c) conceptual inadequacy; (d) insensitivity to social context; (e) Western centrism; and (f) being ahistorical. All these flaws, so glaringly evident with the benefit of hindsight, went overlooked at the time.

As the East-West conflict mixed uneasily with emerging South-North tensions in the 1970s, Latin Americanists proposed various strains of "dependency" perspectives as a formidable challenge to the modernization formula. In a thoughtful review essay, Palma (1978) summarizes and compares three main perspectives from this movement: (a) the theory of "development of underdevelopment" (A. G. Frank); (b) "growth without development" (O. Sunkel); and (c) "dependent development" (F. H. Cardoso). With the East-West conflict unabated, the United States continued to spread the gospel of modernization to the Third World as a main strategy to deter Communism. Meanwhile, on the South-North dimension, the United States found itself blamed and held responsible by poor nations for the unequal control and distribution of the world's economic and information resources. The resulting antagonism was in large part what prompted the United States to withdraw from UNESCO in 1984 (an absence lasting until 2003); President Ronald Reagan had no stomach or patience for the heated "new international information and communication order" debate in which the United States was chief villain.

Of the three perspectives, "growth without development" proved of minor importance, but the implications of theoretical and methodological divergences between "development of underdevelopment" and "dependent development" were most profound. Methodologically, Frank as a political economist proposed a formal *theory* of underdevelopment, which was almost a mirror image of modernization theory it sought to debunk. Cardoso, a Weberian historical sociologist who years later became president of Brazil, rejected formalized theory and instead preferred to use dependency as a *methodology* to account historically for the open-ended and concrete situations of underdevelopment—indeed, Cardoso (1977) criticized U.S. scholars for consuming dependency as a formal theory in Frank's positivistic terms.

Frank theorized that Latin America was incorporated into the international capitalist system, in which the world center through *external* conditioning of local economies created entrenched conditions of underdevelopment for the periphery. Rejecting Frank's exclusive attention on external conditions, Cardoso argued that it was important to grasp "the political alliances, the ideologies, and the movement of structures within the dependent countries" and to analyze how these forces "internalized" the external. He concluded that at least some countries (such as Brazil) in the semi-periphery were able to develop their economies concurrent with continued dependence on the international capitalist structure.

The implications surely are worth revisiting in the age of globalization; yet the influence of dependency perspectives on international communication research has been sparse and uneven. Herbert I. Schiller (1976) was perhaps the best-known critic of cultural imperialism to have drawn, albeit rather cursorily, on Frank's theory of underdevelopment as well as on Immanuel Wallerstein's world-system theory. Otherwise, the theoretical alliance and intellectual flow between radical U.S./European political economists with their Third World (in this case, Latin American) counterparts remained weak and minimal. Amid the almost total absence of analysis written in English on "dependent development" of media and culture, Salinas and Paldan (1979) provided a notable exception. Even among members of the like-minded critical Marxist camp, First World and Third World scholars were divided by a veritable gulf in interests, concerns, and orientations. The divide had obvious material underpinnings, of course: when radical British scholars were occupied with the erosion of the "public sphere" (including public service broadcasting) caused by Thatcherism, Latin American scholars had to grapple with pressing issues of economic survival and structural dependence. It is rather startling that Raymond Williams's brilliant work on Marxist cultural theory and analysis (Williams, 1977) was oriented primarily toward the history and geography of social formation in Britain without connecting explicitly to the wider historical and international context of imperialism. It took someone like Edward Said (1993) to fill this significant void, paving the foundation for the postcolonial work that should form a point of departure for much of the Third World analysis. Stuart Hall, another main figure of British cultural studies, also waited until rather late in his career to start addressing the identity issues related to the race and ethnicity of his own Jamaican immigrant background (Chen, 1996).

In his chapter for this volume, Tsan-Kuo Chang performs an interesting frequency count of keyword combinations in the title of journal articles over time, providing a rough index of major "paradigms" and paradigm change. Such keywords as "modernization," "imperialism" and "dependency" came into significant use in the 1970s. In the 1980s, two significant clusters appeared: imperialism/dependency and modernization/dependency. What these clusters mean is murky, but an educated guess might point to two camps: while the radical perspective linked imperialism to dependency, the pluralist perspective pitted modernization against dependency. Not until the 1990s did "globalization" come into vogue. By the 1990s, coinciding with the end of the Cold War and the rise of neoliberal ideology and rhetoric of a new world order, "globalization" rapidly rose in prominence, with "dependency" sinking to relative obscurity in academic discourses. Moreover, the close affinity of "globalization" with "modernization" suggests the almost unchecked ascendancy of neoliberalism in the post–Cold War milieu. Peter Dahlgren succinctly notes in his chapter that the theoretical traditions of globalization (from social sciences) and post-colonialism (from the humanities) have had relatively little encounter with each other, when in fact they should be very much entwined.

In reconstructing the neoliberal world order after the conclusion of the Cold War, Said (1993, p. xvii) remarks that the United States has displayed "its redolent self-congratulation, unconcealed triumphalism, and its grave proclamation of responsibility." Meanwhile, culture, political values and foreign policies have been reframed euphemistically in terms of "soft power" (Nye, 1990, 2004)—that is, ostensibly no longer dependent on the hard power of economic prowess and military might. Celebrants canonize liberalism as having prevailed over other competing systems and ideologies, ushering in a new era euphorically characterized as "the end of history" (Fukuyama, 1992). At the same time, however, the United States is urged to bolster its "soft power" in order to win the war of public diplomacy (Nye, 2008) and to prevail in the supposed "clash of civilizations" (Huntington, 1993). It seems that earlier proponents of modernization theory such as Huntington have not really changed their position, despite the veneer of seemingly different sets of rhetoric. Like the modernization project, the current soft power and "civilizing" missions are still geared toward advancing the vital interests of Washington. The wars in Iraq and Afghanistan, as they contrarily sapped vital resources from an ailing economy, have flown in the face of naïve and wishful predictions about the United States reaping a "peace dividend."

Chang's chapter begs a big question: What accounts for the contexts in which such shifts in keyword combinations take place? Chang is no fan of "cultural imperialism" and attributes its long life cycle to "group think." He favors Castell's concepts of "network society" and "network state," but as Benson discusses in his chapter, whether this optimistic version of technological determinism can be taken at face value is an open question. It is about time: vigorous debates on globalization and anti-globalization discourses have occurred in other social science disciplines (Held & Mc-Grew, 2007), but technological dazzle evidently is mesmerizing enough to significantly mute such voices in the field of international communication. After all, "network society" does not take anything away from the realities of global domination.

What counting these terms reminds us is that academic fads come and go, moving in tandem with the reigning political environment. No one is arguing for keeping a vulgar theory of cultural imperialism, but the concept still deserves intellectual currency as long as global domination persists. The chapter by Colin Sparks is a clarion call to resurrect the relevance of cultural imperialism as an explanatory framework. Not that competing discourses will die away; but the field needs juxtaposition, new arguments, and energetic debates. As Alfred Whitehead (1925) once said, "The clash of doctrines is not a disaster, it is an opportunity."

Hegemony

In starting his project on the intellectual history of the twentieth century, Peter Watson (2001) sought input from scholarly specialists on the intellectual thought of the non-Western world. Much to his amazement, almost all of them—experts on the history and cultures of India, China, Japan, South and Central Africa, and the Arab world—concurred that during the century nothing matching the achievements of the Western world had come out of non-Western contexts. Since the nineteenth century, all these old civilizations had fallen short in their varied and rushed attempts to respond to the challenges and ramifications of Western cultural imperialism, leaving a legacy of "cultural shock" that still lingers.

During the latter half of the nineteenth century, China declined from what had been a closed yet seemingly self-sufficient and proud empire to semi-colonial status and humiliation at the hands of Western and Japanese colonial powers. Early modernists at the outset of the twentieth century (such as Yan Fu, Zhang Binglin, and Liu Shipei), shocked into searching for Western prescriptions, thought they had found answers in Charles Darwin, Thomas Huxley, and Herbert Spencer. (It was said that China's intellectual elite revered Western scholars as Gods and their treatises as sacred—an exaggerated portrayal but symbolic of the cultural mind-set of the era.) With China's indigenous identity shattered, these seekers came to accept the claim that all civilizations must obey the "scientific" iron law of social evolutionism, in which only the fittest could survive at each stage along a trajectory of linear development. Liu Shipei (1884–1919), the first to translate the *Communist Manifesto* into Chinese, stands out as a vivid example of this Westernized worldview: he declared that Western countries, already at the "modern" stage, thus enjoyed stability, whereas China was still loitering in the "pre-modern" stage with its precarious cycles of chaos. Chinese intellectuals seeking to reinterpret Chinese canonical texts in light of Western body of knowledge firmly believed that China was lagging behind the West by an entire historical chapter.

With several notable exceptions, the next generation of modernists—

many of whom had been educated in the West—took an equally if not more radical approach toward their traditional Chinese heritage. The intellectual cohort of the 1920s acquired a more intimate and nuanced understanding of the West and shifted the targets of admiration to such contemporary figures as John Dewey, Bertrand Russell, and Harold Laski, along with the late Karl Marx, whose translated texts were beginning to circulate in China. The emblematic figure of anti-traditional enlightenment, Lu Xun, advised young people to read nothing but Western books, holding that Chinese books were so out of touch with reality as to be incapacitating. The liberal intellectual Hu Shi was equally anti-traditional, but returning from the United States armed with Dewey's "scientific method," he energized a short-lived but vigorous revolution in the study of Chinese classics. Many others who had internalized the ethos, paradigms, and exemplars of Western scholarship likewise reoriented their studies of China's history, geography, literature, and society with remarkable accomplishments. In this period, intellectuals who firmly rooted their interests in the fertile ground of indigenous texts and experiences but systematically dissected their subjects with the theoretical and methodological advances adapted from the West went a long way toward integrating and enriching both cultural traditions. It is not surprising that many "masterpieces" produced during that transitory golden age (1920s–1940s) are being reissued with a vengeance, to widespread accolades from today's Chinese academic community.

The contours of this brief intellectual history (see Yu, 2007, pp. 272–91) have notable implications. First, China's loss of self-confidence in the face of Western cultural assaults has been keenly felt, but is by no means unique or exceptional. Otherwise, Watson (2001) would have gladly given a pride of place to what were generally regarded as seminal intellectual contributions from Indian, Japanese, Islamic or African (i.e., except Chinese) civilizations. Western hegemony is undeniably a universal fact. Second, Western cultural supremacy has permeated every field of modern scholarship, with the active collaboration of local elites in Third World countries. Although this influence may provoke little epistemological concern in the natural sciences, it is obvious cause for consternation in the humanities and social sciences, where cultural premises and values are deemed of cardinal import. For a young and immature field of study called international communication, what this means is that scholars everywhere must learn *from* the West, then unlearn, and proceed to relearn *with* the West. Most vital of all, we must seek feasible ways to cross cultural borders and achieve truly multicultural interaction. We need to develop agendas for expanded South-North and South-South dialogue with such aims in mind.

At the same time, scholars hoping to make these breakthroughs are still encumbered with social Darwinist postulates about the required "stages" through which each civilization must pass. This perspective finds its latter-day incarnations in modernization theory and also in Marxist doctrine— both carriers of old ideas in different guises. According to modernization theory, the media played a critical role in stimulating empathy to facilitate the passing of "traditional" society through the "transitional" phase to attain the "modern" threshold (Lerner, 1958). Marxist dogma about "stages" of history has not plagued our field simply because Western Marxists are not particularly interested in media, but it certainly frustrated several generations of Chinese academics in other fields; into the 1970s, historians strapped into ideological straitjackets still were trying futilely to determine when feudal and capitalist "stages" had begun and ended so as to substantiate the official claim that new China had surpassed all other earlier stages to enter the more advanced stage of socialism. Even worse than the impediments to understanding, of course, was the great damage to lives and careers wreaked by this academic charade.

Finding a New Point of Departure

Modernization theory is a prime example of the theoretical and methodological failings of trying to mimic the natural sciences in the social sciences. Now discredited but not abandoned, the assumptions of modernization theory are still widespread in academic literature; Inglehart and his associates (Inglehart and Welzel, 2005; Norris and Inglehart, 2009), for example, represent major recent attempts at reviving modernization theory in "globalized" terms. The quest to establish universally valid "laws" of human society with little regard for cultural values and variations thankfully, however, seems to be running out of steam. The development of microhistory, the interest in "local knowledge" among anthropologists (following Geertz, 1983), and the challenges of epistemological reflexivity posed by continental European thought (such as phenomenology and hermeneutics) are all ways of reckoning, if belatedly, with the important dimensions of empathetic understanding and subjective consciousness in the study of humanity. By now it seems obvious that no culture or theory is one size that fits all. At the same time, the "local" cannot be parochial; rather, it is dialectically interactive with the "global." The recognition that few places are culturally homogeneous anymore and that everyone must contend with the emerging motifs of multi-ethnic and multi-cultural complexities has reached to the very heights of Western academia itself. In a matter of decades, for instance, the movement to incorporate non-Western and non-white authors into the U.S. university canon has been spearheaded by Stanford University and the Ivy League.

In this volume, concern with the local and global and their interrelationship extends beyond geography to theory, method, and epistemology. Contributors are seeking new approaches to "cosmopolitan theories"—by which we mean a constellation or system of interlinking concepts that, through continuous cycles of creative synthesis from global perspectives, is provisionally accepted as having robust explanatory power. Such theories are neither fixed nor a priori Western; rather, they are open to constant contestation and dynamic change. Scholars of international communication need the cultural confidence and epistemological autonomy to make their mark on global or cosmopolitan theory, which necessarily will entail borrowing, recasting, or reconceptualizing Western theories—the more the better, whatever help us elucidate and analyze rich local experiences and connect them to broader processes, whatever broaden our horizons and expand our repertoire, as long as we are not beholden to any purported final arbiter of universal truth. And in the event no suitable theories are available, we are obliged or challenged to create new ones.

As I point out later in this volume, connecting the local with the global does not give us license to abuse local experiences to *fit* or validate global theories; instead, we should use "global" theories to help *illuminate* local experiences. My chapter argues for adopting an approach that commences with reflecting on the internal logic and context of local experiences, gradually moving up the ladder of abstraction, and meeting dynamically with what are considered suitable theories in the larger globalized contexts. Thus, local experiences eventually may be endowed with broader and general significance.

Other contributors complement this project by combining thoughtful conceptual work with keen attention to specifics. As Luckmann (1978) argues, the logic of science *is* the logic of social science, but the explanatory aims are different: the structure of everyday life and the meanings of human action have to be interpreted reflexively and intersubjectively. It is also important to pay attention to different textures of the agency-structure interaction in different contexts: for example, when Western scholars seek to debunk the ideology of news professionalism as upholding the status quo, this ideology may empower individual journalists in China and other authoritarian countries to make a difference (Lee, 2001).

In this spirit, drawing on empirical evidence from recent Chinese media studies, Judy Polumbaum tries in her chapter to borrow Anthony Giddens's theory of structuration as a starting point for conducting grounded research on the interaction between human agency and social structure. Moreover, she promotes Pierre Bourdieu's "field" of production as a framework to look at how external forces may contribute to expanding or circumscribing the elastic range of possibilities, or how actors may fortify established interests, promote emerging social formation, or yield new creativities. For her, the primary goal of research is to gain rich insights into how the world really works rather than to test propositions in a positivistic manner of causal attribution.

Silvio Waisbord begins by criticizing "area studies" for failing to contribute to a common set of questions and unifying theories in international communication. Let it be recalled that in the immediate wake of the Cold War, the idea of terminating area studies and absorbing them into mainstream disciplines of the humanities and social sciences gained some currency; but alarm over the U.S. shortage of area specialists on al Qaeda and Afghanistan during the "war on terror" gave area studies new academic and institutional life. To me, it might make more sense to promote "*area-based* studies" that combine culturally contextualized area knowledge with theoretically informed pursuits. Waisbord advocates "cosmopolitan scholarship" characterized by "sensitivity to comparative and global questions and approaches and engagement in globalized debates." To this end, he recommends three strategies: (a) analyzing neglected areas in order to rethink arguments and broaden analytical horizons; (b) conducting comparative research so as to provide more solid and nuanced theoretical conclusions; and (c) examining transborder flows and global questions. For each of the three strategies he also cites thought-provoking research topics.

Peter Dahlgren proposes a broadened normative theory of "civic cosmopolitanism" to advance globalized democratic politics and to anchor the analysis of international communication. Dahlgren argues that cosmopolitanism is a necessary element for civic agency in the modern globalized world, and the character of the media is a precondition for such agency because without the media the ideal of democracy would not have been spread so far and so deep. He urges moving the cosmopolitan moral stance into concrete political praxis, for cosmopolitan citizenship has a responsibility to engage with global others. While acknowledging a universalistic core in globalized democratic politics, we should be sensitive to different modes of democratic praxis due to contingencies of circumstance. Dahlgren concludes: "Democratic civic agency needs to incorporate the cosmopolitan perspective and pay more attention to morality as an analytic dimension for understanding political agency as an expression of subjectivity. Cosmopolitanism needs to analytically further engage with the media, and look beyond moral categories to situated political practices." How to translate this reflective piece of normative theory into empirical projects of sorts will be a big challenge.

Rodney Benson offers a critical comparative analysis of three European-influenced master terms—public sphere (Jürgen Habermas), field (Bourdieu), and network (Manuel Castells, Bruno Latour)—and their implications for research in transnational or non-Western contexts. Given his complex arguments, I can only highlight three salient points here. First, as Benson argues, "As one moves from Habermas/Peters and Bourdieu on the one hand to Castells and especially Latour on the other hand the ontological accounts become more fluid, the epistemological accounts (to the extent they are elaborated) become more relativist, and the politics become more open-ended." Second, the public sphere project is most useful for internet democracy and in need of critical interrogation, but it draws a line in the sand against authoritarian projects. Field theory holds some promise for investigating the processes of identity formation, the unequal distribution of resources, and the importance of symbolic and economic power. Castells retains an interest in power and democratic politics but his theory is too flexible and ahistorical, whereas Latour's micro-empirical approach refuses the big picture. Third, it would nonetheless be fruitful to draw upon and engage with any or all of these theories, but with reflexivity, to facilitate empirical research for international communication.

Writing from the perspective of cross-cultural and comparative literary studies, Zhang Longxi eloquently argues that the "translation" of meanings within or between languages and cultures is a communicative act of border-crossing, a goal to which all cosmopolitan scholars have a moral responsibility, despite difficulties, to make a contribution. The cosmopolitan spirit assumes that "different peoples at great distances from one another with very different cultures and histories can understand each other and be brought together to form a common humanity." He draws on the most fascinating historical episodes of utopian and demonized representations of China in Europe during the seventeenth and eighteenth centuries, by the Jesuits (who saw China as the "European vision of Cathay" and Confucius as the "patron saint" of the Enlightenment) versus the Catholic Church (which fanned the "Chinese rites controversy"), to illustrate some of the issues confronting East-West understanding. At the end of the day, he rejects as contradicting historical facts and textual evidence any formulations of dichotomized, essentialized, and opposite "modes of thinking" that are alleged to cause the incommensurability of cultural values and ideas between East and West.

For decades, the standard frame of reference for comparing media systems has been *Four Theories of the Press* (Siebert, Peterson, & Schramm, 1956). Despite its vast and long-standing influence, this framework has been criticized for its Cold War bias, Western centrism, and conceptual flaws (Nerone, 1995; see also Servaes's chapter in this volume). Almost fifty years later came the more thoughtful work of Hallin and Mancini (2004), who compared four dimensions of media systems—the structure of media markets, professionalism, political parallelism, and the role of the state— across 18 advanced democracies in western Europe and North America. They derived three Western models: (a) the north Atlantic or liberal model; (b) the northern European or democratic corporatist model; and (c) the Mediterranean or polarized pluralist model. Hallin and Mancini (2012) further assembled a group of scholars from the non-Western world (China, Brazil, Russia, Poland, and South Africa), whose case studies were intended to subject the original framework to critical scrutiny. The ongoing dialogue between the "most similar systems" of the Western world and the "most dissimilar systems" of the non-Western world is a fruitful experiment for conceptual improvement and theory building. As part of this extended discussion, Paulo Mancini maintains in his chapter that the polarized pluralist and especially hybridized models are more applicable to non-Western countries, where mass parties are not everyday experience and the media are instruments of state intervention and elite maneuvering. Besides questioning the Western/non-Western dichotomy, it is always vital to ask what variables, dimensions, or indicators are valid for comparative research. If imposing such a concept and yardstick as "media professionalism" on the non-Western world is seen as unacceptable (as some may argue), what would be a valid alternative?

Michael Curtin observes in his chapter that there is no need to "internationalize" film studies because it has from the beginning been "international," with its origin in the likes of Harold Innis. This is at best an exception to the general pattern of intellectual parochialism and Western dominance; Innis and other globalists are rarely in the bibliography for students of journalism and mass communication in the United States. Curtin proposes the concept of "media capitals," which tend to be located in major port cities with dense transnational networks of hybridized culture and cultural interaction, creative migration, and concentrated capital resources for production and distribution. He argues that the nation's political capitals, because of the entrenched institutions of censorship and clientelism, rarely emerge as media capitals—with the intriguing theoretical implication that political centrality means media/culture marginality. It should be noted that the historical antecedents of the empire and the legacy of post-colonial conditions may be instrumental in the shaping of "media capitals." Moreover, these media capitals do not challenge the dominance of Hollywood; Hong Kong and Mumbai have become major film hubs, but few of their films make an impact beyond neighboring countries.

Arvind Rajapopal uses South Asia as a site of communicative modernity to offer a densely interpretive chapter on post-colonial visual culture. His central argument is that "[g]reater visibility in public does not ensure more rationality, nor does a greater density of information flow assure less violence or more democratization." New media reactivate rather than supplant or erase earlier media forms, and media expansion makes social divisions more visible instead of promoting unity. Non-Western forms of "seeing" tend to validate, not disrupt, the existing rules of social space. Post-colonial visual culture extends a "split public" between religion and politics, without rendering either of them transparent to the other. While media spectacles are an extension of commodity logic in the West, they are only a site of heterogeneous factors brought together to enhance the marketability of the commodity in the post-colonial South Asia.

Revisiting "Cultural Imperialism"

Finally, I would like to revisit the enduring theme of culture/media imperialism, by way of the provocative chapter by Colin Sparks, because this topic invokes a host of interesting theoretical, ideological, and methodological debates. Sparks does not like such terms as cultural imperialism or media imperialism, but argues that we should understand international communication as being shaped by the *cultural* consequences of imperialism. He is explicitly critical of capitalism as a force or source of imperialism. As a pronounced feature of the contemporary world system, he notes that states in the advanced countries tend to colonize international communication through direct or indirect uses of the media.

To me, Sparks's argument speaks in important ways to the core issues of how we can assure this analysis is holistic on the one hand but not totalistic on the other. A holistic perspective does not reduce the whole to distinct parts; the whole is larger than the sum of parts, but this does not preclude or exclude a detailed analysis of the constituent formation. In other words, we cannot be content with viewing just the wood to the neglect of the trees, or vice versa; for aesthetic and ethical reasons we need a balanced landscape of the two elements to round up a fuller picture. Schiller (1976), for example, attacked an assortment of tourism, advertising, public relations, entertainment, news media, and education in the United States as a neat package of "cultural imperialism." It is laudable not to compartmentalize "cultural imperialism," but this "abstract" and essentialized formulation may risk moving dangerously close to being a totalistic discourse. As such, it may scorn any analyses of nuanced differences and the interaction between cultural genres, and looks unfavorably to anything short of utopian once-and-for-all solutions, such as waging a partial yet crucial resistance movement of cultural intifada and guerrilla wars. Frank (1969) warned that Latin America had no choice other than "underdevelopment" or "revolution." Likewise, Schiller (1976) urged Third World countries to extricate themselves from the international capitalist system as a precondition for purging cultural imperialism. The prospect of mass extrication is, realistically speaking, so slim as to render any impatient and totalistic project most likely a recipe for inaction. Equally important is the question of where Third World countries should extricate themselves to? The sad fact is that extrication does not promise cultural independence—and independence is not synonymous with liberation—as it is clear that before our eyes are so many post-imperialist Third World countries run by nationalist, chauvinistic, sectarian, or brutal regimes with the whole pathology of dictatorial power. I recall these seemingly ancient examples primarily in view of their contemporary resonances. Even more important, how are we to understand and sort out the complex, highly contested, and often contradictory meanings of "cultural consequences" in the way of multilayered structures, relationships, and interactions between media genres, content flow, transfer of institution and technology, ideological effect, and the all-encompassing "way of life"? It should also be kept in mind that no modern culture is self-sufficient, fully autonomous, or out of touch with others, as Said (1993) and Hall (1996) have emphasized the open, hybridized, and mutually interactive characters of modern culture.

Imperialism with or without Final Guarantees?

Sparks argues that "[s]hifts in economic power are usually accompanied by a shift in military power and a shift in cultural power." This implies that the economic power of capitalism may precede and create certain cultural consequences of imperialism. Three points can be briefly noted. First, if Michael Curtin is right in arguing that "media capitals" tend to be far away from the nation's political centers and concentrated in rowdy port cities that are disdained by national elites, then the link between economic forces and political forces seems significantly weakened. We are at least reminded of these competing and yet inconclusive hypotheses. Second, is economic power necessarily a "determining" locomotive of cultural power? The fact that Japan's unparalleled international economic power in the 1970s and 1980s was accompanied by its relatively weak presence of international cultural power, plus as-yet dubious evidence on the emerging cases of China, India, and Russia, makes me wonder if a nation's ability to transform its economic power into cultural power is necessarily assured. Third, most seriously, if we opt not to quarrel with Sparks's claim, the task remains one of fully conceptualizing where the analysis of capitalism's imperialist cultural consequences should begin or end.

The intramural dispute between radical political economists and culturalists seems to throw important light on this last question. Murdock and Golding (1977, p. 17) started by taking Theodor Adorno, Raymond Williams, and Stuart Hall to task for doing "a top-heavy analysis in which an elaborate autonomy of cultural forms balances insecurely on a schematic account of economic forces shaping their production." Golding and Murdock (1991, p. 27) reiterated the central importance that should be accorded to explaining "how the economic dynamics of production structure public discourse by promoting certain cultural forms over others." Their criticism has to be interpreted against Williams's seminal work (1977) on Marxist cultural theory, which redefines the concept of "determination" not in terms of "reflection" but in terms of "mediation." Williams further develops the concept of "mediation" to mean that the economic base may primarily "set the limits" (passively) and "exert pressures" (actively) on the ideological field. By the same token, Stuart Hall (1996) thinks of the "materialism" of Marxist theory in terms of "determination (of the cultural) by the economic in the *first* instance." He criticizes political economists' steadfast position with respect to "determination (of the cultural) by the economic in the *last* instance" has long been "in the depository of the last dream or illusion of theoretical *certainty*" (italics in original).

Hall (1996) characterizes his theoretical stance metaphorically as "Marxism *without* final guarantees." The material base is a point of departure for establishing "the open horizon of Marxist theorizing" (in Hall's terms), for defining the direction and setting the limits of cultural production. However, the actual processes and outcomes of cultural formation and counterformation are more open-ended, more autonomous, and more intensely contested than what political economists would postulate—in fact, as Hall maintains, the outcomes are "without guaranteed closures," to the extent that the cultural may in some cases even depart from the contours of the economic. Insofar as Sparks (1996, p. 95) was critical of Hall for not investigating the material base of Thatcherism, we may reasonably understand him to be a defender of the "cultural imperialism *with* final guarantees" position, as determined by the logic of capitalism. With or without final guarantees, it is essential to specify and analyze a complex chain of conceptual building blocks that straps global capitalism to the posited cultural consequences of imperialism. To this end, how profitable is it to draw on a rejuvenated version of, say, the historically interpretive framework of "dependent development" that focuses on the dialectical interactions among the "triple alliance" of the state, the dominant classes, and the international capitalist structure (Cardoso & Faletto, 1979; Evans, 1979)? In the age of globalization, furthermore, how can cultural consequences react upon the material base?

Political Economy versus Audience Decoding

Cultural imperialism would seem to have enduring relevance as long as media globalization radiates from metropolitan centers—and indeed, from one primary center. Despite the rise of regional hubs of cultural production, media globalization still is hard to distinguish from Americanization. The United States is the only genuine global media exporter across a range of media, and home to media conglomerates that are both vertically and horizontally integrated to span the entire spectrum of forms and genres. These conglomerates, built on the elusive benefits of synergy and the ephemeral icon of consumer choice, are either U.S.-owned outright (Disney, Time Warner, and Viacom) or nominally "foreign" (Sony, Bertelsmann, Vivendi-Universal, and News Corporation) but with their most important operations and markets in the United States. These companies

compete and cooperate in an intertwined way: they set up cross ownership, produce revenue sharing and joint ventures, engage in coproduction
and co-purchasing, and swap local outlets (Tunstall & Machin, 1999, pp.
64–66). Entertainment is the priority; meanwhile, many scholars have expressed concern that journalism may be increasingly McDonaldized and
trivialized, overwhelmed by the emphasis on infotainment, gossip, and
scandal that pander to the instant gratification of mass consumers (e.g.,
Gunther & Mughan, 2000).

None of the global conglomerates has been able to make the inroads
it would desire in the China market. But all are trying, as international
appetites for American-style cultural products become ever more vital to
corporate survival. In this volume, Jaap van Ginnenken presents a fascinating case of a globalized media product—*Avatar*, the first 3-D mega-
blockbuster—to illustrate how tried-and-tested Hollywood formulas have
re-emerged in new technological guise. He points out five well-worn colonial motifs that endure despite all the technological dazzle, namely: (a)
underdeveloped "virgin" land; (b) primitive national tribe; (c) indigenous
natural worldviews; (d) imperial intervention; and (5) the beautiful native
girl. It is tempting to interpret the *Avatar* phenomenon as the center of
world capitalism imposing its particular system of manufactured cultural
images, forms, and meanings on the world audience.

However, as Liebes and Katz (1993) have demonstrated, audiences
negotiate with the media over meanings in accordance with their own
cultural assumptions. Van Ginnenken likewise highlights the contradiction between the control exercised over production and the "relative autonomy" of meaning-making in reception. In short, focusing primarily on
the political economy of media ownership and control without sufficient
sensitivity to the process of audience decoding may result in overestimat-
ing the weight of cultural domination and homogenization. On the other
hand, paying sole attention to audience decoding without situating it in
the structural constraints of product availability as dictated by the logic
of contemporary political economy may lead to minimizing the weight of
cultural domination. Once again, we face questions of agency-structure interaction. Once again, more empirical investigation is required.

Concluding Remarks

I begin this chapter by criticizing the parochial orientation of U.S. scholarship that has distorted the study of international communication for de-

cades, and the willing collaboration between the tutor and the tutored that has supported such academic hegemony. Besides critiquing established approaches to studying media and communications outside Anglo-American contexts, contributors to this volume have offered a way forward for studying the issue of media and globalization.

We take seriously the continued relevance of nation-states while remaining attuned to the ways in which media and communications is now a thoroughly "globalized" space. We have examined different dimensions of the world-historical nature of media and communications: institutions and power, states and governance, policy and regulation; economic capital, political economy, and production of journalism, media, network, and culture industry; cultural geography, meaning, and public sphere; issues of identity, values and cosmopolitanism; and visual culture. Furthermore, we have situated these issues of pertinence to international communication scholars in relation to questions of relevance to the field of media and communications at large.

To suggest alternatives aimed at truly "internationalizing" international communication, we believe that the point of departure must be precisely the opposite of parochialism—-namely, a spirit *of cosmopolitanism*. In sum, we reject both America-writ-large views of the world and self-defeating mirror images that reject anything American or Western on the grounds of cultural incompatibility or even cultural superiority. Scholars worldwide have a moral responsibility to foster global visions and mutual understanding, which requires that we listen to one another patiently, try to put ourselves in the shoes of others, and stand prepared to negotiate and contest painstakingly over language, meanings, evidence, and states of mind. Metaphorically, this forms symphonic harmony that is nonetheless made of cacophonic sounds. In this light, I might be forgiven for making a bolder claim that our ultimate goal is not only to internationalize "international communication" as a subfield, but rather that international communication will provide a vital force, site, and opportunity to revitalize the whole agenda and landscape of media and communication studies. This claim resonates with the classical spirit of "sociological imagination" (Mills, 1959) that calls for examining media and communication issues from global and historical perspectives.

Should this volume give rise to the unfortunate yet inevitable impression of overemphasizing the conceptual and methodological flaws of U.S. scholarship, it is because only through critical reflection will any new beginnings have a chance. My utmost admiration, nevertheless, goes to Said

(1993), who framed his criticism of the culture of imperialism—along with Third World resistance against the empire—in terms of the grand narratives of enlightenment and emancipation. He did not countenance reaction driven by xenophobia or cultural nationalism. I recall as well the philosopher who once described the meaning of philosophy to me as "having no knockout statements so the conversation can go on." This is a good maxim for the enterprise we hope to foster—an ongoing dialogue in the cosmopolitan spirit that tries to traverse borders, identify shared values, and reach common ground while respecting differences.

This book grows out of an international conference organized jointly by the Department of Media and Communication and the Center for Communication Research at the City University of Hong Kong. Professor Elihu Katz, as a living testimony of the development of both U.S. and international communication research for more than half a century, was invited to deliver the conference's keynote address under the university's Distinguished Lecture program. Let the truth be told about the story of this remarkable career and life in his own words and in his own chapter by someone who has inspired us all.

REFERENCES

Berelson, B. (1959). The state of communication research. *Public Opinion Quarterly* 23 (1): 1–5.

Berger, C. R., & Chaffee, S. H., eds. (1987). *Handbook of communication science.* Beverly Hills, CA: Sage.

Berger, C. R., Roloff, M. E., & Roskos-Ewoldsen, D. R., eds. (2010). *The handbook of communication science.* Los Angeles, CA: Sage.

Cardoso, F. H. (1977). The consumption of dependency theory in the United States. *Latin American Research Review* 12 (3): 7–24.

Cardoso, F. H., & Faletto, E. (1979). *Dependency and development in Latin America.* Berkeley: University of California Press.

Chen, K. H. (1996). The formation of a diasporic intellectual: An interview with Stuart Hall. In D. Morley & K.-H. Chen, eds., *Stuart Hall: Critical dialogues in cultural studies* (pp. 484–503). London: Routledge.

Curran, J., & Park, M.-J., eds. (2000). *De-Westernizing media studies.* London: Routledge.

Czitrom, D. J. (1982). *Media and the American mind: From Morse to McLuhan.* Chapel Hill: University of North Carolina Press.

Evans, P. B. (1979). *Dependent development: The alliance of multinational, state, and local capital in Brazil.* Princeton, NJ: Princeton University Press.

Frank, A. G. (1969). *Latin America: Underdevelopment or revolution.* New York: Monthly Review.

Fukuyama, F. (1992). *The end of history and the last man.* New York: Free Press.

Geertz, C. (1963). *Agricultural involution: The process of ecological change in Indonesia*. Berkeley: University of California Press.

Geertz, C. (1983). *Local knowledge: Further essays in interpretive anthropology*. New York: Basic Books.

Golding, P., & Murdock, G. (1991). Culture, communications, and political economy. In James Curran & M. Gurevitch, eds., *Mass media and society* (pp. 15–32). London: Arnold.

Gunther, R., & Mughan, A., eds. (2000). *Democracy and the media: A comparative perspective*. New York: Cambridge University Press.

Hall, S. (1996). The problem of ideology: Marxism without guarantees. In D. Morley & K.-H. Chen, eds., *Stuart Hall: Critical dialogues in cultural studies* (pp. 25–46). London: Routledge.

Hallin, D. C., & Mancini, P. (2004). *Comparing media systems: Three models of media and politics*. New York: Cambridge University Press.

Hallin, D. C., & Mancini, P., eds. (2012). *Comparing media systems beyond the Western world*. New York: Cambridge University Press.

Hardt, H. (1992). *Critical communication studies: Communication, history, and theory in America*. New York: Routledge.

Held, D., & McGrew, A. G. (2007). *Globalization/anti-globalization: Beyond the great divide*. Cambridge: Polity.

Huntington, S. (1993). The clash of civilizations. *Foreign Affairs* 71 (3): 22–49.

Inglehart, R., & Welzel, C. (2005). *Modernization, cultural change and democracy: The human development sequence*. New York: Cambridge University Press.

Lasswell, H. D. (1927). *Propaganda technique in the World War*. New York: Knopf.

Lazarsfeld, P. (1952–53). The prognosis for international communications research. *Public Opinion Quarterly* 16 (4): 481–90.

Lazarsfeld, P., & Merton, R. K. (1971). Mass communication, popular taste, and organized social action. In W. Schramm & D. F. Roberts, eds., *The process and effects of mass communication* (pp. 554–578). Urbana: University of Illinois Press.

Lee, C.-C. (2001). Rethinking the political economy: Implications for media and democracy in Greater China, *Javnost–the Public* 8 (4): 81–102.

Lerner, D. (1958). *The passing of traditional society: Modernizing the Middle East*. New York: Free Press.

Lerner, D., & Schramm, W., eds. (1967). *Communication and change in the developing countries*. Honolulu: East-West Center Press.

Liebes, T., & Katz, E. (1993). *The export of meaning: Cross-cultural readings of Dallas*. Cambridge: Polity.

Luckmann, T. (1978). Philosophy, social sciences and everyday life. In T. Luckmann, ed., *Phenomenology and sociology* (pp. 217–56). London: Penguin.

Merton, R. K. (1972). Insiders and outsiders: A chapter in the sociology of knowledge. *American Journal of Sociology* 77:9–47.

Mills, C. W. (1959). *The sociological imagination*. New York: Oxford University Press.

Murdock, G., & Golding, P. (1977). Capitalism, communication, and class relations. In J. Curran, M. Gurevitch & J. Wollacott, eds., *Mass communication and society* (pp. 12–43). London: Arnold.

Nerone, J. C., ed. (1995). *Last rights: Revisiting four theories of the press.* Urbana: University of Illinois Press.

Norris, P., & Inglehart, R. (2009). *Cosmopolitan communications: Cultural diversity in a globalized world.* New York: Cambridge University Press.

Nye, J. S. (1990). *Bound to lead: The changing nature of American power.* New York: Basic Books.

Nye, J. S. (2004). *Soft power: The means to success in world politics.* New York: Public Affairs.

Nye, J. S. (2008). Public diplomacy and soft power. *Annals of the American Academy of Political and Social Science* 616 (1): 94–109.

Palma, G. (1978). Dependency: A formal theory of underdevelopment or a methodology for the analysis of concrete situations of underdevelopment? *World Development* 6:881–924.

Pool, I. de sola (1973). Communication in totalitarian societies. In I. de sola Pool & W. Scharmm, eds., *Handbook of Communication* (pp. 462–511). Chicago: Rand McNally.

Pool, I. de sola., & Schramm, W., eds. (1973). *Handbook of communication.* Chicago: Rand McNally.

Pye, L. W., ed. (1963). *Communications and political development.* Princeton, NJ: Princeton University Press.

Rogers, E. M. (2003). *Diffusion of innovations.* New York: Free Press.

Said, E. W. (1993). *Culture and imperialism.* New York: Knopf.

Salinas, R., & Palden, L. (1979). Culture in the process of dependent development: Theoretical perspectives. In K. Nordenstreng & H. I. Schiller, eds. *National sovereignty and international communication* (pp. 82–98). Norwood, NJ: Ablex.

Schiller, H. I. (1976). *Communication and cultural domination.* White Plains, NY: International Arts and Sciences Press.

Schramm, W. (1964). *Mass media and national development.* Stanford, CA: Stanford University Press.

Schramm, W., & Lerner, D., eds. (1976). *Communication and change, the last ten years—and the next.* Honolulu: University Press of Hawaii.

Siebert, F. S., Peterson, T., & Schramm, W. (1956). *Four theories of the press: The authoritarian, libertarian, social responsibility, and Soviet communist concepts of what the press should be and do.* Urbana: University of Illinois Press.

Smelser, N. J. (1976). *Comparative methods in the social sciences.* Englewood Cliffs, NJ: Prentice-Hall.

Sparks, C. (1996). Stuart Hall, cultural studies and Marxism. In D. Morley & K.-H. Chen, eds., *Stuart Hall: Critical dialogues in cultural studies* (pp. 71–101). London: Routledge.

Thussu, D. K., ed. (2009). *Internationalizing media studies.* London: Routledge.

Tipps, D. C. (1973). Modernization theory and the comparative study of societies: A critical perspective. *Comparative Studies in Society and History* 15 (2): 199–226.

Touraine, A. (1997). *What is democracy?* Boulder, CO: Westview Press.

Tunstall, J. (1977). *The media are American.* New York: Columbia University Press.

Tunstall, J., & Machin, D. (1999). *The Anglo-American media connection.* New York: Oxford University Press.

Wang, G., ed. (2011). *De-Westernizing communication research: Altering questions and changing frameworks.* London: Routledge.

Watson, P. (2001). *The modern mind: An intellectual history of the 20th century.* New York: HarperCollins.

Whitehead, A. N. (1925). *Science and the modern world.* New York: Free Press.

Williams, R. (1977). *Marxism and literature.* New York: Oxford University Press.

Yu, Y.-S. (2007). *Zhishiren yu zhongguo wenhua de jiazhi* [Intellectuals and the value of Chinese culture]. Taipei: China Times Press.

NOTE

1. I owe a debt to Professor Judy Polumbaum for helping me to make this chapter more lucid and readable.

CHAPTER TWO

Window Shopping

On Internationalizing
"International Communication"

Elihu Katz

When Professor Lee asked me to accept his invitation to open this conference, I immediately agreed—that is, until he told me what it is about. Whereupon I demurred, protesting that I hardly know anything about international communication and certainly nothing about internationalizing it. CC persisted, however, and challenged me to reconsider my own research and writing and to decide which of us is right. We made a bet, so to speak, for which the cost (at least to me) is that I have spent the past six months trying to decide whether I have any standing in this field. He said that it would be OK, as an oldtimer, if I were to share whatever I found, even autobiographically. It occurred to me only later that CC might be worrying that he had asked the wrong person to write an introduction to his book on media imperialism (Lee, 1980) some thirty-five years ago!

So, let us do exactly that. In part 1 of what follows, I will unashamedly review what I think I have done that might qualify me *in* international communication, even if, at the time, I did not think of this work as explicitly international. I will do this chronologically, more or less, as if I were searching my CV for keywords. Following which, in part 2, I will try to make some observations about what, if anything, I have learned on this narcissistic safari, as I try to find meaning in the series of relevant projects on which I shall report, and especially on their sequence. You'll have to decide which of us won the bet, CC or me.

Part I

The place to begin, I think, is as a graduate student recruited by Paul Lazarsfeld to join in analysis of a massive data set concerning public opinion and media use in four Arab nations, plus Greece and Turkey. This was the study made famous by Daniel Lerner (1958), then of MIT, under the title *The Passing of Traditional Society*, subtitled *Modernizing the Middle East*, and well remembered in several of the papers being presented at this conference. It was commissioned by the Voice of America at the outset of the Cold War in the 1950s. My role in the project was a minor one (Katz, 1952) but I remember being impressed by Lerner's introduction of the concept of "empathy," which he attributed to the kind of media exposure that produced a substantive reply to a survey question such as, "What would you do if you were Prime Minister?" Or what would you write about if you were editor of the local newspaper? Rather than answering, as most people did, "Who me, editor of a newspaper?" there were other, more media-literate respondents who could imagine themselves in these roles. These were the newly modernizing individuals, Lerner argued, they had psychological access to the world outside the village; they were the harbingers of a radical transformation. In his introduction to Lerner's book (1958), David Riesman translated "empathy," somewhat skeptically perhaps, as "window shopping." In separate papers, published later, Lazarsfeld (1952) and Charles Glock (1952) spoke of the theoretical and methodological potential of extending communications research internationally.

During the same period, I began work on my dissertation which, ultimately, appeared as *Personal Influence*, coauthored with Lazarsfeld (Katz & Lazarsfeld, 1955). The aim of the book was to redirect attention away from the power of the media to effect short-run change in opinions and attitudes and toward the more complex, and more sociological, interaction between mass media and interpersonal networks. Ultimately, this "two-step flow of communication," proposed by Lazarsfeld in the 1940s resulted in a revival of interest in the process of diffusion of innovation. Rather than focus on individual change, diffusion research aimed to track the spread of change throughout a community over time (Rogers, 1962; Katz, Levin & Hamilton, 1963). This shift in emphasis reconnected the mainstream search for the persuasive powers of the media with sister sciences interested in such things as the spread of fashion, social movements, technological change, and epidemics. Outstanding in this respect was the pioneering work of rural sociologists whose studies of the diffusion and adoption of new farm practices had been a continual concern (Katz, 1960). These sociologists then turned their attention to programs of initiating and evaluating projects of rural development overseas. Their technological emphases complemented the projects of development and modernization that occupied political science-oriented scholars at MIT, Stanford, and elsewhere. Both of these trends were rather ill-fated, in that they were criticized for being too self-serving of the Western powers that supported them, as this volume will remind us. Yet, it led to the healthy realization that diffusion was a primordial process that is invoked to explain how Christianity, for example (Stark, 1997) managed to make its way around the world long before there were media of mass communication.

A very different kind of international communication occupied me as I began to commute between the Universities of Chicago and Jerusalem. Together with Brenda Danet, then a student, later a colleague, we found interest in problems of intercultural communication between Western-style bureaucrats confronting the mass of new-immigrant clients who had arrived in Israel from more traditional societies (Katz & Danet, 1973). Our observations came not from media content or from survey research, but from protocols of face to face encounters with customs officials, traffic policemen, health workers, and so on. Anecdotally, at first, we found passengers bargaining with bus drivers over the fare, or arguing over proper behavior in a queue. We met health officers in well-baby clinics preaching family planning over the objections of their clients' husbands. We studied the language of appealing to authority—implicitly invoking reciprocity, altruism, and norms—and learned much about how the representatives of these disparate cultures perceived each other.

After a few years in Israel, somebody decided that I was just the right person to head the task force that would, finally, introduce television broadcasting. Israelis had resisted the introduction of television for some years, until the so-called Six Days War convinced them that it was no use continuing to debate the pros and cons of TV, once the Arab states had all established their own channels, and no less important, after Israel began to realize that it was an occupying power. However unqualified I was, administratively and technologically, how could one decline this kind of invitation? And I did not (Katz, 1971). I will not tell you this story, however, even though it involved an intercultural clash between me and what seemed to me the suddenly alien culture of the CBS capitalists who had been commissioned to help in the process. At the same time, it was the beginning of my love affair with the public broadcasting of the BBC. I am mentioning this episode not only for its intrinsic interest but because it was also a prelude to a sequence of subsequent work that, finally, deserves to be labeled international communication research.

The first of the projects that followed my short career as an impresario was a grant from the Ford Foundation via the International Institute of Communication to trace the transplantation of television broadcasting from the capitals of the West to the Third World. The object was to observe the process whereby television "diffused" from the capitals of the West to what were then known as developing countries. In other words, I was given the opportunity to observe elsewhere what I myself had done in Israel. My partner in this project was Professor George Wedell who, like me, had taken leave from his university (Manchester) to serve as first secretary general of the Independent Broadcasting Authority, Britain's newly established commercial channel. Between us, and with the assistance of Dov Shinar and Michael Pilsworth, we studied the "promise" and the "performance" of television in twelve countries on three continents (Katz & Wedell, 1977). While the rhetoric of "promise" resounded with slogans relating to "national integration," "cultural renaissance," and "economic development," we found, in the 1970s, that television broadcasting was narrowly concentrated in the major cities, and that the popular programs were American reruns. Students of programming flow confirmed this pattern (Nordenstreng & Varis, 1974; Tunstall, 1976; Schiller, 1969) at the time, even though it would soon change, as the popularity of local programming overcame that of imported programs—although the formats of those programs may still originate elsewhere (cf. Sorokin, 1941 on stimulus diffusion). We thought of naming our book *Waiting for Kojak*, but we lost our nerve.

Research that accompanied these projects—economic and political—were equally subject to protests of self-interest and paternalism. Here, too, there were loud outcries against "cultural imperialism." Several papers in this conference review the relabeling of these studies as modernization, then imperialism. It was alleged (Schiller, 1969) that Hollywood films and American sitcoms had created new forms of dependence, taking the place of colonialism and economic exploitation by the West against the rest. These debates led Tamar Liebes and myself (Liebes & Katz, 1990) to undertake a study of the cross-cultural "reception" of the U.S. nighttime soap opera *Dallas*. *Dallas* captivated audiences almost everywhere—although there were a few exceptions, like Japan. Our study organized focus groups (of three couples each) in six different sub-cultures to view episodes of the program in their own homes. We wanted to see whether viewers in the several subcultures varied from each other in their attitudes and understandings, and more generally whether there was evidence for or against the allegation of "cultural imperialism." We called our book *The Export of Meaning*.

While blockbuster programs like *Dallas* bring the world together—albeit not at the same time—certain "media events," such as the live broadcasting of historic occasions, can do so even better, and what's more, at one and the same time! This is the most dramatic attribute of the electronic media since the telegraph; it made possible being present and active in more than one place at the same time. This third of the three projects I want to describe was a partnership with Daniel Dayan of Paris that began in 1977 when Anwar Sadat of Egypt came to talk peace with Israel, and continued until 1992, when our book was published (Dayan & Katz, 1992). It deals with a genre of television that fulfills the Durkheimian function of integrating a nation or the world. It invites people everywhere to sit down with their closest others in celebration of a ceremonial occasion to which they are personally invited—almost like Christmas or Thanksgiving or the Passover Seder—with the knowledge that everybody else in the same society or the whole world is co-present. Thus, Israelis and Egyptians cheered Anwar Sadat, whose three-day visit was broadcast live—linking the two countries via TV for the first time. Much of the Western world watched too, but it was ignored in the other Arab states. Nobody doubts that this rare example of media diplomacy contributed to the peace treaty that was signed shortly thereafter—but also to the subsequent assassination of President Sadat. Another classic example of this kind of international communication is the live confrontation between John Paul II and the Communist rulers of the Polish people. Again, it is widely believed that this ceremonial visit of the first Polish pope—as broadcast live on Polish national television and, later, distributed on film—was a first push toward the dismantling of the Eastern European regimes. Not all "media events" are "conquests" of this kind, however. The Olympics and the World Cup (Mondial) are "contests." And the live broadcast of the Kennedy funeral or the funeral of Princess Diana, which engaged the whole world, not as somebody else's trauma but as our own. These are three different "scripts," of course, but each is an interruption of routine—a broadcasting holiday, so to speak—that invites our participation and affirmation.

Let me include mention of my paper on the coverage of the first Gulf War (Katz, 1992). It applies as well to the massacre at Tiananmen Square. These events saw the emergence of media coverage aiming at a world audience, not a national one. No less important, their reports were live and direct from the scenes of the action—from the roof in Baghdad, if you recall. My point is that they circumvented the role of the editor who could give it context. We were offered an embedded view, so to speak, describing something to us and to the world, but without explaining under whose auspices this was taking place. It was an ostensible beginning of "broadcasting without frontiers," but it raised a new set of problems. It focused on the live broadcasting of popular protest.

I will conclude this list almost where it began by reporting on my membership n a recent project centering on communications and diasporas (Katz & Blondheim, 2010). We tried to understand how "imagined communities" (with a dutiful nod to Benedict Anderson [1983]) held together, even in dispersion, and in the absence of any tangible contact with a remembered homeland. Our focus was on the Jews, though we might equally have focused on the Chinese, because that was the case we knew best. More than imagination was involved, of course. There were economic and cultural ties—and premodern channels of communication that were invented and activated. And it seems more than coincidence that the Jews subsequently made major contributions to the establishment of media institutions, new and old, beginning with the telegraph (Blondheim, 1994).

Part II

Even if some of this is relevant to the theme of the conference, the real question is "What have I learned?" Let me try to answer, sometimes based on findings from these studies and experiences, sometimes based on the inspiration of calling them back into consciousness.

1. A first point to make, I think, is that international communication preceded national communication, rather than vice versa. As the history of diffusion research makes clear—the case of early Christianity, for example—messages moved freely across cultural divides and natural borders, long before these were organized into nations, and long before the era of mass communication. Of course, problems of rhetoric, reception, and resistance prevailed even then.

2. Indeed, it might be said that media and messages and, of course, language served as building blocks for the consolidation of nations, as we learn

from scholars such as Gabriel Tarde (1898) and Benedict Anderson (1983), and their followers (such as Jaap van Ginneken, 1992). Translations of the Bible into the spoken languages of different regions in Europe reinforced the emergence of national entities.

3. Once established, I think it is fair to say that nations did their best to interfere with the flow of communication across their borders. Nations began to patrol the traffic in communications. Internally, they tried to educate and entertain, to inform citizens of what they were expected to know and deny them what they were not expected to know, while externally they tried to use communication to expand empire as the ancient Egyptians (Innis, 1951) and modern-day Hollywood have tried to do, or to disinform and defame their enemies. The International Telecommunications Union still allocates broadcasting frequencies and still attempts to control the reach of national signals, though that has become all but impossible in today's age of satellites.

4. If technological theories of media can help explain the emergence of nation-states and mega-structures like the Protestant denominations (Eisenstein, 1980), for example, the self-same theory should predict that the free flow of information—that is, the internationalization of international communication—should contribute to the rise of global structures and the demise of nation-states. Is this what we are now seeing as the former prerogatives of nations are being overruled by the globalization of human rights and of economics? Monroe Price (2002) and several of the volume's chapters here (Sparks, for one) suggest that it is too soon to make such generalizations, and that nations still exert sovereign power, and that they surrender sovereignty only under the umbrella of formal treaties. Yet, the famous case—undocumented, I believe—of East Germans tuning into the relative prosperity of Germans on the other side of the Wall is a good example of international communication. It may not coincide with the theory of "revolution of rising frustration" that developmentalist researchers have advised us to reject, but it comes pretty close.

5. Even when messages reach their destinations, there is no assurance that they will be decoded as their senders intend. Most of the history of research on mass communication has been devoted to the study of effects, that is, the success of mass persuasion campaigns in the very short run. And, ironically, what we have to show is only how surprisingly ineffective the media are in this domain. Even though we hardly believe it ourselves, the truth is that propaganda and advertising don't persuade very well, either domestically or, a fortiori, internationally (Schudson, 1984). If diffusion

research shows greater success, it is because it is more about things than about ideas and because research tends to report on things that take off rather than on failures. In any case, it is worth noting that persuasive effects, however much studied, are hardly the most interesting types of effects. If I invoke only my own experience with international projects, as reviewed here, I would highlight (1) the near-universal success of the BBC in gaining the trust of most of the world (from the study of Arab countries); (2) that the institutionalization of broadcasting and likely the new media as well—administration, technology, content—look much alike the world over and that governments are losing control of the media to international interests who consort with them; (3) that communication and culture are rapidly superseding geography in the creation of international alliances (Kraidy & Khalil, 2009) even while breaking the national audience into segments and networks (Turow, 2006; Katz, 1996). (4) that the critical abilities of viewers everywhere are more fully developed than is usually thought, but that the everyday of mutual understanding required for cross-cultural communication still has a long way to go; (5) that exceptional "media events" can nevertheless gather the whole world together and unite it in a shared heartbeat as in the Diana funeral or for a favorite football team; (6) that the live broadcasts of Sadat and the pope prove that the media can sometimes contribute to peace and reconciliation, even while the same media can be used by nations and groups to terrorize the world as in 9/11—also a kind of "media event" (Katz & Liebes, 2007; Dayan, 2009)—and as in the threats of President Mahmoud Ahmadinejad.

6. Let me conclude where I began, by returning to Lerner's concept of empathy and to Riesman's window shopping. Recall that Lerner was proposing that the media—those were the days of radio—affect modernization by expanding individual horizons, inviting identification with theretofore unfamiliar roles, and enlisting participation in a newly opened public sphere. Without spelling it out, Lerner was suggesting that a major effect of media exposure is identification with remote others and the trying on of new identities. In using, or perhaps misusing, the concept of empathy, he was pointing to the idea of identification, which, astonishingly, is almost altogether absent in the catalog of media effects. It is a central concept in cinema studies—who doesn't identify with the stars?—but has been strangely missing in media studies. Although the concept is too individualistic to fully explain the developmental process, it also implies, indirectly, that the media contribute to the creation of polities and public spheres.

The concept of empathy has suddenly reappeared—sixty years later—in connection with the new genre of communications research that deals with "distant suffering," to quote Luc Boltanski (1999). There is a sudden rush of interest in the emotional, cognitive, and, especially, moral aspects of mediated witnessing of widespread tragedy. Under what conditions, these authors ask, do people rise to the challenge of doing something to right a wrong, or save a life, in response to what they see on the nightly news or learn about from the Internet? When do people get up from their TV sets to demand that their governments intervene? When do people mobilize to donate money to cope with a far-away disaster? In the past, this question had hardly been asked (Ball-Rokeach, Rokeach, & Grube, 1984 is an exception), and has resurfaced only now in the writings of authors such as Ellis (2000), Peters (2001), Chouliaraki (2006), and in the collection edited by Frosh and Pinchesvki (2009). It follows the unnerving assertions that there are "no more secrets," as Meyrowitz (1985) has taught us, and now, even worse, that "there are no more excuses." We have run out of ways of saying "I didn't know!" It is in this connection that the concepts of "empathy" and "compassion" have been resurrected in order to explain everyday arousal and action, and to revive the idea that the media have the power to empower.

I am not now thinking of media events, which bring the potential power of television into full view. I am thinking, rather, of the everyday effects—including those of the nightly news—that we dismissed as limited. Lazarsfeld found comfort in the idea that effects were limited, arguing that it was safer for democracy that broadcasters and their oligarchs cannot easily arouse listeners and viewers to do their bidding. Sometimes we regret this, of course, as when we observe how difficult it is to induce people to stop smoking, for example. So perhaps we should applaud those of our colleagues who have refused to abandon studies of the conditions under which media can be effective in the short run, especially with respect to the suffering of others. Is so-called compassion fatigue just another case of "limited effects" or are viewers actually motivated to respond but unable to identify the means that might enable them to do so (cf. Wiebe, 1951)? We should be asking again, as Hallin and Mancini (1984) once did, whether there are cultural differences involved here. Is it still true that while Americans view the nightly news (or whatever news they view nowadays) that they have another beer and go off to sleep, while Italians news viewers, upset by what they have just seen, don their overcoats and go off to the piazza to discuss it with their friends before going to register their feelings at the local offices of the political parties or trade unions? It is time to renew more problem-oriented comparative studies that go beyond the structural emphases of the Columbia group, and beyond even the comparative work that the Hallin/Mancini team (2004) has done more recently. It is widely thought in the United States, for example, that the tragedy of Haiti enlisted an unusually large outpouring of support in money and in services. Is this true? Is it equally true of other countries? How did this compare with the response to the East Asian tsunami of several years ago, or the tragedies of Darfur or Kosovo or Rwanda? If there are big differences here, we should be asking about the parts played by media systems and media images along with differences in cultural proximities and available means.

As far as images are concerned, Iyengar and Kinder (1987) have suggested in a study of the depiction of homelessness that the very personification of social problems that is characteristic of television leads viewers to conclude that the victim is to blame for his/her own plight, while the ostensibly cold statistics of homelessness are more likely to direct viewers' attention to systemic problems. Paul Slovic (1997), for one, disagrees. His experiments seem to show that an individual victim or person in need arouses more sympathy than a group of such people, or, a fortiori, a statistic of their helplessness. And what of protest and revolution? Have we any comparative evidence of arousal to action in defiance of oppression that can be attributed to the media? There seems to be some evidence from Eastern Europe in 1989, when large numbers of provincial Czechs took to the streets to express solidarity with their fellow countryman massed in Wenceslas Square. More recent protests in Korea provide an additional example—but, by now, the new small media have entered the scene. Whether these new media are the new media of collective action is a matter of growing debate (see, e.g. Gladwell, 2010).

David Riesman's somewhat cynical translation of empathy as "window shopping" is probably closer to the facts. It is a lot easier, of course, to tour the tragedies of the world with the ever dwindling number of foreign correspondents than to do anything about it. It is rather closely linked to Lazarsfeld and Merton's (1948) "narcotizing dysfunction." Limited effects, that is, is still the better bet. But even Riesman's more sober view goes some way to explaining the overthrow of the Berlin Wall.

REFERENCES

Anderson, B. (1983). *The imagined community.* New York: Verso.
Ball-Rokeach, S. J., Rokeach, M., & Grube, J. (1984). *The great American values test: Influencing behavior and belief through television.* New York: Free Press.

Blondheim, M. (1994). *News over the wires*. Cambridge, MA: Harvard University Press.

Boltanski, L. (1999). *Distant suffering: Morality, media and politics*. Cambridge: Cambridge University Press.

Chouliaraki, L. (2006). *The spectatorship of suffering*. London: Sage Publications.

Dayan, D. (2009). Sharing and showing: Television as monstration. *Annals of the American Academy of Political and Social Science* 625 (1): 19–31.

Dayan, D., & Katz, E. (1992). *Media events: The live broadcasting of history*. Cambridge, MA: Harvard University Press.

Eisenstein, E.L. (1980). The emergence of print culture in the West. *Journal of Communication* 30 (1): 99–106.

Ellis, J. (2000). *Seeing things*. London: Cambridge University Press.

Frosh, P., & Pinchevski, A. (2009). *Media witnessing: Testimony in the age of mass communication*. New York: Palgrave Macmillan.

Gladwell, M. (2010). Small change. *New Yorker*, 4 October. Retrieved from http://www.newyorker.com/reporting/2010/10/04/101004fa_fact_gladwell.

Glock, C. Y. (1952). The comparative study of communications and opinion formation. *Public Opinion Quarterly* 16 (4): 512–23.

Hallin D. C., & Mancini, P. (1984). Political structure and organizational form in U.S. and Italian television news. *Theory and Society* 13 (40): 829–50.

Hallin, D. C., & Mancini, P. (2004). *Comparing media systems*. Cambridge: Cambridge University Press.

Innis, H. (1951). *The bias of communication*. Toronto: University of Toronto Press.

Iyengar, S., & Kinder, D. (1987). *News that matters: Television and American opinion*. Chicago: University of Chicago Press.

Katz, E. (1952). *Communication and political attitudes in four Arabic countries*. New York: Bureau of Applied Social Research, Columbia University.

Katz, E. (1960). Communications research and the image of society: Convergence of two traditions. *American Journal of Sociology* 65 (5): 435–40.

Katz, E. (1971). Television comes to the people of the book. In I. L. Horowitz, ed., *The use and abuse of social science* (pp. 249–71). New Brunswick, NJ: Transaction Books.

Katz, E. (1992). The end of journalism? Notes on watching the war. *Journal of Communication* 42 (3): 5–13

Katz, E. (1996). And deliver us from segmentation. *Annals of the Academy of Political and Social Science* 546 (1): 22–33.

Katz, E., & Blondheim, M. (2010). Four diaspora dreams. In M. Blondheim & E. Katz, eds., *Communication and diaspora*. Unpublished manuscript, Department of Communication, Hebrew University.

Katz, E., & Danet, B., eds. (1973). *Bureaucracy and the public: A reader in official-client relations*. New York: Basic Books.

Katz, E. and Lazarsfeld, P.F. (1955). *Personal influence: The part played by people in the flow of mass communication*. Glencoe, IL: Free Press.

Katz, E., Levin, M. L., & Hamilton, H. (1963). Traditions of research on the diffusion of innovation. *American Sociological Review* 28:237–52.

Katz, E., & Liebes, T. (2007). No more peace: How disaster, terror and war have upstaged media events. *International Journal of Communication* 1:157–66.

Katz, E., & Wedell, E. G. (1977). *Broadcasting in the Third World*. Cambridge, MA: Harvard University Press.

Kraidy, M. M., & Khalil, J. F. (2009). *Arab television industries*. London: Palgrave Macmillan.

Lazarsfeld, P. F. (1952). The prognosis for international communication research. *Public Opinion Quarterly* 16 (4): 481–90.

Lazarsfeld, P. F., & Merton, R. K. (1948). Mass communication, popular taste and organized social action. In W. Schramm, ed., *Mass communication*. Urbana: University of Illinois Press.

Lee, C. C. (1980). *Media imperialism reconsidered: The homogenizing of television culture*. Beverly Hills, CA: Sage Publications.

Lerner, D. (1958). *The passing of traditional society: Modernizing the Middle East*. New York: Free Press.

Liebes, T., & Katz, E. (1990). *The export of meaning: Cross-cultural readings of "Dallas."* New York: Oxford University Press.

Meyrowitz, J. (1985). *No sense of place*. New York: Oxford University Press.

Nordenstreng, K., & Varis, T. (1974). *Television traffic—a one-way street? A survey of and analysis of the international flow of television programme material*. Research Report No. 70. Paris: UNESCO.

Peters, J. D. (2001). Witnessing. *Media, Culture & Society* 23 (6): 707–23.

Price, M. E. (2002). *Media and sovereignty: The global information revolution and its challenge to state power*. Cambridge, MA: MIT Press.

Riesman, D. (1958). Preface to D. Lerner, *The passing of traditional society: Modernizing the Middle East*. New York: Free Press.

Rogers, E. M. (1962). *Diffusion of innovations*. New York: Free Press.

Schiller, H. I. (1969). *Mass communication and American empire*. Boston: Beacon Press.

Schudson, M. (1984). *Advertising: The uneasy persuasion*. New York: Basic Books.

Slovic, P. (1997). "If I look at the mass I will never act": Psychic numbing and genocide. *Judgment and Decision Making* 2 (2): 79–95.

Sorokin, P. (1941). *Social and cultural mobility*. New York: Free Press.

Stark, R. (1997). *How the obscure, marginal Jesus movement became the dominant religious force in the Western world in a few centuries*. New York: HarperCollins.

Tarde, G. ([1898] 1969). Opinion and conversation. In T. Clark, ed., *Gabriel Tarde: On communication and social influence*. Chicago: University of Chicago Press.

Tunstall, J. (1976). *The media are American*. London: Constable.

Turow, J. (2006). *Breaking up America*. Chicago: University of Chicago Press.

Van Ginneken, J. (1992). *Crowds, psychology and politics: 1871–1899*. New York: Cambridge University Press.

Wiebe, G. D. (1951). Merchandising commodities and citizenship on television. *Public Opinion Quarterly* 15 (4): 679–91.

CHAPTER THREE

Beyond Lazarsfeld

International Communication Research and Its Production of Knowledge

Tsan-Kuo Chang

A good theory should be seen as one perspective among others rather than as a catch-all explanation.

—Johan Galtung (1990)

In a *Public Opinion Quarterly* article, Paul Lazarsfeld (1952–53, p. 483) argued that "since the domestic area will not have many opportunities in the years to come, the *new ideas* in communications research . . . will have to be picked up and developed in the international field if they are not to be neglected altogether" (emphasis added). He went on to say that "there are certain comparative possibilities in the sphere of international communications research which will open up *new and rather exciting subjects* for investigation." What Lazarsfeld suggested is that the new ideas might be better developed contextually, sociologically, historically, and methodologically outside U.S. research settings. Although he did not elaborate, the new and exciting ideas certainly should include new concepts, new theories or new perspectives, and new ways of doing research as well as new knowledge and new insights. This has not been the case, however. While the body of studies of international communication has grown significantly over the past decades, the production and accumulation of knowledge have been less impressive. In fact, the field has been regurgitating old ideas and stale perspectives without keeping abreast with the changes of the times.

Since Lazarsfeld's prognosis there has been little reflection on the state of the field of international communication research, which picks up where he had left off. With the growth of the literature in international communication that had by the early 1980s reached "almost landslide proportions" (Hur, 1982, p. 531), the Lazarsfeld article appears to have been forgotten and mostly vanished from many ensuing studies on the structure and processes of international communication. Stevenson sought to define international communication as a field in 1992, but made no reference to Lazarsfeld even though the latter's insights and projection of the future direction of international communication research had more or less anticipated what was to come 40 years later. This study has no intention to accord the Lazarsfeld article status as a milestone or a canonical text in international communication research. Nevertheless, the article serves as a useful departure point to tackle the production of knowledge in international communication research.

Against the backdrop of the sociology of knowledge, this study is informed by three perspectives to assess the extant literature in international communication research: Johan Galtung's life cycle of theories (1971), Erving Goffman's keying in frame analysis (1974), and Thomas Kuhn's "paradigm testing" (1970). The assessment is not intended to be either a quantitative meta-analysis (Wolf, 1986) or a critical bibliographic or citation analysis of existing studies on international communication. As indicators of the state of mind in research, the data reported are used mainly to externalize the arguments made within the context of the three perspectives. They help provide empirical answers to the conceptual questions, but by no means offer statistical tests of any hypothesis implied by the individual perspective or their combination.

The purpose of this study is threefold: first, to examine how the key concepts or theories in international communication research emerge and fluctuate over time; second, to determine the relationship between the modes of thinking in international communication research as manifested in the literature and the historical-social setting in which they occur; and third, to explore the group mind of international communication researchers as knowledge producers through their scholarly outputs as recorded in journal articles and books. As bearers of intellectual activities, international communication scholars and researchers constitute a professional group that carries certain epistemological interests in the world of cross-national communication and occupies a specific position in knowledge production regarding what that world is, how it is to be observed, and why it turns out the way it does.

Sociology of Knowledge and
International Communication Research

To determine the trajectory of international communication research that Lazarsfeld had charted for his successors over the past 60 years is to examine the mode of thought or the group mind of scholars who have come "to find expression in certain theories, doctrines, and intellectual movements" (Wirth, in Mannheim, 1936, p. xxviii) since his prognosis. Although he was among the few towering figures who have established communications research as a discipline and whose legacy continues to inspire or invoke debates in the community of scholars,[1] Lazarsfeld was not alone in his thinking. To paraphrase Mannheim (1936, p. 3), it is, strictly speaking, incorrect to say that the single scholar thinks and does research; rather, it is more correct to insist that he or she participates in thinking and doing further what other researchers have thought and done before. The sociology of knowledge perspective therefore provides a useful framework to comprehend the particular style of thought among international communication scholars in the historical-social setting.

Because of "its concern with the role of knowledge and ideas in the maintenance or change of the social order," as Wirth (1936, in Mannheim, 1936, p. xxix, emphasis added) put it, the sociology of knowledge "is bound to devote considerable attention to the *agencies or devices through which ideas are diffused* and the degree of freedom of inquiry and expression that prevails." In social sciences research, the devices through which ideas are diffused include predominantly books and journal articles that are published throughout the years, especially those that have been frequently cited in the literature. Quoting Merton (1967, pp. 36–37), Simonson (2006, p. 6) wrote, in the introduction to the November 2006 volume of the *Annals of the American Academy of Political and Social Science*, that "any classic text worth reading is worth rereading periodically, for 'what is communicated by the printed page' changes as a result of changes in the readers and the worlds they inhabit." The frame of reading and the interpretation of its content have been altered in ways that Goffman called "breaking frame" (1974).

To some extent, the prognosis article is such a text. In discussing comparative research opportunities, Lazarsfeld had anticipated what Katz and his colleague reported in *The Export of Meaning* (1990), indicating that there "can be little doubt that the meaning of news will be very different from one culture to another, and that we cannot know in advance what these variations will be" (Lazarsfeld 1952–53, p. 486). Substituting the TV show *Dallas* for the word "news," this statement summarized succinctly what turns out to be the reception theory in cross-national research. Re-reading the article in the contemporary context adds a new perspective to Lazarsfeld's excitement that we "should be grateful for the sudden upsurge of interest in international communications" when radio—the new medium at that time—changed the media landscape.

Since the mid-1990s, the proliferation of nation-state-based 24/7 TV news channels has reconfigured the world of global media terrain beyond recognition or imagination. Along with such well-established traditional channels as BBC and CNN, the rise of Al Jazeera as a formidable voice from the Middle East has been followed by a rush of countries to establish global channels through satellites to present the news from their own national perspectives: China's CCTV-9 (2000), Russia Today (2005), France 24 (2006), Iran's Press TV (2007), Japan's NHK World TV (2009), Venezuela's TeleSur (2010), and the CNC World (2010) of China's Xinhua News Agency. Ranging from the democratic to authoritarian countries, these channels compete at the global level to serve as the voice of the host country and to report the world from its own vantage point. Arguably, the emergence of these various brands of satellite TV outlets represents a form of media nationalism that seeks to claim a legitimate space in the global marketplace of ideas, not a form of media imperialism as was conceived in the old order when the U.S. brand roamed the world. As such, the playing field of international communication has been leveled, changing not only the ways audiences may be exposed to the flow of news and other cultural products across national borders but also the rule of the game for the global media. The shift prompted Tunstall (2008, p. 10) to declare that national and regional media are stronger than international media in his book *The Media Were American: U.S. Mass Media in Decline.*

If "what is communicated . . . changes as a result of changes in the readers and the worlds they inhabit" (Simonson, 2006, p. 6) and if "changes in communications alter cultures—expanding, changing, and destroying them" (Greig, 2002, p. 225), then it is theoretically imperative to scrutinize how the changes in the global media environment have been reflected in the life cycle of existing concepts or theories central to the field of international communication inquiry. Thanks to the penetration of the Internet into every corner of the world, it is difficult to imagine that cultures everywhere are not affected by it in one way or another. For one thing, the intellectual context of thinking and doing research has changed. When there is a conceptual shift, will the questions to be asked, the observation of facts, or the method of investigation remain unchanged? If the empirical has been transformed from one state of being to another, will the theoretical derived from the past observation continue to be relevant? Like cars and fashions, as Galtung (1971, p. 93) argued in the early 1970s, theories "have their life-cycle, and whether the obsolescence is planned or not there will always be a time-lag in a structure with a pronounced difference between center and periphery. Thus the tram workers in Rio de Janeiro may carry banners supporting Auguste Comte one hundred years after the center of the Center forgot who he was." A compelling question is, why would Comte become known in a place several thousand miles away from his home base in the first place?

Life Cycle of Theories in International Communication Research

The life cycle of a theory is the autobiography of an idea through time and space. Galtung's comment on Rio de Janeiro centered on the diffusion of theories between developed and developing/underdeveloped countries in academic research. Explicitly, the hegemonic structure in international social science research has created an unequal setting in which peripheral countries suffer from the theories and methods imported from the core nations. Part of the reason is the deficiency of theories and methods developed in the Western countries that fail to take into account local knowledge and experiences, not to mention the lack of awareness among the community of scholars of the intellectual need to understand the objects of their investigation (Curran & Park, 2000). In international communication research, the tendency to view "the rest of the world as a forgotten understudy," as Curran and Park (2000, p. 3) reckoned, has reached a plateau where "US- and UK-based media academics are beginning to feel embarrassed." Embarrassed they should be, because there is always a danger when groupthink or the absence of alternative perspectives crowds out competing explanations. In the context of group decision, one of the theoretical and epistemological issues involved in groupthink is the shift of conceptual cohesiveness from a multidimensional to a unitary construct and its power to affect the views of others (Street, 1997). Groupthink occurs not only because of individual attributes of members but also because of circumstances of their deliberations (Neck & Moorhead, 1995). In social science inquiries, the body of literature certainly counts as part of the deliberative circumstances among researchers. In the case of international communication research, groupthink appears in the fact that, some 40 years after its inception, the banner of cultural imperialism as a theory continues to be carried by scholars in many parts of the world, including Latin America (e.g., Vilas, 2002) where the dependency theory was first formulated to challenge the knowledge claim of the modernization perspective, even though the global media landscape has been greatly transformed.

In the 1980s, the thesis of cultural imperialism was considered by both its proponents and critics as a "dominant paradigm" in the field of international communication. Whether it has achieved a theoretical status as a paradigm in the Kuhnian sense of the notion is debatable.[2] For the lack of a better term, this study will use *paradigm* testing to address the issue of theoretical juxtaposition as explications in international communication research. As will be discussed later, the proposition of paradigm testing as an analytical design does not necessarily imply the existence of competing paradigms in international communication inquiry. Nor does it attempt to provide a critical test of the validity of different theories involved in the historical and empirical context. A number of scholars and researchers have offered insightful critiques and challenges to the conceptual inadequacy and epistemological weakness of cultural imperialism in various texts (Chadha & Kavoori, 2000; Curran & Park, 2000; Curtin, 2007; Fejes, 1981; Fortner, 1993; Golding & Harris, 1997; Hamm & Smandych, 2005; Lee, 1980; Lee, 1988; McPhail, 2002, 2010; Roach, 1997; Salwen, 1991; Thussu, 2006; Tomlinson, 1991; Wang, Servaes, & Goonasekera, 2000).

In this study, the concept of cultural imperialism is taken as is, not what it may refer to. It is the concept itself that is being historically examined, not its content. The thesis is used as a case to exemplify the life cycle of theories in international communication research. The survey of its genesis and application as a key concept and theory in international communication is meant to be illustrative, not exhaustive, of its general footprint in the literature. Although the exact origin of the idea of *cultural imperialism*[3] is difficult to pinpoint, it is commonly accepted that it was first proposed in the late 1960s as a theoretical articulation to address the structure and processes of the domination of U.S. media at the expense of other countries' indigenous media industry in the international arena. From Africa to Latin America, there has been no shortage of theoretical and empirical studies that seek to uncover the structural factors underlying such an imperialistic configuration and its implications for international relations.

Since the 1960s, the world's media setting has evolved dramatically both within and between countries. The Internet and its surrounding digital communication technologies have particularly created new opportunities and challenges to the traditional media in areas of content production, distribution, and consumption. Over the past decades, countries around the world have witnessed the end of the Cold War between the two superpowers, the collapse of communism in eastern Europe, the breakup of the Soviet Union, the demise of the New World Information and Communication Order, and the widespread of the Internet as a powerful democratic platform for civil society and global communication. In light of these sociopolitical and technological transformations, the thesis of cultural imperialism[4] apparently exhibits a remarkable shelf life with no sign of abating (see table 1). Facts come and go. Any theory that has endured for more than four decades in a field of intellectual inquiry does not exist by itself in a philosophical vacuum. It must be perpetuated by those who continue to see its relevance and centrality to the contemporary world.

Theories have power (Alford & Friedland, 1985). Take modernization in international communication research in the 1950s and the 1960s. The power of modernization theory can be characterized, according to Alford and Friedland (1985), as follows: policy impact (a driving force of national development); interpretation of actions (internal, as opposed to external, solutions to underdevelopment); arousing consciousness of social groups (creating empathy in peasants); hegemony over categories of language (modern vs. traditional as frames); and demarcation of boundaries between the public and the private (ownership and regulation of media systems). As will be shown later, displacing modernization, the thesis of cultural imperialism has shaped the way journalists come to perceive the international reality.

Table 1 offers a snapshot of the enduring power of the thesis of cultural imperialism over time. In international communication, the year 1969 is a milestone, both conceptual and technological. Conceptually, Herbert Schiller published an influential book entitled *Mass Communications and American Empire*. His central argument is that "[t]he *emerging imperial network* of American economics and finance utilizes the communications media for its defense and entrenchment wherever it exists already and for its expansion to locale where it hopes to become active" (1969, p. 3, emphasis added). The linkage between the U.S. economic and finance system and its media system at the international level sets the stage for the notion of cultural imperialism to emerge as it soon began to spread in the literature. If Schiller broke the ground, then Wells (1972) plowed the field. Eventually, Tunstall (1977) paved the way for the expansion of cultural imperialism thesis in international communication research. Although critical of the original ideas of Schiller and Wells and their evidence, Tunstall nevertheless helped accentuate the thesis. While he questioned the claim of the cultural imperialism thesis "that authentic, traditional and local culture in many parts of the world is being battered out of existence by the indiscriminate dumping of large quantities of slick commercial and media products, mainly from the United States" (Tunstall, 1977, p. 57), he accepted

TABLE 1. The Life-Cycle of Cultural Imperialism in International Communication Research

Citing Text	Cited Text[a]
McPhail (2010)	Schiller (1969), Tunstall (1977)
Chakravartty & Zhao (2008)	Tunstall (1977)
Kamalipour (2007)	Dorfman & Mattelart (1975), Schiller (1969), Tunstall (1977), Wells (1972)
Thussu (2006)	Boyd-Barrett (1977), Dorfman & Mattelart (1975), Galtung (1971), Schiller (1969), Tunstall (1977), Wells (1972)
Hamm & Smandych (2005)	Galtung (1971), Schiller (1969)
McPhail (2002)	Tunstall (1977)
Thussu (2000)	Boyd-Barrett (1977), Dorfman & Mattelart (1975), Galtung (1971), Schiller (1969), Tunstall (1977), Wells (1972)
Fortner (1993)	
Lee (1980), Schiller (1971), Tunstall (1977)	
Frederick (1993)	Boyd-Barrett (1977), Lee (1980), Schiller (1971)
Tomlinson (1991)	Fejes (1981), Lee (1980), Dorfman & Mattelart (1975), Tunstall (1977)
Fejes (1986)	Lee (1980), Schiller (1971), Tunstall (1977)
Lee (1980)	Boyd-Barrett (1977), Schiller (1969), Tunstall (1977), Wells (1972)
Tunstall (1977)	Schiller (1969), Wells (1972)

[a]Both the citing and cited texts are chosen for the purpose of illustration only. They are not meant to suggest they are the most cited texts in the field. The citing texts are selected to show the life-cycle or timeframe. The cited texts include only those published in the 1960s, 1970s, and 1980s that are considered central to the knowledge production of cultural imperialism as a thesis. The entries do not imply that the citing texts include no recent publications, especially those published during the past three decades; nor do they suggest that other books published between 1960s and 1980s were not consulted by various authors and editors. Some of the cited texts were used by the authors in the edited volumes, not necessarily by the editors.

that "the Anglo-American media are connected with imperialism, British imperialism" (p. 63). With a question mark after the words "Media Imperialism?" in chapter 2, Tunstall challenged the broad stroke of cultural imperialism by offering his own conceptualization. As will be discussed later, it is a matter of conceptual abstraction or rekeying, with the concept involved being located at different levels and implying different units of analysis.

Since its publication, Tunstall's 1977 book began to take on a life of its own. From the late 1970s to 2010, as shown in table 1, the book has been obligingly cited, often in connection with the works by Schiller (1969), Wells (1972), and Dorfman and Mattelart (1975). I don't intend to engage in any deliberation over which work is more influential in the field of international communication research. A compelling question is how the concept of cultural imperialism has persisted over time in academic research and journalistic practices. If we agree that the thesis of cultural imperialism was specifically presented by Schiller in 1969, its shelf life has been extended consistently in many journal articles and books during the past four decades, suggesting that it is still very much alive today. What is most intriguing is that by 2008, Tunstall apparently had abandoned the thesis of cultural imperialism in favor of what he called new nationalism in his book *The Media Were American: U.S. Mass Media in Decline* (Tunstall, 2008, p. 344). Yet, citing Tunstall in 2010, McPhail opted for the 1977 book, not the 2008 one, as if nothing had happened, when Tunstall had couched the 2008 book out of his earlier conceptual frame and into another.

The year 1969 was also significant in international communication not because of Schiller's book but because of a major milestone that was mostly overshadowed by the landing of the first man on the moon. ARPANET, the world's first packet switching network created by BBN (Bolt, Beranek and Newman), went online in October 1969, connecting four computers at UCLA, UC Santa Barbara, Stanford, and University of Utah in the United States. It was the predecessor of today's Internet although the scale was much smaller and its use was restricted to the United States only. Since then, the number of computers connected to the Internet has grown from four to hundreds of thousands worldwide at a speed and pace unimaginable, as shown by the mind-boggling tangled web mapped by the U.S. Company Lumeta in 2004. By April 2008, the Internet had expanded to over 450,000 nodes, with many more top-level domains and nodes added on a regular basis. It means countries around the world are now highly interconnected and interdependent. In light of this structural transformation, as Chang (2010, p. 12) argued, the field of international communication research requires new perspectives that go "beyond extant theories that were developed some 40 years ago." He singled out cultural imperialism as one such theory "that seems to be largely rooted in the territorial and physical relevance of an old media landscape" (p. 12).

When Schiller published his 1969 book, the international media landscape was indeed dominated by American multinational corporations. In Tunstall's view, "a non-American way out of the media box is difficult to discover because it is an American, or Anglo-American, built box. *The only way out is to construct a new box*, and this, with the possible exception of the Chinese, no nation seems keen to do" (1977, p. 63, emphasis added). He was both right and wrong. He was right because a new media box has actually been built that is non-American (e.g., Al Jazeera or CNC World); he was wrong because other than China many countries are now capable of building their own media boxes (e.g., Russia, Iran, Japan, and Venezuela). This is probably why, in *The Media Were American*, Tunstall spent a significant amount of space tracing the emerging national media centers and their challenges to U.S. media domination, hence setting up the basis for the proposition that the U.S. mass media have been in decline since 1950. Throughout the book, however, what is not spoken tends to speak louder than what is said. In the genealogy of knowledge production, it is telling that in *The Media Are American*, Tunstall went to great lengths defining media imperialism and tackling its consequences; three decades later, the word imperialism is not even indexed in *The Media Were American*. Not until the last part is it mentioned in passing in the context of nationalism vs. imperialism (p. 344).

Similar to his earlier declaration of *The Media Are American*, Tunstall's proclamation of *The Media Were American* explicitly announces the demise of an old order that has been replaced by a new one with a fresh set of national media systems and international arrangements of market relations. Given the growth of nation-state-based satellite TV channels, the U.S. media indeed no longer take the high command in the global media marketplace, let alone exercising their supreme authority in content production and dissemination. Tunstall discussed this new pecking order mostly against the backdrop of cultural and media nationalism. He failed to explain why, leaving a pressing question unanswered: What happens to media imperialism if media nationalism has been on the rise? The latter appears to have superseded the former largely because much of the historical evidence and key issues Tunstall used to buttress the thesis of media nationalism took place before the 1970s. From the 1977 *The Media Are American* to the 2008 *The Media Were American*, Tunstall made an interesting conceptual turn, but missed a great opportunity to explicate its theoretical significance. It should be illuminating to see whether the central concept and thesis in international communication research that Tunstall helped spread, but discarded some 30 years later, continues to be codified in the literature. If the life cycle in table 1 is any indication, the 1977 book may have a shelf life for yet many years to come unless scholars and researchers seek outside the frame (Goffman, 1974) of what is contained in the book for opposing versions of reality in international communication, as Tunstall did himself.

The notion of cultural imperialism appears not only in scholarly works, but also in journalistic reports. It has become part of the vocabularies in the mainstream media as fait accompli of some sort. In 1992, when Euro Disneyland opened its theme park in the suburb of Paris, the *New York Times* (9 April 1992, p. C1, emphasis added) reported this way: "The French intelligentsia have been taking potshots at the 4,800-acre Euro Disneyland . . . , dubbing it a 'cultural Chernobyl' and denouncing the '*imperialism of Mickey*.'" Nearly two decades later, the *Economist* (31 May 2008, p. 89, emphasis added) carried a story with very much the same theme: "The French film industry is more often given to introspective agonising about *American cultural imperialism* or the tyranny of the market than to self-congratulation." These two stories demonstrated the extent to which the received knowledge of cultural imperialism has somehow taken root in the news.

From the 2008 report in the *Economist* to McPhail's 2010 book, it is striking that the idea of cultural imperialism has persisted in academic and journalistic circles for more than 40 years after it was first proposed in the 1960s. This intriguing phenomenon deserves to be closely interrogated, especially when the Internet has fundamentally altered the global media environment. Quantitatively, expansion of daily audiences in units of millions takes place at a speed and pace previously unthinkable. Qualitatively, convergence of a single platform for all forms of media has become a reality. Economically, the decline of traditional media, particularly newspapers and commercial TV in terms of audience size and advertising revenues, has led to a reconfiguration of the markets that affects the flow of various media content.

How does the Internet affect the global media landscape and the form of international communication? First, with the global network made possible by the Internet, countries around the world are densely connected. Access points to this global network, however, still remain local. They are bounded by the political and social interests of territorial governments. Who controls the Internet is therefore of significant importance to international communication "to determine what is to be delivered and how" (Chang, 2010, p. 13). Second, although globalization implies a weakened nation-state, the new form of state in today's information age is the network state (Carnoy & Castells, 2001, p. 14), in which each node—the nation-state—is linked to other nodes "that are equally necessary for the performance of the state's functions." Given this networked structure at the global level where the flows move in many directions, how does cultural imperialism take place?

This study contends that the theory has lagged far behind the new reality. In international communication research, the state of theory is either underdeveloped in the first place or misguided by the traditional ways of thinking and conceiving the world, or both. Simply put, there is a lack of alternative perspectives. Groupthink still permeates in the intellectual enterprise in the field of international communication. For one thing, theorists of cultural imperialism have failed to take note of the technological innovations and the shift of content production and distribution from corporate interests to user-generated concerns (e.g., Web 2.0) that have largely reshaped the form and content of global media.

Technologically, the new global media environment defies traditional conceptions, requiring theoretical rethinking of what is to be seen and how to see it. Why would a theory formulated at a time when countries were not as connected as they are today continue to be relevant to the network society created by the ubiquitous Internet? When the object of observation has changed, would the focus of conceptual lens capture the same image as it appeared before? Implied in these questions are layers of conceptual focus and their different theoretical formulation. This has implications for international communication research. As Alford and Friedland (1985) argued, "theories themselves must be analyzed at different levels, which cannot be reduced to each other" (p. 392). Epistemologically, Thomas Kuhn (1970) reasoned convincingly that no existing theory should be tested in isolation by itself. Goffman's (1974) notion of "keying" in frame analysis is relevant. A theory provides a frame that is keyed to see the reality in some way.

Keying of Concepts in International Communication Research

In his seminal book *Frame Analysis*, Goffman (1974, p. 11) argued that "once a term is introduced . . . it begins to have too much bearing, not merely applying to what comes later, but reapplying in each chapter to what it has already applied to." The essence of his arguments—that there is a linear presentation in conceptual formulation and articulation embedded "in some sort of logical sequence" (p. 11)—is central to this study's contention. Introducing a term is very much like keying. Keying of concepts concerns how an idea might be called by different researchers over time. Concepts are ingredients of theories, but they are not theories per se. As Alford and Friedland (1985, p. 394) put it, "Concepts always contain a theory of the causes and consequences of the essential attributes of the phenomena located and defined by the concept." Moreover, in a historical view "concepts are properties of the social relations of production of knowledge" (Aford & Friedland, 1985, p. 27).

In international communication, imperialism is certainly a concept. As a theory, it is more complex, involving a set of interrelated statements that seek to describe and explain in a systemic manner how and why international relations may function the way they do. In this study, cultural imperialism is used as an encompassing concept to include all types of communication-related forms of imperialism, which have been coined in the literature. Technically, the choice of which adjective (*media, cultural, communication,* or *informatic*) to precede the word imperialism appears to be largely wordplay or what Goffman (1974) called "keying" that frames what is to follow or to be expected. In the cognitive orientation of the world, Goffman (1974, p. 443, emphasis added) argued, "Wordplay seems to celebrate the power of the context *to disqualify all but one reading,* more than it disconfirms the workings of this force." In the ladder of abstraction, the four concepts are located at different levels. Below the most abstract concept, *culture,* they slide up or down as a key with a slight different tone.

A theory can be considered as a frame that sets specific boundaries with its key concepts to look at the reality, a form of theoretical bracketing. The insistence on a specific word or the priority of one particular word over other words misses the most fundamental question: How does cultural imperialism stack up against other competing theories such as dependency, reception (Liebes & Katz, 1990), or globalization? In fact, these terms (media imperialism, cultural imperialism, communication imperialism, and informatic imperialism)[5] consist of two kinds of concept: primary and secondary. The primary concept is imperialism whereas the secondary concepts are media, cultural, communication, and informatic. What the secondary concepts bracket out is largely methodological categories as to the type of data and the unit of analysis that might be required, not necessarily the underlying process. To paraphrase Alford and Friedland (1985), an imperialistic state of international relations has to exist in some form before the concept of imperialism could become accepted. In international communication research, scholars of cultural imperialism insist on defining, and thus changing, the secondary term, when it is the primary concept that should be reexamined. If they already see "imperialism" in international communication, what lies beyond the rim of an "imperialistic" frame tends to be unattended. Absence of other concepts therefore precludes alternative perspectives from being discussed because they are considered to be irrelevant or insignificant. Addition of a secondary concept does not break the primary framework.

This inquiry will address four different primary concepts—imperialism, modernization, dependency, and globalization—and their interrelationships that have emerged in international communication research before and after Lazarsfeld's prognosis to determine their conceptual genealogy in the historical context. The source of data came from JSTOR, "one of the world's most trusted sources for academic content" with "over one thousand leading academic journals across the humanities, social sciences, and sciences" (http://about.jstor.org/content-collections; retrieved 20 October 2010). The database includes 2,832 journals in 53 disciplines, varying from African American Studies to Zoology.[6]

Using "international communication" as the keyword in the full text, a search of articles and book reviews published in all eight languages (English, Dutch, French, German, Italian, Latin, Portuguese, and Spanish) returned, as of 8 October 2010, a total of 2,415 listings. Almost all the publications (99.2%) were in English, with the remaining items in three other languages: Spanish (9), French (8), and German (3). Because of the concentration of English publications, there might be a "historical bias" that Anglo-American researchers in North America and Europe have "towards citing each other" (*Economist*, 13 November 2010, p. 82). If the plea can only be heard in English, deWesternizing media studies (Curran & Park, 2000) would be an exercise in futility.

Through the keyword search *in the full text*, this study treats each listing in the database as an equal unit of analysis regardless of its length. As opposed to the search *in the item title*, a full text search has the advantage of retrieving all entries involving the central concepts under investigation. A random check of 10 percent of articles over time found that the full text search captured items that were largely relevant to the theories of international communication. These keywords indeed index what was theoretically discussed in the texts.

Table 3 reports the genealogy of the four central concepts identified in the literature from the 1920s to the 2000s: imperialism, modernization, dependency, and globalization. Each concept is assumed to underline an implicit theory of knowledge. The order of sequence (from imperialism to globalization) is arranged roughly according to their appearance in the literature, not necessarily their exact genesis. Overall, a given concept does not appear to have any significant bearing on what other concepts might be used in different lines of thought. Within each realm of investigation, however, there is some consistency in that the use of later concepts does not replace the prior ones or diminish their usage in research.

The concept of imperialism clearly has a long history in international

TABLE 2. Articles and Book Reviews of International Communication Research, 1929–2009[a]

Year	"International Communication" in Full Text[b]		
	Articles	Reviews[c]	Total[d]
<1929	4.6%	2.5%	4.1%
1930–1939	1.7	2.1	1.8
1940–19 49	3.7	4.5	3.6
1950–59	7.0	9.7	7.6
1960–1969	9.2	14.1	10.2
1970–1979	14.8	13.0	14.4
1980–1989	21.3	20.5	21.1
1990–1999	22.7	23.8	22.6
2000–2009	15.1	11.6	14.3
Total	1,899	516	2,415

[a]As of October 27, 2010 when the database was accessed, there were a total of 2,832 journals in 53 disciplines. Although JSTOR has been comprehensive, the database does not necessarily include all journals that are published in the eight languages.

[b]"International communication" was used as the exact phrase in the *full text* in the JSTOR search.

[c]Entries are book reviews and are used a proxy of the number of books published during the decade. It should be noted that a few reviews looked at the same book, but were published in different journals.

[d]Based on the JSTOR search results, entries represent the number of articles and reviews published in eight languages: English, Dutch, French, German, Italian, Latin, Portuguese, and Spanish. In fact, almost all the publications were in English (99.2%). A breakdown of the number of articles and reviews published in different languages is: English, 2,395; Dutch, 0; French, 8; German, 3; Italian, 0; Latin, 0; Portuguese, 0; and Spanish, 9.

communication research, but did not appear frequently in the literature until the 1970s. Over the last four decades, it has remained prevalent in various social science disciplines, suggesting a common intellectual concern over the potential impacts of cross-national communication. As a concept, modernization emerged most visibly in the 1960s, while during the previous three decades it was fairly obscure. This pattern evidently supports the campaign of modernization as the goal of national developments in many parts of the world since then and through the 2000s. The dependency concept offers some clue as to how a theory might rise to challenge the existing one that purports to explain the same phenomenon. In the 1960s and the 1970s, modernization projects in Africa and other places were found to be a failure and the theory was largely discredited in social science research; dependency as an alternative perspective surged significantly in the literature in the following decades. Like that of imperialism, its current usage probably reflects contemporary concerns over the real intention of the spread of globalization around the world. Such scholarly concern is best expressed by Vilas (2002) in an article that was simply entitled "Globalization as Imperialism." While the notion of globalization might be traced to Marx's ideas in the nineteenth century, the concept itself only appeared in the JSTOR database in the 1980s, signaling an increasing intellectual attention to this particular phenomenon.

The above discussion of keying in international communication research does not directly address the relationship between the concepts that underscore different theories in the field, especially in the era of network

TABLE 3. Genealogy of Theories in International Communication Research, 1929–2009[a]

Year	Imperialism	Modernization	Dependency	Globalization
<1929	0.5%	—	1.3%	—
1930–1939	1.2	0.5	—	—
1940–1949	3.5	0.5	0.6	—
1950–1959	6.3	3.3	—	—
1960–1969	6.3	11.9	2.5	—
1970–1979	15.3	17.6	15.9	—
1980– 989	23.5	26.7	33.1	3.6%
1990–1999	21.6	21.0	29.3	34.9
2000–2009	21.6	18.6	17.2	61.4
Total	255	210	157	166

[a]Each of four key words—*imperialism, modernization, dependency,* and *globalization*—was used in combination with the exact phrase "international communication" in the *full text* in the JSTOR search. Because of the small number of book reviews published over time (imperialism, 38; modernization, 27; dependency, 14; and globalization, 17), the two categories were combined.

society. As documented (Chang et al., 2009; Himelboim, Chang, & Mc-Creery, 2010), although the global network is open, the flow of news is very much closed within the network itself. Whether the media outlets are state-owned or privately owned, for example, the number of outgoing links in foreign news is almost nonexistent, particularly so under the state-dominated system. Considering the advent of sophisticated software that automatically creates linkages between websites, apparently it is not the technological considerations that lead to the absence of hyperlinks. Explanations for the missing links have to be sought beyond the hyperlinks themselves. The thesis of cultural imperialism obviously cannot offer convincing explanation for this structural deficiency. What are the alternative perspectives? The question can be best answered by paradigm testing.

Paradigm Testing in International Communication Research

The notion of paradigm is borrowed from Thomas Kuhn's classic work, *The Structure of Scientific Revolution* (1970). The term *paradigm* refers to "the entire constellation of beliefs, values, techniques, and so on shared by members of a given community" and "the concrete puzzle-solutions, employed as models or examples, can replace explicit rules as a basis for the solution of the remaining puzzles of normal sciences" (Kuhn, 1970, p. 175). Because Kuhn restricted the use of paradigm to the normal sciences, the field of international communication research apparently would not fall within the range of his conception. As such, the application of the concept to the explanation of international communication phenomenon does not necessarily suggest there are *competing paradigms* in the field. In fact, whether international communication research could even be considered pre-paradigmatic in the Kuhnian sense is open to debate. To claim cultural imperialism as a paradigm is therefore to stretch its status as *the* dominating theoretical perspective in the field. Nevertheless, his discussion of comparing competing theories to determine which theory best explains the facts is germane to gauging the production of knowledge in international communication research.

Although Kuhn did not call it as such, for lack of a better word the notion of "paradigm testing" is used here to capture the tension between two competing theories within the same field of inquiry, which seek to account for the facts. If Kuhn's paradigm shift or scientific revolution is any hint, the challenge of competing theories apparently comes from outside, not necessarily from inside, the dominant paradigm itself, which, if successful, may eventually lead to the collapse of the existing paradigm. When enough members of the "in-group" abandon the old paradigm, a new one from the "out-group" may replace it and the world is seen anew. Again, "paradigm testing" in international communication research implies the existence of competing theories, not the presence of rival paradigms, if any. It is useful to quote Kuhn's idea in its entirety:

> All historically significant theories have agreed with the facts, but only more or less. There is no more precise answer to the question whether or how well an individual theory fits the facts. But questions much like that can be asked when theories are taken collectively or even in pairs. It makes a great deal of sense to ask which of two actual and competing theories fits the facts *better*. (Kuhn, 1970, p. 147, emphasis in original)

In international communication, if the facts are examined against the thesis of cultural imperialism, the U.S. domination in the global cultural market would indeed be supported by the historical data of unequal flows in many countries around the world. According to Kuhn, however, this is not good enough as evidence to lend convincing support to the theory. As used in this study, paradigm testing requires that a theory be pitted against a theoretical "other" or another competing theory. Several theories can be used to explain the form of international communication flows of cultural products: cultural discount, cultural proximity, cultural imperialism, cultural diffusion, and globalization. The empirical data have to be carefully analyzed and the theory of cultural imperialism has to be pitted against other alternative perspectives to determine how it stacks up in comparison. In other words, it is not adequate to examine a theory in isolation as a valid explanation of a given phenomenon when other theories may become viable candidates.

Although the design is not ideal, the JSTOR database offers some proxy means to compare whether opposing theories in international communication research might be juxtaposed in pairs. It is assumed that when two different concepts appear in the same text, they are brought together presumably because of their relevance to each other. On the other hand, if different concepts that describe the phenomenon of international communication do not even turn up in the same space, they would literally be outside the conceptual domain (Goffman, 1970), hidden from view. Chances are therefore low for the rival theories to be considered collectively or for one theory to be evaluated against the other. Table 4 shows the results of paired concepts in the literature as recorded in JSTOR.

One observation becomes immediately visible. In most cases, the four key concepts do not have much co-appearance in the same texts, indicating that a significant number of studies (almost 90%) in international communication research concentrated on a single perspective. The high degree of mutual exclusion suggests a lack of comparison of potential contending accounts. It also highlights a form of groupthink in that alternative perspectives are often excluded in the literature. Of the small number of studies that cover concepts in pairs, the evidence nonetheless points to increasing awareness of challenging ideas. This is particularly evident when globalization is paired with either modernization or imperialism, an equation that largely echoes recent debates as to whether globalization is an extension of modernization or a form of imperialism in disguise. The same can be said of the pairing of dependency with imperialism and modernization in the decades between 1970s and 1990s.

Conclusion and Discussion

Because of the rapid changes in the media landscape and the loss of media jobs as well as the growth of personal communication devices, some scholars and researchers have argued that there is a crisis in international communication (e.g., Sparks, 2000). Although I do not share such an alarmist

TABLE 4. "Paradigm Testing" in International Communication Research, 1929–2009*

Year	Imperialism/ Dependency	Modernization/ Dependency	Modernization/ Globalization	Imperialism/ Globalization
<1929	2.2%	—	—	—
1930–1939	—	—	—	—
1940–1949	2.2	—	—	—
1950–1959	—	—	—	—
1960–1969	2.2	2.8%	—	—
1970–1979	13.0	13.9	—	—
1980–1989	32.6	33.3	2.6%	2.3%
1990–1999	34.8	41.7	41.0	25.6
2000–2009	13.0	8.3	56.4	72.1
Total	46	36	39	43
% of Combined Total	11.2	9.8	10.4	10.2

*The pair of key words was used in combination with the exact phrase "international communication" in the *full text* in the JSTOR search.

view, I have increasingly come to believe that most international communication studies have produced little knowledge that is both solid in the ways it has been produced and sound in its claim of validity across national borders, especially comparative research in news and advertising (Chang et al., 2001; Chang et al., 2009).

The key question this study seeks to answer is: Why and how does international communication research as a field of intellectual inquiry produce a body of knowledge through empirical studies that have mostly followed the same school of thought? Two general conceptual frameworks guided the present study: the sociology of knowledge and the powers of theory. The former concerns ontological and epistemological issues in international communication research; the latter addresses theoretical, ideological, and practical matters of theory in this field. If the findings in this study are any indication, the field of international communication research has exhibited a groupthink mentality in its conceptual approach. Scholars and researchers have yet to think outside the box of international communication inquiry, or, more specifically, the body of literature that has been established in this field.

Groupthink often leads to stagnation or failure. At the abstract level, the mind-set of groupthink excludes alternative perspectives that should be relevant to international communication scholars and researchers who are engaged in the production of knowledge, especially when the received knowledge is delimited within certain geographical territories and defined by a specific perspective. Any empirical research is always bound by the particular context of space and time, within which ideas and ways of seeing and doing things are formulated. But knowledge does not necessarily recognize any national borders although there are historical conditions under which knowledge is generally being produced. The form of international communication is complex. Its determinants vary from country to country. Many competing explanations therefore can be applied to the same facts, depending on how they are theoretically conceived and methodologically analyzed.

For any theory to be valid in its knowledge claim about the reality of the social world, it has to be tested comparatively. Examining how a theory in international communication may fit the historical facts is neither adequate nor convincing. The world is as diverse as the number of countries in it. Perspectives of the reality are bound to be different when it is viewed from different locales. The relationship between theory and the facts is therefore changeable. As Galtung (1990) argued, "a good theory should never leave us with the idea that the world is made once and for all" and "will always have some empty boxes for the reality not yet there, for potential as opposed to empirical reality" (p. 102). A good theory "should be seen as one perspective among others rather than as a catch-all explanation" (p. 100). In international communication, this is especially true because its attributes are more multidimensional than a national one for experimenting different permutations and combinations, as Lazarsfeld had long recognized.

Lazarsfeld's prognosis is worth rereading in the contemporary setting, particularly against the backdrop of the debate over "Washington Consensus" vs. "Beijing Consensus." In discussing the importance of comparative research, he had offered in the early 1950s a recipe for inquiry about what was to come in today's world as a result of the tension between the free market and democracy. In the United States, he said (1952–53, p. 487) that social scientists "tend to assume that economic laissez-faire and political liberty go together. So let us study the formation of opinion and attitudes in countries where the two principles have developed independently and where economic state control has apparently not interfered with political freedom." This proposal to investigate the connection or the lack of it between marketization and democratization has yet to be fully addressed in social sciences research.

In international communication inquiry, comparative research has generated more heat than light. Part of the reason is that, over the past four decades, the field as a whole has engaged in research activities that are stuck in an outdated mode of replaying past experience without serious intellectual attempt to go beyond the conceptual boundaries of existing frameworks in knowledge production. The "dominant" model of cultural imperialism no longer fits the world of nations that are interconnected and interdependent in a global network society. For any theory of international communication to find the goodness of fit, it will have to clear the frame that contains scholars and researchers in a groupthink mind-set.

REFERENCES

Alford, R. R., & Friedland, R. (1985). *Powers of theory: Capitalism, the state, and democracy.* Cambridge: Cambridge University Press.

Boyd-Barrett, O. (1977). Media imperialism: Towards an international framework for the analysis of media systems. In J. Curran, M. Gurevitch, & J. Woollacott, eds., *Mass communication and society* (pp. 116–35). London: Edward Arnold.

Carnoy, M., & Castells, M. (2001). Globalization, the knowledge society, and the Network State: Poulantzas at the millennium. *Global Networks* 1:1–18.

Chadha, K., & Kavoori, A. (2000). Media imperialism revisited: Some findings from the Asian case. *Media, Culture & Society* 22:415–32.

Chakravartty, P., & Zhao, Y., eds. (2008). *Global communications: Toward a transcultural political economy*. Lanham: Rowman & Littlefield.

Chang, T.-K. (2010). Changing global media landscape, unchanging theories? International communication research and paradigm testing. In G. J. Golan, T. J. Johnson, & W. Wanta, eds., *International communication in a global age* (pp. 8–35). New York: Routledge.

Chang, T.-K., Berg, P., Fung, A. Y.-H., Kedl, K. D., Luther, C. A., & Szuba, J. (2001). Comparing nations in mass communication research, 1970–1997: A critical assessment of how we know what we know. *Gazette* 63: 415–34.

Chang, T.-K., Huh, J., McKinney, K., Sar, S., Wei, W., & Schneeweis, A. (2009). Culture and its influence on advertising: Misguided framework, inadequate comparative design and dubious knowledge claim. *International Communication Gazette* 71 (8): 1–22.

Curran, J., & Park, M.-J., eds. (2000). *De-Westernizing media studies*. London: Routledge.

Curtin, M. (2007). *Playing to the world's biggest audience: The globalization of Chinese film and TV.* Berkeley: University of California Press.

Dorfman, A., & Mattelart, A. (1975). *How to read Donald Duck: Imperialist ideology in the Disney comic.* New York: International General.

Fejes, F. (1981). Media imperialism: An assessment. *Media, Culture and Society* 3:281–89.

Fejes, F. (1986). *Imperialism, media, and the good neighbor: New Deal foreign policy and United States shortwave broadcasting to Latin America.* Norwood, NJ: Ablex.

Fortner, R. S. (1993). *International communication: History, conflict, and control of global metropolis.* Belmont, CA: Wadsworth.

Frederick, H. H. (1993). *Global communication and international relations.* Belmont, CA: Wadsworth.

Galtung, J. (1971). A structural theory of imperialism. *Journal of Peace Research* 8:81–117.

Galtung, J. (1990). Theory formation in social research: A plea for pluralism. In E. Oyen, ed., *Comparative methodology: Theory and practice in international social research* (pp. 96–112). London: Sage.

Goffman, E. (1974). *Frame analysis: An essay on the organization of experience.* New York: Harper Colophon.

Golding, P., and Harris, P., eds. (1997). *Beyond cultural imperialism: Globalization, communication and the new international order.* London: Sage.

Greig, J. M. (2002). The end of geography? Globalization, communications, and culture in the international system. *Journal of Conflict Resolution* 46:225–43.

Hamm, B., & Smandych, R., eds. (2005). *Cultural imperialism: Essays on the political economy of cultural domination.* Peterborough, ONT: Broadview Press.

Himelboim, I., Chang, T.-K., & McCreery, S. (2010). International network of foreign news coverage: Old global hierarchies in a new online world. *Journalism & Mass Communication Quarterly* 87 (2): 297–314.

Hur, K. K. (1982). International mass communication research: A critical review of theory and methods. In M. Burgoon & A. E. Doran, eds., *Communication Yearbook 6* (pp. 531–54). Beverly Hills, CA: Sage.

Kamalipour, Y. R., ed. (2007). *Global communication.* 2nd ed. Belmont, CA: Thomson Wadsworth.

Katz, E. (1987). Communication research since Larzarsfeld. *Public Opinion Quarterly* 51: S25–S45.

Kuhn, T. S. (1970). *The structure of scientific revolutions.* 2nd ed., enlarged. Chicago: University of Chicago Press.

Lazarsfeld, P. F. (1952–53). The prognosis for international communications research. *Public Opinion Quarterly* 16:481–90.

Lee, C.-C. (1980). *Media imperialism reconsidered: The homogenizing of television culture.* Beverly Hills, CA: Sage.

Lee, S.-N. P. (1988). Communication imperialism and dependency: A conceptual clarification. *Gazette* 41:69–83.

Liebes, T., & Katz, E. (1990). *The export of meaning: Cross-cultural readings of Dallas.* New York: Oxford University Press.

Mannheim, K. (1936). *Ideology and utopia: An introduction to the sociology of knowledge.* San Diego: Harcourt Brace & Company.

McPhail, T. L. (2002). *Global communication: Theories, stakeholders, and trends.* Boston: Allyn and Bacon.

McPhail, T. L. (2010). *Global communication: Theories, stakeholders, and trends.* Malden, MA: Blackwell.

Merton, R. K. (1967). *On theoretical sociology: Five essays, old and new.* New York: Free Press.

Neck, C. P., & Moorhead, G. (1995). Groupthink remodeled: The importance of leadership, time pressure, and methodological decision-making procedures. *Human Relations* 48:537–57.

Roach, C. (1997). Cultural imperialism and resistance in media theory and literary theory. *Media, Culture & Society* 19:47–66.

Salwen, M. B. (1991). Cultural imperialism: A media effects approach. *Critical Studies in Mass Communication* 8:29–38.

Schiller, H. I. (1969). *Mass communications and American empire.* New York: A. M. Kelly.

Simonson, P. (2006). Introduction. *Annals of the American Academy of Political and Social Science* 608: 6–24.

Sparks, C. (2000). Media theory after the fall of European communism: Why the old models from East and West won't do any more. In J. Curran and M.-J. Park, eds., *De-Westernizing media studies* (pp. 35–49). London: Routledge.

Stevenson, R. L. (1992). Defining international communication as a field. *Journalism Quarterly* 63:543–53.

Street, M. D. (1997). Groupthink: An examination of theoretical issues, implications and future research suggestions. *Small Group Research* 28:72–93.

Tomlinson, J. (1991). *Cultural imperialism.* Baltimore: Johns Hopkins University Press.

Thussu, D. K. (2000). *International communication: Continuity and change.* London: Arnold.

Thussu, D. K. (2006). *International communication: Continuity and change.* 2nd ed. London: Hodder Arnold.

Tunstall, J. (1977). *The media are American: Anglo-American media in the world.* New York: Columbia University Press.

Tunstall, J. (2008). *The media were American: U.S. mass media in decline.* New York: Oxford University Press.

Vilas, C. M. (2002). Globalization as imperialism. *Latin American Perspectives* 29:70–79.

Wang, G., Servaes, J., & Goonasekera, A., eds. (2000). *The new communication landscape: Demystifying media globalization.* London: Routledge.

Wells, A. (1972). *Picture-tube imperialism? The impact of U.S. television on Latin America.* Maryknoll, NY: Orbis Books.

Wolf, F. M. (1986). *Meta-analysis: Quantitative methods for research synthesis.* Beverly Hills, CA: Sage.

NOTES

1. See "Politics, Social Networks, and the History of Mass Communications Research: Rereading Personal Influence," *Annals of the American Academy of Political and Social Science* (November 2006).

2. Kuhn (1970) used the term *paradigm* in two different senses. "On the one hand, it stands for the entire constellation of beliefs, values, techniques, and so on *shared by* the members of a given community. On the other, it denotes one sort of element in that constellation, the *concrete puzzle-solutions* which, employed as models or examples, can replace explicit rules as a basis for the solution of the remaining puzzles of normal sciences" (p. 175, emphasis added). It should be evident that cultural imperialism as a theory has not been shared by the members of international communication research community; nor has it offered any concrete puzzle-solutions to the problems of international communication.

3. In this study, the term *cultural imperialism* is used as an encompassing concept to include all types of communication-related forms of imperialism that have been coined in the literature. As will be discussed later, the addition of an adjective word (e.g., *media, cultural, communication,* or *informatic*) to precede *imperialism* appears to be merely a form of keying to frame the thesis in a particular way.

4. There are, of course, other major concepts in international communication that can be addressed. But no other concepts appear to come closer to the impacts of cultural imperialism as received knowledge in both academic and journalistic communities.

5. Using the exact phrase in the full text search, 65 items in the JSTOR database include "cultural imperialism" in the text, with the earliest one published in the *Yale Law Journal* in 1946 and the majority of them (81.5%) appearing in the last three decades (1980–2009). For the concept "media imperialism," 15 items were published in the 1980s and 1990s. Only two items referred to the concepts "communication imperialism" and "informatic imperialism": one in a footnote and the other in the text.

6. The JSTOR database does not include any of the journals related to communication research, except for *Public Opinion Quarterly*. This means that journals that are most likely to publish international communication studies have been excluded, making the analysis incomplete.

CHAPTER FOUR

Beyond Modernization and the Four Theories of the Press

Jan Servaes

Lerner's model is, at least, an approximation of the Western experience and must not be accepted as a developmental inevitability. Lerner's attempt to generalize to a universal process from rather limited historical experience should be treated with great caution. The model is an ethnocentric identification of Western (especially American) middle-class values and images.

—Chin-Chuan Lee (1980, p. 21)

Perhaps the main feature in the philosophy of American exceptionalism is the argument that the United States is unique, but at the same time its values and interests are universal.

—Hemant Shah (2011, p. 148)

Differences or diversity cannot and will not stop understanding and communication, but ignoring them will.

—Georgette Wang (2011c, p. 271)

The above opening quotes are just three among a selection of available critical assessments of the Western bias in international and development communication (see the list of references for starters). Together they could be summarized in a few succinct points that

- Question and broaden the epistemological and ontological assumptions on which our scientific field is based. We need to look for ways to complement the still dominant Western positivistic perspectives with interpretive social constructivist approaches, which might contribute to a more universalistic interpretation of reality.

- At the level of the so-called Kuhnian paradigm discussion the original model of modernization has been complemented/replaced by other models, such as dependency, multiplicity, globalization. However, these alternatives tend to be driven by a Western missionary zeal for outward expansion. More attention needs to be paid to perspectives which are inward looking and less determined by "imperialistic" objectives.

- Consequently, our methods and techniques for inquiry need to be reconsidered in view of the above considerations. The limitations of quantitative methods and findings have become obvious. However, qualitative inquiries also need to be critically assessed. An integration of quantitative and qualitative techniques from a participatory perspective may provide more adequate and relevant answers.

- Comparative cross-national or intercultural research too often starts from an implicit Western bias. Models and frameworks developed in a Western context are used as templates for evaluation and comparison. A genuine indigenous starting point may be needed.

If the above is "common knowledge," why hasn't the mainstream of international and development communication research embraced these obvious considerations? That could be the conclusion emerging out of the findings of three scholars who have been assessing the "richness" of the field in a historical perspective: Jo Ellen Fair, Hemant Shah, and Christine Ogan. They each, either alone or with their graduate students, by examining journal articles, books, and book chapters wanted to highlight the directions that the research took in different periods, broadly defined as from 1958 to 1986, from 1987 to 1996, from 1997 to 2005, and from 1998 to 2007.

In the 1958–86 period models predicting either powerful effects or limited effects informed the research: "Communication has been a key element in the West's project of developing the Third World. In the one-and-a-half decades after Lerner's influential 1958 study of communication and development in the Middle East, communication researchers assumed that the introduction of media and certain types of educational, political, and economic information into a social system could transform individuals and societies from traditional to modern. Conceived as having fairly direct and powerful effects on Third World audiences, the media were seen as magic multipliers, able to accelerate and magnify the benefits of development" (Fair, 1989, p. 145).

In the 1987–96 period, "Lerner's modernization model completely disappears. Instead, the most frequently used theoretical framework is participatory development, an optimist postmodern orientation, which is almost the polar opposite of Lerner who viewed mass communication as playing a top-down role in social change. Also vanishing from research in this latter period is the two-step flow model, which was drawn upon by modernization scholars" (Fair & Shah, 1997, p. 10).

The two more recent periods, which partly overlap, 1997–2005 and 1998–2007, provide new findings that may be surprising to some. I quote from Shah's essay first:

First, Lerner's model of media and development has reappeared in the 1997–2005 time period after totally disappearing in the 1987–1996 period. Second, only two other theories from the traditional US-based behavioral science approach, social learning theory and knowledge gap, appear in the 1997–2005 period. The third trend to note is that the two most prominently mentioned theories in 1997–2005—participatory communication and social learning—reflect two popular development communication project orientations that were mentioned as innovations in the 1987–1996 study: participatory development and edu-tainment (Shah, 2007, p. 13).

Shah explains the persistence of "old" ideas, especially Lerner's model (1958, 1977), from a technological deterministic perspective: "Each new technological innovation in the postcolonial world since 1958—television, satellites, microwave, computers, call centers, wireless technology—has been accompanied by determined hope that Lerner's modernization model will increase growth and productivity and produce modern cosmopolitan citizens" (Shah, 2007, p. 24; see also Shah, 2011).

Also Ogan and her students (2009) conclude that studies have moved away from mass communication and toward Information and Communication Technologies' (ICTs') role in development, that they infrequently address development in the context of globalization, and often continue to embrace a modernization paradigm despite its many criticisms. They argued, "We believe that the more recent attention to ICTs has to do with the constant search for the magic solution to bringing information to people to transform their lives, allowing them to improve their economic condition, educate their children, increase literacy and the levels of education and spread democracy in their countries. Despite years of research that tells us that information is necessary but insufficient to bring about this change, ICTs have become the most recent iteration of the holy grail for development. And even if communication scholars know better because critical scholarship written over the last 30 years has told them so, newcomers to this field from other information-based disciplines may not have such close acquaintance with that literature. Furthermore, because of the appeal of the modernization paradigm, there is a tendency to forget that it cannot work" (Ogan et al., 2009, pp. 667–68).

In other words, there may be more at stake than ignorance. It may well be that the Western bias in international communication was and is a convenient way for the powers that be to maintain the status quo, assisted by a community of academics who, as Pierre Bourdieu eloquently argued, are a conservative lot sui generis (Servaes, 2012).

It is my intention to provide some additional ammunition in this chapter by looking at the historical context in which international communication evolved, questioning some of the assumptions on which the so-called Four Theories of the Press were based, and briefly outlining a possible way out of the current stalemate.

The Historical Context for the "Western Bias"

The proclamation of the Four Freedoms by President Franklin Roosevelt on 6 January 1941 (Freedom of Speech, Freedom of Expression, Freedom from Want, and Freedom from Fear), the launch of the Marshall Plan in 1947 after the Second World War, the establishment of the Bretton Woods financial system and the creation of the World Bank, the IMF, the United Nations, and its regional and specialized affiliates, all led to what Amy Staples (2006) called the birth of development, or what Eric Louw (2010) has characterized as the Pax Americana.

Many developing countries saw the "welfare state" of the North Atlantic nations as the ultimate goal of development. These developing nations were attracted by the new technology transfer and the model of a centralized state with careful economic planning and centrally directed development bureaucracies for agriculture, education, and health as the most effective strategies to catch up with the industrialized countries. This perspective has been typified by many, including myself, as the modernization paradigm (Servaes, 1999, 2008).

Modernization accelerated the growth of a Westernized elite structure and of urbanization. Latham (2000) explains how social science theory helped shape American foreign policy during the Kennedy administration and resulted in the Alliance for Progress with Latin America, the Peace Corps, and other U.S. development aid programs worldwide. It was assumed that, with the help of foreign aid, the rural backward areas would be developed in the area of agriculture, basic education, health, rural transportation, community development, and so forth. As a result, government bureaucracies were extended to the major urban centers. In fact, the United States was defining development as the replica of its own political-economic system and opening the way for the transnational corporations. Christopher Simpson (1994, 1998), Rohan Samarajiva (1987), and Hemant Shah (2011), who examined the beginnings of the development communication concept, find that the seminal work by Daniel Lerner (1958) and Wilbur Schramm (1954) was a spin-off from a large and clandestine audience research project conducted for the Voice of America by the Bureau of Applied Social Research. Some of their research reports still remain classified by the CIA. They note the strong influence exerted by the demands of psychological warfare, in the context of the Cold War, on the early studies of communication in the United States: "Exploratory work on the early period suggests the following pattern of net influence flows: marketing research to communication research; marketing and communication research to psychological warfare; from psychological warfare to communication and development" (Samarajiva, 1987, p. 17).

Similar observations have been made by other scholars (see, e.g., Ambrose, 1983; Krige & Barth, 2006; McMichael, 2008; Roberts, 2006; Schiller, 1969, 1976; Smythe, 1981; Smythe & Van Dinh, 1983; or Tunstall, 1977).

The broadcasting system was used mainly for entertainment and news. Radio was a channel for national campaigns to persuade the people about specific and select health and agricultural practices. According to Robert White (1988, p. 9): "The most significant communication dimension of the modernization design in the developing world has been the rapid improvement of the transportation, which linked rural communities into market towns and regional cities. With improved transportation and sources of electric power, the opening of commercial consumer supply networks stretched out into towns and villages carrying with it the Western consumer culture and pop culture of films, radio and pop music. Although rural people in Bolivia or Sri Lanka may not have attained the consumption styles of American middle-class populations, their life did change profoundly. This was the real face of modernization."

Communication for Development

From the 1950s onwards, communication models became increasingly central to the programs of development being undertaken. The basic idea was that communication stimulates and diffuses values and institutions that are favorable to achievement, mobility, innovations, and consumption, or, what it means to "become modern." According to Lerner (1958), the general psychological conditions captured by the concept of empathy stimulated mobility and urbanization, which, in turn, increased literacy and consequently economic and political participation—all essential to the modernization process. The media would serve to stimulate, in direct and indirect ways, the conditions of "psychological mobility" that were considered crucial to economic development. In other words, central in Lerner's 1958 study was the argument that empathic persons have a higher degree of mobility, meaning a high capacity for change, and were more future oriented and rational than so-called traditional people. The driving concepts behind the link between communication and development were basically of a quantifiable and linear nature: How much and in what ways can communication contribute to the process of modernization? Such questions relied primarily on transmission models of communication derived from work in information engineering, in political campaigns, and the diffusion of ideas. Based on Lerner's concept of empathy, Inkeles and Smith (1974) concluded their comparative analysis of six developing countries that "modern" people increasingly trust the mass media more than personal media for world news. Hence, in their opinion, modern people prefer national and international news rather than sports, religious, or local news.

Building on Lerner's work, Wilbur Schramm (1964) took a closer look at the connections between mass communication and modernizing practices and institutions. He suggested that there are at least three indispensable functions performed by the mass media in a modern or modernizing society: they are "watchdogs," "policy makers," and "teachers" for change. Schramm proposed that every country should aim at a minimum level of mass media facilities: 10 copies of daily newspapers, five radio receivers, two cinema seats, and two television receivers per 100 inhabitants. Reflecting the influence of the two-step flow theory of communication and the stress on attitudes and attitudinal change, Schramm saw modern communication media as supplementing and complementing the oral channels of a traditional society. Schramm suggested that the mass media functioned as mobility multipliers. The relative popularity of these models within the development literature and practices of the time can be traced to three attributes associated with this way of conceptualizing the communication process. First, because they identified communication basically as the transfer of information focused on efficiency or effects. This was true both in a social sense, such as in Rogers's (1962) diffusion of innovation theory (which has changed somewhat in the course of five editions, as observed by Hoffmann 2007), as well as in a technological deterministic sense (for which McLuhan 1964 is the chief proponent). McLuhan (1964) sees technology as a value-free and politically neutral asset in bringing about the modernization of under-developed countries. He argued that technology gradually creates a totally new human environment. This "totally new human environment" was that of the modern society. In other words, technology is an inexorable force in development, irresistible and overwhelming. Rogers (1962, 1986, 2003) stressed the adoption and diffusion processes of cultural innovation. Mass media are important in spreading awareness of new possibilities and practices, but at the stage where decisions are being made, personal communication is far more likely to be influential. Therefore, the general conclusion is that mass communication is less likely than personal influence to have a direct effect on social behavior.

Also, the communication models fit neatly into the nature and mechanics of mass or mediated communication, an emergent and powerful force at that time. In other words, communication was primarily about the manipulation of messages and people for the purposes of directed development. Implicit in this formulation was the idea that media messages are like a "bullet" or "hypodermic needle," whose effects are quickly and efficiently inserted into the consciousness of receivers. Over the years—as documented by Hornik (1988), Leeuwis and Van Den Ban (2004) and in the historical meta-analysis summarized in the introduction—this may have changed slightly but not fundamentally.

A Critical Assessment of the Modernization Paradigm

Since the 1960s, communication and modernization has come under attack from distinct sides in different parts of the world. The most important points of this criticism of the modernization view of communication can be summarized as follows (further elaborated in Servaes, 1999, 2008):

1. Empirically, what has been studied are primarily specific, quantitatively measurable, short-term, and individual effects that are generalized in a questionable manner. When testing Lerner's thesis, for instance, several

scholars, including Schramm and Ruggels (1967), have found little evidence of any single pattern of mass media growth in relation to literacy, urbanization, and per capita income. Rather, the evidence showed that these patterns vary widely by region, environment, or culture.

2. This approach starts from basic positivistic and behavioristic positions that presuppose a linear, rational sequence of events, planned in advance and with criteria of rationality determined externally. The assumption is that human behavior can be explained in terms of independent, isolated, and direct causalities, as has been the case with the behavioristic stimulus-response model. The process of communication through mass media is compared to the communication process in face-to-face situations. The transmission of information is viewed as an isolated and linear activity, with a beginning and an end. This concept, which is directly derived from the mechanistic information theory, is, in my opinion, difficult to transfer to processes of human interaction where the context, in which the transmission or communication process occurs, form an integrated and substantial part of the overall process.

3. Positivism assumes "reality" can be "objectively" and empirically grasped, and rarely questions these assumptions. Indeed, the normal mode is to laugh off those who do, or request they empirically invalidate empiricism. In many cultures, however, the immeasurable (i.e., that which cannot be named, described or understood through any form of reason) is regarded as the primary reality. Rather than a stimulus-response switchbox, people are regarded as active, creative, purposeful creatures. Writing about the Brahmin view of "oneness and subjectivity," Jayaweera and Amunuguma (1987, p. 41) say such challenges "are not likely to be considered seriously by social scientists . . . who purport to live in the real world of empirical science. But then their 'real world' . . . is being shown up to be mostly a fiction, and that, by the most scientific among them, the high-energy physicists."

4. In most Sender-Receiver models the social context in which communication takes place is absent. Therefore, according to Thomas (1982, p. 84), "the entire notion of a Sender-Receiver relationship may tend to obscure the process of information transmission as it occurs at the social level of behavior." The notion of intentionality is still considered to be a basic aspect of any definition of communication. This notion assumes implicitly—in the "uses and gratifications" theory even explicitly—that each human activity can be explained on the basis of a subjective definition provided by the actors themselves. In other words, human behavior

is not conditioned by one's place in a social context (system or subsystem, social group or class), but by the individual's self-defined place and impact on his or hers environment. This results in dominant and dominated man-man relationships that are consistent with the anti-historical dominant man-environment relationship that constitutes the Western world view of history. More specifically, the two-step-flow hypothesis neglects the fact that a great amount of information flows directly from the media to users without passing through an opinion leader. Furthermore, the concept of opinion leader has proven to be far too simple. It can be said, for instance, that change can and should occur from below by those who need it on their own behalf.

5. Little attention is given to sociological and contextual factors except for commercial and ideological reasons. By motivating individuals to aspire to mobility and higher standards of living, the media, in editorial material as well as advertising, are creating the kind of consumer demand that maintains the dependence of Third World economies on the West. Partly because of the high proportion of imported programs, partly because of imitation, the dominant message of the media is conservatism, materialism, and conformism. Even schools and educational TV programs reinforce this kind of ideas. At the same time, by omitting advertising from much research and only concentrating on the content of editorial material, these researchers divert attention away from the principal intended object of the mass media, namely to produce and market to advertisers the means to complete the marketing of consumer goods and services. Therefore, Dallas Smythe (1981, p. 250) argues that "in this way, they [these researchers] naturally protect from investigation the blind spot: the audience and its work."

6. As a result of the underlying ethnocentrism and endogenism one takes for granted that results derived from U.S. campaigns can be extrapolated toward Third World settings, or that the media hardware as well as software has to be imported from "outside." This rather deterministic perspective has had very negative consequences, especially in the field of technology transfer. Therefore, one could argue for an integrated and multidimensional approach in which communication technology has to be considered as a complement to the development process. However, in reality, one often observes that technologies are under the control of those with power and will be used in ways consistent with those interests or remain inaccessible to the majority of the population, or both.

7. The static and ahistorical manner of studying communication processes leads to the supposition of a stable social system where social har-

mony and integration prevails and where class struggle or social conflicts and contradictions are non-existent. Rao (1986, p. 202) says such research "equals a long series of empirical-analytical, fragmentary, piecemeal studies, guided by the dichotomy of facts and values, directed by the interested to steer social technology for status-quo purposes, and epistemologically handicapped by the Kantian tradition of confining reality to predefined categories which are applied to it."

The Four Theories

Traditionally, in communication sciences one used to refer to the book by Siebert, Peterson, and Schramm (1956) for a positioning of the relationship between media and society, or, the so-called normative media theories. Siebert, Peterson and Schramm started from the assumption that "the press always takes on the coloration of the social and political structures within which it operates. Especially it reflects the system of social control whereby the relations of individuals and institutions are adjusted" (Siebert, Peterson, & Schramm, 1956, pp. 1–2). The four models they identified have become critiqued since for being too Western-centric and for making unrealistic universalistic claims. Additions such as the "development model" and the "democratic-participatory model" were introduced (for an overview, see, e.g., Hachten, 1996; Hachten and Scotton 2007; Merrill, 1974, 1979, 1989; McQuail, 2005; Nerone, 1995; or Servaes, 1989). However, Siebert's starting thesis was never questioned. The above-mentioned authors also think that, as summarized by John Merrill (1979), "media systems are, of course, closely related to the kinds of governments in which they operate; they are, in essence, reflective and supportive of the governmental philosophy. When viewed in this way, it is possible to say that all press systems are enslaved—tied to their respective governmental philosophies and forced to operate within certain national ideological parameters" (Merrill, 1979, p. 153).

Three of the more recent contributions to the tradition of comparative media theories and systems are the work by Christians et al. (2009), the overview presented by Daniel Hallin and Paolo Mancini (2004), and the assessment of recent social and media changes in central and eastern Europe by Karol Jakubowicz (2007). Of these three, Hallin and Mancini's work is the one most often quoted and used in comparative analytical ways (see, for instance, the recent overview of European journalism education, edited by Terzis, 2009).

Hallin and Mancini (2004) distinguish between three models: the North Atlantic or Liberal Model (which includes Britain, United States, Canada, and Ireland), the Northern European or Democratic Corporatist Model (Austria, Belgium, Denmark, Finland, Germany, Netherlands, Norway, Sweden, and Switzerland), and the Mediterranean or Polarized Pluralist Model (France, Greece, Italy, Portugal, and Spain). A fourth model has been added by Karol Jakubowicz (2007), who, assessing the central and eastern European region and quoting Hallin and Mancini, argues that, since the falling apart of the former Communist bloc, central and eastern European journalism has embraced the liberal or Anglo-American version of professional journalism. While many local people (including journalists) initially welcomed the "spreading of the gospel of democracy" (especially the financial benefits that accompanied it) into their world, this new love affair has lost some of its glamour lately, especially since the 2008–9 global financial meltdown has had a sobering ripple effect on all sectors of society, including the post-Communist version of journalism with its blind belief in unbridled individual freedom and free market principles. However, because of the strong historic role of the state, "the Democratic Corporatist Model, we suspect, will have particularly strong relevance for the analysis of those parts of Eastern and Central Europe that share much of the same historical development" (Hallin & Mancini, 2004, p. 305).

In view of the recent economic crisis, the far too optimistic hint by Hallin and Mancini (2004, p. 301) that "there is . . . a clear tendency of convergence toward the Liberal system" against the two other models may need to be re-assessed. Hallin & Mancini warn against simplistic generalizations—there are important differences among and within the media systems they grouped together—and plead for more comparative historical and ethnographic research on the subject. They also make an effort to assess how the three models "might relate to other systems" in the so-called developing world: "Even though the Liberal Model has dominated media studies and has served as the principal normative model against which other media systems have traditionally been measured, it is probably the Polarized Pluralist Model, more than the other two, that is most widely applicable to other systems as an empirical model of the relation between media and political systems. We suspect that scholars working on many parts of the world—eastern Europe and the former Soviet Union, Latin America, the Middle East and all of the Mediterranean region, Africa, and most of Asia—will find much that is relevant in our analysis of Southern Europe, including the role of clientelism, the strong role of the state, the role of media as an instrument of political struggle, the limited development of mass circulation press, and the relative weakness of common professional norms" (Hallin & Mancini, 2004, p. 306).

Hallin and Mancini's comparative analysis still overemphasizes political, technological and economic conditions, and implicitly disregards, apart from the proverbial lip service, the importance of cultural dimensions in media systems and societies. By collapsing almost all non-Western countries and regions under one category, they do injustice to the complexity, specificity, and richness of local, national, and sociocultural systems. For instance, in the African context, the anthropological analysis of the African political and media system by Francis Nyamnjoh (2005, 2007) or the philosophical observations by people like Kwame Appiah (2005, 2006) and Molefi Kete Asante (2007) are far more sophisticated and multifaceted than the Polarized Pluralist Model may make us believe.

A More Complex and Integrated Framework
for Normative Media Theories

Already in the eighties (see, e.g., Servaes, 1982, 1989; Servaes & Tonnaer, 1992) I have argued in favor of a triple and dialectically integrated framework for the study of the so-called normative media theories: at a philosophical, a political-economic, and a culturalist-anthropological level. Christians et al. (2009, p. 16) use a more or less similar typology: a philosophical level focusing on normative traditions; a political one assessing models of democracy; and the different roles the media can play. We consider the role of the media part of the culture at large.

My critique was that the classic models are based on, on the one hand, a too restricted (Western) description of concepts like "freedom," "democracy," "objectivity," and so on, which allow little or no generalizations; and that, on the other hand, reality often doesn't comply with the principles defined in philosophical terms. Traditional principles such as the freedom of the press and professional journalism practices, I contended, need a radical rethinking in order to become an integral aspect of the process of democratization in both media and society. I am glad to notice that this 'coupling of journalism and democracy' was the theme of a recent special issue of *Journalism*, edited by Beate Josephi, who concluded: "All panelists (Nerone, Zelizer, George, Waisbord, i.a. [inter alia]) agreed that the dominance of the journalism and democracy paradigm found to date in scholarly literature has led to a distortion in the way journalism is perceived" (Josephi, 2013, p. 441).

The increasing multiplicity and convergence of ICTs, the Internet, and social networks, the deregulation of media markets, and the cultural globalization/localization of media products and services forces a re-assessment of international communication. Multi-tasking on different media platforms and the 24/7 news circles challenge journalists not only in technical ways but force them to reconsider classic notions of balance, objectivity and bias (Thussu, 2008). This also accounts for the interpretation of concepts such as cultural and press freedom in, for instance, the post-communist world (Casmir, 1995; De Smaele, 1999; Jakubowicz, 2007), Asia (Iyer, 2001), Latin America (Beltran, 1993; Fox, 1988) or Islamic society (Hussain, 2006); a discussion on journalism ethics and universal versus particular values (Christians & Traber, 1997; Karikari, 1996; Preston, 2007; Ukpabi, 2001), journalism in a Buddhist (Dissanayake, 2006; Gunaratne, 2007) or Confucian/Chinese (Chen, 2004; Gunaratne, 2005) tradition; or deontological codes and practices in different parts of the world (Mendel, 2008; Pigeat & Huteau, 2000).

Christians et al. (2009) identify four distinct yet overlapping roles for the media: the monitorial role of a vigilant informer collecting and publishing information of potential interest to the public; the facilitative role that not only reports on but also seeks to support and strengthen civil society; the radical role that challenges authority and voices support for reform; and the collaborative role that creates partnerships between journalists and centers of power in society, notably the state, to advance mutually acceptable interests. Each role could be associated with a specific set of competencies, which the journalist or knowledge worker of the future needs to acquire in order to perform adequately. In other words, competencies are characteristics that individuals have and use in appropriate, consistent ways in order to achieve a desired performance. These characteristics include knowledge, skills, aspects of self-image, social motives, thought patterns, mind-sets, and ways of thinking, feeling, and acting (Dubois & Rothwell, 2004; Irigoin et al., 2002; Hofstede & Hofstede, 2005). The journalistic competencies needed to operate in today's complex world are manifold and are almost impossible to acquire during a regular journalism program. They range from core or generic competencies (e.g., communication, teamwork) to managerial competencies (e.g., empowering others, decision making) and technical or specialist competencies related to specific jobs within the journalism profession. In other words, a competency is measured by identifying the behaviors or tangible results (outcomes) produced by their use in the context of the work performed.

For Instance: Thailand

If we return to the earlier argument made by Hallin & Mancini that most countries in Asia are leaning towards a Polarized Pluralist Model and apply this to the case of Thailand, we are faced with a complex picture. Thailand was once recognized as the country with the most liberal media system in Southeast Asia. Thailand has also been boasting about its constitution as being one of the most democratic in the region (Chongkittavorn, 2000, p. 37).

Therefore, as Thailand has never been colonized in a formal sense, the country provides an interesting case study. Advocates of the Liberal Model claim that if the press were regulated it would become a servant of the state. Privately owned media competing in a free market, they argue, can ensure complete independence from the government. The fourth estate is ensured by the market relationship between the press and its audience. Ideally, through their buying power, consumers, not the government, act as the controllers of press output (Wheeler, 1997, p. 129).

Unfortunately, the privately owned media in Thailand do not operate in this ideal way. As the media rely largely on advertisement revenues, it is hard to keep them away from external political and economic pressures. Since its inception in 1932 the Thai democracy has always been an oligarchy, governed by an ever-changing coalition of elites (Lertvicha, 1987; Nelson, 2004). Hence, it is difficult to stop the nature of corruption in Thailand as journalists chose their careers and media increase income by censoring themselves, and for the most part they reliably transmit the message of the rulers to the people (Lertrattanavisut, 2004; Phongpaichit & Priryarangsan, 1994). Furthermore, under the concept of "lèse majesté," the media cannot cover news about the royal family in a disrespectful or critical way.

Within such a frame, the political situation in Thailand has turned into turmoil, with the Thai people roughly divided into two groups. The first group consists of the grass roots that were happy with former prime minister Thaksin's populist policy and those advocating globalization and a total neo-liberalism. The second group consists of the suburban middle class and intellectuals who advocate the king's sufficient economy concept (Likhitsomboon, 2006, 25; Prasirtsuk, 2007). Each group claims to promote a more sufficient economy and civic and just society (Wasi, 2003, p. 136).

Several characteristics make the Thai media system different from most other media systems in Asia (see Cheypratub, 1995; Chongkittavorn, 2000; McCarco, 2000; Servaes, 1999; Servaes, Malikhao, & Pinprayong, 2009; Siriyuvasak, 2004, 2005; Supadhiloke, 2007, 2008; Taveesin & Brown, 2006). Or, as Lauren Kogen, who assessed the relevance of the Hallin & Mancini model in the case of Thailand, concludes: "Citizens unsatisfied with the Thai version of democracy are protesting against the current regime, and continue to be suppressed, sometimes violently, by the state. During such uncertain times, civil society, the corporate world and the government will be facing off to try to find a way to balance power in the new system" (Kogen, 2010, p. 343). Whether Thais opt for total liberalization or a sufficient economy or a mixture of both, the Thai democratic and media system will remain difficult to comprehend from a Western perspective.

Challenges Ahead

Each from their specific vantage point, the following scholars provide unique insights and perspectives for a better understanding of what the future has in store: Bhambra (2007), on modernity; Braman and Sreberny-Mohammadi (1996), on globalization and localization as "interpenetrated globalization"; Cimadevilla and Carniglia (2004), on sustainability and rural development; Friedmann (1992), on empowerment; Geertz (1983), on local knowledge and "blurred genres"; Gunaratne (2005, 2011), on Asian philosophical perspectives; Hall and du Gay (1996) and Bera and Lamy (2008), on cultural identity; Lie (2003), on intercultural communication spaces; Thornton and Cimadevilla (2010), on participation; Tremblay (2007), on the relationship between communication and sustainable development; and Wronka (2008), on social justice and human rights.

This also implies that the cultural perspective has to be fully embraced, as argued by southern scholars such as Kwame Anthony Appiah (2005, 2006), Wimal Dissanayake (2006, 2011), Mohan Dutta (2011), Guo-Ming Chen (2004, 2011), Hattam (2004), Shelton Gunaratne (2005, 2011), Swaminathan (1994), Majid Tehranian (2007), and Georgette Wang (2011a).

Gunaratne (2005) attempts to de-Westernize communication theory. He interprets press theories from the perspective of Eastern philosophy and the emerging theory of living systems. He also draws from quantum physics, post-Parsonsian systems thinking, and world-systems analysis to derive a more humanocentric theoretical framework that reflects the integration of Eastern ontology with Western epistemology.

Hattam (2004) advocates for a socially engaged Buddhism that involves a creative and dialectical attitude toward Buddhist teachings as a middle way. It attempts to apply these principles to the highly complex and increasingly globalized world. A range of socially engaged perspectives are outlined including those from Nagarjuna, the Dalai Lama, Thich Nhat Hanh, Sulak Sivaraksa, and the Think Sangha.

Dissanayake (2006, 2011) argues for a new concept of humanism: "Humanism as generally understood in Western discourse . . . places at the center of its interest the sovereign individual—the individual who is self-present, the originator of action and meaning, and the privileged location of human values and civilizational achievements. However, the concept of the self and individual that is textualized in the kind of classical works that attract the attention of Asian communication theorists present a substantially different picture. The ontology and axiology of selfhood found in Buddhism differs considerably from those associated with European humanism. What these differences signpost is that there is not one but many humanisms" (Dissanayake, 2006, 6).

Many humanisms may lead to what Appiah calls the cosmopolitan challenge: "If we accept the cosmopolitan challenge, we will tell our representatives that we want them to remember those strangers. Not because we are moved by their suffering—we may or may not be—but because we are responsive to what Adam Smith called "reason, principle, conscience, the inhabitant of the beast." The people of the richest nations can do better. This is a demand of simple morality. But it is one that will resonate more widely if we make our civilization more cosmopolitan" (Appiah, 2006, p. 174).

By Way of Conclusion: "Internationalize" Media Education

These are some of the "problems" and "constraints" a genuine "internationalizing" of international communication may have to come to grips with. However, an equally important "internationalization" may need to take place in journalism and media education.

Professional education (of journalists and others) continues to be based on local or national parameters. It has to break out of its national carcass and internationalize. One of the central questions is "how do we escape national stereotypes in journalism education? How do we break the mode of a nationally biased understanding of media and news?" More multicultural and international "authentic" learning experiences, more innovative and critical reflection, more problem solving, social negotiation of information and knowledge, and collaboration are the challenges for journalism educators of the future. This will have a tremendous impact on teaching and learning (Servaes, 2009).

New needs for visual and online literacy will soon lead us into difficulties comparable to that of illiteracy in the nineteenth century. Like the illiterate of those times, the new illiterate will be, as we can clearly see from the diffusion patterns of new technologies, of lower social status, with an associated lower income and level of education. Medium-term developments may lead to a dichotomized social body made of, on the one hand, wealthier, better educated, and new literates having the skills and the means to access and use ICTs and, on the other hand, poorer, less educated, and new illiterates kept out of the new tech scene and deprived of most technologies and hence denied access to an increasing amount of information and culture. Hence, the need for new forms of media education.

Furthermore, in order to promote participation, it is important to reinforce independent and pluralistic media. For media to be able to offer a critical view of government, political and economic systems must enable the media to operate in as open a public sphere as possible. Press freedom is never guaranteed, particularly when media industries are commercialized, even in a democracy. Apart from creating the appropriate political and economic environments for an independent media system, it is crucial to educate journalists to the highest ethical and professional standards possible. How to deal with a permanent overload of information will be the key challenge for journalists and citizens alike, and how to regulate this in a democratic way will be the challenge for public authorities (Servaes, 2005). For both journalists and citizens the capacity and speed to access, retrieve, select, and reproduce information and turn it into knowledge will determine power and facilitate change in the age of globalization.

REFERENCES

Aeusrivonse, N. (2004). Building popular participation: Sustainability of democracy in Thailand. In M. Nelson, ed., *Thai politics: Global and local perspectives*. Nonthaburi, Thailand: King Prajadhipok's Institute.

Ambrose, S. (1983). *Rise to globalism: American foreign policy since 1938*. Harmondsworth, UK: Penguin.

Appiah, K. A. (2005). *The ethics of identity*. Princeton, NJ: Princeton University Press.

Appiah, K. A. (2006). *Cosmopolitanism: Ethics in a world of strangers*. London: Allen Lane.

Asante, M. K. (2007). *An Afrocentric manifesto*. Cambridge: Polity.

Beltran, L. R. (1993). Communication for development in Latin America: A forty-year appraisal. In D. Nostbakken & C. Morrow, eds., *Cultural expression in the global village*. Penang, Malaysia: Southbound.

Bera, M., & Lamy, Y. (2008). *Sociologie de la culture*. Paris: Armand Colin.

Bhambra, G. K. (2007). *Rethinking modernity: Postcolonialism and the sociological imagination*. London: Palgrave Macmillan.

Boyd-Barrett, O. (1977). Media imperialism: Towards an international framework for the analysis of media systems. In J. Curran, M. Gurevitch, & J. Woollacott, eds., *Mass communication and society* (pp. 116–41). London: Arnold.

Boyd-Barrett, O. (1982). Cultural dependency and the mass media. In M. Gurevitch, T. Bennett, J. Curran, & J. Woollacott, eds., *Culture, society and the media* (pp. 174–95). London: Methuen.

Braman, S., & Sreberny-Mohammadi, A., eds. (1996). *Globalization, communication, and transnational civil society*. Cresskill, NJ: Hampton Press.

Casmir, F., ed. (1995). *Communication in Eastern Europe: The role of history, culture, and media in contemporary conflicts*. Mahwah, NJ: Lawrence Erlbaum.

Charoensin-O-Larn, C. (1988). *Understanding postwar reformism in Thailand*. Bangkok: Editions Duang Kamol.

Chen, G.-M. (2004). The two faces of Chinese communication. *Human Communication: A Journal of the Pacific and Asian Communication Association* 7 (1): 25–36.

Chen, G.-M. (2011). Moving beyond the dichotomy of communication studies: Boundary wisdom as the key. In G. Wang, ed., *De-Westernizing communication research: Altering questions and changing frameworks* (pp. 157–71). New York: Routledge.

Cheypratub, S. (1995). *Sue muan chon lae karn pattana prathet: Nen chao pao prathet Thai* [Mass media and development: The case of Thailand]. Bangkok: Chulalongkorn Publishing House.

Chongkittavorn, K. (2000). Thailand: A troubled path to a hopeful future. In L. Williams & R. Rich, eds., *Losing control: Freedom of the press in Asia* (pp. 219–38). Canberra: Asia Pacific Press of the Australian National University.

Christians, C., Glasser, T. L., McQuail, D., Nordenstreng, K., & White, R. A. (2009). *Normative theories of the media: Journalism in democratic societies*. Urbana: University of Illinois Press.

Christians, C., & Traber, M., eds. (1997). *Communication ethics and universal values*. Thousand Oaks, CA: Sage.

Cimadevilla, G., & Carniglia, E., eds. (2004). *Comunicación, ruralidad y desarrollo: Mitos, paradigmas y dispositivos del cambio*. Buenos Aires: Instituto Nacional de Tecnología Agropecuaria (INTA).

Daorueng, P. (2004). Thai civil society and government control: A cyber struggle? In S. Gan, J. Gomez, & U. Johanan, eds., *Asian cyberactivism: Freedom of expression and media censorship*. Bonn: Friedrich Naumann Foundation.

de Smaele, H. (1999). The applicability of Western models on the Russian media system. *European Journal of Communication* 14 (2): 173–90.

Dissanayake, W. (2006). Postcolonial theory and Asian communication theory: Towards a creative dialogue. *China Media Research* 2 (4): 1–8.

Dissanayake, W. (2011). The production of Asian theories of communication: Contexts and challenges. In G. Wang, ed., *De-Westernizing communication research: Altering questions and changing frameworks* (pp. 222–37). New York: Routledge.

Dubois, D., & Rothwell, W. J. (2004). *Competency-based human resource management.* Palo Alto, CA: Davies-Black Publishing.

Dutta, M. (2011). *Communicating social change: Structure, culture, and agency.* New York: Routledge.

Fair, J. E. (1988). A meta-research of mass media effects on audiences in developing countries from 1958 through 1986. PhD diss., Indiana University.

Fair, J. E. (1989). 29 years of theory and research on media and development: The dominant paradigm impact. *Gazette* 44:129–50.

Fair, J. E., & Shah, H. (1997). Continuities and discontinuities in communication and development research since 1958. *Journal of International Communication* 4 (2): 3–23.

Fox, E. (1988). *Media and politics in Latin America: The struggle for democracy.* London: Sage.

Friedmann, J. (1992). *Empowerment: The politics of alternative development.* Cambridge, UK: Blackwell.

Geertz, C. (1983). *Local knowledge: Further essays in interpretive anthropology.* New York: Basic Books.

Gunaratne, S. (2005). *The dao of the press: A humanocentric theory.* Cresskill, NJ: Hampton Press.

Gunaratne, S. (2007). A Buddhist view of journalism: Emphasis on mutual causality. *Communication for Development and Social Change* 1 (3): 197–210.

Gunaratne, S. (2011). Emerging global divides in media and communication theory: European universalism versus non-Western reactions. In G. Wang, ed., *De-Westernizing communication research: Altering questions and changing frameworks* (pp. 28–49). New York: Routledge.

Hachten, W. (1996). *The world news prism: Changing media of international communication.* Ames: Iowa State University Press.

Hachten, W., & Scotton, J. (2007). *The world news prism: Global information in a satellite age.* 7th ed. Malden, MA: Blackwell.

Hall, S., & Du Gay, P., eds. (1996). *Questions of cultural identity.* London: Sage.

Hallin, D., & Mancini, P. (2004). *Comparing media systems: Three models of media and politics.* New York: Cambridge University Press.

Handley, P. (2006). *The King never smiles: A biography of Thailand's Bhumibol Adulyadej.* New Haven, CT: Yale University Press.

Hattam, R. (2004). *Awakening struggle: Towards a Buddhist critical social theory.* Flaxton, Queensland: Post Pressed.

Hoffmann, V. (2007). Five editions (1962–2003) of Everett Rogers's *Diffusion of Innovations. Journal of Agricultural Education and Extension* 13 (2): 147–58.

Hofstede, G., & Hofstede, G. J. (2005). *Cultures and organizations: Software of the mind.* London: McGraw Hill.

Hornik, R. (1988). *Development communication: Information, agriculture, and nutrition in the Third World.* New York: Longman.

Hsiung, J., ed. (1985). *Human rights in East Asia: A cultural perspective.* New York: Paragon House.

Hussain, M. Y., ed. (2006). *Media and Muslim society.* Kuala Lumpur: International Islamic University Malaysia.

Inkeles, A., & Smith, D. (1974). *Becoming modern: Individual change in six developing countries.* Cambridge, MA: Harvard University Press.

Irigoin, M. E., Whitacre, P. T., Faulkner, D., & Coe, G., eds. (2002). *Mapping competencies for communication for development and social change: Turning knowledge, skills, and attitudes into action.* Washington, DC: Change Project/U.S. Agency for International Development.

Iyer, V., ed. (2001). *Freedom of information: An Asian survey.* Singapore: Asian Media Information and Communication Center.

Jakubowicz, K. (2007). *Rude awakening: Social and media change in central and eastern Europe.* Cresskill, NJ: Hampton Press.

Jayaweera, N., & Amunugama, S., eds. (1987). *Rethinking development communication.* Singapore: Asian Media Information and Communication Center.

Josephi, B. (2013). De-coupling journalism and democracy: Or how much democracy does journalism need? *Journalism* 14: 441–45.

Karikari, K., ed. (1996). *Ethics in journalism: Case studies of practice in West Africa.* London: Panos.

Klausner, W. (1997). *Thai culture in transition.* Bangkok: Siam Society.

Kogen, L. (2010). Savage deregulation in Thailand: Expanding Hallin and Mancini's European model. *Media, Culture & Society* 32 (2): 335–45.

Komin, S. (1988). Thai value system and its implication for development in Thailand. In D. Sinha & H. Kao, eds., *Social values and development: Asian perspectives.* New Delhi: Sage.

Komin, S. (1991). *Psychology of the Thai people: Values and behavioral patterns.* Bangkok: National Institute of Development Administration.

Krige, J., & Barth, K.-H., eds. (2006). *Global power knowledge: Science and technology in international affairs.* Washington, DC: History of Science Society.

Latham, M. (2000). *Modernization as ideology: American social science and "nation building" in the Kennedy era.* Chapel Hill: University of North Carolina Press.

Lee, C.-C. (1980). *Media imperialism reconsidered: The homogenizing of television culture.* London: Sage.

Leeuwis, C., & Van Den Ban, A. (2004). *Communication for rural innovation: Rethinking agricultural extension.* 3rd ed. Oxford: Blackwell.

Lerner, D. (1958). *The passing of traditional society: Modernizing the Middle East.* New York: Free Press.

Lerner, D. (1977). Communication and development. In Lerner, D. and L. Nelson, eds., *Communication research: A half-century appraisal.* Honolulu: University Press of Hawaii.

Lertrattanavisut, P. (2004). *Toxinomics.* Bangkok: Open Books Publishing.

Lertvicha, P. (1987). Political forces in Thailand. *Asian Review* 1:58–66.

Lie, R. (2003). *Spaces of intercultural communication: An interdisciplinary introduction to communication, culture, and globalizing/localizing identities.* Cresskill, NJ: Hampton Press.

Likhitsomboon, P. (2006). Acharn of Faculty of Economics, Thammasat University, Retorted the alliances and some academics: Stop deceiving the people. 8 July.

(in Thai) http://www.konpanfa.com/index.php?option=com_content&task=vie w&id=107&Itemid=28.

Louw, E. (2010). *Roots of the Pax Americana: Decolonization, development, democratization and trade.* Manchester: Manchester University Press.

MacBride, S., ed. (1980). *Many voices one world: Toward a new more just and more efficient world and information order.* London: Kogan Page.

Mann, R., & Youd, R. (1992). *Buddhist character analysis.* Bradford on Avon: Aukana Meditation Trust.

Mattelart, A. (2007). *Diversite culturelle et mondialisation.* Paris: La Decouverte.

McCarco, D. (2000). *Politics and the press in Thailand: Media machinations.* London: Routledge.

McLuhan, M. (1964). *Understanding media.* New York: Signet Books.

McMichael, P. (2008). *Development and social change: A global perspective.* 4th ed. Thousand Oaks, CA: Pine Forge Press.

McQuail, D. (2005). *McQuail's mass communication theory.* 5th ed. London: Sage.

Mendel, T. (2008). *Freedom of information: A comparative legal survey.* Paris: UNESCO.

Merrill, J. (1974). *The imperative of freedom: A philosophy of journalistic autonomy.* New York: Hastings.

Merrill, J. (1979). *Media, messages, and men: New perspectives in communication.* New York: Longman.

Merrill, J. (1989). *The dialectic of journalism: Towards a responsible use of press freedom.* Baton Rouge: Louisiana State University Press.

Morris, N. (2001). *Bridging the gap: An examination of diffusion and participatory approaches in development communication.* Washington, DC: Change Project/U.S. Agency for International Development.

Mulder, N. (1985). *Everyday life in Thailand: An interpretation.* Bangkok: DK Books.

Mulder, N. (2000). *Inside Thai society: Religion, everyday life, change.* Chiang Mai, Thailand: Silkworm Books.

Nederveen Pieterse, J. (2010). *Development theory: Deconstructions/reconstructions.* 2nd ed. London: Sage.

Nelson, M., ed. (2004). *Thai politics: Global and local perspectives.* Nonthaburi, Thailand: King Prajadhipok's Institute.

Nerone, J., ed. (1995). *Last rights: Revisiting four theories of the press.* Urbana: University of Illinois Press.

Nyamnjoh, F. (2005). *Africa's media, democracy and the politics of belonging.* London: Zed Books.

Nyamnjoh, F. (2007). Africa in the new millennium: Interrogating Barbie democracy. *Communication for Development and Social Change* 1 (2): 105–11.

Ogan, C. L., Bashir, M., Camaj, L., Luo, Y., Gaddie, B., Pennington, R., Rana, S., & Salih, M. (2009). Development communication: The state of research in an era of ICTs and globalization. *International Communication Gazette* 71 (8): 655–70.

Phongpaichit, P. (2002). Recent popular movements in Thailand in global perspective. *Asian Review* 15:1–20.

Phongpaichit, P., & Baker, C. (1998). *Thailand's boom and bust.* Bangkok: Silkworm Books.

Phongpaichit, P., & Priryarangsan, S. (1994). *Corruption and democracy in Thailand.* Bangkok: Faculty of Economics, Chulalongkorn University.

Pigeat, H., & Huteau, J. (2000). *Deontologie des medias: Institutions, pratiques et nouvelles approaches dans le monde.* Paris: UNESCO.

Prasirtsuk, K. (2007). *From political reform and economic crisis to coup d'etat: The twists and turns of Thai political economy, 1997–2006.* Bangkok: Thammasat University.

Preston, N., ed. (2007). Global ethics. *Social Alternatives* 26 (3): 3–4.

Rajadhon, A. (1987). *Some traditions of the Thai.* Bangkok: Sathirakoses Nagapradipa Foundation.

Rao, S. (1986). *The agenda of Third World communication research: A critical review. Media Asia* 13 (4): 201–8.

Roberts, A. (2006). *A history of the English-speaking peoples since 1900.* London: Phoenix.

Rogers, A. (2005). *The state of communications in international development and its relevance to the work of the United Nations.* New York: United Nations Capital Development Fund.

Rogers, E. M. (1962). *Diffusion of innovations.* New York: Free Press.

Rogers, E. M. (1986). *Diffusion of innovations.* 3rd ed. New York: Free Press.

Rogers, E. M. (2003). *Diffusion of innovations.* 5th ed. New York: Free Press.

Samarajiva, R. (1987). The murky beginnings of the communication and development field: Voice of America and the passing of traditional society. In N. Jayaweera & S. Amunaguma, *eds., Rethinking development communication* (pp. 3–19). Singapore: Asian Media Information and Communication Center.

Schiller, H. (1969). *Mass communications and American empire.* Boston: Beacon Press.

Schiller, H. (1976). *Communication and cultural domination.* White Plains, NY: International Arts and Sciences Press.

Schramm, W., ed. (1954). *The process and effects of mass communication.* Urbana: University of Illinois Press.

Schramm, W. (1964). *Mass media and national development: The role of information in the developing countries.* Stanford, CA: Stanford University Press.

Schramm, W., & Ruggels, W. (1967). How mass media systems grow. In D. Lerner & W. Schramm, eds., *Communication and change in the developing countries.* Honolulu: University Press of Hawaii.

Servaes, J. (1982), *De nieuwsmakers.* Kapellen: De Nederlandsche Boekhandel.

Servaes, J. (1989). Beyond the four theories of the press. *Communicatio Socialis Yearbook* 8: 107–19

Servaes, J. (1999). *Communication for development: One world, multiple cultures.* Cresskill, NJ: Hampton Press.

Servaes, J. (2005). Knowledge is power (revisited): Internet and democracy. *Media Development* 52 (4): 42–50.

Servaes, J. (2007a). Harnessing the UN system into a common approach on communication for development. *International Communication Gazette* 69 (6): 483–507.

Servaes, J., ed. (2007b). Communication for development: Making a difference. Background paper for the World Congress on Communication for Development, World Bank's FAO Communication Initiative, Washington, DC, October.

Servaes, J., ed. (2008). *Communication for development and social change*. Los Angeles, CA: Sage.

Servaes, J. (2009). Back into the future? Re-inventing journalism education in the age of globalization. In G. Terzis, ed., *European journalism education* (pp. 519–39). Bristol, UK: Intellect.

Servaes, J. (2012) Homo academicus: Quo vadis? In Silvia Nagy-Zekmi & Karyn Hollis, eds., *Global academe: Engaging intellectual discourse* (pp. 85–98). New York: Palgrave Macmillan.

Servaes, J., Malikhao, P., & Pinprayong, T. (2009). Communication rights are human rights: A case study of Thailand's media. In A. Dakroury, M. Eid, & Y. Kamalipour, eds., *The right to communicate: Historical hopes, global debates, and future premises* (pp. 227–54). Dubuque, IA: Kendall Hunt Publishers.

Servaes, J., & Tonnaer, C. (1992). *De nieuwsmarkt: Vorm en inhoud van de internationale berichtgeving*. Groningen: Wolters-Noordhoff.

Shah, H. (2007). Meta-research of development communication studies, 1997–2005: Patterns and trends since 1958. Paper presented to International Communication Association, San Francisco, 24–27 May.

Shah, H. (2011). *The production of modernization: Daniel Lerner, mass media, and the passing of traditional society*. Philadelphia: Temple University Press.

Siebert, F., Peterson, T., & Schramm, W. (1956). *Four theories of the press*. Urbana: University of Illinois Press.

Simpson, C. (1994). *Science of coercion: Communication research and psychological warfare 1945–1960*. New York: Oxford University Press.

Simpson, C., ed. (1998). *Universities and empire: Money and politics in the social sciences during the Cold War*. New York: New Press.

Siriyuvasak, U. (2004). *Anakhot sue seri nai rabob Thaksin roo tan Thaksin* [The future of free media in the Thaksin administration: Knowing Thaksin]. Bangkok: Kor Kid Duay Khon Publishing.

Siriyuvasak, U. (2005). A genealogy of media reform in Thailand and its discourses. In S. Wangvivatana, ed., *Media reform going backward?* Bangkok: Thai Broadcast Journalists Association and Friedrich-Ebert Stiftung.

Smythe, D. W. (1981). *Dependency road: Communication, capitalism, consciousness and Canada*. Norwood, NJ: Ablex.

Smythe, D. W., & Van Dinh, T. (1983). On critical and administrative research: A new critical analysis. *Journal of Communication* 33:117–27.

Sparks, C. (2007). *Globalization, development, and the mass media*. Los Angeles, CA: Sage.

Staples, A. (2006). *The birth of development: How the World Bank, Food and Agriculture Organization, and World Health Organization changed the world, 1945–1965*. Kent, OH: Kent State University Press.

Stiglitz, J. (1998). *Towards a new paradigm for development: Strategies, policies, and processes*. October. Geneva: Prebisch Lecture, UNCTAD.

Supadhiloke, B. (2007). Right to communicate, media reform, and civil society in Thailand. *Communication for Development and Social Change* 1 (4): 323–38.

Supadhiloke, B. (2008). Participatory communication and sufficiency economy in Thailand. *Journal of Global Communication* 1 (2): 101–17.

Swaminathan, M., ed. (1994). *Uncommon opportunities: An agenda for peace and equitable development*. Report of the International Commission on Peace and Food. London: Zed Books.

Taveesin, N. J., & Brown, W. (2006). The use of communication technology in Thailand's political process. *Asian Journal of Communication* 16 (1): 59–78.

Tehranian, M. (2007). *Rethinking civilization: Resolving conflict in the human family*. London: Routledge.

Terzis, G., ed. (2009). *European journalism education*. Bristol: Intellect.

Thomas, S. (1982). Some problems of the paradigm in communication theory. In D. C. Whitney & E. Wartella, eds., *Mass communication review yearbook 3*. London: Sage.

Thornton, R., & Cimadevilla, G., eds. (2010). *Usos y abusos del participare*. Buenos Aires: Instituto Nacional de Tecnología Agropecuaria.

Thussu, D. K. (2008). *News as entertainment: The rise of global infotainment*. London: Sage.

Tremblay, S., ed. (2007). *Developpement durable et communications: Au-dela des mots, pour un veritable engagement*. Quebec: Presses de l'Université du Quebec.

Tunstall, J. (1977). *The media are American: Anglo-American media in the world*. New York: Colombia University Press.

Ukpabi, C., ed. (2001). *Handbook on journalism ethics: African case studies*. Windhoek, Namibia: Media Institute of Southern Africa.

Wang, G. (2011a). Orientalism, occidentalism and communication research. In G. Wang, ed., *De-Westernizing communication research: Altering questions and changing frameworks* (pp. 58–76). New York: Routledge.

Wang, G., ed. (2011b). *De-Westernizing communication research: Altering questions and changing frameworks*. New York: Routledge.

Wang, G. (2011c). After the fall of the Tower of Babel. In G. Wang, ed., *De-Westernizing communication research: Altering questions and changing frameworks* (pp. 254–75). New York: Routledge.

Wangvivatana, S., ed. (2005). *Media reform going backward?* Bangkok: Thai Broadcast Journalists Association and Friedrich-Ebert Stiftung.

Wasi, P. (2003*). Sufficient economy and civic society* [in Thai]. Bangkok: Mau Chao Ban.

Wheeler, M. (1997). *Politics and the mass media*. Oxford: Blackwell Publishers.

White, R. (1988). *Media politics and democracy in the developing world*. London: Center for the Study of Communication and Culture.

Wronka, J. (2008). *Human rights and social justice*. Los Angeles, CA: Sage.

CHAPTER FIVE

Professional Models in Journalism

Between Homogenization and Diversity

Paolo Mancini

This chapter is focused on the discussion of the possible contradiction between the homogenization and fragmentation of professional models in journalism following our *Comparing Media Systems* (Hallin & Mancini, 2004). One of the most frequent criticisms raised about our book concerns the homogenization hypothesis that we discussed in the last chapter of the book. We observed that in all the countries that we analyzed, a clear tendency was emerging: most of the differences in professional journalism observable in the second part of last century were disappearing or had already disappeared. Professional journalism in the 18 countries of our study was becoming closer to what we had defined as the North Atlantic or liberal model, particularly as practiced in the United States and in Great Britain, and that other authors had already defined as the liberal model (Curran, 1991; Waisbord, 2000) or the Anglo-American model (Chalaby, 1996). All those features (partisanship, comment orientation, elite press, and so forth) that could be observed in other models, being very different from those that were inherent to the liberal model, were progressively disappearing. In particular, we stressed how the level of partisanship clearly found in most of continental journalism in Europe up to the 1980s was dramatically decreasing.

I still believe that, yes, the tendency toward homogenization characterizes most of the professional models in western European countries, but, if we look beyond that part of the world, I have to admit that, no, that same tendency is not so clearly emerging; rather, it is openly contradicted. In the final chapter of *Comparing Media Systems*, we stressed that because of increasing commercialization and the secularization of society, which led to the decline of traditional mass parties in favor of more individualized, media-centered forms of political mobilization, and the consequence of technological innovation, the differences that up to few years before had marked professional journalism in Western democracies were disappearing.

The development of the European Union and then the attention devoted to the formation of a single, unified economic market have favored the exchange of experiences, fostering the adoption of one single professional model. These changes can be seen as pushing European media systems closer to the liberal model, centered around commercial media and mostly information-oriented journalism in which market forces are dominant, as well as are more individualized forms of political communication, which are rooted in the culture of marketing and consumption. These forces are significant in most of the rest of the world as well but not to the extent that a unique, unifying model of professional journalism is emerging.

On the contrary, in many parts of the world beyond the Western one, journalism appears to be something completely different from what most of the scholarly community assumes it ought to be. It is not just that the professional procedures of the dominant Western model of professional journalism (neutral journalism, the separation between news and comment, accuracy, and so forth) do not exist and are not applied, but journalism itself, its own raison d'être, is something else from what it is expected to be in the Western world.

Even if journalists perceive that there exists a dominant model of journalism whose practices and principles are spreading around the world, even if they may claim to follow and to apply this normative framework, nevertheless in their everyday activity they perform in a completely different way. At least there exists a gap between the theory of journalism and its everyday practice. A very vivid picture of this contradiction has been given by Silvio Waisbord (2000):

> Even if we consider the liberal model in its own terms, without addressing the adequacy of its theoretical bases and prescriptions for the existence of a democratic press, it is obvious that its chances of becoming effective were at odds with South American politics. Its visibility

in public discourse contrasted with the realities of press systems. Its prospects ran against conditions that differed glaringly from original contexts coupled with questionable commitment of press barons. It was improbable that a liberal press would develop in antiliberal capitalist societies, considering that owners rhetorically exalted liberalism but ceaselessly courted states, supported military interventions and only (and vociferously) criticized government intrusion that affected their own political and economic interests." (p. 51)

With this statement, Waisbord touches on many points that need to be discussed at length, focusing around one major question: the difference between what journalism is supposed to be in our Western view and what journalism is in real practice in many other parts of the world.

Another reason for abandoning the idea of professional homogenization is the increasing fragmentation of the media system. There are two main aspects to be considered: the increasing commercialization of the media system, and technological innovation. The first point is very well illustrated by the experience of Fox News: to compete within a very crowded market and essentially to compete with its most direct competitor, CNN, Fox News has clearly chosen its own market niche composed mostly of conservative people. Rupert Murdoch's television network offers a product that fits very well with the expectations of a conservative audience whose beliefs have been pushed even further rightward by reactions to President Obama's health care reform and by the Tea Party movement. The ideal of neutral, objective, detached journalism is progressively disappearing on Fox News.

Of course, the commercialization process was already well developed when we wrote *Comparing Media Systems.* Indeed, Elihu Katz had written that article with the very appealing title "And Deliver Us from Segmentation" (Katz, 1996) in which he pointed out that, because of the segmentation of the market linked to the process of commercialization, there was the risk of the disappearance of the wider public sphere, including all the different interests acting in the society, in which all these different voices could meet and discuss problems of general interest. In 1992 Daniel Hallin himself had written another paper in which he discussed the possible weakening of that strong ideology of neutrality and objectivity that characterized U.S. journalism in the '60s and '70s because of the increasing fragmentation of the mass media market.

Today, the Internet, and technological innovation in general, pushes even further the process of fragmentation: blogs and social networks favor the birth and the development of "micro" niches of users who are drawn together by a common affiliation and by the sharing of common feelings, interests, habits, and beliefs. These "virtual communities," as Rheingold (2000) has named them, introduce specific practices and routines that very often are of very particular nature and that, moreover, are aimed at reinforcing a common affiliation and pre-existing feelings and opinions.

All these observations underscore the importance of abandoning the traditional Western-centrism of media studies (and, more important, the Western-centrism that very often directs professional education in journalism), the assumption that Western journalism, what Jean Chalaby (1996) defines as the Anglo-American model, *is journalism*. In many parts of the world journalism is something completely different and the tendency toward the adoption of a unique professional model today seems to be contradicted both by increasing commercialization and the Internet.

Instrumentalization and the Diffusion of the Polarized-Pluralist Model

In a very general way it could be said that if we observe countries beyond the Western world, journalism is no longer an instrument to spread news but, first of all, it is an instrument to take an active part in the decision-making process, to intervene in the public arena, to influence not just the construction of a consensus but the actions of government, to promote the interests, both economic and political, of the groups that own the media outlets. In *Comparing Media Systems* we used the word "instrumentalization" to stress that, contrary to the mythical idea of liberal journalism, whose main goal ought to be the construction of an informed citizen, in many parts of the world the diffusion of news is exactly an "instrument" to reach particular goals that do not pertain solely to the distribution of knowledge within a community. In particular, our study found that instrumentalization was to be found in the so-called Mediterranean or polarized-pluralist model.

In a written comment after his first reading of *Comparing Media Systems*, Stylianos Papathanassopoulos, one of our Greek colleagues whom we had asked to comment on the initial draft of our book, reported a widely circulated statement among the political community in Greece: when a new government is established politicians aiming at important government positions are not afraid to tell the appointee prime minister: "If you don't give me a ministry, I [will] start a newspaper." We defined "instrumentalization as the control of the media by outside actors, parties, politicians, social groups or movements, or economic actors, seeking political influence, who use them to intervene in the world of politics" (Hallin & Mancini, 2004, p. 37). In this case the candidate minister who is starting a newspaper, or threatening to do so, is not at all interested in spreading news and in facilitating the distribution of knowledge. He wants to start a newspaper to be used against the prime minister who has not given him the opportunity to become a minister in the government. He is not interested either in fostering political participation or in narrowing the links between political actors and citizens. He is just interested in influencing the decision-making process to better guarantee his own interests and, in this case, to get a position of high responsibility.

This attitude seems very widespread outside the Western world. As to Russia, Svetlana Pasti has written, "Like ordinary people, journalists must manage through common sense and effort to find a niche in the new prosperous Russia. Therefore they serve the interests of those who possess political and economic capital, i.e. the state and business elite" (Pasti, 2005, p. 109). Outside eastern Europe, the situation doesn't seem to be very different: discussing journalism in Southeast Asia, Duncan McCargo writes, "In short, rapid economic growth and rapid social change gives media a heightened political salience, and empowers media to be much more potent political actors in their own right than has generally been the case in the West" (McCargo, 2012). In most of the cases instrumentalization is linked to clientelism as Chin-Chuan Lee has demonstrated as to the media in Taiwan (Lee, 2000).

What has been described in these previous statements was characteristic of Western journalism when it was born and it still represents an important reason for its existence today in many parts of the world. Instrumentalization is one of the main features of what we have defined as the "Mediterranean or polarized-pluralist model": in the view of many scholars who refer to our interpretive schema, the polarized-pluralist model seems to be a widely diffused model outside the Western world, with its strong prevalence of partisan media, a tendency to instrumentalization of the media by political and economic elites and their use as tools of bargaining and maneuvering among those elites, frequent state intervention and involvement in the media system, lesser development of journalistic professionalism, and lower newspaper circulation.

But there is no doubt that even the polarized-pluralist model may assume very particular forms beyond the Western world. In most cases, it mixes with a dramatic influence of mass media commercialization, very close to the competitive situation that is possible to observe in the liberal model and the already quoted influence of the ideal principles of liberal professionalism. These principles could direct the behavior of reporters if they don't clash with their everyday activities, which are also determined by the instrumentalization practices that we just discussed. But in most cases the principles of liberal journalism constitute a sort of "false ideology" of the profession (false as in most cases it is not really applicable) that is taught in schools, that is illustrated in textbooks, and that, in omes way or another, constitutes a continuous reference for all discussions around the profession, influencing both those who are already part of it, those who want to enter it, and those who interact with it in different ways. In this way a situation of hybridization may emerge. I shall return to this later.

Political Parallelism beyond the Western World

The forms that the polarized-pluralist model of journalism assumes beyond the Western world may be different from what was possible, and still is possible, to observe in some of the countries studied in *Comparing Media Systems*. One of the major differences seems to lie in the experience of mass parties that was so important in the European context (and in a minor degree in the United States too); political parallelism was one of the most important features affecting the relationship between media and politics in our polarized-pluralist model. Both the experience of mass parties and the idea of political parallelism are deeply tied to the particular political history of western Europe and can hardly be observable beyond that area. Indeed, in western Europe there were patterns of development centered around multiparty democracy, built around the competition of mass parties and other organized groups, such as unions, that are rooted in broad socioeconomic interests. European mass parties historically have represented the most important means to participate in the life of the community and to address problems of general interest. They have had a strong influence in many processes of socialization, including the mass media, which in the strongest forms of party-press parallelism played the roles of diffusing political "faith" and information to members and of reinforcing and linking together the organization of the party. The mass party systems of western Europe provided a clear structure to political conflict mostly centered around the Left-Right spectrum, and media tended to have stable relationships with these groups, or stable ideological identities rooted in their conflicts, or both. The print media in most of the West, and the broadcast media in many countries, were born within this framework of ideological links and affiliations.

But this is a very particular political history. In other countries political parties tend to be relatively shallow and transient: they do not have deep social roots or clear ideological identities; they tend to appear and disappear very quickly; neither voters nor political leaders have strong, stable attachments to them. In many cases we face personalized parties, with political organizations, in most cases very weak organizations, built around the figure of a single politician or businessman who decides to enter the political arena for specific goals and interests. A very good prototype of this is represented by Berlusconi's Popolo della libertà. This is a party without a real organizational structure that is dependent on the symbolic, charismatic, and economic resources of its founder. Similar structures may be found in many other countries as well and particularly in eastern Europe and in Asia.

In many parts of the world the specific kind of political parallelism that was tied to the historical experience of mass parties is today replaced by completely different forms of parallelisms. News media overlap with a range of different organizations: with ethnic or religious organizations that very often represent interests that are not just based on ethnicity and religion but that also embrace political and economic constituencies or interests. Very often news media overlap with different forms of business organizations and interests to the point that, mostly in relationship to central and eastern Europe, scholars have described this as "business parallelism" (Ornebring, 2010). This is a very complex form of instrumentalization, also observable in Western countries, that mixes together business, politics, and the news media within a system of reciprocal clientelistic links, with reciprocal advantages and disadvantages. As Colin Sparks has observed, "there exist a close set of relations between politicians, businessmen and the media that leads to a routine interchange between different groups in post-communist countries" (Sparks, 2000, p. 42). Sparks himself defines "political capital" as the "overlapping between economics, politics and the media" (Sparks, 2000, p. 42).

Not differently, Duncan McCargo uses the formula "partisan polyvalence" to indicate the weakness of traditional political parallelism and how the media in East Asia may be used for (and may be instrumentalized by) a multiplicity of different goals, such as supporting one political figure (or one political program) and pursuing business goals at the same time. The news media can also shift from one goal to another in a very brief period of time without losing their traditional formula and readership.

Alina Mungiu Pippidi has been studying corruption for many years and she argues that "in societies based on particularism rather than free competition media outlets are not ordinary business ventures. Rather, investors use their channels for blackmail or for trading influence" (Mungiu Pippidi, 2010, p. 126). And Alena V. Ledeneva confirms this: "[T]he black PR discourse is symptomatic of a situation where certain defects of formal institutions, weakness of political parties, lack of independent media, disrespect for the law create incentives for informal practices to spread" (Ledeneva, 2004, p. 36). Peter Gross adds that "the profit making incentive of some media owners was simply married to the political use of the media, which is to say, some media owners are also politicians" (Gross, 2003, p. 87).

So, if we look beyond the Western world, what we see is that the news media play a mixture of different roles within which the provision of news and the goal of facilitating an informed citizen are not the major objectives. They undergo different forms of parallelism: the traditional political parallelism, which was characteristic of many news outlets in the Western world in past years, is not the most important one, and very frequently it mixes with "business parallelism."

The idea of "political parallelism" presupposes the existence of strong party organizations that are active in different sectors including the production of news. But, and this is the main difference, the experience of mass parties is a Western experience, deeply rooted in Western history and in the economic context within which they were born and developed. They are the product of specific economic, social, and cultural conditions that do not exist or are very different beyond the Western world today. They are—better, they were—the product of those "cleavages" that characterized the European situation in the nineteenth and twentieth centuries and that motivated their existence.

Of course, political parties exist beyond the Western world but they are very different organizations: as already said, very often they assume the form and the structure of "personal parties" built around the figure of one single politician and around the specific interests and symbolic connotations of this single figure. Their ideological dimension is very weak. The system of common values that was at the very root of European mass parties does not exist either, and therefore a "culture" to be transmitted is almost completely absent. News media are not means to socialize people to the culture of their own group.

In other situations, party organizations are weak and volatile: they are established for particular goals and under particular contingencies but when these contingencies disappear, the parties, too, suddenly either disappear or change their nature and name. This is what has happened very frequently in eastern Europe, where the shift from communism to democracy has given rise to a situation of uncertainty and continuous change in which stable party organizations have not been able to develop. Parties are not broadly inclusive organizations and the number of members is limited: they act essentially at the electoral moment, thus confirming the well-known typology of Angelo Panebianco and the existence of the so-called electoral-professional party (Panebianco, 1998) supported by professionals in the field of communication, press, advertising, and being active just in the moment of an election campaign. This form of party organization also confirms the instrumental role of the news media: they are mostly used at election time when they have to produce consensus around single political figures or specific political programs and proposals, but stable political parallelism doesn't exist because stable and strong political organizations don't exist either. Religious parties are very common beyond the Western world; in their experience, too, parallelism assumes forms very different from those that it is possible to observe in Europe.

About the Nature of the State

Another important difference between what it is possible to observe in the Western world and what is observable beyond the Western world as to the relationship between politics and news media lies in the very nature of the state. We are used to referencing the existence and the activity of news media to our specific idea of the state and then to the question of its government. Indeed, following the thesis of the polarized-pluralist model, in many countries in the Western world the relationship between state and news media is very strict: news media are an instrument for different organizations to compete for government within a stable and consolidated state organization. In the polarized-pluralist model and in the democratic-corporatist model too, news media are strongly connected to the state. They depend on it not just for rules ensuring their freedom but also for a framework of different interventions aimed at making possible a better and more comprehensive pluralism and therefore making possible, also through economic subsidies, the existence of papers and other media outlets representing the voice of different minority organizations. Very often this is an occasion through which parties in government try to shape and to influence news media to get more support for their actions.

But the form of state we are referring to is very rare beyond the Western world: in many countries and in many parts of the world, including in eastern Europe (where we have a large amount of evidence), the state is still something that has to be constructed in a stable and consolidated manner. First, it is not a unitary actor behaving in an organized and homogeneous way (Grzymala-Busse & Jones-Luong, 2002; McCargo, 2012), as we often assume in the Western world. It includes many different parts that very often act in a contradictory way and not rarely compete and struggle with each other. Very often, rather than "nation building" we face a situation of "state building," as the existing state is weak, is contradictory, and often acts in a confusing way. This is what is possible to observe in most of the so-called transitional democracies: "Oligarchs, political parties and president on one hand and international financial institutions or regional trade associations on the other, all have access to the nascent state structures and exert considerable pressures on the process of state formation" (Grzymala-Busse & Jones-Luong, 2002, p. 533).

The construction of the state is a question of struggle among elites. In this situation the state can't play any role in facilitating a free market of ideas and pluralism, neither stressing freedom of the press nor its neutrality, as we assume it ought to do. Rather, news media are used instrumentally by the different elites to compete for the formation and the control of the state. In this situation, as we have seen, political parallelism is just one of the many components that direct the behavior of the media.

In an opposite way, there are social contexts in which the state plays a much more important role that not rarely ends in censorship, and this doesn't just apply to authoritarian and totalitarian regimes but also to many young democracies as well. As McCargo (2012) argues:

> The dominant order of state-media relations, especially as regards electronic media, is that states interfere wherever they can. This is particularly true in middle-income developing countries, where newspaper readership is typically low, yet most people have ready access to television and radio. But the idea of state intervention is also complicated by questions concerning the nature of the state itself. In many developing countries, the state has a patrimonial character and is used as a vehicle for rent-seeking. In other words,

the state or certain elements thereof has been captured by private, elite interests. In great swathes of the developing world, the much-vaunted distinction between public and private, on which so many heuristic categories and so much of the basic tool kit of social science relies, turns out to be something of an urban myth. Under such circumstances, state intervention in media is the norm rather than the exception. The same applies to censorship: rather than imagining that media is free to report whatever it wishes, unless subject to specific external interference, in much of the world it is safe to assume that such freedom is always highly contingent. (p. 213)

Very often, both in the newborn democracies in the moment of "state building" and in those countries on the path toward democracy where a strong state already exists, there is mixture of formal and informal rules that doesn't facilitate an independent and neutral role for the media. Indeed, in these situations the media are part of the many negotiation practices that take place among elites as the space for reciprocal accommodation exists because of either the prevalence of informal rules or the contradiction that often exists between formal and informal rules (Borocz, 2000; Park, Kim, & Sohn, 2000; Ledeneva, 2004). In this case, too, the state can't be that guarantor of press freedom and independence as it is assumed to be in the most classic liberal model.

The weakness of the state and its brutal intervention in limiting freedom of the press seems to be a characteristic in all those countries that are on the path toward democratization and in most transitional democracies (Voltmer, 2012). The so-called developmental state (Clark, 2000) contradicts our Western view of the state and its role also in regard to the news media. That framework of interventions, warrants, and attitudes that we expect in our view of the state should not be expected where this particular state doesn't exist.

The discussion about the role of the state may be viewed also in a different light. As the successful book by the English journalist John Kampfner (2010) has put before Western public opinion, in many countries, mostly in East Asia, there is a completely different idea of both state and government and their role. In its attempt to improve the economic status of the country's citizens the state can limit press freedom and influence the behavior of the news media to establish that harmony whose roots are to be found in Confucian philosophy (Gunaratne, 1999). The possibility of criticism by the media is therefore limited to pursuing harmony in the press-government relationship that may persuade citizens to be part of a society in which conflicts are rare and are not welcome, and in which they are stimulated to collaborate to reach the common good and to improve the life conditions of the entire community.

This is a completely different view from the Western idea of the state, where, on the contrary, the role of the press is rooted in the oppositional design that allots to journalists the duty to control and limit the power of the rulers. As is well known, this interpretation of the role of the press is not just part of professional education and everyday professional practice in the so-called liberal model, but it was clearly stressed by Jürgen Habermas (1989), who, as Niklas Luhmann (1998) has pointed out, saw the birth of the public sphere as an instrument of the struggle between the absolute power of the king and the newborn needs of the bourgeoisie. This view, very much rooted in Western political philosophy, could be enlarged to understand, still in the oppositional logic, the relationship between the press and the rulers in today's society. The press found, and is still finding, its primary goal in the attempt to control power holders. In Western world common sense and in the professional culture of the journalists this oppositional view of the relationship between the press and the government has produced the well-known catchword of "watch-dog" journalism. This may have a hard time in contexts where, on the contrary, a different view of this relationship prevails that is based on the Confucian harmonic design.

Which Interpretive Categories?

With this, we have reached a central point and it seems necessary to revive an old concept that has been used for many years: "cultural imperialism." In this case, these words aren't about the export of meaning and cultural product, as they were in the original work of Herbert Schiller and his followers, but they concern the interpretive frameworks we apply to look at realities beyond the Western world. It is not easy to admit this, but there is a cultural imperialism that is linked to our own work as scholars and, specifically, as media scholars. Very frequently we pretend to observe realities beyond our own using our own interpretive categories, which are taken, as Curran and Park already observed in 2000, from "a tiny handful of countries" (Curran & Park, 2000, p. 3). "The tiny handful of countries" refers to our Western experience. Therefore, for instance, we assume that the idea of the mass party that was (and partially still is) so influential in Western history is some sort of universal category that is possible to apply everywhere, as mass parties represent the principal instrument for political participation and for the life of democracy and also affect journalistic performance. Equally, very often it is assumed that the state as we have experienced it in the Western world is the only possible form of state, whereas, instead, this idea of the state is profoundly rooted in specific historical conditions. The idea of "democracy" itself, as developed in the Western world, may be questioned by different frameworks of cultural values and historical conditions. This point has been discussed by political scientists and particularly by all those who have criticized Samuel Huntington's thesis on democratization.

In other words, in the field of media studies, as in many other social scientific fields, very often it is assumed that our history is *the* history. On the basis of our particular experience and the interpretive categories that "this specific history" produced we can observe and interpret social realities that come from completely or partially different experiences. Most of the time, to be culturally correct, we don't pretend to export our models of how things ought to be done; we are not normative at that point, but, perhaps unconsciously, we observe different realities with our own eyes. Undoubtedly, we suffer from an almost unavoidable Western bias. With regard to the news media, we are not only pushed to believe that whatever deviation from the ideal type we have constructed on the basis of our own experience has to be interpreted as degeneration or bad functioning, but we apply our interpretive categories to realities where these categories don't find room. In part, this is almost unavoidable: the categories that we apply cannot but be based on our own history and experience. To avoid this sort of "interpretive imperialism" we could abstain from analyzing countries beyond our own experience, but there is no doubt that this does not serve scientific inquiry.

Could we avoid stating that clientelism is clientelism wherever it occurs? That corruption is corruption everywhere? Again, avoiding these sorts of statements would badly serve scientific inquiry. Nevertheless, we have to be aware that to interpret these phenomena correctly we have to place them within the set of particular conditions within which they developed in each part of the world. Journalism doesn't grow up in a vacuum: it is the product of specific historical, economic, social, and cultural conditions that have very local roots.

Journalism Culture as a "Shortcut" to Avoid Our Western Bias

Indeed, as a conclusion to this paper, I would like to advance the idea of journalism culture as a possible means to avoid our almost unavoidable "Western bias." Indeed, the concept of "journalism culture," at least in the way in which it is conceived in this chapter, may be useful because it offers two advantages. First, it allows journalism to be placed in the widest social and political context in which it develops. The idea of journalism culture may include all those technical skills and practices necessary for everyday work and the assumptions of a very broad nature regarding the political culture of each country and the role of professional journalism within this set of expectations. Unlike other professions, such as medicine or engineering, journalism is not a neutral, aseptic profession that can be separated from the surrounding social, cultural, and political reality. Like many other professions, journalism is made up of skills that we could define as being technical and specialist, but their cultural and political dimension is so important and their relationships with other social subsystems are so frequent and profound that it is impossible to isolate the specific type of professionalism from the society in which it develops. For this reason, the concept of journalism culture not only allows us to view journalism as a profession, with its own routines, practices, and specific ethics (that can have some sort of universal nature), but also to link this profession to the country's more general culture and especially to its political culture. Indeed, journalism doesn't grow up in a vacuum. This simple, almost commonplace statement is shared by many scholars and, nevertheless, most of the time it remains a sort of dead letter that doesn't produce any further interpretive improvement. Since the classic *Four Theories of the Press*, many media scholars have stressed the need to place journalism within a broader context. At the very beginning of their book, Siebert, Peterson, and Schramm wrote in 1956: "The thesis of this volume is that the press always takes on the form and coloration of the social and political structures within which it operates. Especially it reflects the system of social control whereby the relations of individuals and institutions are adjusted" (Siebert, Peterson, & Schramm, 1956, p. 1). Nevertheless, as some critics have pointed out (Nerone, 1995), *Four Theories of the Press* seems to assume one model, the libertarian model and its "social responsibility" derivation, as a sort of ideal model independently from the surrounding social context; at least it is conceived as the one that constitutes the basis for the evaluation of all the others. An interpretive category, rooted in Western world experience, has become the category to interpret and to judge journalism in other parts of the world. On the same path as Siebert, Peterson, and Schramm is Herbert Gans, who concluded his seminal work *Deciding What's News* with these words: "This study has, thus far, ignored the intriguing possibility that journalists and their firms are pawns of larger and more basic social processes to which they unwittingly respond. Perhaps journalists perform unintended or unrecognized (latent) functions for the nation and society as a whole which are necessary enough to force journalists to act as they do" (Gans, 1979, p. 290).

All these statements and many others (Schudson, 1995; Cook, 2006; Hanusch, 2009) have not been followed by studies and interpretations that have placed journalism within the social contexts in which it develops. In most cases, in Western media studies, journalism has been studied as a closed system in itself; the stated connections with the broader society have been forgotten and very few works have been able to address them in a productive way. Journalism procedures, routines, and professionalization processes have been analyzed as if it were possible to abstract them from each single social context. Progressively, mass media have been studied in themselves and this attitude has grown with the development of the media studies field that has produced, on the one hand, a positive academic autonomy from other scientific fields, but, on the other, has separated the mass media from their social and political context, undermining a better understanding of their functioning.

The second reason to prefer the expression "journalism culture" is that this concept may represent a very useful tool for comparative research because, at least in the sense I'm proposing it, it is deeply rooted in the different national contexts that can therefore confront each other (Hanitzsch, 2007). But in spite of its importance, the concept of journalism culture is very hard to study empirically. Different proposals have been advanced to catch it empirically (Servaes, 1999; Hanitzsch, 2007), but the difficulty remains. This concept is multifaceted, maybe contradictory in its different aspects, and is difficult to transform into quantitative indicators; it deals with factors of cultural and emotional nature that the people we interview in our studies rarely are willing to express freely and sincerely. The complexity of this concept is very well synthetized by the expression that Richard Hoggart used several years ago to introduce *Bad News*. He used the expression "the cultural air we breathe" in the light of the specific topic of that book and to indicate how news, and its interpretation, has to be placed within a framework of a sort of common sense that tells us that "some things can be said and others had best not to be said" (Hoggart, 1981). Michael Schudson has further developed his idea: "Hoggart has written that the most important filter through which news is constructed is the cultural air we breathe, the whole ideological atmosphere of our society, which tells us that some things can be said and that others had best not to be said. That cultural air is one that in part ruling groups and institutions create but it is in part one in whose context their own establishment takes place" (Schudson, 2005, p. 189). Some years before this sentence Schudson himself had already pointed out the importance of the cultural environment within which journalists work: "The news then is produced by people who operate often unwittingly within a cultural system, a reservoir of stored cultural meanings and patterns of discourse. . . . news as a form of culture incorporates assumptions about what matters, what makes sense, what time and place we live in, what range of considerations we should take seriously" (Schudson, 1995, p. 14).

This cultural heritage is what permeates journalism culture and practices everywhere; it is the product of history and particular social, cultural, economic, and political conditions. This heritage is very hard to observe empirically and it is almost impossible to define in precise terms. It is "the cultural air we breathe": something that is in the air, that is volatile, that goes with the wind, and that, nevertheless, is there in that specific place where we breathe it.

The concept of journalism culture may be very useful in understanding why our word today is "hybridization" (Norris & Inglehart, 2009). On the one hand, globalization is something that nobody can deny. Journalists practice a profession that has some kind of universal nature and this universal nature goes around the entire world through movies, textbooks, seminars, global events, education, media ownership, media concentration, and so forth. This universal nature is first of all rooted in the idea (and practice) of news as a good for the market, news as a product to be sold and to be consumed. Today, market and news are strictly interrelated as they were when the idea of the "marketplace of ideas" was born in the Western world. This universal nature takes shape essentially in a whole of professional rules, and may be identified in what is called the liberal model of professional journalism. The influence of the liberal model of journalism is something very hard to deny: it depends on the strong tendency toward commercialization but also on the influence that Western thought (and our own scholarship and education efforts) exercises consciously and unconsciously.

Nevertheless, the universal nature of journalism takes shape in relation to the different cultural contexts where it occurs. As Barbie Zelizer puts it, "Despite the prevalence of arguments of journalism's universal nature, the culture of journalism presupposes that journalistic conventions, routines and practices are dynamic and contingent on situational and historical circumstances" (Zelizer, 2005, p. 211). This is the reason why many authors, in connection to the interpretive framework proposed in *Comparing Media Systems*, have talked of a situation of hybridization (Voltmer, 2012; Dobek-Ostrowska, 2012; Chadwick, 2013) between what we defined as the liberal model of professional journalism and the polarized-pluralist model where we found that instrumentalization was, and still is, a very common feature. Indeed, if one looks beyond the Western world the set of conditions that feature the polarized-pluralist model seem to construct the common framework even if with specific features that vary country by country.

The liberal professional model mixes together with local conditions, producing a hybrid that we tend to look at and to interpret on the basis of our Western categories. In some ways the hybridization between the liberal and the polarized-pluralism model that, following our *Comparing Media Systems*, is seen by several scholars as the most appropriate model to explain professional journalism beyond the Western world, may suffer from the Western bias deriving from the application to different realities of categories that are deeply rooted in the Western experience within which they were conceived.

REFERENCES

Borocz, J. (2000). Informality rules. *East European Politics and Society* 14 (2): 348–80.

Chalaby, J. (1996). Journalism as an Anglo-American invention: A comparison of the development of French and Anglo-American journalism, 1830s–1920s. *European Journal of Communication* 11 (3): 303–26.

Chadwick, A. (2013). *The hybrid media system.* Oxford: Oxford University Press.

Clark, C. (2000). Modernization, democracy and the developmental state in Asia: A virtuous cycle or unraveling strands? In J. Hollifield & C. Jilson, eds., *Pathways to democracy.* New York: Routledge.

Cook, T. (2006). The news media as a political institution: Looking backward and looking forward. *Political Communication* 23 (2): 159–73.

Curran, J. (1991). Rethinking the media as a public sphere. In P. Dahlgren & C. Sparks, eds., *Communication and citizenship.* London: Routledge.

Curran, J., & Park, M. J. (2000). Beyond globalization theory. In J. Curran & M. J. Park, eds., *De-Westernizing media studies*. London: Routledge.

Dobek-Ostrowska, B. (2012). Italianization (or Mediterraneanization) of the Polish media system? Reality and perspective. In D. Hallin & P. Mancini, eds., *Comparing media systems beyond the Western world*. Cambridge: Cambridge University Press.

Gans, H. (1979). *Deciding what's news*. New York: Pantheon Books.

Gross, P. (2003). New relationships: Eastern European media and the post-Communist political world. *Journalism Studies* 4 (1): 79–89.

Grzymala-Busse, A., & Jones Luong, P. (2002). Reconceptualizing the state: Lessons from post-Communism. *Politics and Society* 30 (4): 529–54.

Gunaratne, S. (1999). The media in Asia. *International Communication Gazette* 61 (3–4): 197–223.

Habermas, J. (1989). *The structural transformation of the public sphere: An inquiry into a category of bourgeois society*. Cambridge, MA: MIT Press.

Hallin, D. (1992). The passing of the "high modernism" of American journalism. *Journal of Communication* 42 (3): 14–25.

Hallin, D., & Mancini, P. (2004). *Comparing media systems*. Cambridge: Cambridge University Press.

Hanitzsch, T. (2007). Deconstructing journalism culture: Toward a universal theory. *Communication Theory* 17: 367–85.

Hanusch, F. (2009). A product of their culture. *International Communication Gazette* 71 (7): 613–26.

Hoggart, R. (1981). Foreword. In Glasgow University Media Group, ed., *Bad News*. London: Routledge & Kegan Paul.

Kampfner, J. (2010). *Freedom for sale*. New York: Basic Books.

Katz, E. (1996). And deliver us from segmentation. *Annals of the American Academy of Political and Social Science* 546:22–33.

Ledeneva, A. (2004). *How Russia really works: The informal practices that shaped post-Soviet politics and business*. Ithaca, NY: Cornell University Press.

Lee, C. C. (2000). State, capital and the media: The case of Taiwan. In J. Curran & M. J. Park, eds., *De-Westernizing media studies*. London: Routledge.

Luhmann, N. (1998). *Observations on modernity*. Stanford, CA: Stanford University Press.

McCargo, D. (2012) Partisan polyvalence: Characterizing the political role of Asian media. In D. Hallin & P. Mancini, eds., *Comparing media systems beyond the Western world*. Cambridge: Cambridge University Press.

Mungiu Pippidi, A. (2010). The other transition. *Journal of Democracy* 21 (1): 120–27.

Nerone, J., ed. (1995). *Last rights: Revisiting four theories of the press*. Urbana: University of Illinois Press.

Norris, P., & Inglehart, R. (2009). *Cosmopolitan communication*. Cambridge: Cambridge University Press.

Ornebring, E. (2010). *Latvia*. Unpublished report for the Media and Democracy in Central Eastern Europe project, Department of Politics and International Relations, Oxford University.

Panebianco, A. (1998). *Political parties: organization and power.* Cambridge: Cambridge University Press.

Park, M. J., Kim, C. N., & Sohn, B. W. (2000). Modernization, globalization, and the powerful state. In J. Curran & M. J. Park, eds., *De-Westernizing media studies.* London: Routledge.

Pasti, S. (2005). Two generations of contemporary Russian journalists. *European Journal of Communication* 20 (1): 89–115.

Rheingold, H. (2000). *The virtual community.* Cambridge, MA: MIT Press.

Schudson, M. (1995). *The power of news.* Cambridge, MA: Harvard University Press.

Schudson, M. (2005). Four approaches to the sociology of news. In J. Curran & M. Gurevitch, eds., *Mass media and society.* London: Hodder Arnold.

Servaes, J. (1999). *Communication for development: One world, multiple cultures.* Cresskill, NJ: Hampton Press.

Siebert, F., Peterson, T., & Schramm, W. (1956). *Four theories of the press.* Urbana: University of Illinois Press.

Sparks, C. (2000). Media theory after the fall of European communism: Why the old models from East and West won't do anymore. In J. Curran & M. J. Park, eds., *De-Westernizing media studies.* London: Routledge.

Voltmer, K. (2012). How far can media systems travel? Applying Hallin and Mancini's comparative framework outside the western world. In D. Hallin & P. Mancini, eds., *Comparing media systems beyond the Western world.* Cambridge: Cambridge University Press.

Waisbord, S. (2000). Media in South America. Between the rock of the state and the hard place of the market. In J. Curran & Park, M. J., eds., *De-Westernizing media studies.* London: Routledge.

Zelizer, B. (2005). The culture of journalism. In J. Curran & M. Gurevitch, eds., *Mass media and society.* 4th ed. London: Hodder Arnold.

CHAPTER SIX

Conditions of Capital:
Global Media in Local Contexts

Michael Curtin

Allow me to begin with an alternative proposition: the field of international communication studies doesn't need "internationalizing," at least so far as film and media studies are concerned. From the beginning, film studies has been thoroughly international, both theoretically and epistemologically. It conceived of cinema as a cultural phenomenon of modern nation-states and set out to delineate the distinctive features of national cinemas, comparing each against the others. Concerned about the intrusive impact of Hollywood exports on societies around the world, film scholars sought to counterbalance it with a profound and ongoing appreciation of French, Egyptian, and Indian cinemas, among others (Nowell-Smith, 1999). They celebrated the growth of international film festivals, supported national film policies, and developed an impressive ensemble of university courses and textbooks that sustained and explained the distinctive histories and practices of national cinemas worldwide. More recently, scholars have challenged and interrogated the national cinemas model (Hjort & Mackenzie, 2000; Vitali & Willemen, 2006; Durovicova & Newman, 2010), but film scholarship nevertheless remains anchored to national points of reference.

Similar observations could be made about studies of publishing and electronic media. Harold Innis (1972), a founding figure, wrote expansive histories of communication from the very dawn of human history to the modern era, describing the communicative features of empires, theocracies, and feudal regimes, but when it came to the modern era, his analysis focused on national media systems situated within an international context. He reflected on power imbalances and transborder flows, but largely he compared and contrasted the distinguishing features of national media. Others followed this lead, which is understandable given the significant influence of sociology on the field of communications. Sociological paradigms were built on the assumption that communication was largely a national systemic concern, and in those situations where it breached national borders it was explored as a disruptive or transgressive influence. This led to the most common and enduring conception of transnational communication as media imperialism, an insidious menace that raised the specter of cultural homogenization on a global scale. Even today, critics point to the ubiquity of American media products such as *Batman*, *CSI*, and Lady Gaga, and they portray the world's masses as vulnerable, even gullible, subjects in a circuit of culture that feeds corporate conglomerates and impoverishes national modes of expression and public life (Schiller, 1969; Guback, 1969; Miller et al., 2008). Many scholars and government policy makers have argued that national governments and international institutions are the best hope for containing the imperial tide, pointing to policies that limit imports, foster indigenous production, and promote responsible citizenship (McBride, 1980).

So perhaps we need not internationalize our scholarly endeavors so much as we should explore alternative approaches to the issues raised above. To what extent are national frameworks and perspectives useful, or to what extent do they obscure recent trends engendered by media globalization? Global studies researchers proceed from a different set of assumptions, acknowledging the enduring significance of national systems and expressing concern about the unequal distribution of economic and cultural power, but this school of thought moves beyond a foundational focus on national concerns to explore the interactive dynamics that unfold at a variety of levels. These scholars say media globalization has no uniform logic and no central command center but is rather a push-pull process with many unexpected outcomes (Tomlinson, 1999). The interactions between global, national, and local institutions are therefore radically contextual and complex. Researchers point to examples of local media competing with dominant global counterparts in many parts of the globe, and they pay attention to the ways that popular culture appropriates, reconfigures, and reinterprets global hegemonic texts. Although conscious of systemic patterns of power, global studies scholars are especially alert to local contingencies, differences, and disjunctures (Appadurai, 1996). They see the world less as a mosaic of interlocking and discrete national entities than as a collage of diverse, layered, and transversal elements. They furthermore argue that national governments are not necessarily the best antidote to globalization, since they too are characterized by unequal structures of power that advance the interests of elites through the fabrication of supposedly indigenous values and cultural artifacts. With respect to China, these researchers are quick to point out the many internal differences that belie the fiction of national unity as promoted by the Communist Party (e.g., Pan, 2010). Global studies scholars therefore acknowledge that national political action can be a site for contesting cultural domination from afar but they also aim to uncover other important locations of cultural struggle and to explain them within the context of globalization.

Although the foregoing approaches differ in significant ways, they share a set of central research questions with respect to modern media: What are the relations between global, national, and local institutions? What are the patterns of dominance and subordination? Where are the centers of creativity and cultural power? How do these relations of power affect creative workers and media users? How do they affect the socio-cultural fortunes of human communities? What are the essential principles that inform the production, circulation, and social uses of modern media? Such questions are implicitly spatial, which helps to explain persistent concerns about boundaries and relationships. Yet it is curious that spatial concerns are not more explicitly foregrounded in communications research. If film and media scholars were to do so, they might place more emphasis on the study of cities, and in particular the study of port cities, rather than the study of nations. This might present us with different ways of thinking about cultural power in the contemporary global media environment.

In ancient and medieval times, imperial regimes exerted their influence across space by subduing local populations and building alliances with groups that controlled strategic fortresses, towns, and cities. This was superseded by the modern system of states that were predicated on the establishment of fixed political boundaries and the internal cultivation of national populations. Under both systems, political and cultural power often coincided so that centers of creative activity developed around the centers of political rule. But capitalism subsequently endowed many cities around the world with resources that grew from commercial and industrial activity rather than political power and military conquest. Especially important in this regard were seafaring cities—such as Bombay, Lagos, Beirut, and

Hong Kong—that functioned as centers of trade, finance, manufacturing, and culture.

Port cities often operated in between the grand empires or on the margins of powerful states. They were places where the *exchange* of goods, ideas, and cultural artifacts was the basis of metropolitan prosperity. As modern publications, movies, and sound recordings expanded the geographical range of popular media, these cities were especially well situated to facilitate the transversal circulation of cultural goods and influences. They became centers of regional media economies that transcended national borders and they furthermore served as launching pads for the circulation of cultural products even further afield—Bombay movies to the Gulf States, African high life music to the Americas, and Chinese *wuxia* (martial arts) novels to Southeast Asia. Such cultural flows accelerated in the latter part of the twentieth century with the emergence of satellite television, digital recordings, and Internet communication. At first, these new technologies seemed to serve the interests of Western media conglomerates based in Hollywood, New York, and London, but over time they facilitated counter-flows within and between regions, and from the margins to the centers. These circulations also enabled new ways of thinking about one's affinities with others and about one's place in the world. Some dreamed of life in Hollywood but many others looked to cities like Bombay and Beirut with respect to fashion, culture, and lifestyle (Mitra, 2010). For those that were politically disempowered within their material locale, such cultural centers provided imaginary alternatives to the constraints and indignities they suffered in everyday life.

National governments were uneasy with cultural competition from afar, whether it came from Hollywood or Mumbai, cities that I refer to as media capitals. And they grew even more unsettled as it became easier to circulate popular music and screen media in the digital era. At the same time that cultural products were moving more fluidly across national borders, so too were capital, technology, and commercial goods, eventually tying countries into an interdependent global economic system (Harvey, 1990; Castells, 1996). As states saw their cultural and economic sovereignty eroding, their decision-making and administrative power were similarly constrained by forces from afar. They felt pressure from dominant Western powers to allow transnational media to flow freely and they felt exasperated by a rising enthusiasm among their citizens for cultural options from afar. If governments tried to set import quotas on movies, consumers would turn to black market video discs. If states banned satellite dishes, audiences would turn to the Internet. Such developments helped to heighten tensions between global hegemons, national governments, and port cities from which many transnational media products emanated.

As suggested above, these dynamics are not simply (inter)national, they are truly global: multidimensional, intersecting, conflictual, and systemic. They demand attention to national institutions and international relations but they also require the investigation of agents, forces, and locations beneath and between the nation-state. My recent research attempts to address these global cultural dynamics through the analysis of "media capital," a concept that at once directs attention to the leading status of particular cities and to the principles and processes that promote the concentration of resources in specific locales (Curtin, 2004, forthcoming, in progress). In this essay, I focus on the struggles between the Chinese state and Hong Kong film industry since the 1997 transfer of sovereignty, considering the spatial and power dynamics of their relationship in the past, present, and future. I inquire as to why the Chinese film industry has shifted its geographical center of gravity over time: from Shanghai to Singapore to Hong Kong, and most recently to Beijing. Rather than a nationally rooted commercial cinema, the Chinese film industry has been mobile, dynamic, and transnational for much of its history. This example raises intriguing questions about the contested relations between global, national, and local media. But before turning to this particular case study, I explain the principles of media capital and then describe the institutional characteristics and enabling conditions that encourage media resources to accumulate in particular cities. I offer Bombay as a fairly clear example of a successful media capital that operates relatively autonomously from the West. And finally, I turn to Chinese media, noting the rise and demise of Hong Kong as a media capital and exploring the Chinese state's role in disciplining its cultural competitor, as it endeavors to exert its "soft power" aspirations abroad. Compared to Mumbai, the Chinese case offers a contrasting example of a strong state battling for cultural supremacy at home and abroad. Although the state has been arguably successful in many respects, the chapter concludes by explaining that the principles of media capital suggest why, under current conditions, Beijing is unlikely to become a media capital and unlikely to extend its cultural influence globally or even regionally.

What *Is* Media Capital?

Although the range of forces and factors at play are various and complex, one can nevertheless discern three key principles as playing a structuring role in screen industries around the world since the early twentieth century: (1) the logic of accumulation, (2) trajectories of creative migration, and (3) contours of socio-cultural variation.

The logic of accumulation is not unique to media industries, since all capitalist enterprises exhibit innately dynamic and expansionist tendencies. As David Harvey (2001, pp. 237–66) points out, most firms seek efficiencies through the concentration of productive resources and through the expansion of markets so as to fully utilize their productive capacity and realize the greatest possible return. These tendencies are most explicitly revealed during periodic downturns in the business cycle when enterprises are compelled to intensify production or extensify distribution in order to survive, or both. Such moments of crisis call for a "spatial fix," says Harvey, as capital must on the one hand concentrate and integrate sites of production so as to reduce the amount of time and resources expended in manufacture and on the other hand it must increase the speed of distribution in order to reduce the time it takes to bring distant locales into the orbit of its operations. These *centripetal* tendencies in the sphere of production and *centrifugal* tendencies in distribution were observed by Karl Marx more than a century earlier when he incisively explained that capital must "annihilate space with time" if it is to overcome barriers to accumulation (Marx, 1973, p. 539). As applied to contemporary media, this insight suggests that even though a film or TV company may be founded with the aim of serving particular national cultures or local markets, it must over time re-deploy its creative resources and reshape its terrain of operations if it is to survive competition and enhance profitability.[1] Implicit in this logic of accumulation is the contributing influence of the "managerial revolution" that accompanied the rise of industrial capitalism (Chandler, 1977). Indeed, it was the intersection of capitalist accumulation with the reflexive knowledge systems of the Enlightenment that engendered the transition from mercantile to industrial capitalism. Capitalism became more than a mode of accumulation, it also became a disposition toward surveillance and adaptation, as it continually refined and integrated manufacturing and marketing processes, achieving efficiencies through the concentration of productive resources and the extension of delivery systems (Giddens, 1990).

The second principle of media capital emphasizes trajectories of creative migration. Audiovisual industries are especially reliant on creative labor as a core resource due to the recurring demand for new prototypes (i.e., feature films or television programs). Yet the marriage of art and commerce is always an uneasy one, especially in large institutional settings, and therefore the media business involves placing substantial wagers on forms of labor that are difficult to manage. As Asu Aksoy and Kevin Robins (1992, p. 12) observe, "Whether the output will be a hit or a miss cannot be pre-judged. However, the golden rule in the film business is that if you do not have creative talent to start with, then there is no business to talk about at all, no hits or misses." In fact, attracting and managing talent is one of the most difficult challenges that screen producers confront. At the level of the firm this involves offering attractive compensation and favorable working conditions, but at a broader level it also requires maintaining access to reservoirs of specialized labor that replenish themselves on a regular basis, which is why media companies tend to cluster in particular cities.[2]

Geographer Allen J. Scott contends that manufacturers of *cultural* goods tend to locate where subcontractors and skilled laborers form dense transactional networks. Besides apparent cost efficiencies, Scott points to the mutual learning effects that stem from a clustering of interrelated producers. Whether through informal learning (such as sharing ideas and techniques while collaborating on a particular project) or via more formal transfers of knowledge (craft schools, trade associations, and awards cer-emonies) clustering enhances product quality and fuels innovation. "Place-based communities such as these are not just foci of cultural labor in the narrow sense," observes Scott (2000, p. 33), "but also are active hubs of social reproduction in which crucial cultural competencies are maintained and circulated."

This centripetal migration of labor encourages path dependent evolu-tion, such that chance events or innovations may spark the appearance of a creative cluster, but industrial development depends on a spiral of growth fueled by the ongoing migration of talent in pursuit of professional oppor-tunities. Locales that fail to make an early start in such industries are subject to "lock-out," since it is difficult to disrupt the dynamics of agglomeration, even with massive infusions of capital or government subsidies. The only way a new cluster might arise is if a dominant media capital were to falter or if a new cluster were to offer an appreciably distinctive product line.

Despite the productive power and structural advantages of media capi-tals, the symbolic content of media products attenuates their geographical reach. That is, the cultural distance between, say, Chinese filmmakers and Turkish or Indian audiences introduces the prospect that the meaning-fulness and therefore the value of certain products may be undermined at the moment of consumption or use. Although the centripetal logics of accumulation and of creative migration help us identify concentrations of media capital, the centrifugal patterns of distribution are much more complicated, especially when products rub up against counterparts in distant cultural domains that are often served, even if minimally, by competing media capitals.

Cities such as Cairo, Mumbai, Hollywood, and Hong Kong lie across significant cultural divides from each other, which helps to explain why producers in these cities have been able to sustain distinctive product lines and survive the onslaught of distant competitors. These media capitals are furthermore supported by intervening factors that modify and complicate the spatial tendencies outlined above. Consequently, the third principle of media capital focuses on contours of socio-cultural variation, demonstrating that national and local institutions have been and remain significant actors in the global cultural economy.

During cinema's early years of industrial formation, market forces and talent migrations fostered the growth of powerful producers such as Hollywood, but governments around the world reacted to Hollywood's growing influence by developing policies as early as the 1920s to limit imports and to foster local media production. Attempts to develop local filmmaking institutions often proved difficult, but many countries were nevertheless successful at promoting radio and later television (most of them public service broadcasters) that produced popular shows and attracted substantial audiences. Broadcasting seemed an especially appropriate medium for intervention, since many of its cultural and technological characteristics helped to insulate national systems from foreign competition. The ensuing parade of broadcast news and entertainment punctuated daily household routines, interlacing public and private spheres, thereby situating national culture in the everyday world of its audiences (Scannell, 1991; Silverstone, 1994; Morley, 2000).

It should also be pointed out that state institutions were not the only actors to organize and exploit the contours of socio-cultural variation. Media enterprises have for decades taken advantage of social and cultural differences in their production and distribution practices, especially by employing narratives and creative talent that resonate with the cultural dispositions of audiences within their spheres of influence. They furthermore made use of social networks and insider information to secure market advantages, and they invoked ethnic and national pride in their promotional campaigns. Contours of socio-cultural variation have provided and continue to provide opportunities to carve out market niches that are beyond the reach of powerful but culturally distant competitors.

Overall, media capital is a concept that at once acknowledges the *spatial* logics of capital, creativity, culture, and polity without privileging one among the four. Just as the logic of capital provides a fundamental structuring influence, so too do forces of socio-cultural variation shape the diverse contexts in which media are made and consumed. The concept of media capital encourages us to provide dynamic and historicized accounts that delineate the operations of capital and the migrations of talent, while at the same time directing our attention to socio-cultural forces and contingencies that can engender alternative discourses, practices, and spatialities. Such an approach furthermore aims to address the supposed tension between political economy and cultural studies scholarship—and between the media imperialism and global studies approaches—by showing how insights from each of these schools can productively be brought to bear on the study of film and television.

What *Are* Media Capitals?

Media capitals are powerful geographic centers that tap human, creative, and financial resources within their spheres of circulation in order to fashion products that serve the distinctive needs of their audiences. Their success is dependent on their ability to monitor audience preferences, tap the popular imagination, and operationalize resources within their cultural domain. A media capital's preeminence is therefore relational: its bounty flows outward while in turn it gathers and exploits the very best human and cultural resources within its sphere of circulation. Its preeminence is dynamic and contingent, for it is subject to competition from other cities that aspire to capital status. Dubai, for example, is self-consciously attempting to challenge the leadership of Beirut within the sphere of Arab satellite television and Miami has recently arisen as a transnational competitor to Mexico City. Thus, the concept of media capital encourages a spatial examination of the shifting contours of accumulation and dissemination, which both shape and are shaped by the imaginary worlds of audiences. Such research seeks to understand why some locales become centers of media activity and to discern their relations to other locales. Media capitals emerge out of a complex play of historical forces and are therefore contingently produced within a crucible of transnational competition. Cities as diverse as Hollywood, Mumbai, and Lagos operate as media capitals within their respective spheres of circulation. Although qualitatively different in many respects, cities that become media capitals exhibit a shared set of characteristics with respect to institutional structure, creative capacity, and political autonomy.

Institutionally, media capitals tend to flourish where companies show a resolute fixation on the tastes and desires of audiences. In order to cater to such tastes, they adopt and adapt cultural influences from near and far, resulting in hybrid aesthetics. Such eclecticism and volatility is moderated by star and genre systems of production and promotion that help to make texts intelligible and marketable to diverse audiences. The bottom line for successful firms is always popularity and profitability. Although often criticized for pandering to the lowest common denominator, commercial film and TV studios are relentlessly innovative, as they avidly pursue the shifting nuances of fashion and pleasure. In the early stages of development, a media capital may be characterized by small businesses with an opportunistic outlook, many of them chasing the latest trend with abandon, churning out products on shoestring budgets and releasing them into the market with little promotion or strategic calculation. As media capitals mature, however, firms begin to formalize their institutional practices and in most cases they begin to integrate production, distribution, and exhibition within large corporations. Profitability is derived from structured creativity that feeds expansive (and expanding) distribution systems. Marketing considerations become woven into the conceptual stages of project development and financing. Media capitals therefore emerge where regimes of capital accumulation are purposefully articulated to the protean logics of popular taste. The mercantilist opportunism of an emerging filmmaking community gives way to industrialized modes of production and distribution.

Just as importantly, media capital tends to thrive in cities that foster creative endeavor, making them attractive destinations for aspiring talent. The research literature on industrial clustering shows that creative laborers tend to migrate to places where they can land jobs that allow them to learn from peers and mentors, as well as from training programs that are sponsored by resident craft organizations (Porter, 1998). Job mobility and intra-industry exchanges further facilitate the dissemination of skills, knowledge, and innovations. Thus a culture of mutual learning becomes institutionalized, helping to foster the reproduction and enhancement of creative labor (Scott, 2000). Workers are also inclined to gravitate to places that are renowned for cultural openness and diversity (Florida, 2005). It's remarkable, for example, that the most successful media capitals are usually port cities with long histories of transcultural engagement.

It's furthermore noteworthy that national political capitals rarely emerge as media capitals, largely because modern governments seem incapable of resisting the temptation to tamper with media institutions.[3] Consequently, media capitals tend to flourish at arm's length from the centers of state power, favoring cities that are in many cases are disdained by political and cultural elites (e.g., Los Angeles, Hong Kong, and Mumbai). Successful media enterprises tend to resist censorship and clientelism, and are suspicious of the state's tendency to promote an official and usually ossified version of culture. Instead, commercial media enterprises absorb and refashion indigenous and traditional cultural resources while also incorporating foreign innovations that may offer advantages in the market. They do this even though such appropriations tend to invite criticism from state officials and high-culture critics. The resulting mélange is emblematic of the contradictory pressures engendered by global modernity, at once dynamic and seemingly capricious yet also shrewdly strategic. The choice of location is no less calculated: media capital tends to accumulate in cities that are relatively stable, quite simply because entrepreneurs will only invest in studio construction and distribution infrastructure where they can operate without interference over extended periods of time.

Mumbai as a Media Capital

Mumbai is a useful example of a prosperous port city that has grown to become an influential media capital. It is a city that has been a commercial nexus for centuries, enjoying transcontinental trading relations with Persia, Egypt, and Greece during ancient times and later becoming the central node of the British imperial shipping and railroad networks in South Asia. The expansion of the railroads in the late 1800s and explosive growth of the city's cotton industry made Bombay a prosperous mecca for merchants and job seekers. As a result, almost every Indian language and many foreign languages are spoken in Mumbai. Marathi, the state language, is dominant, followed by Gujarati, Hindi, Bengali, and Urdu. English is commonly used in commerce and government. Such diversity has brought periods of ethnic and religious strife, but Bombay/Mumbai nevertheless has long been considered one of the most cosmopolitan and tolerant cities in India.

Today Mumbai remains India's principal seaport, the railhead for two major trunk lines, and country's principal airport, handling almost two-thirds of India's international flight traffic. The stock exchange, established in 1875, and commodity markets make Mumbai the most important financial center in South Asia. The local economy—initially renowned for banking, shipping, and textile manufacturing—has diversified since independence to include plastics, printing, and pharmaceuticals. Given the constant flow of people and goods, it's not surprising that Mumbai is also an important center for illicit trade in currencies, gemstones, precious metals, and human flesh. Closely connected to mafia networks in Karachi and Dubai, the underworld societies of Mumbai have exerted a powerful influence on trade, real estate, and the movie industry. Mumbai is also an aspirational locale, where the wealthy live lavishly and the more modestly endowed can sample the ambiguous gift of cosmopolitan modernity. Both onscreen and off, the city has come to symbolize the attractions and trepidations of big city life, with many popular melodramas representing it as the quintessential urban locale of South Asia (Prakash, 2006; Mitra, 2010).

Mumbai's status as a port city is intimately intertwined with its history as a cultural center. During the British Raj, Parsi migrants from Persia rose to become wealthy and influential players in the shipping, shipbuilding, and financial industries. They also launched the city's popular commercial theater troupes that shrewdly intermingled a range of performance traditions, including Shakespearean drama, Persian lyric poetry, and Hindu folk dances. Lavishly staged, Parsi theater was renowned for spectacle and melodrama, often with historical or mythological themes. During the nineteenth century, these theater companies traveled throughout India and Southeast Asia, playing to appreciative crowds (Gupt, 2005; Ganti, 2004). Their appropriation of diverse cultural influences no doubt derived from Parsi awareness that, as a minority population, the commercial success of their theatrical endeavors would depend on their ability to negotiate differences.

Some of these theatrical troupes made the transition to cinema, which first arrived in Bombay in 1896, and as filmmakers they earned renown for borrowing from a broad range of sources in order to satisfy the growing demands of moviegoers. By the 1920s, the city was widely recognized as a leading center of Indian movie production and its accomplishments were all the more impressive given the fierce competition from Western imports. The arrival of sound technology in 1931 posed new challenges for Bombay filmmakers, since there existed no "natural" candidate for spoken dialog. Bombay itself was polyglot, and was surrounded by territories where Marathi and Gujarati prevailed. No doubt aware that language would affect the patterns of movie distribution, filmmakers gravitated to Hindustani, a mixture of Hindi and Urdu that was used by the trading classes in north and central India. As the lingua franca of the bazaars, Hindustani was furthermore a fitting choice because Bombay was tied to these locales via historical trade routes and the Indian railway. Moreover, Hindi was the most widely spoken language in India and Urdu was a foundational idiom for populations in northern India and what is today Pakistan. The two share a common grammatical structure and much vocabulary. Hindustani was therefore accessible to Hindi and Urdu speakers, as well as somewhat accessible to speakers of other Indo-Aryan languages.

"This led to a peculiarity," observes Tejaswini Ganti (2004, p. 12). "Bombay became the only city where the language of the film industry was not congruent with the language of the region. . . . The fact that cinema in the Hindi language developed in multi-lingual Bombay, rather than the Hindi-speaking north, disassociated Hindi films from any regional identification, imbuing them with a more 'national' character. As a result of circulating in a national market, Hindi cinema also developed its own idiom and style [that] does not necessarily correspond to any particular regional variant of Hindi." Cinematic Hindustani was therefore a language that many could access, but none could claim, making Bombay films appear as transcultural as the theatrical tradition from which the city's film industry emerged. The Hindustani language furthermore insulated against Western imports and spurred the development of a lucrative popular music industry (Punathambekar & Kavoori, 2008). These cultural characteristics helped Bombay movies to establish broad if haphazard circulation patterns across many parts of colonial India, including what is today Pakistan, Sri Lanka, and Bangladesh. Their success allowed producers to invest in ever more lavish on-screen spectacles, which in turn enhanced their competitive edge over regional competitors from Calcutta, Hyderabad, or Madras. With their resolute focus on popular taste, film (and later television) companies incorporated diverse cultural influences while nevertheless disciplining their hybrid aesthetics to star and genre systems that rendered texts popular and marketable in various contexts. Distribution concerns were thoroughly integrated into the conception, financing, and production of products, ensuring a healthy circulation of popular fare.

Mumbai furthermore benefited from its reputation as a center of creative endeavor. Talent was attracted to the city not simply because jobs were available but also because it was renowned for a creative community that had institutionalized a system of mutual learning. The city was generally welcoming to diverse populations and, as a seaport, had a long history of cultural and economic exchange with outsiders. It was a stable and prosperous locale that became renowned as a trendsetter among the middle class and aspiring middle class of South Asia.

After India became in 1947, tensions between commercial filmmakers and the national government became an enduring feature of the industry (Jeffrey, 2006). For a variety of complex reasons, however, the Indian government eventually capitulated to the pervasive influence of Mumbai media, anointing it with official industry status in 1998, which opened the door to new financing opportunities from the private sector as well as government programs aimed at bolstering media enterprises. The state furthermore passed legislation that legitimized commercial satellite television, providing lucrative distribution channels for television programming, feature films, and popular music. Synergies among the three have fueled the fortunes of these industries, which most likely would have languished on their own. Although the term "Bollywood" raises the hackles of many industry insiders, Ashish Rajadhyaksha (2003) has quite correctly pointed out that the term at least provides a means of coming to grips with the complex interconnections among commercialized and globalized media institutions headquartered in the Indian city of dreams. Mumbai is the undisputed center of financing, production, and distribution, serving as a magnet for creative talent, a bazaar for media merchants, and a palimpsest for cultural influences from near and far.

As this very brief historical sketch indicates, Mumbai's status as a media capital traces its roots to commercial circulations, human migrations, ethnic diversity, cultural hybridity, linguistic opportunism, and underworld machinations. Admired by the masses and disdained by the nation's elite, the city matured at the center of India's economy but on the margins of political power. Mumbai's fortune as a media capital rests not only on its centrality but also on its marginality. It is in many respects the emblematic melting pot of the Indian nation and yet it is in many respects remarkably Western. It exists at the center of flows, yet it's also on the periphery of both India and the West. Bollywood therefore must mark its distance from New Delhi and from Hollywood if it is to survive as a media capital. For the attraction of its screen media resides in their perceived distance from the disciplinary logic of the Indian state and the cultural logic of Hollywood.

Contested Capital in Chinese Screen Media

The commercial Chinese movie industry was, during its prime, a fundamentally transnational medium. Expansive and mobile, it emerged in the

1920s in Shanghai and Hong Kong, and soon expanded into export markets in Southeast Asia. During the 1930s, the mainland movie market was beleaguered by war and revolution, so the center of Chinese commercial cinema shifted south to Singapore, only to be buffeted yet again by waves of nationalist fervor on the Malay Peninsula during the 1950s. The industry then relocated to Hong Kong, where it matured and flourished, serving local audiences but also fashioning products with an eye to overseas markets (Fu, 2003, 2008; Uhde & Uhde, 2000; Zhang, 2004). Chinese movie executives pursued opportunities wherever they arose and the industry was therefore proto-global in orientation, even if its products were not ubiquitous worldwide. It was anchored moreover by a resident creative community that tapped talent and resources from near and far, making Hong Kong the central node in the intricate circuits of Chinese popular culture.

Although transnational in orientation, it was also quite local in many respects. In the latter decades of the twentieth century Hong Kong filmmakers shot most of their productions on the streets of the city and consciously fashioned their movies for local fans. Hong Kong's film culture was then renowned for midnight premieres, where cast and crew would mingle among the moviegoers, taking the pulse of the audience and sometimes adapting the final cut of the film accordingly (Teo, 1997; Bordwell, 2010). Movies were made for locals and their response was considered as a rough predictor of potential success in overseas markets such as Malaysia, Singapore, and Taiwan. The creative community made its home in a colonial city, among a population that had largely migrated from elsewhere and was then in the process of developing a distinctly indigenous but also cosmopolitan identity. Moviemaking was a local business with a translocal sensibility (Zhang, 2010). Aspiring Chinese talent moved to Hong Kong from many parts of Asia—and even as far afield as Europe and North America—seeing the city as the most promising place to build a career. Movie executives similarly saw it as the best place to raise financing, recruit labor, and launch projects.

The movie business operated outside the reach of national politics, sheltered by the benign neglect of the British colonial regime. Producers cobbled together feature films in a freewheeling fashion and at a ferocious pace, turning out popular products, occasional gems, and a good deal of rubbish. Nevertheless the tempo, scale, and diversity of production helped to foster a flexible ensemble of film companies that provided job opportunities to thousands of professionals as well as training for those that aspired to join the industry. Hong Kong became a magnet for talent from near and far, and became an incubator for creative experimentation (Curtin, 2007). It was home to Tsui Hark, Maggie Cheung, and Leonard Ho. Home to Ann Hui, Peter Chan, and Michelle Yeoh. Home to Peter Pau, Wong Kar-wai, and Christopher Doyle. It was also home to a vibrant ensemble of newspapers, music labels, and broadcasting stations.

In 1997, the People's Republic of China reclaimed Hong Kong after more than a century of British rule. The terms of transfer provided a fifty-year transition in which the city would operate as a relatively autonomous Special Administrative Region, but it was clear from the beginning that Beijing intended to exert its authority and many believed that government scrutiny of the media industries would increase. This posed a problem for Hong Kong film companies that were accustomed to producing satirical and ribald comedies, as well as fantasy, horror, and crime stories. The city's creative class grew nervous as the deadline for transition approached, for the very genres that had proven most prosperous were likely to become targets of censors and propaganda officials. Consequently, many producers, directors, and actors began to explore job options abroad and even those that remained in place quietly began moving resources and families overseas in case of an official crackdown (Chan, 2009). The industry also entered into a cycle of hyperproduction, spewing out as many movies as possible, hoping to maximize profits before the fateful moment of transition. This flooded the market with low-grade products that alienated loyal audiences both at home and abroad. Hong Kong's reputation suffered tremendously as a result, most tragically with its audiences, who by the late nineties had grown accustomed to cultural alternatives from Tokyo, Seoul, Europe, and Hollywood that were readily available at movie multiplexes, on video, and over the Internet. No longer willing to risk the expense of a theater ticket for a Hong Kong feature film, consumers bought (or downloaded) pirated Chinese movie videos that sold for only a fraction of the retail price (Wang, 2003). As audiences turned a cold shoulder to the industry, so too did media professionals in other parts of Asia. Distributors stopped buying, producers stopped collaborating, and directors declined to use Hong Kong talent on their projects. In the decade following the handover, the industry's transnational network of audiences, distributors, and creative talent slowly dissolved (Curtin, 2007; Chan, Fung, & Ng, 2010; Bordwell, 2010).

In retrospect, anxieties about the handover to Chinese sovereignty were somewhat exaggerated and the industry was therefore ill-served by the opportunistic mentality that prevailed throughout much of the 1990s and into the new century. In fact, it suffered less from censorship than it did from a fear of censorship that fueled self-destructive cycle of overproduction. The Beijing leadership therefore didn't need to dip its hands directly into the messy mechanics of content regulation. Instead, it kept its distance and withheld assistance during a time when the Hong Kong industry was under tremendous stress. Interestingly, the Chinese leadership hatched numerous joint ventures with Hollywood partners while snubbing the Hong Kong industry, whose films were treated as foreign imports for seven long and turbulent years after the city's return to Chinese sovereignty. The PRC government essentially starved the industry at a moment of crisis and only opened the door to the mainland market slowly after it was sure it had the upper hand in its relationship with "Hollywood East."

In the years following the handover, movie companies started shuttering their operations, support services evaporated, and talent dispersed. To make matters worse, PRC policies regarding censorship remained cloudy, so that many producers urged caution with respect to content issues, fostering a culture of self-censorship that further alienated audiences, especially those in important overseas markets such as Taiwan, Singapore, and Malaysia. As the irreverent and innovative qualities of Hong Kong media products diminished, export revenues declined and producers were confronted with two options: focus on the tiny domestic market of the SAR itself or enter into projects (usually coproductions) with mainland media partners.[4] The former would entail significant downsizing while the latter would require feature films that were fashioned as much for PRC censors as audiences. The Beijing government furthermore sent signals that it would brook no challenges to the supremacy of state institutions such as China Film and China Central Television (CCTV). If Hong Kong firms were to participate in the rapidly growing mainland media economy, they would do so within parameters established by the Communist Party (Yeh & Davis, 2008; Yeh, 2010; Davis, 2010).

Today, Hong Kong is but one node in a geographically dispersed circuit of deal-making and creative endeavor that is increasingly driven by the exigencies of the mainland market. Filmmakers must be attentive to government officials that explicitly make use of import policies, subsidies, and regulations to shape movie messages and to nurture the development of large national enterprises that they hope will someday compete with their Hollywood counterparts. They favor big movies with big stars. The themes and dialogue are cautious, even at times stilted, but the production values are growing more competitive with global standards and much of this has to do with the skills and insights that Hong Kong talent bring to these coproductions. Indeed, the leading box office performers during the first decade of the 2000s were Hong Kong–PRC blockbusters. Most were historical dramas (e.g., *Hero*, 2002; *Red Cliff*, 2008; *The Warlords*, 2008), which were safe with censors because they displaced controversial issues onto a distant past and were furthermore acceptable to officials because they promoted the image of China as a grand and ultimately united civilization with a long and distinguished history (Wang, 2009; Zhao, 2010).

Audiences in East Asia outside the PRC seem to sense the caution and calculation behind these efforts, and many moviegoers consequently opted for Hollywood products, which are arguably no less cautious or calculated. The difference is that Hollywood filmmaking is periodically rejuvenated by sleeper films and independent features. It also has a film rating system that makes it possible for filmmakers to target particular segments of the audience and to explore mature themes and offbeat topics. These structural mechanisms have allowed innovative projects—such as *Juno* (2007), *Slumdog Millionaire* (2008), and *The Hurt Locker* (2009)—to break through the institutional inertia and the insider dealings of the industry. As currently constituted, the mainland movie industry has no such mechanisms. Instead, there is a yawning gap between state-sanctioned feature film extravaganzas (all of them G-rated) and sadly undernourished mid-range and independent movies (Zhang, 2010; Chan, Fung, & Ng, 2010; Song, 2010). Chinese independent films are micro-budgeted projects that are either destined for the international festival circuit or they are opportunistic features that are produced largely for the satellite television market. The former are seen as unprofitable art cinema that rarely make it into theaters while the latter tend to be "main melody" films that are subsidized by the state and conform to ideological guidelines that favor uplifting characters and pro-social themes (Song, 2010).

Television likewise suffers from various institutional constraints, so that mainland China—which has by far the world's largest national television audience—remains a net importer of programming (Keane, 2010). Low-cost genres (talk, reality, and variety) flourish, but few are innovative and those that are find themselves quickly besieged by imitative competitors (Keane, Fung, & Moran, 2007). Drama and comedy—signature genres of the world's most successful television enterprises—remain underdeveloped, largely because of the same caution and calculation that prevails in the movie business. Besides the constraints on content, mainland television enterprises also suffer from structural limitations. Shanghai and Guangzhou media have exploded in size and Hunan provincial television has proven itself to be a shrewd innovator, but most TV companies are run by provincial or municipal units of government that are eager to maintain their authority and ownership status. This makes it difficult for companies to merge and makes it difficult to shake out the weakest performers (Diao, 2008). Provincial and municipal TV enterprises are hampered as well by regulations that favor the state-sanctioned national champion, China Central Television, which in a stunning conflict of interest is also the organization that overseas national television ratings. Provincial and municipal telecasters are furthermore discouraged from building overseas distribution channels, a privilege that largely belongs to Beijing-based institutions that nest snugly under the wing of the state, where they are closely monitored for content and tone.

If today there is a geographic center to Chinese media, it is within the Communist Party offices in Beijing, not because the party micromanages the day-to-day operations of television and film enterprises but rather because it systematically doles out favors and franchises to those that acknowledge its supremacy. The party leadership is quite successful at keeping a leash on domestic players and at exploiting joint venture partners from overseas.[5] The PRC government has cagily manipulated both Western and Hong Kong movie companies to serve its own ambitions, which are to build a movie infrastructure that will ultimately be popular with national audiences and competitive with Hollywood, both at home and abroad. To the extent that it has succeeded, it is largely because China's moviegoing public is expanding at a breathtaking pace, with box office receipts of $2.7 billion in 2012, making it the second largest theatrical market in the world ("China box office round-up," 2013). Television is undergoing a similar growth trajectory, with CCTV announcing that its 2010 annual advertising auction drew $1.9 billion in revenue, rising more than 15 percent over the preceding year (Coonan, 2010b); by 2013, that figure had doubled.

Yet despite these impressive figures, mainland media have little influence abroad, casting barely a ripple through media markets in Korea, Taiwan, or Japan, let alone Europe or the United States. This is due largely to the fact that PRC cinema has, since its inception, been an instrument of the state, a bridge between the Communist Party and the people. Since the 1980s, the government has reorganized and marketized the national economy so that media institutions now operate in a more decentralized fashion. They pursue audiences as they might pursue media consumers, but their overriding mission is to serve the party and media ownership remains squarely in the hands of the state (Zhu, 2003; Diao, 2008). This system of control is fairly obvious to viewers on the mainland who commonly seek alternatives via the Internet and the DVD black market. Young people especially rely on Internet viewing, employing a host of strategies to circumvent the "Great Firewall" in order to acquire products that could never find their way into cinemas or onto the airwaves (Barboza, 2010; Chua & Iwabuchi, 2008). As for overseas markets, audiences seem occasionally interested in historical dramas that emanate from the mainland, but their tastes are quite diverse and they have access to a great range of media products and services. Mainland movies have therefore performed modestly overseas and television exports have proven to be of little interest to audiences in Hong Kong, Taipei, and Singapore. As for projecting soft power even further afield in Asia, state media products have enjoyed little success in Tokyo, Seoul, or Bangkok.

Conclusion

By breaking outside a national perspective and applying a global lens to the development of media institutions in East Asia, one begins to appreciate the pervasive tensions between national and cosmopolitan media, between state imperatives and the dynamic principles of media capital. Beijing's apparent success at controlling its domestic film industry runs counter to what many critics and researchers see as the unrelenting global expansion of Western media conglomerates. It raises the prospect of a new center of cultural power based in the national capital under the watchful eye of the state, suggesting that, under certain conditions, state regimes may indeed be able to assert their cultural influence domestically, and may furthermore be able to tame the power of nearby competitors in cities such as Hong Kong. Yet the regime's apparent triumph also constrains its explicit soft-power ambitions. For Beijing is unlikely to become a global media capital so long as it is remains the seat of national government. This is because media capital flourishes at cultural crossroads, not at the centers of political power. Beijing may build and manage a vast domestic media infrastructure, but it is likely to struggle in its efforts to influence popular culture beyond its borders. This is because media capitals tend to prosper at a distance from state power—Mumbai vs. New Delhi, Lagos vs. Abuja, Miami vs. Mexico City. Although London has been successful as a media capital, that's largely because its creative industries tend to be resolutely capitalistic and are insulated from state pressures by a common law tradition that sets limits on state power. Even the national public broadcaster, the BBC, has a long tradition of creative independence and insulation from the political imperatives of the ruling regime. If Chinese media can someday achieve this level of relative autonomy, Beijing might indeed emerge as a transnational media capital, but until that time its creative cluster is perhaps more appropriately seen as a national center or media hub. London is an exceptional case—perhaps a rare historical accident—and one doubts, for example, that Washington or Riyadh or Moscow could ever be media capitals.

As for Hong Kong, the (soft) nationalization of its film industry helps to explain why its status as a media capital is declining. Once known for its rambunctious, reflexive, and visceral cinema, the city's creative community has shriveled and the talent that remains has capitulated to a system that is built around the cautious, calculated blockbuster feature film that will appease state censors, party officials, and major financial backers. Audiences matter, but not the way that they used to matter when the Hong Kong industry was in its prime, and not the way they continue to matter to filmmakers in Los Angeles or Mumbai. Hollywood and Bollywood both have been successful because of their ongoing fixation on audience preferences. Their popularity in large and diverse domestic markets has in turn translated into overseas profitability, so that both industries now place a premium on global audiences and routinely consider them during the conception and financing of new products (Schuker, 2010). Chinese commercial cinema has by comparison turned inward and one therefore wonders where (and if) a new center of gravity will emerge in the Chinese film industry. Will it remain a national industry nestled in Beijing under the watchful eye of the state or might a transnational media capital reemerge in one of the seaport cities along China's coast? For if China is truly to assert its soft power, it seems less likely to do so as a state-driven media regime than as a popular culture industry situated at a cosmopolitan crossroads.

REFERENCES

Aksoy, A., and Robins, K. (1992). Hollywood for the 21st century: Global competition for critical mass in image markets. *Cambridge Journal of Economics* 16:1–22.

Appadurai, A. (1996). *Modernity at large: Cultural dimensions of globalization.* Minneapolis: University of Minnesota Press.

Barboza, D. (2010). For Chinese, Web is the way to entertainment. *New York Times,* 18 April, p. B1.

Bordwell, D. (2010) *Planet Hong Kong: Popular cinema and the art of entertainment.* 2nd ed. http://www.davidbordwell.net/books/planethongkong.php.

Castells, M. (1996). *The rise of the network society*. Malden, MA: Blackwell.

Chan, P. (2009). A discussion with producer/director Peter Ho-San Chan on global trends in Chinese-language movie production. Interview, Taiwan Cinema website, Government Information Office, Republic of China (Taiwan), 2 April. http://www.taiwancinema.com/ct.asp?xItem=58252&ctNode=124&mp=2.

Chan, J. M., Fung, Y. H., and Ng, C. H. (2010). *Policies for the sustainable development of the Hong Kong film industry*. Hong Kong: Chinese University of Hong Kong Press.

Chandler, A. (1977). *The visible hand: The managerial revolution in American business*. Cambridge: Belknap Press of Harvard University Press.

China box office round-up 2012: China becomes world's second biggest market. (2013). *Screen Daily*, 21 January. http://www.screendaily.com/china-box-office-round-up-2012-china-becomes-worlds-second-biggest-market/5050843.article.

Chua, B., and Iwabuchi, K. (2008), *East Asian pop culture: Analysing the Korean wave*. Hong Kong: Hong Kong University Press.

Coonan, C. (2010a). Chinese B.O. totals $1.14 bil. *Variety*, 19 October. http://www.variety.com/article/VR1118025904.html?categoryid=1278&cs=1&query=china+box+office.

Coonan, C. (2010b). Ads auction up 15.5% for CCTV. *Variety*, 8 November. http://www.variety.com/article/VR1118027181.

Curtin, M. (2004). Media capitals: Cultural geographies of global TV. In J. Olsson & L. Spigel, eds., *Television after TV: Essays on a medium in transition* (pp. 270–302). Durham, NC: Duke University Press.

Curtin, M. (2007). *Playing to the world's biggest audience: The globalization of Chinese film and TV*. Berkeley: University of California Press.

Curtin, M. (Forthcoming). Global media capital and local media policy. In J. Wasko, G. Murdock, & H. Sousa, eds., *Handbook of political economy of communication*. Malden, MA: Blackwell.

Curtin, M. (In progress). *Media capital: The cultural geography of globalization*. Manuscript.

Davis, D. W. (2010). Market and marketization in the China film business. *Cinema Journal* 49 (3): 121–25.

Diao, M. M. (2008). Research into Chinese television development: Television industrialisation in China. PhD diss., Macquarie University, Sydney.

Durovicova, N., & Newman, K., eds. (2010). *World cinemas, transnational perspectives*. New York: Routledge.

Florida, R. (2005). *Cities and the creative class*. New York: Routledge.

Frater, P. (2008). Hollywood weighs China yin-yang. *Variety*, 1 August. http://www.variety.com/article/VR1117989939?refCatId=2520&query=yin+yang.

Fu, P. (2003). *Between Shanghai and Hong Kong: The politics of Chinese cinemas*. Stanford, CA: Stanford University Press.

Fu, P. ed. (2008). *China forever: The Shaw brothers and diasporic cinema*. Urbana: University of Illinois Press.

Ganti, T. (2004). *Bollywood: A guidebook to popular Hindi cinema*. New York: Routledge.

Giddens, A. (1990). *The consequences of modernity.* Stanford, CA: Stanford University Press.

Guback, T. H. (1969). *The international film industry: Western Europe and America since 1945.* Bloomington: Indiana University Press.

Gupt, S. (2005). *Parsi Theatre: Its Origins and Development,* Calcutta: Seagull Books.

Harvey, D. (1990). *The condition of postmodernity.* Malden, MA: Blackwell.

Harvey, D. (2001). *Spaces of capital: Towards a critical geography.* New York: Routledge.

Hjort, M., & Mackenzie, S., eds. (2000). *Cinema and nation.* New York: Routledge.

Innis, H. (1972). *Empire and communications.* Toronto: University of Toronto Press.

Jacobs, J. (1984). *Cities and the wealth of nations.* New York: Random House.

Jeffrey, R. (2006). The mahatma didn't like the movies and why it matters. *Global Media and Communication* 2 (2): 204–24.

Keane, M. (2007). *Created in China: The great new leap forward.* London: Routledge.

Keane, M. (2010). Keeping up with the neighbors: China's soft power ambitions. *Cinema Journal* 49 (3): 130–35.

Keane, M., Fung, A. Y. H., & Moran, A. (2007). *New television, globalisation, and the East Asian cultural imagination.* Hong Kong: Hong Kong University Press.

Marx, K. (1973). *Grundrisse: Foundations of the critique of political economy.* New York: Vintage.

McBride, S. (1980). *Many voices, one world: Communication and society, today and tomorrow; Towards a new more just and more efficient world information and communication order.* New York: Unipub.

Miller, T., Govil, N., McMurria, J., Wang, T., & Maxwell, R. (2008). *Global Hollywood: No. 2.* London: British Film Institute.

Mitra, S. (2010). Localizing the global: Bombay's sojourn from the cosmopolitan urbane to Aamchi Mumbai. In M. Curtin & H. Shah, eds., *Reorienting global communication: Indian and Chinese media beyond borders.* Urbana: University of Illinois Press.

Morley, D. (2000). *Home territories: Media, mobility, and identity.* New York: Routledge.

Nowell-Smith, G. (1999). *The Oxford history of world cinema.* New York: Oxford University Press.

Pan, Z. (2010). Enacting the family-nation on a global stage: An analysis of CCTV's spring gala. In M. Curtin & H. Shah, eds., *Reorienting global communication: Indian and Chinese media beyond borders.* Urbana: University of Illinois Press.

Pang, L. (2010). Hong Kong cinema as a dialect cinema? *Cinema Journal* 40 (3).

Porter, M. (1998). Clusters and the new economics of competition. *Harvard Business Review* (November): 77–90.

Prakash, G. (2006). The idea of Bombay. *American Scholar* 75 (2): 88–99.

Punathambekar, A., & Kavoori, A., eds. (2008). *Global Bollywood.* New York: New York University Press.

Rajadhyaksha, A. (2003). The "Bollywoodization" of the Indian cinema: Cultural nationalism in a global arena. *Inter-Asia Cultural Studies* 4 (1): 25–39.

Scannell, P. (1991). *A social history of British broadcasting.* Cambridge: Blackwell.

Schiller, H. I. ([1969] 1992). *Mass communication and American empire.* 2nd ed. Boulder, CO: Westview.

Schuker, L. A. E. (2010). In depth: Plot change: Global forces transform Hollywood films. *Wall Street Journal Asia*, 2 August, p. 14.

Scott, A. J. (2000). *The cultural economy of cities*. Thousand Oaks, CA: Sage.

Silverstone, R. (1994). *Television and everyday life*. New York: Routledge.

Song, T. (2010). Independent cinema in the Chinese film industry. PhD diss., Queensland University of Technology, Queensland.

Teo, S. (1997). *Hong Kong cinema: The extra dimensions*. London: British Film Institute.

Tomlinson, J. (1999). *Globalization and culture*. Chicago: University of Chicago Press.

Uhde, Jan, and Uhde, Yvonne Ng. (2000). *Latent images: Film in Singapore*. Singapore: Oxford University Press.

Vitali, V., & Willemen, P., eds. (2006). *Theorising national cinema*. London: British Film Institute.

Wang, S. (2003). *Framing piracy: Globalization and film distribution in greater China*. Lanham, MD: Rowman & Littlefield.

Wang, T. (2009). Understanding local reception of globalized cultural products in the context of the international cultural economy: A case study on the reception of *Hero* and *Daggers* in China. *International Journal of Cultural Studies* 12:299–318.

Wong, A.-L., ed. (2002). *The Cathay story*. Hong Kong: Hong Kong Film Archive.

Yeh, E. Y. (2010). The deferral of pan-Asian: Critical appraisal of film marketization in China. In M. Curtin & H. Shah, eds., *Reorienting global communication: Indian and Chinese media beyond borders*. Urbana: University of Illinois Press

Yeh, E. Y., & Davis, D. W. (2008). Re-nationalizing China's film industry: Case study on the China Film Group and film marketization. *Journal of Chinese Cinemas* 2 (2): 37–51.

Young, D. (2010). News Corp sells controlling stake in China TV channels. *Reuters*, 9 August, http://www.reuters.com/article/idUSTRE67810L20100809.

Zhang, Y. (2004). *Chinese national cinema*. New York: Routledge

Zhang, Y. (2010). Transnationalism and translocality in Chinese cinema. *Cinema Journal* 49 (3): 135–39.

Zhao, Y. (2010). Whose *Hero*? The "spirit" and "structure" of the made-in-China blockbuster. In M. Curtin & H. Shah, eds., *Reorienting global communication: Indian and Chinese media beyond borders* (pp. 161–82). Urbana: University of Illinois Press.

Zhu, Y. (2003). *Chinese cinema during the era of reform: The ingenuity of the system*. Westport, CT: Praeger.

Notes

1. Monopoly rents are an exception, but as shown in this chapter, monopoly rents have proven less tenable in an era of changing technologies and increasing transborder flows.

2. Although it does not address media industries specifically, an extensive litera-

ture discusses the impact of human capital on the clustering of business firms in particular locations (Jacobs, 1984; Porter, 1998; Florida, 2005).

3. London, the national capital of the United Kingdom, is an exception, largely because of the residual advantages of empire that made it such an important maritime and financial center. Its importance as a center of media activity has been perpetuated largely because it has exploited its access to the wealthy global Anglophone market and because the state has exercised restraint in its oversight of creative institutions.

4. Recently, a third option has begun to present itself. The terms of the Closer Economic Partnership Agreement between the PRC and Hong Kong has made it possible for filmmakers to target the provincial Guangdong market (Pang, 2010). It is still too soon to know whether this possibility will provide greater autonomy to the Hong Kong industry.

5. News Corporation and Warner Bros. have both thrown in the towel after more than a decade of failed joint ventures, and the general consensus among Western executives is that India is a better bet for investment these days (Frater, 2008). Most prominently in this regard is News Corporation's decision to sell its ownership stake in Star TV, which generated a flurry of press coverage (e.g., Young, 2010).

CHAPTER SEVEN

The Enduring Strength of Hollywood

The "Imperial Adventure" Genre and Avatar

Jaap van Ginneken

During the last decade of the twentieth century, we have witnessed the disintegration of the Soviet Union, the Warsaw Pact, and the eastern European bloc of Communist countries, as well as the emergence of the Internet as an instrument of globalization. The ensuing "free market" euphoria led to a series of economic bubbles and their bursting around non-Western currencies, dot-com shares, and housing mortgages—culminating in the worldwide credit crisis of 2008.[1]

Today, we are witnessing the rapid emergence of new powers such as Brazil, India, and China, not so much because of "development aid," but rather because these countries turn out to be large and diversified enough to kick off cycles of capital accumulation and productivity gains on their own.

One major question remains: To what extent will these profound changes affect the global landscape of international/intercultural/inter-ethnic communication and media? The debate on a New World Information and Communication Order (NWICO), within the framework of the United Nations Organization for Education, Science and Culture (UNESCO), was sidelined long ago, due to fierce opposition from the dominant media powers: the major Anglo-Saxon countries and their closest allies, representing the largest and most of all the richest media home markets in the world.

Recent years have finally seen the emergence of some significant non-

Western media and media groups. Yet the media materials circulating between continents do still mostly originate from the Western world. This holds for news agency dispatches and syndicated journalism, books and translations, comic strips and video games, toy characters and gadgets. It holds for news pictures and films, television series and formats, as well as movies. True, Hong Kong, Bombay, and other cities have become major film hubs, but few of their movies make an impact beyond the immediate neighboring countries and overseas diasporas of Chinese and Indians, for instance.

To fathom the implications of this state of affairs, we need to focus not on alternative cinema but on worldwide blockbusters instead (Stringer, 2003), which help shape the global conscience, its view of history, geography, and society. The website IMDb provides an elaborate database on movies. Among other things, it carries up-to-date numbers on the "Worldwide box office" revenue generated by individual movies during their theatrical releases. This is also the basis for an all-time blockbuster list. Recently, it had 390 movies that had made more than two hundred million dollars in cinemas up to that point.[2] Let us consider a further breakdown.

Who Makes Global Blockbusters? The Pyramid and the Prism

Of these almost four hundred movies, 70.3 percent mentioned a single producing country: namely, in 67.9 percent (or more than two-thirds) of cases, the United States alone; in a meager 2.3 percent, a country other than the United States. These latter few percent involved four times another Anglo-Saxon country, thrice a European country, and twice Japan. By contrast, 29.7 percent, or almost a third, of the films were listed as international co-productions. Of these, 27.4 percent (or more than a quarter) of all the blockbusters also mentioned the United States as a participant; a miniscule 2.3 percent did not. By far the largest part of the co-productions, or 19.2 percent of the blockbusters overall, mentioned another Anglo-Saxon country (Canada, the United Kingdom and Ireland, Australia and New Zealand), 15.9 percent a continental European country (mostly Germany, because of a special tax law there), and only three films involved Japan.

So the United States remains the mammoth in this field, with even its closest allies playing only a marginal role. Other countries are rather insignificant. Hong Kong was mentioned three times as a territory participating in a production, the People's Republic of China and Taiwan once (for the same brilliant *wuxia* movie, *Crouching Tiger*). But India was not mentioned at all (*Slumdog Millionaire* was not listed as an Indian production, though partly in Hindi).[3] Nor was any other country from other continents listed: none from Asia and the Pacific, Central and South America, Africa, or the Middle East.

Most blockbusters listed one of the "seven sisters" among the Hollywood studios as the prime participating company: Universal (43), Warner (42), Disney (including Buena Vista, 35), Twentieth Century Fox (including Fox 2000, 32), Paramount (29), Columbia (22), and the relative newcomer Dreamworks (20). Even lesser American studios registered many more hits than (originally) European companies, such as Polygram (3) and Gaumont (1). Sony was mentioned once. A key question is of course why the United States is so far ahead of all others. Is it just its political and economic, cultural, and linguistic clout worldwide? Or are there other structural factors as well?

One major factor is of course that in Hollywood, filmmaking is unequivocally a commercial affair. Participants make an investment and a calculation about how they plan to recoup their money. They gamble, but cover their risks—usually by not departing too far from the ideological mainstream. Films are also "tested" on U.S. audiences before release. If needed, new scenes are shot, other scenes are re-edited. Sometimes, a completely new ending is added (usually more upbeat), until the whole proves to "work" with audiences.

In Europe and elsewhere, filmmaking is often approached in a more "arty" way, by contrast, with government subsidies playing a key role. Producers often cave in to "auteur" directors. But the most important factor is this: the United States is already a mosaic society of immigrant groups, including many recent ones who are not always fluent in English yet. European countries have long lived with more or less monolithic linguistic and cultural reference frames. Most popular French and German films, Italian and Spanish ones, therefore, do not cross cultural borders very well.

Hollywood learned from the start to make movies that crossed lines between communities relatively easily by playing on very primary reactions to impressive "production values": elaborate sets and props, grandiose spectacle and special effects—always employing the latest in technology, however expensive—a cast of recognizable stars, and an attendant star system, with festivals and awards, paparazzi and gossip.

Among the almost four hundred blockbusters on the list, furthermore, there were at least forty different series of sequels of two or more films. Apparently, such recognizable formulas can be marketed globally with ease—

across the Atlantic and Pacific Oceans—supported by fast food chains and soft drink companies with considerable clout. They also tie in with games and television series, toys and figurines, posters and clothing, books and comics—alliances making each separate release a multi-billion enterprise. The numbers also seem to be suggesting an accelerating trend on this score.

One key question remains as to what extent this American and G7 predominance affects non-Western audiences. Who can have his or her voice heard on the world stage, and who remains largely silent? The nature of the problem may be illustrated by a crude comparison. The makers of most blockbusters form a kind of pyramid or prism. They are mostly white males with English as their mother tongue, multi-millionaires or aspiring to become one as soon as possible. They look at the rest of the world from the perspective of the major Western urban centers—although most do apparently see themselves as cosmopolitan and liberal.

On a more fundamental level, however, they have usually internalized a mid-Atlantic view of global history and geography, its central myths and legends. Even if they feel they have just freely "thought up creative fantasies," they often unwittingly reproduce clichés from a pre-existing body of folklore and popular culture (pulp novels, comic strips)—often harking back to colonial and segregationist days. So many blockbusters remain ethnocentric, even today: they tend to make non-Westerners look at the world through Western eyes.

But their effect is not always simple, as there is always a "negotiation of meaning" throughout the entire process—from production to reception. The latter has been well demonstrated by early studies on the differing interpretation of central themes in the supposedly "Texan" blockbuster television series *Dallas* by American, Dutch, Israeli, and immigrant viewers there, and ultimately also Japanese (Ang, 1985; Liebes & Katz, 1990).

"Cultural Encounter" Genres and Stereotypes

One of the central notions in film studies is that of "genre," which is derived from a French term for kind or category. The notion was long taken for granted, although a closer look reveals that there are many different, often overlapping and contradictory, ways to distinguish genres. The dominant theme may play a role, or the way in which it is treated, for instance. Genres often bring their own idiom or grammar. Newer films often refer back to famous scenes and characters in earlier "classical" films in the same category, either explicitly or implicitly. Part of the joy of looking at such films is being able to recognize and decode such "inter-textual" references to predecessors (Altman, 1999; Neale, 2002).

Within the aforementioned list of almost four hundred bestselling blockbusters of all time, "intercultural encounters" often play a major role. One may select some 80 movies or 20 percent in which this is clearly the case, and group them into a dozen categories for closer inspection. Within these categories, one may try to identify "meta-narratives" and "sub-texts" through discourse analysis and similar approaches, and illustrate these with case studies of some prominent and overly familiar examples. But other observations may deal with recurring choices in casting and props, images and sounds. Various academic disciplines, sub- and inter-disciplines, have wrestled with the question of the possible influence of such tropes and clichés.

Like many social sciences, international/intercultural/interethnic communication and media studies are primarily an Anglo-American affair today. Yet, dominant Anglo-American media images have always been critically dissected, often by scholars with some kind of privileged tie to other cultures. The mere reproduction of stereotypes by such media does of course not necessarily lead to their internalization, as the *Dallas* studies point out. Yet it may be illuminating to try and analyze their hidden logic. Popular culture and film studies have increasingly done so over the last generation. Some early examples were Nederveen Pieterse's study (1992) on "blackness," Dyer's study (1997) on "whiteness," Shohat and Stam's study (1994) on "Eurocentrism," and Bernstein and Studlar's study (1997) on "Orientalism" in film.

I myself long taught a video-illustrated course on dominant Western media images of other cultures for students coming from all continents. I developed two English books for it: an earlier one on *Understanding Global News* (1998), and a later one on *Screening Difference* (2007) in the movies. Whereas some of the aforementioned film studies also included rather technical analyses of unfamiliar art house movies, I chose to focus mostly on a discussion of commercial successes in plain, everyday language. The chapters were built around the detailed dissection of some ten different intercultural encounter genres, series, and prime examples—one at the time.

Animated cartoons made for children provided a good appetizer about a wide range of overly familiar stereotypes, for instance, the four major 1990s Disney productions on exotic boys from the Middle East and Africa, respectively (*Aladdin* and *Lion King*), and about exotic girls from the Americas and Asia (*Pocahontas* and *Mulan*). After that introduction, I switched to a largely chronological grid. In religious movies, Old Testament movies have a clear tendency to include anti-Arab elements (e.g., successive versions of *The Ten Commandments* as well as *The Prince of Egypt*); many pre-war New Testament movies had a tendency to include anti-Jewish elements (partly revived in *The Passion of the Christ*). Antiquity movies, in turn, treat Greece rather differently from Persia (e.g., *Troy, Alexander, 300*).

Of course the cinematic history of European overseas expansion is shot through with familiar tropes. Wilderness adventure has various sub-genres: monster movies (e.g., the successive versions of *King Kong*), jungle man movies (e.g., the successive versions of *Tarzan*), and castaway/survivor movies (e.g., the successive versions of *Robinson Crusoe* and its present-day "reality television" spin-offs). The clichés of the western genre are of course also overly familiar: even a worthwhile revisionist western like *Dances with Wolves* is unable to break clear of all of them. British colonial adventures in turn are of course U.K. centric: whether supposedly historical (*Lawrence of Arabia* or the successive versions of *Anna and the King*) or fictional (the successive versions of *Alan Quatermain*—the key model for the later *Indiana Jones*).

Several special themes stand out. Romantic and erotic encounters between white Western men and "colored" non-Western women show a particular hidden logic, for instance, whether situated in the Pacific (the successive versions of *The Mutiny on the Bounty* as well as almost all other South Seas movies) or in East Asia (the successive Geisha-type movies and movies about China). At the same time "Us" versus "them" is of course at the heart of all armed confrontation abroad: in the spy sub-genre (*James Bond*), the lone commando sub-genre (*Rambo*), and the limited military expedition overseas genre (*Black Hawk Down*). Science fiction further projects these intercultural themes into space and into an imaginary future (e.g., the *Star Trek* and *Star Wars* series).

All these genres and films turn out to be ethnocentric in a wide variety of ways: from supposed "research" to overt wish-fulfillment fantasies about characters and story lines. That's the case not only because they obviously prefer Western authors and Western accounts, often dating back to the days of colonialism and segregation, and still bearing many traces of them, or because they mostly consult Western experts or submit to Western pressure groups (e.g., for religious or patriotic movies). It's also because these ideological orientations do determine a wide range of cinematic details that we will usually tend to overlook.

Time and again, it can be demonstrated that even technical choices concerning light, color, and camera movements, for instance, are used in a highly ideological manner. The choice of (the ethnicity of) actors, their makeup, and their costumes is often ideological. The props, sets, and design are often oriented in similar ways, as are the sound and music, language and speech. In sum, they often reflect the legacy of a large variety of imperial adventure movies. Even where they ostensibly try to "revise" the original drift, they mostly remain mired in the same old idiom and grammar.

Of course similar things also hold for Chinese or Indian or other films aimed at a large home audience. On the one hand, they remain "open" texts that can be "read" in a variety of ways. On the other hand, they are often built around "saming" and "othering." They flatter their own people and denounce the enemy. But their influence abroad is very limited, in contrast to Hollywood blockbusters.

James Cameron and the *Avatar* Project

Soon after the publication of the *Screening Difference* book, the 3D super-mega-giga blockbuster *Avatar* was released. On the one hand, it seemed to be a unique and standalone project. On the other hand, it seemed to be an adept re-combination of all the aforementioned genres, a kind of *Emerald Forest* meets *Dances with Wolves*, or *Indiana Jones* meets *Star Wars*. To what extent was it able to break free of the accumulated body of clichés, or did it inevitably remain mired in it?

We should begin to emphasize that director James Cameron is an extremely versatile filmmaker. Born to a Canadian family that later moved to California, he had done the first treatment of *Spiderman* there, wrote the first version of *Rambo*, wrote and directed the successful science fiction movies *Terminator, Alien,* and the *Abyss,* and the romantic disaster movie *Titanic*—the highest grossing film up to that day (Robb, 2002). He always showed great affinity with natural science, advanced technology, and special effects, and was one of the first blockbuster directors to get involved in the development of a new generation of 3D systems after the turn of the millennium. He had also made underwater documentaries, as well as covered mythical and biblical themes (*Exodus Decoded, The Lost Tomb of Jesus*).

Cameron claimed the earliest inspiration for *Avatar* came from a dream his mother had reported when he was young. Just after the mid-seventies he said he had developed a first screenplay along those lines, and just before the mid-nineties a more elaborate script. But he had to wait ten more years for imaging technology to catch up. Filming started in April 2007, and the film was finally released in time for the Christmas season in late

2009. The term *avatar* originally referred to a Hindu god incarnating in a human body, but it had meanwhile become video game speak for a figure onscreen representing the player. In this case, the characters are supposedly deep asleep in the human world when they are wide awake in the alien world, and vice versa.

The story is set in 2154 on the moon Pandora of a planet in a distant galaxy. A terrestrial corporation has financed a huge space program to send a large-scale armed expedition there in order to mine the rare substance "unobtainium," which is worth "twenty million a kilogram." But the corporation runs into opposition from aboriginals, the Na'vi. A small group of explorers is trained to inhibit native bodies as "avatars," to win the locals over or infiltrate them, or do both. At the very last moment, one of those scientists dies and has to be replaced by his "genetically identical" twin brother. This Marine veteran, Jake, who is in a wheelchair, is the central protagonist of the movie.

The film paints an extremely enchanting fantasy world. It uses the very latest in "synthetic" imaging techniques, blending real actors with elaborate computer animation. It is the first major 3D blockbuster of a new generation, where special glasses suggest an in-depth view. The story and characters seem highly original at first. But upon closer inspection, they turn out to borrow heavily from the entire "intercultural encounter" film library I discussed in my book *Screening Difference*. We will see that it also harks back to specific scenes and story lines in a wide range of similar previous "imperial adventure" movies.

A key question is whether *Avatar* became the greatest blockbuster so far in spite of the fact that it recycled all clichés of the genre, or exactly because it did. Even at a running time of more than two-and-a-half hours, a fantasy movie can be much more efficient if it works with all the stereotypes already pre-installed in the audience's minds. In Hollywood movies, this is often called "research": making a prior inventory of all narratives and visuals on a particular topic, and taking it from there. For major Disney animation features, it is even standard procedure. So let us look at how five major themes of *Avatar* resonate with its forerunners.

1. The Theme of the Underpopulated "Virgin" Land

Films and sequences start with an "establishing shot" of a location that sets the scene and the tone for what follows. Good examples are the 1492 "discovery of America" sequences in archetypal Columbus movies (at least three of which were almost simultaneously released upon the 500th anniversary of the landing). They show an aerial shot of immaculate vegetation, suggesting uninhabited "virgin lands" belonging to nobody, and thus seemingly offering themselves up for exploration and exploitation. *Avatar* starts with very similar shots. Somewhat later, there often is an imperative counter-shot. In Columbus movies, we observe the encroachers from and through the foliage as an obviously native hand pushes the branches aside, alerting us to a possible impending confrontation.

Further to the interior of the discovered land, majestic waterfalls are often a key feature of the landscape. They may cover grotto entrances or passages to secret valleys behind them. They denote the deepest heart of the newly penetrated land, between upstream rivers and lakes. The first major Western explorers of Africa went looking for the origins of the Nile, found a lake and falls, which they then named after the British queen Victoria. It has become the arch template for such settings.[4]

The features of that precise landscape and Mount Kilimanjaro also played a key role in the visuals of Disney's African *Lion King*, for example (largely plagiarized from the preceding Japanese *Kimba*, by the way). The first major Western explorers of present-day Zaire explored the higher reaches of the Congo River. Think of Joseph Conrad's terrifying *Heart of Darkness*—also a major source of inspiration for Francis Ford Coppola's Vietnam War movie, *Apocalypse Now*.[5]

The "heart of darkness" itself is located in a forest, of course: not just any forest, but a dense rain forest. The largest remaining one still stretches all the way from the Amazon Basin to the Orinoco River in the north. Near the mouth of the latter river lies a small island that had become a key motif in imperial adventure fantasies, the imaginary location of the aforementioned *Robinson Crusoe* by Daniel Defoe (recycled in present-day popular "reality television" formats).

Such natural settings are of course inhabited by wild and exotic animals, which are used to scare readers and viewers alike in imperial adventure narratives. *Indiana Jones*, *The Mummy*, and their like also capitalize on such animals in a desert environment. Disney's *Tarzan* and *Lion King* even reduce Africa to a tourist safari park and entirely blot out the natives, as a potential source of embarrassment. *Avatar* in turn scares its audiences with sci-fi versions of the same familiar tropical zoo, ranging from "scorpions, lizards and bats" to "hyenas, panthers and rhinos" (according to explanations in the script).

The superlatives of scary animals in such movies are prehistoric monsters, surviving in those very same deep unexplored interiors, derived from the dinosaurs in *The Lost World* by Conan Doyle, spilling over into the original *King Kong* story co-authored by Edgar Wallace, and also revived in *Godzilla* and *Jurassic Park*. In *Avatar*, they find their parallel in the appearance of smaller and larger dragon-like animals, which are then domesticated.[6]

Matinee audiences for intercultural encounter and imperial adventure movies are also habitually scared with masses of creepy smaller animals (bats, rats, spiders, and so forth) as well as with repulsive animal food. Think of the recurring fried beetles, baby snakes, sheep eyeballs, live monkey brain dishes, etcetera, that are standard fare in the *Indiana Jones* series. In *Avatar*, the natives eat beetle larvae as a delicacy, and live worms as a sacred medicine. They send shivers through the theater—exactly as intended—and further help to "otherize" the aliens.

2. The Theme of the Primitive Native Tribe

We have seen that the imperial adventure story primarily feeds on two major predecessors: the American "cowboys and Indians" story (with "cowboys" including early settlers and later cavalry) and the European "colonial adventure" story (with the travails of British, French, and other pioneers in Africa, Asia, and elsewhere).[7]

In the original versions, ethnic difference between the explorers and the natives is highlighted in a wide range of different ways. In traditional Western thinking, "skin color" was the prime signifier of "race," as can be seen in all popular visual arts. First, the explorers are and remain lily white, to such an extent that they often hardly show a suntan—even after decades in the tropics (as in the case of *Tarzan*). Many often have exaggerated light blond hair and exaggerated light blue eyes (as in the case of *Lawrence of Arabia*).

The natives, with skins ranging from beige to brown, are seen and emphatically depicted as "colored" by contrast, with East Asians as "yellow," Native Americans as "red," and Africans as "black" (in comic strip versions by Disney and others, they are often literally given such primary colors). In *Avatar*, the natives are assigned the primary color cyan blue, in order to stay away from this real-life race heritage, but still remain within the same repertoire.[8] Most also have the long black hair of Native Americans, but some also show the fashionable braids of African Americans.

Second, the whites in imperial adventure movies are implicitly seen and depicted as of "normal" height—even though the male heroes themselves may sometimes be slightly above average. Asians are mostly seen and depicted as slightly smaller on average, and therefore sneaky. Africans are often seen and depicted as slightly larger on average and therefore implicitly threatening. They are also larger in a sexual sense, in the "rape and lynching" lore of the segregationist southern United States.

In *Avatar*, the natives are made considerably larger than the explorers. Their ethnicity is a mix of Native American and African. They are also somewhat "animalized" and explicitly ascribed "feline" characteristics. Jake's love interest, Neytiri, hisses like a cat whenever threatened, for instance. The Na'vi natives move rapidly through the trees, swinging on lianas—as in *Tarzan*. The colonel therefore derogatively calls them "blue monkeys." But the clan leader retorts that the colonel "smells" in turn (another key signifier of racial difference).

The other senses are also enlisted. In *Avatar* and many such movies, views of the jungle are overlaid with the sound of an isolated pan flute to denote quiet nature, contrasted with massive drums (and sometimes collective chants), denoting the disquieting presence of a threatening tribe nearby—for instance, in *King Kong*. A warrior also shouts "an ululating warning"—familiar from North African Arabs and North American natives. Cameron even took great care to have ethno-linguists develop a local language—as Gene Roddenberry had already done with great success for the original *Star Trek* TV series, which he created and produced.[9]

3. The Theme of the Indigenous Natural Worldview

Avatar illustrates that the "creative avant-garde" in the Western metropolitan centers that holds itself to be "most advanced" is trying to rehabilitate the seemingly most backward natural religions of indigenous peoples and rain forest tribes—by slightly adapting them to their own tastes as they are purged of their multitude of personal gods and turned into a new kind of abstract pantheism.[10]

That is the idea that the entire universe and planet Earth, as well as its plants and animals, form a godlike perfect whole—the equilibrium of which should be respected rather than disturbed. Such Greenpeace ethics emerged in a range of previous blockbusters, particularly "revisionist" depictions of "Indians" with a superior morality—as in the aforementioned *Emerald Forest* and *Dances with Wolves*. They embody the "noble savages" of the Enlightenment philosophers. At one point, the hero of *Avatar* notes (Cameron, 2007, p. 84 in the script): "They don't even have a word for 'lie'—they had to learn it from us."

The privileged way to experience this connectedness is through Zen-like meditation, *Avatar*'s heroine suggests (p. 64): "When you hear nothing, you will Hear everything. When you see nothing, you will See everything." Within the media, chroniclers of religion were first and foremost to point to this noteworthy aspect of the New Age fairy tale. A commentator in the *New York Times* noted "Cameron's long apologia for pantheism . . . Hollywood's religion of choice for a generation now." A reviewer for a major Christian film website added that the film was "a virtual apotheosis of Hollywood mythopoeia," as it "is not so much something that has never been done as something that everything else has been trying to be or preparing for," citing among other things "hippie politics" with "eco-spiritual and pacifist themes" (Greydanus, 2009).

This environmental consciousness seems to have taken hold at "five minutes to midnight," when the world's climate is already changing, raw materials seem to be running out, the rain forests are dwindling, and biodiversity is shrinking at an alarming rate, with unique plant and animal species dying out every single day. It is a secular religion worshipping Mother Nature and Mother Earth.

The earth goddess Gaia has maintained subtle balances so far—just like Pandora's equivalent goddess Eywa. This theme is underlined by the exalted design and visuals of *Avatar*, some of them harking back to the first lyrical documentaries about the strange alternative underwater universe by the famous French diver Jacques Cousteau and to the idyllic photo and film reports commissioned by the American National Geographic Society, its magazine and television arms.

The living totem of the tribe is an ancient sacred willow tree, the "well of souls" that helps the natives connect to their forefathers. "Signal transduction" connects all living organisms to an "electrochemical network" of energy, a force field that exists between plant tendrils, animal antennae, and human neurons. Each of the billions of trees has ten thousand connections to other trees—"more than a human brain."

The Na'vi are also capable of thought transmission. "It's a global network" with "uploading and downloading," the movie explains, in an obvious reference to the global Internet. The aggressive invaders threaten to cut such vital connections, sometimes literally. But near-dead people can be revitalized by restoring "the bond." The network is symbolized by a kind of blue-green spiritual luminescence reminiscent of ghost movies.

In *Avatar*, the key figures of this religion are the clan leader and his wife, the high priestess. They are also the parents of the local heroine, and the future in-laws of the hero from Earth: Jake. In the course of the film he turns into the archetypical prophet/liberator hero overly familiar from western and colonial folklore. He is a kind of Moses from Exodus in the Old Testament, or Jesus from the Gospels in the New Testament, But also *Lawrence of Arabia, Indiana Jones,* and many others, whose inborn superiority and charisma as "natural leaders" is demonstrated in their interaction with local crowds.

They are the eternal non-natives who soon turn into better natives than the natives themselves—who feel forced to show their deference and respect. In *Avatar,* Jake becomes the military leader of the uprising, gets to marry "the princess" as his prize, and impregnate her. He will thus become "the new king" or at least the father of the new king, a colonial era fantasy par excellence (already in the twisted popcult version of *Pocahontas, Alan Quatermain,* and other films).

Tribal life is also signified by the usual props in *Avatar:* the teeth of wild animals as a warrior necklace, rings lengthening the neck, feathers as headgear, like typical "Indians," the skulls of wild animals on gates and totems. The tribe gathers and chants around a bonfire, as in the famous Bali monkey dance paraphrased in an early version of *King Kong.* They use an intoxicating drink and fragrant herbs for purification and initiation rituals.

When assembling, the tribe even looks like a hippie "Woodstock in the jungle"—so says the script. When praying, they do so "in concentric rings of people, all plugged-in and softly chanting." When mobilizing, they radiate "a dark primeval energy." We are not far from the stirring human sacrifice and cannibal scenes in *Alan Quatermain,* and similar ones in the *Indiana Jones series* (e.g., *The Temple of Doom*).

4. The Theme of Imperial Armed Intervention

The basic premise of *Avatar* is simple. It is basically "cowboys and Indians" catapulted into distant space and into the far future, as in *Star Trek* and *Star Wars*—and by extension, colonialism and neocolonialism catapulted into future space. The home country/planet of the invaders is running out of the necessary resources; they intervene militarily elsewhere to obtain them.

The mineral "unobtainium" on Pandora is like the gold mines in Africa for the British imperial hero Alan Quatermain, or like the references to Middle East oil wells that Disney inserted throughout the *Aladdin* movie. The *Avatar* script contains explicit references to meddling in oil-rich countries like Nigeria and Venezuela, and implicit ones to the confrontations around Iran and Iraq. The script also contains references to "development aid" as a lubricant for unequal exchange. The carrots supplementing the stick: roads, clinics, schools, and the inevitable learning of . . . English.

Such action and war movies have traditionally been primarily aimed at adolescent boys at home, as "armchair conquistadores." They seem to promote their enlistment for military service overseas only a few years later—as a more virile adventure.[11] They tend to glamorize Western technological superiority, from the eternal gadgets of the British spy James Bond to the electronic savvy and overwhelming firepower demonstrated in most American war movies—an implicit warning to overseas audiences. The relation of *Avatar* to such displays is ambivalent. On the one hand, it impresses us with its oversized weapons; on the other hand, it seems to frown upon their actual use—as natives denigrate the invading soldiers as cowardly, "hiding inside machines."

The movie "shocks and awes" us with these huge contraptions, but we can "read" these scenes as industry promotion, pacifist propaganda, both or neither. It begins with "Mitsubishi MK-6 ampsuits—human-operated walking machines 4 meters tall." They resonate with the giants in ancient folklore and the Golem, with harnessed knights on horses in the medieval armory, but also with Hollywood inventions such as *The Hulk* and *Robocop*. Then there are "Samson tilt rotors: big as a Blackhawk"—familiar from the movie with the same name about a failed military expedition in Somalia.[12]

To confront this "overwhelming force," the native tribes use only some of their traditional means. They put on war paint and utter war cries to try and scare their adversaries away. They use martial arts techniques familiar from man-to-man combat in Asian movies; they are also "Zen" in their concentration and focus. They use the bows and poison-tipped arrows of native peoples everywhere, as well as their white imitators such as *Tarzan* and *Rambo*. Yet when they try to scale the fence around the invaders' compound, they are easily mowed down by gunfire. They are still like the Indians trying to scale the palisades around the cavalry fort.

Toward the end of the film, this confrontation is gradually drawn into the usual orgy of stylized violence, as an air fleet of invading troopships and gunships squares off against a swarm of dragons—some jockeyed by the natives, and the mythical largest one by the new non-native leader Jake. It is esthetically choreographed: with many victims, but little of their suffering in sight. This is also a catharsis—as the good guys win, of course. The final battle takes fifty pages, half as much as the rest of the script taken together. It is made elegant, but also comic book cartoonesque ("Kapow, Kaboom").

Most interesting of all are the two liminal characters ultimately leading these opposing forces. On the one hand, there is the unsympathetic gung-ho colonel of the mining company's security detail, with a crew cut and multiple scars to denote him as an experienced veteran fighter. And on the other hand is the sympathetic paraplegic reincarnated in his local avatar who comes to the defense of a seemingly desperate cause. As an avatar, he is also a kind of mulatto—and a turncoat who becomes a hero. Not Navy but Na'vi. The colonel to Jake: "How does it feel to betray your own race?"

This is indeed a surprising twist for an American action movie. But maybe even more surprising is that it leaves the further structure of the archetypical imperial adventure story largely untouched. This is also illustrated by a final theme.

5. The Theme of the Beautiful Native Girl

Dating within one's own group has always and everywhere been considered normal; crossing group boundaries is "not done" but sometimes strangely attractive, from the classic *Romeo and Juliet* play to the modern *West Side Story* musical.

In the original imperial adventure genre, and according to the early Hollywood production codes, interracial romance and miscegenation were completely out of the question. In later novels and movies, the taboo was slowly circumvented—as it was in real life, timidly at first, and under various clandestine pretexts. White men abroad often felt drawn to exotic girls (*Suzie Wong*); white women being attracted to exotic men abroad was even more problematic (*The Sheik*). It was the sinful lure of transgressing cultural taboos, of tasting the "forbidden fruit." But after a passionate fling, the native partner was often made to die in such scripts, so that the white hero (or heroine) could return to a regular life and marriage at home.

Of course the semi-nudity and suggestive dancing by the locals had often added to their immediate sexual appeal—for instance, in cinematic Polynesia. In *Avatar*, according to one review, "the girls are sexy enough to be easy on the eyes, but not too sexy for the comfort level of typical parents." The first review in the *New York Times* added that "the humanoid Na'vi come with supermodel dimensions (slender hips, a miniature-apple rear, long articulated digits" and "slanted eyes") (Dargis, 2009).[13]

Neytiri's attire is a difficult Hollywood compromise between prudish covering and provocative uncovering of shoulders or legs (compare *Pocahontas*). The script itself describes the love interest of the hero in *Avatar*: "lithe as a cat, with . . . nubile breasts . . . devastatingly beautiful." Fortunately, at age 18 she has just ceased to be under age. Jake's white superior reproaches him: "You got a little local pussy." After he has made love to Neytiri, his native rival erupts: "You mated with this woman?" On the last page of the script, we learn that she is "obviously pregnant" (Cameron, 2007, pp. 90–105). The girl is played by Zoe Saldana, who also played the "ethnic other" of Uhura in *Star Trek*.[14]

Interestingly enough, "surplus libido" was often ascribed to such cultural others of the opposite sex. They were supposed to be more animalistic, primitive, childish, or at least very much lower class. Lower on the ladder of civilization, therefore more uninhibited, authentic, and attractive. This theme also derived from illicit relations between male masters and female slaves in the U.S. South, between settlers and servants in the European colonies, later between millions of military men and prostitutes in South, Southeast, and East Asia. The theme also runs from the successful classical opera *Madama Butterfly* to its present-day knockoff musical *Miss Saigon*.

Of course most multiracial societies were characterized by grave inequalities. For a "colored" girl to become the potential fiancée or even a marriage prospect for an ordinary white man, she had often to be elevated to the status of a local "princess" in a story—thus almost equaling him in status—to the extent that even a mere chieftain's daughter was depicted as royalty (*Pocahontas*). This is also a theme in one of the original fictional stories about the colonial hero Alan Quatermain—the Indiana Jones of his day. It is the central theme of the romance in *Avatar* as well.

In *Pocahontas* and *Avatar*, there is a further twist. The superior attractiveness of white men in general is further underlined by the fact that the local princess had already been promised to a local partner/fiancé, but she immediately drops him after receiving "a sign" and upon first encountering " the real one." This is a theme in the mythical (but twisted) *Pocahontas* story: in the Disney version she literally falls for the very first young white man she sees setting foot on American soil—and begins kissing him within minutes . . . in the very same sequence. This theme is also maintained in *Avatar*, even though it takes them slightly longer. In the end the native rival cedes, and recognizes the white man's superiority (if not physically then at least characterwise).

This is related to another recurrent racist theme, which we have already pointed out. The white hero soon proves to be a better native than the natives themselves: in fighting and riding local animals, in using local weapons and strategies. This is the central theme of *Tarzan*, but also of all other imperial heroes such as *Alan Quatermain, Lawrence of Arabia, Tintin, Indiana Jones, Rambo*—and Jake in *Avatar.* The interesting thing is that a movie like *Avatar* may be explicitly anti-imperial, but its narrative structure implicitly retains many pro-imperial traits that derive from the large body of predecessors by which it is inspired. The "free fantasy" of the writer and director feeds on pre-existing stereotypes in their heads, often without them being aware of it.

Avatar's Revival of Hollywood's Strength

The unprecedented success of *Avatar* came along at a crucial moment. Hollywood had seemed to be severely affected by the 2008 economic crisis, the decline of DVD sales, and the rise of illegal copying. Twelve hundred professionals participated in a three-day conference on the state of the industry in Los Angeles, convened by the Producers Guild of America. The *New York Times* reported that "the big studios are cutting back" on the number of productions, largely limiting themselves to "bloated sequels, bloated remakes," whereas "half of the independent distributors in the United States have folded over the past couple of years" (Barnes, 2010).

Whereas it is said that a cat has nine lives, Hollywood may turn out to have ten. Technological advances have always helped restore its preeminence, outdistancing both producers overseas and illegal copiers. In this case, there had already been some renewed experiments with 3D, even by Cameron himself. But *Avatar* became the first mega-blockbuster to demonstrate the attractiveness of this revolution. Movie theaters around the world were adapted in a hurry, and manufacturers of television screens also launched themselves into the breach—even contemplating new ways to get rid of the cumbersome stereoscopic glasses.

Nine and a half months after its release, on 1 October 2010, movie databases already listed *Avatar* as the highest grossing film ever, calling it a "must see" event. It was also a hit in emergent markets such as China, the natural beauty and cultural legacy of which had inspired some of its unique "floating mountains" scenery.[15] The outlay for *Avatar* had been estimated at an unprecedented $300 million for production, with $150 million more for marketing. But the worldwide theatrical box office receipts (ticket sales) were calculated to be $2.8 billion that far—not including video rentals, television rights, merchandizing, and other revenues of further multiple billions. That was already 50 percent more than the runner-up *Titanic*, also made by James Cameron, a dozen years earlier. The director quickly opened talks with Twentieth Century Fox over two possible sequels.

Other directors quickly followed suit. Steven Spielberg (of the *Indiana Jones* series and many others) was involved in developing an alternative 3D system for which one would no more need special glasses. George Lucas had already rushed into converting his half dozen *Star Wars* films into 3D. Disney was adapting the next installment of *Pirates of the Caribbean*. As a matter of fact, all major studios and blockbuster directors were in the process of hastily shifting major projects to 3D, including a wide array of remakes and sequels already in the pipeline. So *Avatar* proved not only "more of the same" but also the ultimate catalyst for another revolution in Hollywood.

Avatar's Cultural Reception

Meanwhile, *Avatar* had also been rather well received by reviewers. Websites Metacritics and Rotten Tomatoes each aggregated 35 early reviews into scores of 84 percent and 94 percent positive, although the film got "only" three Oscars (as opposed to six for *The Hurt Locker*). Spin-offs included books, music, videos (including a documentary on Cameron's entire life and work), action figures—and of course a first-person "shooter" video game available for all existing game machines, where the player has to choose sides between the invaders and the invaded. There is no Pandora/Na'vi theme park ride at this point, but it will no doubt come about.

But let us return to the question with which we began this essay. What did *Avatar* mean, or what was it made to mean, by viewers around the world belonging to various groups? Early television researchers had alerted us to the possibility of alternative "readings" by other cultures. We have seen that the blockbuster was shot through with contradictory messages, both subliminal and supraliminal. The *Chicago Tribune* even called it "the season's ideological Rorschach blot," after the ambiguous ink stain used to uncover unconscious feelings in psychotherapy.

It seemed apt that it was the first blockbuster movie for which one explicitly had to put on special glasses, in order just to be able to see it as intended. Some people deemed the movie nihilistic, others rather utopian. An article in the *New York Times* noted that over the very first month it had "found itself in the crosshairs of a growing number of interest groups, schools of thought and entire nations": feminists and anti-smoking activists, liberals and conservatives, the Kremlin and the Vatican and whatnot.[16]

Like most people of his social category, Cameron had always felt sympathy for environmentalism and indigenous people. But after *Avatar* he now felt obliged to take an even clearer stand, as Native American groups pressed him to take up the defense of the remaining "real Pandoras" in the world. For instance, in the Amazon Basin, where thirteen native tribes felt threatened by a dam project.[17] The Indians invited him to join a three-day protest. He flew in, put on war paint, and showed them his movie on DVD: for many, it was the first encounter with such modern technology. The meeting predictably became a media event, was filmed in high definition, and shown by television channels around the world (Itzkoff, 2010a).

But there seemed to be a paradox. The first review in the *New York Times* had noted that it was ironic that *Avatar* "feeds you an anti-corporate line in a corporately financed entertainment." It was distributed by Twentieth Century Fox, the Hollywood movie arm of the most global of all media empires—Rupert Murdoch's News Corp.[18] The blockbuster was also promoted worldwide by the usual broad alliance of powerful U.S. corporations. Coca Cola supported the worldwide marketing campaign with specially marked *Avatar* cans and bottles. McDonalds distributed toys of half a dozen major characters with its Happy Meals in half a dozen major countries. Mattel announced that it would produce a line of *Avatar* action figures.

Even more surprising: *Avatar* was embraced as a powerful symbol by people and groups fighting for freedom and resistance against foreign domination. Soon, news channels around the world showed Palestinian demonstrators against Israel, in Nablus on the West Bank, painted blue and dressed like Pandora's Na'vi.[19] Evo Morales, the first indigenous president of dirt-poor and landlocked Bolivia, praised *Avatar* for its "profound show of resistance to capitalism and the struggle for the defense of nature." He maintained tense relations with the United States, which was actively opposing a number of his social reforms. The aforementioned Christian film website had already noted about *Avatar:* "It's noble primitives and warmongering Westerners, imperialist and expansionist guilt and no blood for oil, Cortez and Custer and George W. Bush in one fell swoop." Another website called it "the essence of the white guilt fantasy, laid bare."

So even if such a movie may be chockfull of age-old "imperial adventure" themes, it may still be experienced as an anti-imperial statement overall. Such a complex product has multiple threads running through it that can be "read" in contradictory ways. Audiences "negotiate" its meaning to themselves and their situation. The message of movies does therefore always remain polysemic: audiences with different experiences in varying contexts can extract their own messages from them. That remains a central finding of international/intercultural/interethnic studies of communication and media.

REFERENCES

Note: More detailed references in Van Ginneken (2007). News items, basic reporting, and key reviews mostly came from the *International Herald Tribune*. The official script of Avatar was downloaded from http://www.foxscreenings.com. Page numbers refer to this document. The global blockbuster list and gross worldwide revenues refer to http://www.imdb.com, 2010. Many American reviews can be found on http://www.rottentomatoes.com. I have also consulted an early version of the elaborate Wikipedia entry on the movie for further leads.

Altman, R. (1999). *Film/genre*. London: British Film Institute.
Ang, I. (1985). Dallas—*Soap opera and the melodramatic imagination*. London: Methuen.
Barnes, B. (2010). Facing crisis: Hollywood producers turn skills to survival. *International Herald Tribune*, 25 May.
Bernstein, M., & Studlar, G., eds. (1997). *Visions of the East: Orientalism in film*. London: I. B. Tauris.
Cameron, J. (2007). *Avatar:* Official movie script. Hollywood: Twentieth Century Fox Film Corporation.
Dargis, M. (2009). "Avatar" triumphs as a high-tech Eden. *International Herald Tribune*, 19 December.
Dyer, R. (1997). *White*. London: Routledge.
Greydanus, S. (2009). *Avatar* (2009). *Decent Films Guide*, http://www.decentfilms.com/reviews/avatar/html.
Itzkoff, D. (2010a). Sci-fi epic becomes a culture-war battleground. *International Herald Tribune*, 20 January.
Itzkoff, D. (2010b). James Cameron on *Avatar, Titanic, Cleopatra*, and the future of 3D. *New York Times*, 19 October.
Liebes, T., & Katz, E. (1990). *The export of meaning—Cross-cultural readings of "Dallas."* Oxford: Oxford Univ. Press.
Neale, S., ed. (2002). *Genre and contemporary Hollywood*. London: British Film Institute.
Nederveen Pieterse, J. (1992). *White on black: Images of Africa and blacks in Western popular culture*. New Haven, CT: Yale University Press.
O'Barr, W. (1994). *Culture and the ad: Otherness in the world of advertising*. Boulder, CO: Westview.
Robb, J. (2002). *James Cameron*. Harpenden, UK: Pocket Essentials.
Said, E. W. (1978). *Orientalism: Western conceptions of the Orient*. London: Penguin.
Shohat, E., & Stam, R. (1994). *Unthinking Eurocentrism: Multiculturalism and the media*. London: Routledge.
Slotkin, R. (1998). *Gunfighter nation: The myth of the frontier in 20th century America*.

Norman: University of Oklahoma Press.

Stringer, J. (2003). *Movie blockbusters*. London: Routledge.

Van Ginneken, J. (1998). *Understanding global news: A critical introduction*. London: Sage.

Van Ginneken, J. (2007). *Screening difference: How Hollywood's blockbuster films imagine, race, ethnicity and culture*. Lanham, MD: Rowman & Littlefield.

NOTES

1. Analyzed in my 2010 Dutch book *Gek met geld—Over financiële psychologie* [Mad with money—About financial psychology].

2. 21 February 2010. Of course such a list has a tendency of overweighing the number of visitors in developed countries, as they pay higher ticket prices.

3. *Crouching Tiger* was the first "pan-Chinese" blockbuster, although it was said that the four main actors could hardly understand each other, as they spoke with entirely different accents: from Beijing and Canton, from Taiwan and Malaysia. (Columbia and Sony participated as well.) *Slumdog Millionaire* was officially an English film, although with an Indian co-producer and with a screenplay based on an Indian novel. Critics have claimed that Chinese and Indian movies can only become worldwide blockbusters if they somehow cater to Western tastes and stereotypes.

4. Think of Henry Morton Stanley's highly dramatized accounts of his travels in these regions looking for David Livingstone and beyond, which became the major source for the *Tarzan* novels by Burroughs. (Neither the movie productions nor the novelist ever set foot in the real Africa, though,)

5. Cameron's college years near Niagara Falls may have further resonated with such primeval features.

6. In recent years, this same theme had already been developed by several series of bestselling novels for both children and adults. Improvements in CGI animation techniques had already enabled their inclusion in blockbuster movies.

7. The Belgian comic strip *Tintin* (the film rights of which have been bought by Steven Spielberg) is a good example—which I have analyzed elsewhere in greater detail in the Dutch book *Striphelden op de divan* [Comic strip heroes on the couch, 2002].

8. Green may have been less of an option, as they would then blend too much into the background.

9. This Klingon became highly popular among "Trekkies" or fans of the series, and a popular "pseudo-foreign" minority language.

10. It is of course no coincidence that environmentalism arose whenever and wherever the natural environment had almost disappeared.

11. It is well documented that such movies have often been facilitated and subsidized by departments of defense, particularly in the United States.

12. The images of trigger-happy and gung-ho GIs with huge guns hanging out of the open doors of helicopter gunships, and scrutinizing the jungle underneath for anything that moves, comes straight out of older Vietnam footage, of course: both

newsreel and Hollywood fiction.

13. Steven D. Greydanus on the Christian website http://www.decentfilms.com. And Manohla Dargis in the *International Herald Tribune*, 19–20 December 2009.

14. There is a whole category of stars in Hollywood devoted entirely to playing certain ethnic roles. People such as Anthony Quinn or Raquel Welch easily switched from Latino to Indian to everything in between. Also think of Yul Brunner who built an entire career on "ancient and exotic tyrant" roles.

15. Within a month, *Avatar* reportedly broke all previous box office records in China, for instance, with receipts exceeding 100 million dollars. Like elsewhere, moviegoers proved to prefer the more expensive 3D theaters over the less expensive 2D ones. According to discussions on some Chinese websites, evictions and similar themes from the film resonated with current domestic controversies. Avatar "beat" the newly released major local movie *Confucius*, favored by the authorities, according to Simon Elegant, in "Letter from China/A little bit of flexibility," *International Herald Tribune*, 5 February 2010.

16. Dave Itzkoff, "Sci-fi epic becomes a culture-war battleground," *International Herald Tribune*, 20 January 2010.

17. They were to be displaced by the $11 billion Belo Monte dam project, creating a 500 square kilometer lake in the basin of the Xingu River (a tributary to the Amazon). It was to provide electricity to São Paulo, Brazil's bustling industrial metropolis.

18. *International Herald Tribune*, 19–20 December 2009.

19. Euronews channel, 12 February 2010.

CHAPTER EIGHT

Resurrecting the Imperial Dimension in International Communication

Colin Sparks

The concept of cultural imperialism dominated thinking about international communication in the 1970s and early 1980s. Subsequently, it has been thoroughly discredited and more or less fallen out of mainstream usage. Today, relatively few writers are ready to engage with theoretical issues involved in the concept of imperialism (Louw, 2011). While there are some more or less casual uses of the concept in studies of the media, and it retains a surprisingly vigorous life in other fields, such as linguistics, in most specialist studies it is firmly relegated to a discussion of the history of media and communication theories (Ndlela, 2009). When imperialism is mentioned in discussions of contemporary realities, it is usually in the context of a discussion of its limitations. Kraidy, for example, set his task as "dissecting the deficiencies of the cultural imperialism thesis" (Kraidy, 2005, p. vi). Even those writers who credit it with some lingering importance in that it did identify real disparities in the provision of cultural resources internationally spend much of their time discussing its shortcomings (Morley, 2006).

In part perhaps this is the consequence of more general intellectual and political shifts during the period, but it also reflects a theoretical realignment of the field. Much of the work on international communication in the last two decades has been dominated by theories that stress regional markets, complex flows, and the relative unimportance of the state in international communication. The dominant current of thinking, globalization, has tended to discount the role of the state in favor of the relations between the global and the local. To the extent that the state has been recognized as a significant factor in cultural exchanges, it is through the lens of "soft power" rather than "imperialism."

This chapter questions whether it is possible to recover anything valuable from the ruins of the cultural imperialism edifice. In order to do that, it first revisits the classical formulations of the theory and considers some aspects of its defining characteristics. It then reviews some of the main criticisms that were leveled against the theory and which were responsible for its loss of influence. In order to re-establish a workable theory, the underlying concept of imperialism is reconsidered and an alternative account to that prominent during the 1970s and 1980s is offered. Building on this, the scope of a redefined theory is advanced. Finally, reasons are given as to why current international developments mean that the concept is likely to become more pertinent in the coming years.

Cultural Imperialism

Cultural imperialism, as has often been pointed out, is an imprecise category: one of its most severe critics argued that rather than see it as a coherent body of thought, "a better way of thinking about cultural imperialism is to think of it as a variety of different articulations which may have certain features in common, but while may also be in tension with each other, or even mutually contradictory" (Tomlinson, 1991, p. 9). This judgment is certainly correct: many writers with quite different intellectual positions employed the term to a variety of ends. There were, however, "features in common" uniting writers with approaches as diverse as Tunstall, Mattelart, and Smith, notably in their stress upon the importance of the United States of America in world media markets (Mattelart, 1979; Smith, 1980; Tunstall, 1977). Despite this methodological, and indeed political, variety, however, from a theoretical point of view there can be little doubt that the main current was of Marxist inspiration and that it was the work of Herbert Schiller that formed the central reference point for the development and diffusion of the concept (Maxwell, 2003, pp. 38–41). He developed the concept most famously in his *Communication and Cultural Domination* and it is worthwhile repeating the definition of cultural imperialism he gives there:[1]

> [T]he concept of cultural imperialism today best describes the sum of the processes by which a society is brought into the modern

world system and how its dominating stratum is attracted, pressured, forced and sometimes bribed into shaping social institutions to correspond to, or even promote, the values and structures of the dominating center of the system. (Schiller, 1976, p. 9)

This brief statement contains both the core of the concept and the key to some of its weaknesses. We can identify four distinct elements that have been central to discussions of cultural imperialism:

1. This is a very broad conception of the issues at stake (Lee, 1980, pp. 41–42). Taken literally, it would include all sorts of pressures, for example structural adjustment programs developed by the IMF, which do not naturally fall within the ambit of culture but which certainly involve pressure to shape social institutions to fit the dominating center of the system. This broad concept of cultural imperialism is sometimes contrasted with the much narrower claim of media imperialism, which Oliver Boyd-Barrett defined as "the process whereby the ownership, structure, distribution or content of the media in any one country are singly or together are subject to substantial external pressures from the media interests of any other country or countries without proportionate reciprocation of influence by the country so affected" (Boyd-Barrett, 1977, p. 117). In practice, this distinction has proved hard to sustain. Boyd-Barrett included both of the Schiller texts cited here in his catalogue of scholars working within the scope of media imperialism and Schiller's own work tended to be highly focused on the international trade in information products, notably television programs (Schiller, 1970).

2. Schiller operates with a core-periphery model of imperialism (Schiller, 1976, p. 14). The system has a center, and it is clear both from the remainder of this text and from Schiller's other work that this center is the United States. He recognizes that in the past the United States was obliged to struggle with and defeat the earlier imperialist centers of Britain and France, notably in the field of international news but also more generally: "Under the banner of the "Free Flow of Information" U.S. media products came to dominate the world" (Schiller 1976, pp. 24–38). Similarly, Schiller is clearly speaking of a "peripheral" country when he discusses the ways in which a society is "brought into the modern world system." This conception of imperialism as fundamentally a relationship between the rich, developed world and the poorer, underdeveloped, world was, and is, one of the theoretical and practical foundations of most, if not all, existing theories of cultural imperialism.[2]

3. Schiller's account makes two distinct claims: first, the media and cul-

tural apparatuses of the United States, aided by the government, dominate the international trade in media, notably in television programming, which newly established broadcasters in developing countries need in order to fill their schedules while remaining within their budgets; second, that the result of the continual consumption of this U.S.-made material is effective propaganda for the ideas and values of the United States, turning the local elite away from the needs of their own populations and facilitating absorption, or at least collaboration, with U.S. enterprises. These two propositions relate to two different inquiries. The first is concerned with the political economy of the international trade in television programs and the ways in which that dovetailed with the policies of the U.S. state. The second makes a claim about the effect of the consumption of this programming upon its audience in a peripheral country, which can only be answered by an investigation into the realities of watching such material.[3]

4. A fourth point, not present in the text quoted above but elaborated later in the same book, was the argument for the development of national communication policies. While he operated with a more complex notion of the problems of cultural domination, recognizing that these existed within countries as well as between them, Schiller's stress on national communication policies in practice came to mean the efforts of elites in the developing world to re-negotiate their relationship with the developed world.[4] If the current arrangements, centered on the free flow of information around the world, were leading to the worldwide domination of U.S. culture at the expense of the national cultures of developing nations, then one way to counter this was to develop national communication policies designed to limit the inflow of alien messages with their damaging effects on the "cultural integrity of weak societies" (Schiller, 1970, p. 109). Just as it was a central part of the industrialization process of countries like the United States to protect infant manufacturing industries until such time as they were sufficiently developed to be internationally competitive, it was necessary to find ways to protect the cultural life of developing nations. This, Schiller thought, could best be achieved through "responsible international regulation of television programming," most likely through policy changes in UNESCO (Schiller, 1970, p. 125).

This overall position inspired an avalanche of books, articles, and reports, both general and scholarly. In addition, it provided a theoretical basis for a protracted campaign, focused on UNESCO, that purported to change the balance of world communication and to foster national communication policies.

Criticisms and Alternatives

The various critiques of cultural imperialism are extremely well known, and there is little need to recount them exhaustively here. It is, nevertheless, worth sketching four of the more important objections since they provide an insight into the some of the issues that any new theory will have to account for:

1. The tendencies toward regional production noted by Boyd-Barrett and Tunstall were identified as important growth points in the world market for media artifacts. In particular, the developing national television industries of Brazil and Mexico, and later of Japan and Korea, were seen as drivers of regional markets based upon cultural proximity (Sinclair, 1999; Straubhaar, 2007). While the world market for some media artifacts—high-budget films, for example—remains dominated by U.S. products, there are many other areas of cultural exchange that have a much more complex structure.

2. The assumption that there was, or could be, a single national culture that could be defended against U.S. values proved untenable. Every existing society, even in the most successful and developed modern states, exhibits a plurality of cultures, very often themselves a combination of earlier influences from "outside." The "national culture" of every society is the culture of the dominant group and it is one of the mechanisms by which their hegemonic role is consolidated. The United Kingdom provides an obvious example of these tendencies: the national language itself is an accretion of different influences; the diverse population enjoys a variety of different cultures; the norms of "national" culture are unquestionably the norms of the dominant, white, male, metropolitan middle classes. To defend a "national culture" is to defend the position of an elite group, not of a whole people. In some cases, it may be that imported texts articulate suppressed elements of a national culture and allow audiences to celebrate an aspect of their own cultural experience that the broadcasters dominated by the official culture are unable to address (Miller, 1995).

3. The turn toward a conception of the active audience, most markedly in the traditions of cultural studies but also in more empirically oriented research, demonstrated that texts do not have one single reading that will be absorbed by an entire audience either within or across national boundaries (Ang, 1995; Liebes & Katz, 1990). Readings of texts are variable depending upon the cultural resources of their consumers: people watching a U.S. series may absorb U.S. values or they may interpret the same text

in a radically different way. The conditions for the success of an imported program or series depends in part a least on domestic factors, ranging from the established local conventions of broadcasting to scheduling decisions that influence the size of the available audience.

4. The attempt to organize a political struggle around opposition to cultural imperialism took the concrete form of a struggle for a New World Information and Communication Order (NWICO). A great deal of effort went into attempting to influence UNESCO, and into building alliances with the representatives of many unsavory despots who were only too happy to curb the media and impose cultural uniformity on their unfortunate subjects. NWICO became embroiled in the Cold War and it went down to defeat along with the Stalinist allies it had accumulated in its attempt to win acceptance (Hamelink, 1997).

One could both amplify and expand this list of objections: taken together, the evidence against the concept of cultural imperialism advanced by Schiller is simply overwhelming. The new orthodoxy in the study of international communication began from the complexity both of media production and of audience behavior. There are many studies documenting the production and circulation of television programs, cinema films, and other artifacts originating far outside the range of Hollywood. Similarly, there are detailed studies of the ways in which audiences, or at least sections of audiences, within the developed world utilize these non-U.S. media artifacts to construct their own cultural frameworks and identities. Underlying this plethora of studies has been one or other variant of theories of globalization, which replace the concept of imperialism as the organizing element in this framework of thought. This is a notoriously protean group of concepts but we can note one central element which is common to many of the variants: it systematically marginalizes the role of the state.

This marginalization is clearly present in the pervasive slogans of "the global and the local," "glocalization," "think global, act local," and so on. The missing term in all of these formulations is precisely the state. Unless the term "local" really means "national," as indeed it does when one interrogates many of these celebrations of the "local," then the claim is that the poles of contemporary cultural (or indeed almost any other) life are to be located regionally, and thus "below" the level of the state, and globally "above" the level of the state. Unlike the national, neither the local nor the global are equipped with the full apparatus of state power that coerces and regulates social life, culturally and economically. On the contrary, they are much more the field of the free play of economic competition.

Complexity and freedom become the central organizing categories of studies of international communication. There is no doubt that the work that has taken this as its starting point has illuminated some important dimensions of contemporary media and cultural experience. There clearly are many other centers of production of cultural artifacts than simply the United States, and the international trade in these commodities is undoubtedly much more complex than was previously supposed: both Bollywood (India) and Nollywood (Nigeria) produce more movies each year than does Hollywood, and TV Globo (Brazil) is a major source of television fiction. There clearly are sub-national cultures and media organizations, such as Basque and Catalan broadcasting in the Spanish State and Cantonese-language broadcasting in southern China. It is clearly also the case that different social groups, indeed different individuals, increasingly use the resources of new media to construct diets of media consumption that are independent of the programming policies of any broadcaster—local, national, or global. All of these are good reasons for correcting the emphasis on the role of the state.

Although it is important to correct the overemphasis on the state that marked the concept of cultural imperialism, it does not follow that the state is no longer a significant actor, a position exemplified by Bauman's claim that in the epoch of globalization "the military, economic and cultural self-sufficiency, indeed self-sustainability, of the state—any state—ceases to be a viable prospect" (Bauman, 1998, p. 64). This view may have exerted a superficial attraction in the period after the fall of communism, when rivalry between states seemed no longer to be a serious prospect in the age of Pax Americana, although even then the claim that the conclusion applies to "any state" seems much too strong. The fragments of the former Yugoslavia, Rwanda, Somalia, later Afghanistan and a dozen other "failed states" might have been incapable of "self-sustainability," but surely that term could never have been be applied to the United States, or China and India for that matter? Today, should anyone make such a claim it would be immediately rejected as quite incredible.

It is more convincing to argue that there is amongst states what we may call a hierarchy of competences. Some states, pre-eminently the United States, are indeed capable of sustaining themselves in all three of the domains identified by Bauman. Some states, for example the failed states, are clearly not capable of the same sort of self-determination. Others fall between these two poles. Japan, for instance, is economically very powerful and culturally increasingly influential, but politically much weaker. We do not yet live in a post-Westphalian age, and all but the failed states have, to varying degrees, unique characteristics that mark them off from both the local and the global. Specifically, they have the power to coerce (what Max Weber classically described as a monopoly of the legitimate use of violence), which they can employ both to control their own population and to settle conflicts with other states.

If the critique of the classical formulation of cultural imperialism must lead one to reject it, attempts to construct alternatives that do not begin from the centrality of the state system to an understanding of the contemporary world, and see available resources—economic, political, and cultural—as distributed in a fundamentally and systematically unequal way between these states, have proven equally unsatisfactory.

Imperialism Reconsidered

Settling conflicts with other states has, of course, been one of the main geopolitical features of the last twenty years or so. Under a variety of guises, large, powerful states have used their power, political, economic, and military, to coerce other, weaker, states: Serbia, Afghanistan, Iraq, Georgia, and others have all experienced direct military interventions. These uses of the armed might of the state to achieve its ends has given rise to the vigorous contemporary debates about imperialism, and any attempt to reconsider global patterns of cultural life must begin from a reconsideration of what is meant by imperialism in the present period.

Discussions of imperialism have never been exclusively Marxist in inspiration: writers like John Hobson and Joseph Schumpeter historically, and in the present period Niall Ferguson and Michael Mann, have addressed the issues involved from a variety of intellectual standpoints and political positions (Ferguson, 2003, 2004; Hobson, 1902; Mann, 2003; Schumpeter, 1951). Schiller, and others who developed the concept of cultural imperialism, did however work within a broadly Marxist tradition and that has been, since the early years of the last century, the intellectual current most centrally concerned with developing a theory of imperialism (Callinicos, 2009; Kemp, 1967).

As we saw above, one of the key characteristics of the way in which imperialism was conceived by Schiller and others was in terms of the relations of the "center and periphery," with the center in question being the United States. This approach still dominates contemporary discussions, most influentially in the work of Panitch and Gindin. They argue that only the U.S. state is today genuinely imperialist, in that it dominates over the rest of the world state systems, and lesser states are essentially clients of Washington, lacking the capacity for independent action (Panitch & Gindin, 2004).

There is clearly a great deal of evidence to support this view. The United States is by far the largest economy in the world, and it has a military apparatus that is vastly more powerful, and expensive, than any other in the world. As one U.S. commentator put it, "We have a quarter of global GDP (gross domestic product) and 46 per cent of defense spending" (McGregor & Dombey, 2011). Although it seeks allies and supporters for its use of these forces, it is capable, where necessary, of acting independently. By contrast, other large and heavily armed states, like the United Kingdom, have found it impossible to use their armed forces against the will of the United States, at least since the Suez crisis in 1956, and in practice have tended to be a loyal and subservient ally to the United States. In this account, as with earlier versions, the essence of "imperialism" is the domination exerted by large, developed states (the center) over poorer and weaker states (the periphery). This domination, exercised by persuasion, bribery, and coercion, circumscribes the political freedom of developing nations, subordinates their economies to the needs of the center, and helps to ensure that the majority of their people are deprived of the benefits of development. There is, of course, ample evidence that this kind of behavior takes place.

Despite the strength of the evidence, however, there are both theoretical and practical grounds for doubting the validity of this view. In its original formulations, the classical Marxist theory, and indeed contemporaneous formulations by non-Marxists like Schumpeter, focused on conflicts within the developed world. While they were acutely conscious of the ways in which the developed countries dominated and plundered their colonies, they faced the urgent task of explaining why Europe was experiencing the horrors of the First World War. The theory of imperialism was developed to explain how conflicts between imperialist states arose; in other words, they agreed with the liberal Hobson that "the leading characteristic of . . . modern Imperialism [is] the competition of rival Empires" (Hobson 1902, p. 19). This political and military competition, which in that epoch took the form of the annexation of territories and the construction of colonial empires, arose from the increasing scale of capitalist production and of the capitalist firm. As firms came to have a dominant role in their national markets, they more and more faced international competition from capitalists originating in other states, and they increasingly tended to enlist "their" states in these competitive struggles. As Nikolai Bukharin put it: "When competition has finally reached its highest stage, when it has become competition between state capitalist trusts, then the use of state power, and the possibilities connected with it begin to play a very large part" (Bukharin, 1972, pp. 123–24).[5] In contemporary versions of this theory, advanced by, among others, Alex Callinicos and David Harvey, it is the existence of a number of competing large, developed, states that is the condition for imperialism (Callinicos, 2009; Harvey, 2005).

Empirically, this seems a better way to account for the history of the last century or so than does the "unipolar" theory of imperialism. The first half of the twentieth century was dominated by a struggle between the British Empire as the incumbent dominant force and the emerging German empire. Out of the mutual exhaustion of the contenders arose a competition between the United States and the Soviet Union which lasted up until 1991. It is true that, throughout this period, the United States was overwhelmingly the more powerful of the competing states, and this was the motor of its ultimate victory, but it nevertheless faced real opposition and military competition from the Soviet bloc. The period after the collapse of the Soviet Union has indeed been one in which the United States has been the unchallenged dominant player but this has been a relatively brief, and atypical, interlude. The relative decline of the United States and the growth of new economic powers are evidence of the ending of this period. Particularly since the 2008 economic crisis, there is certainly evidence that other states are able to follow policies contrary to the wishes of Washington: arguments between the United States and China over currency, between the United States and Germany over the political economy of economic recovery, between the United States and Russia over the war in Georgia, are all cases where other states have demonstrated independence from the desires of the U.S. government. The shift in the balance of world economic power means that these demonstrations of independence, and the international conflicts that they provoke, are likely to become a more marked feature of the coming years: we are returning to a period in which a powerful incumbent is challenged in its international dominance by new and emerging powers. As Secretary of State Hilary Clinton told the U.S. Senate Foreign Relations Committee: "We are in a competition for influence with China; let's put aside the moral, humanitarian, do-good side of what we believe in, and let's just talk straight realpolitik" and illustrated her point with reference to a contest over rights to natural gas deposits in Papua–New Guinea (Dombey, 2011). More generally, the influential U.S.

magazine *Foreign Affairs* devoted a large section of its March/April 2011 issue to a series of essays grouped under the theme "Will China's Rise Lead
to War?" Charles Glaser opens his contribution with the question "Will
China's ascent increase the probability of a great-power war?" (Glaser,
2011). Fortunately for most of us, he gives an optimistic answer that such
an event can be avoided, provided that the United States makes concessions such as surrendering Taiwan to the People's Republic of China. It
is, however, plain that the economic and military development of China,
although still immeasurably weaker than the United States, is beginning to
pose an increasing challenge to Washington's domination of world affairs.
Inter-imperialist conflict is once again a possibility.

We should, however, be clear as to what inter-imperialist conflict means
and what it does not mean. It is certainly true that conflicts between developed states can take the form of military conflict, but there are many other
less catastrophic ways in which the power of the state is used in inter-state
competition. Trade and currency policy, intellectual property protection,
safety and design standards, international economic aid, and so on are all
ways in which the state is imbricated in protecting and advancing the economic interests of businesses located within its own border. On the other
hand, there are many forms of international economic competition that do
not involve significant state intervention, other than the necessary international agreements that must be present to allow lawful trading in the first
place. If the term "imperialism" is to have any precise and useful meaning,
then it must be used to describe actions of states, rather than what are essentially private economic activities.

The theory of imperialism that emerges from these considerations, and
which fits better with the empirical record, thus differs markedly from that
which informed writers like Schiller. The driving force in producing imperialism is the conflicts between large-scale capitalist enterprises, allied with
"their own" states, seeking to improve their competitive position. Instead
of there being one center, there is an array of competing and conflicting
states of different sizes and power, in some at least of which there is a
co-ordination of political and economic power. The consequences of this
competition involve a struggle for control of weaker and less developed
countries, partly for reasons that are ultimately economic but also for geo-
strategic ones as well.[6] At the start of the twentieth century, this normally
involved formal annexation and the construction of rival colonial empires,
but during the last century this has shifted almost entirely to what Harry
Magdoff called "imperialism without colonies" (Magdoff, 1972). The sub-

ordination of less developed countries often involves brutal exploitation and military violence, but this is not the defining characteristic of imperialism. It is the struggle between developed countries that is the driving force. Within that framework, certain factors will be properly labeled "imperialist" (in a world war, almost all social activities) but others will represent forms of economic competition conducted more or less independently of the state.

Reframing Cultural Imperialism

This revised theory of imperialism has three immediate consequences for any revision of the concept of cultural imperialism. First, it does not rest upon the notion that there is one center: on the contrary, the condition for the modern form of imperialism is that there is competition between different states. Second, it is this competition between the states of the developed world that is the central axis of imperialism, not the domination of the developed over the developing world. Third, it is important to scrutinize very carefully the evidence of international cultural exchanges to determine whether they are simply economic transactions or if they depend upon the exercise of one form or another of state power: only the latter would properly fall under the heading of imperialism.

Following from the fact that it is international competition that is the motor of imperialism, we would expect to find that international trade is characterized by a multiplicity of sources rather than just one: in other words, the theory of imperialism predicts not a single center but a range of different producers competing in the world market. Cultural production does not map directly onto economic strength, but given that economies of scale are to be expected in the production of cultural goods as much as in any other industry, we would expect to find that the serious competitors are among the larger economies as measured by GDP. The United States is by far the largest economy, ranked first in both Nominal GDP and GDP at Purchasing Power Parities (1/1).[7] Those countries that are often cited as sources of alternative flows of cultural material are also quite substantial: Japan (3/3); India (4/11); Brazil (7/8); Mexico (11/14); South Korea (12/15). Since the U.S. economy is, on either measure, around three times the size of the Japanese, and between three and ten times the size of India's, the dominance of the United States across a broad spectrum of cultural production is hardly a surprise. Measured over time, however, the position of the United States, for nearly a century to incumbent power both in economics and culture, is being eroded and its dominance is being challenged (Tunstall, 2008, pp. 360–412).

The international trade in cultural products is dominated by large producers who have distinct "national" home markets. Their trade is primarily within the developed world, as predicted by the theory of imperialism. According to the most recent figures available at the time of writing, News Corporation, probably the most "global" of the global media corporations, remains very heavily focused on the developed world. In 2009, 94 percent of its revenues came from North America, Australia, and Europe (News Corporation, 2009, p. 95). The same applies to other major media corporations: 90 percent of Viacom's 2009 earnings came from the United States and Europe (Viacom, 2010, p. 106); 93 percent of the Walt Disney Company's 2009 revenues came from the United States, Canada, and Europe (Walt Disney Company, 2010, p. 71); for Bertelsmann, 95 percent of 2009 revenues came from Europe and the United States (Bertelsmann, 2009, p. 57); 87 percent of Pearson's sales were in the United States, Canada, and Europe in 2009 (Pearson plc., 2009, p. 97).

None of these facts mean that the penetration of the media products of the developed world into the developing world does not exist, nor that it does not have important consequences, but it does place them in proportion. The companies cited here, and their peers in Europe and the United States, have dominant positions in their home market and compete vigorously in other markets, primarily in the developed world. These are the conditions that give rise to the modern form of imperialism.

The third issue, the degree to which international cultural exchanges actually constitute cultural imperialism, is much more difficult. There are some forms of cultural exchange that clearly fit almost any definition of cultural imperialism: the Voice of America, the BBC World Service, the British Council, and so on, are evidently organizations funded by imperialist states with the specific aim of promoting the ideas, beliefs, and values of their home country. On the other hand, there are many cultural exchanges that do not properly fit into any notion of imperialism: the international sale of a format by a production company is a more or less straightforward example of a trading relationship that does not presuppose state intervention any more than would the sale of the television set upon which the final version of the program will be viewed. In between such extremes lies a variety of cases that require concrete analysis in order to classify them accurately. In making such a classification, seven important points need to be borne in mind:

    1. Neither the concept of imperialism nor the concept of cultural impe-

rialism supposes any consciously aggressive policy on the part of any state or any conspiratorial alliance between top-hatted capitalists and bowler-hatted civil servants. The conflicts that can and do arise originate in the "normal" economic competition between rival capitalist companies and they become imperialist conflicts to the extent that states are drawn into resolving them. States can claim, perhaps sometimes with justification, that their policies are aimed at a "peaceful rise" or at spreading "freedom and democracy," but they can still find that pursuing these ends brings them into conflict with other states.

2. Cultural imperialism can be both offensive and defensive. Discussion has usually turned on the offensive aspects of the phenomenon, for example the drive to negotiate treaties opening audio-visual markets to free trade. There are, however, equally clear examples of the use of state power to prevent foreign entrance into cultural production: the United States, for example, prevents the control of U.S. television stations by foreign nationals by barring them from owning more than 25 percent of the shares. Similarly, the European Union insists on quotas of European production for broadcasters of general channels in the EU.

3. If, as is argued here, imperialism refers to the recruitment of the state to intervene in international relations primarily in order to facilitate economic development, then there must be the demonstrable presence of state action in any international cultural exchange for it to qualify as cultural imperialism.

4. It follows from this that the "imperialist" dimension of cultural imperialism is determined by the presence of state action, not by the nature of the cultural artifact in question. It is not the intrinsic characteristics of a television program, or a language, that make it "imperialist" but the use to state power to ensure that it gains currency. The media are not in themselves "imperialist" even when the conditions specified by Boyd-Barrett actually apply, as for example they have done, historically, in Ireland (Corcoran, 2004, pp. 15–16). There is a long history of British cultural imperialism in Ireland, but the spillover of U.K. signals into the Republic is not part of it.

5. It is essential to distinguish between what may properly be termed "cultural imperialism," which may be briefly defined as the use of state power in the international cultural sphere and the fact that some cultural exchanges are closely connected with imperialism. The international status of the English language is a good example of this. English is not, in itself, an "imperialist" language. Its spread in a number of areas, Ireland most obviously, was indeed closely associated with imperialist policies, but its

contemporary global reach is a product of the fact that for the last two centuries the world's dominant imperialist power has been predominantly English speaking: first the United Kingdom, then the United States. The presence of English in India is not due to the characteristics of the language but to the fact of the long British imperial rule in India: it is not itself cultural imperialism, but rather one of the cultural consequences of imperialism.

6. It is not a necessary condition for cultural imperialism, or for the cultural consequences of imperialism, that they have a particular kind of impact upon their audiences. In some cases, cultural forms that evidently originate in imperial centers are enthusiastically adopted by the population of subject territories: the sport of cricket in India, where it commands a far more central place in the dominant culture than it does in its English place of origin, is an obvious example, and the control of the sport, once located in London, today lies in India. In other cases, cultural phenomena might have quite different meanings in different places, being popular in one and not another, or being reworked into hybrid forms, and so on. The extent and nature of the impact of any cultural phenomenon is a matter for empirical investigation and is independent of the question as to whether that phenomenon occurs as the result of state action or through simple economic exchange. The consequences that earlier theories of cultural imperialism assumed as being intrinsic to the nature of the trade in cultural products are in practice only one possible set of outcomes among many.

7. Not only is the assertion as to the existence of homogeneous "national cultures" extremely difficult to sustain empirically but the theory of cultural imperialism has no place for such a concept, given that most Marxist-inspired theories of the modern state system see it as the result of historical struggle between different class interests rather than as the natural expression of a people. There is no reason to suppose that either the agents (large capitalist corporations and powerful modern states) or the objects of cultural imperialism (states and societies endowed with less economic, political, and military power) are ethnically or culturally homogeneous. There are dominant and subordinate cultures within both the imperialist states and those states that experience their attentions.

Consequences

The first result of applying the above criteria is that it is possible to advance a viable and coherent concept of cultural imperialism that is not subject to the kinds of criticisms that were applied to Schiller's version. It once again becomes a viable project to investigate the ways in which state power and cultural power are intertwined in the production and circulation of cultural artifacts. The second consequence is that the term "cultural imperialism" will be used in a narrower set of circumstances than was the case in the past, although the category of the cultural consequences of imperialism is likely to be quite large.

We can illuminate what this means by considering some of the issues that were at the center of contention during the ascendency of the concept in the 1970s and 1980s. As we noted above, whatever the motives of many of the participants, the struggle over the New World Communication and Information Order was caught up in the inter-imperialist rivalries between the United States and the Soviet Union. Some of the items of contention, for example the close and open alliance between the U.S. State Department and the Motion Picture Association of America in ensuring that trade treaties guaranteed free access to national audio-visual markets, clearly fall within our revised category of cultural imperialism. Others, for example the character of the reporting of Africa, fit better into the category of the cultural consequences of imperialism, both in terms of the social terrain that was being reported and many of the assumptions upon which reporting was (and too often still is) based.

In the future, these concepts will come to have ever greater relevance. Direct economic rivalry between the U.S. incumbent and a new challenger is an obvious feature of the contemporary world, and we saw above how the U.S. secretary of state has begun to formulate that rivalry in terms of strategic conflicts. As China, and other new economic powers such as India, grow stronger so we will see increasing competition and conflict between them and with the Western powers that have dominated the world for two centuries. The analogous situation is with the established and apparently "natural" domination of the British Empire experiencing challenges from Germany at the end of the nineteenth century, and later from the United States and the Soviet Union. Our concern is with the media, not with the general geopolitics of the contemporary world, so we do not have to speculate as to whether this rivalry will have the same consequences as the earlier conflicts: we can simply express the fervent hope that the outcomes this time will be different and much less horrifying.

In media terms, however, we can anticipate at least six possible ways in which these more general economic and political changes will lead to debates and conflicts:

1. Direct rivalry between states in terms of their propaganda efforts. One of the major developments of the last decade or so has been the proliferation of state-backed international broadcasters, who now pose a challenge to the incumbent international broadcasters, both state and private. To quote Hillary Clinton again, on the Middle East: "We [the United States] are in an information war, and we are losing that war.... Al-Jazeera is winning" (Dombey, 2011). In the future, that challenge is likely to widen: China, for example, has recently substantially increased the resources of the former CCTV9 and renamed it CCTV News, while at the same time funding Xinhua to establish a new international news channel. We should recall that such channels do not need to command a mass audience to have a powerful influence on public perceptions. Al Jazeera is an exception in that it commands a fairly wide audience across the Arab world but CNN and the BBC have tiny audiences most of the time in most places. The attention of a small elite audience can be as much a bone of contention as a mass audience.

2. Conflicts over the nature of news and journalism. These state broadcasters are already engaged in a struggle over what constitutes "news" that rests on deeply embedded assumptions in the news cultures of the different countries. Many U.S. journalists, news organizations, and media scholars have a developed and self-conscious sense of the norms of professional conduct. These views are strongly held and frequently expressed, despite the fact that reality sometimes does not correspond to ideology. These views are not in practice shared by journalists formed in other traditions and one only needs to recall the disputes over the coverage of Tibet in 2008 to see that these differences can be expressed by news workers, scholars, and even large numbers of ordinary people.

3. Conflicts over the regulation of international media flows. The protection of cultural industries has been a theme of international trade negotiations since at least the 1947 treaty establishing the General Agreement on Tariffs and Trade (GATT), whose Article IV (d) permitted the retention of screen quotas for cinematic films. The original treaty stated that "screen quotas shall be subject to negotiation for their limitation, liberalization or elimination," but cultural protectionism derived from this article continue to this day (General Agreement on Tariffs and Trade, 1947). The continuing efforts by states to protect the creative industries operating within their territory lead regularly to public altercations. Historically, the pressure to open markets and allow free trade, in general as much as in the creative industries, has come from the most powerful players. As the

locus of economic power shifts, so the offensive and defensive postures will be exchanged. Yesterday's fervent protectionist becomes tomorrow's free trader, and vice versa. We can already see some slight evidence of such reversals in the problems Al Jazeera experienced in getting carriage on U.S. cable channels. The issue of who can own channels and stations is likely to intensify as the balance of economic power shifts.

4. Conflicts over the control of the Internet. The distribution of power in the governance of the Internet reflects the old international order. For example, at the time of writing, the Internet Corporation for Assigned Names and Numbers (ICANN) Board of Directors contains 21 people, one of whom is Chinese (and he is from Taiwan) and two Indians (one of whom has long lived in the United States) (ICANN, 2011). The sub-committee that oversees the root servers reported to the U.S. National Telecommunications and Information Administration's Office of Spectrum Management. As the number of users, and the commercial forces involved, shift towards Asia, so there will be disputes over where decisions are taken, and the composition of the bodies that take them. The World Summit on the Information Society process already illustrated the ways in which such disputes link economic and political forces.

5. Conflicts over the protection of intellectual property. Issues over the widespread copying of computer programs, film and video programs and formats, and music are already well known. Paradoxically, perhaps, this is one area where we might expect to find a decrease in the level of conflict as the economic balance shifts. The ambition of large broadcasters in Asia to become exporters of content, for example, is already changing their attitude toward formats. Instead of the murky processes that led from *Pop Idol* through *American Idol* to *Super Girl*, there have more recently been formal purchases of rights and the signing of co-production agreements.

6. Conflicts over the nature of popular culture. International conflicts find expression in popular cultural artifacts. One need only think of Hollywood representations of Japanese, Russians, and Communists to see how international struggles can map quite closely onto ideologies and this is likely to continue in the future. At the same time, shifting economic power results in the popularization of cultural forms with a different national origin: the shift from cricket to basketball in the Caribbean is one well-known example. A similar shift can be traced in the visual styles of animation following the economic development of Japan, which seems likely to continue in the burgeoning Chinese industry. So, too, the sites and content of popular culture change: there is a considerable distance between an evening

spent in a western bar or pub and an evening of Chinese KTV (karaoke television).

Some of these issues are already evident in the contemporary media while others are certain to become important in the next decade. Cataloguing such changes empirically can be performed within any theoretical framework or none at all. If we wish to analyze and explain them, however, then an appropriate theoretical account is essential. The issues all have a simple economic dimension, but they are also, to a greater or lesser extent, also involved in the actions of states, and an adequate theory must be able to account for both of these. It is for this reason that imperialism, cultural imperialism, and the cultural consequences of imperialism are once again an essential part of the theoretical framework for the study of international communication.

REFERENCES

Ang, I. (1995). *Watching* Dallas: *Soap opera and the melodramatic imagination.* London: Methuen.

Bauman, Z. (1998). *Globlization: The human consequences.* Cambridge: Polity Press.

Bertelsmann. (2009). *Annual report.* Gütersloh: Bertelsmann.

Boyd-Barrett, O. (1977). Media imperialism: Towards an international framework for the analysis of media systems. In J. Curran, M. Gurevitch, & J. Woollacott, eds., *Mass communication and society* (pp. 116–35). London: Edward Arnold.

Bukharin, N. (1972). *Imperialism and world economy.* London: Merlin.

Callinicos, A. (2009). *Imperialism and global political economy.* Cambridge: Polity.

Corcoran, F. (2004). *RTÉ and the globalization of Irish television.* Bristol, UK: Intellect.

Dombey, D. (2011). US struggling to hold role as global leader, Clinton says. *Financial Times,* 2 March. Retrieved 7 March 2011, from http://www.ft.com/cms/s/0/5ff5669c-4508-11e0-80e7-00144feab49a.html#axzz1FCm5vqgK.

Ferguson, N. (2003). *Empire: How Britain made the modern world.* London: Allen Lane.

Ferguson, N. (2004). *Colossus: The rise and fall of the American empire.* London: Allen Lane.

Frank, A. G. (1967). *Capitalism and underdevelopment in Latin America: Historical studies of Chile and Brazil.* New York: Monthly Review Press.

Galtung, J. (1971). A structural theory of imperialism. *Journal of Peace Research* 8 (2): 81–117.

General Agreement on Tarrifs and Trade (GATT). (1947). *WTO legal texts.* 30 October. Retrieved 27 April 2011, from http://www.wto.org/english/docs_e/legal_e/gatt47_01_e.htm.

Glaser, C. (2011). Will China's rise lead to war: Why realism does not mean pessimism. *Foreign Affairs* 90 (2): 80–91.

Hamelink, C. (1997). World communications: business as usual? In M. Baillie & D. Winseck, eds., *Democratising communication? Comparative perspectives in information and power* (pp. 407–25). Cresskill, NJ: Hampton.

Hardt, M., & Negri, A. (2000). *Empire.* Cambridge, MA: Harvard University Press.

Harvey, D. (2005). *The new imperialism.* Oxford: Oxford University Press.

Hobson, J. (1902). *Imperialism: A study.* London: George Allen and Unwin.

International Monetary Fund. (2010). World economic outlook database. October. Retrieved 14 February 2011, from http://www.imf.org/external/pubs/ft/weo/2010/02/weodata/index.aspx.

Internet Corporation for Assigned Names and Numbers (ICANN). (2011). *Board of directors.* Retrieved 29 April 2011, from http://www.icann.org/en/general/board.html.

Kemp, T. (1967). *Theories of imperialism.* London: Dennis Dobson.

Kraidy, M. (2005). *Hybridity, or the cultural logic of globalization.* Philadelphia: Temple University Press.

Lee, C.-C. (1980). *Media imperialism reconsidered.* Beverly Hills, CA: Sage.

Liebes, T., & Katz, E. (1990). *The export of meaning: Cross-cultural readings of Dallas.* Oxford: Oxford University Press.

Louw, P. E. (2011). Revisiting cultural imperialism. In H. Wasserman, ed., *Popular media, democracy and development in Africa* (pp. 32–45). Abingdon: Routledge.

Magdoff, H. (1972). Imperialism without colonies. In R. Owen & B. Sutcliffe, eds., *Studies in the theory of imperialism* (pp. 144–70). London: Longman.

Mann, M. (2003). *Incoherent empire.* London: Verso.

Mattelart, A. (1979). *Multinational corporations and the control of culture: The ideological apparatuses of imperialism.* Brighton, UK: Harvester.

Maxwell, R. (2003). *Herbert Schiller.* Lanham, MA: Rowman & Littlefield.

McGregor, R., & Dombey, D. (2011). Defense: a question of scale. *Financial Times,* 6 March. http://www.ft.com/cms/s/0/695f48d8–4823–11e0-b323–00144fe-ab49a.html#axzz1FvhvUx4v.

Miller, D. (1995). The consumption of soap operas: "The young and the restless" and mass consumption in Trinidad. In R. Allen, ed., *To be continued . . . soap operas around the world* (pp. 213–33). London: Routledge.

Morley, D. (2006). Globalisation and cultural imperialism reconsidered: Old questions in new guises. In J. Curran & D. Morley, eds., *Media and cultural theory* (pp. 30–43). London: Routledge.

Ndlela, N. (2009). African media research in the era of globalization. *Journal of African Media Studies* 1 (1): 55–68.

News Corporation. (2009). *Annual report.* New York: News Corporation.

Panitch, L., & Gindin, S. (2004). *Global capitalism and American empire.* London: Merlin Press.

Pearson plc. (2009). *Report and accounts.* London: Pearson.

Rothkopf, D. (1997). In praise of cultural imperialism? *Foreign Policy* 107:38–53.

Schiller, H. (1970). *Mass communications and American empire.* New York: Augustus M. Kelley.

Schiller, H. (1976). *Communication and cultural domination.* White Plains, NY: M. E. Sharpe.

Schumpeter, J. (1951). *Imperialism and social classes.* Oxford: Basil Blackwell.

Sinclair, J. (1999). *Latin American television: A global view.* Oxford: Oxford University Press.

Smith, A. (1980). *The Geopolitics of information: How Western culture dominates the world.* London: Faber.

Straubhaar, J. (2007). *World television: From global to local.* London: Sage.

Tomlinson, J. (1991). *Cultural imperialism.* London: Pinter.

Tunstall, J. (1977). *The media are American: Anglo-American media in the world.* London: Constable.

Tunstall, J. (2008). *The media were American: US mass media in decline.* Oxford: Oxford University Press.

Viacom. (2010). *Transition report persuant to Section 13 or 15 (d) of the Securities Exchange Act of 1934.* New York: Viacom.

Walt Disney Company. 2010. *Annual reports pursuant to Section 13 or 15(d) of the Securities Exchange Act of 1934.* Burbank, CA: Walt Disney Company.

NOTES

1. Schiller was, of course, a consistent critic of imperialism, both in general and in its specific cultural form, but it is possible to find positive accounts of cultural imperialism to place alongside celebratory theories of imperialism such as Niall Ferguson's: "It is in the general interest of the United States to encourage the development of a world in which the fault lines separating nations are bridged by shared interests. And it is in the economic and political interests of the United States to ensure that if the world is moving toward a common language, it be English; that if the world is moving toward common telecommunications, safety, and quality standards, they be American; that if the world is becoming linked by television, radio, and music, the programming be American; and that if common values are being developed, they be values with which Americans are comfortable" (Rothkopf, 1997, p. 45).

2. This conception, sometimes using the terms "metropolis" and "satellite," has been extremely influential in a wide range of fields (Frank, 1967). Galtung, in a famous article, wrote: "Imperialism is a relation between a Center and a Periphery nation so that: (1) there is harmony of interest between the center in the Center nation and the center in the Periphery nation, (2) there is more disharmony of interest within the Periphery nation than within the Center nations, (3) there is disharmony of interest between the periphery in the Center nation and the periphery in the Periphery nation" (Galtung, 1971, p. 83).

3. It is worth noting that Schiller operated with a model of effects very similar to that of Wilbur Schramm and other development scholars (Schiller, 1970, pp. 109–15).

4. It is worth noting, however, that the charge of assuming a uniform international media market often laid against proponents of cultural imperialism cannot be sustained. Boyd-Barrett, for example, recognized the existence of regional markets for news and media as a potential challenge to the dominance of the core (Boyd-Barrett, 1977, p. 134).

5. This state-centered approach differs radically from that of Michael Hardt and Antonio Negri, who argue that contemporary capitalism has outgrown the state system and therefore there is no longer any basis for the geopolitical conflicts that so marked the twentieth century. The conflicts of imperialism have been replaced by the conflict between "Empire" and "Multitude." As they put it: "The distinct national colors of the imperialist map of the world have merged and blended in the imperial global rainbow" (Hardt & Negri, 2000, p. xiii). In essence, this is a theory of globalization rather than imperialism.

6. So the British Empire seized Gibraltar, Malta, Cyprus, Aden, and Singapore not to exploit the denizens, loot raw materials, or export capital, but for the obvious military advantages they presented.

7. Gross Domestic Product can be measured in several ways. The most common measure is Nominal GDP in U.S. dollars, but an alternative is GDP at Purchasing Power Parities (PPPs). There is no obvious reason for preferring either measure, although in terms of the amount of human effort that is expended in cultural production the PPP measures seem more likely to give a better picture of national capacity. Both measures are provided by the International Monetary Fund, and the rankings here are based on their figures for 2010. The first number is the country's place in the ranking of GDP at PPPs, the second that in the ranking of Nominal GDP ("World Economic Outlook Database," 2010).

CHAPTER NINE

De-Westernization and Cosmopolitan Media Studies

Silvio Waisbord

James Curran and Myung-Jin Park's (2000) *De-Westernizing Media Studies* offered an eloquent, much-needed call to expand the geographical and intellectual frontiers of communication and media studies. It aimed "to contribute to a broadening of media theory and understanding in a way that takes account of the experience of countries outside the Anglo-American orbit" (Curran & Park, 2000, p. 11). Featuring a dozen chapters from around the world, the book makes a normative argument for why the field needs to be more inclusive and worldly. It stands as a prime example of the latest push toward the "internationalization" of media studies (Thussu, 2009). There is no shortage of studies published in English that examine recent changes in media systems (Fox & Waisbord, 2002; McCargo, 2008; Romano & Bromley, 2005; Sakr, 2007; Voltmer, 2006), journalistic practices (de Burgh, 2005), mediated politics (Lilleker & Lees-Marshment, 2005; Strömbäck & Kaid, 2008), and journalistic ethics (Ward & Wasserman, 2010) around the world. Amid "the globalization of everything," including academia during the 1990s, Curran and Park's volume makes a strong case for breaking away from academic parochialism. De-Westernization implies opening up analytical horizons by considering cases from around the world that are not known either due to language obstacles or disinterest. Given that the importance of the non-West is not news for non-Westerner scholars, Curran and Park's goal is primarily to encourage curiosity about other regions among Anglo-American researchers.

Since its inception, the field of media studies has had a distinctive Western, and particularly Anglo-American, accent. The field emerged out the convergence of theories and questions rooted in the tradition of the social sciences in the West during the inter-war period (Katz et al., 2003). Expectedly, the analytical focus and theories have been Western, and specifically U.S. theories. The Western-centric character of media studies is not surprising. Research questions that have dominated the field, such as media effects, journalistic practices, and media and public opinion, mainly reflected the priorities of scholars in the United States and western Europe who laid the foundations of the field. Likewise, theoretical frameworks were grounded in the epistemological premises and analytical traditions of political, psychological, and sociological theories developed in the West. Whereas the field has maintained its position as the meeting ground for interdisciplinary and transdisciplinary research, it has been largely concentrated on issues relevant in the United States and fundamentally drew from Western social thought. Nor is the field of media studies unique in its Western centrism. Similar arguments have been made about the social sciences and humanities, particularly in recent years. Informed by multiculturalism, deconstructionism, and subaltern studies, scholars have criticized the Western focus and intellectual categories in social analysis (Rudolph, 2005).

Amid similar debates across academic disciplines, Curran and Park's book raises questions about the purpose, the strategies, and the academic politics of the "de-Westernization" of media studies. Is the goal to enrich the pool of studies published in English? Question the provincialism of the field? Promote theory-building that draws on a larger set of cases? What methodologies and analytical strategies are adequate to de-Westernize? Should it be through the institutionalization of non-Western research in Western academia? Should be it through the study of global questions and analysis? Who needs de-Westernization? Western and non-Western scholars alike? Is it a debate primarily relevant to Western academia? Or should it also apply to academic debates in the global South? These questions lack obvious answers.

In this chapter, my goal is to discuss the purpose and strategies of the "de-Westernization" of media studies. Given my particular interests in media studies, the analysis focuses on the study of the press and politics. The argument presented here is as follows. "De-Westernization" should nurture cosmopolitan scholarship characterized by sensitivity to comparative and global questions and approaches and engagement in globalized debates. It not should lead to the balkanization of the field in "area studies" that cover various regions of the world. Instead, it should lead to the "de-centralization" of theories and research agendas in ways that foreground globalized perspectives and questions. De-Westernization is not simply about accommodating international research and perspectives in the field. Instead, it is about globalizing research in ways that foreground questions and arguments that draw from various media and political systems. Cosmopolitan media studies should be guided by theoretical and empirical questions that are relevant across geographical and academic borders.

Why Area Studies Are a Problematic Way to "De-Westernize" Media Studies

One could argue that "de-Westernization" of media studies should be accepted without hesitation. De-Westernization is unquestionably good and desirable. After all, who would argue that ignoring the world is fitting for academic life? An analytical mind open to the world defines intellectual work and academic imagination (Bourdieu, 1988; Mills, 1959). It is why cosmopolitanism, particularly in recent decades, has been celebrated (Appiah, 2007; Held, 1995). A worldly, inquisitive, curious mind embodies Immanuel Kant's understanding of cosmopolitanism as hospitality to foreigners. It is why provincialism is a pejorative adjective that conjures what academic minds should not be. It is why theorists believe that international education is critical for nurturing a cosmopolitan mind (Hansen, 2008; Nussbaum, 1996). Ignoring the majority of media systems in the world is unbecoming to intellectual openness. Yet to argue that the study of non-Western media is necessarily good is insufficient. The history of media research in the West amply demonstrates that the purpose of studying non-Western societies is ambiguous. The study of non-Western media has been driven by various and even opposite goals: to legitimize and promote Western ideals about press/media systems, to critically interrogate Western premises, and to explore other societies and media systems.

Because de-Westernization has ambiguous goals, it is important to clarify its purposes. De-Westernization should be more than an effort to make media studies in the West less parochial and more welcoming to research from around the world. The production of knowledge about non-Western media can coexist with an academic mind-set that remains unaware and untouched by global ideas and findings. In fact, both may develop in parallel without entering into a productive dialogue or challenging each other to rethink premises and analytical foci. Neither the availability of non-Western cases in the West nor growing receptiveness to research about non-Western societies inevitably leads to abandoning provincialism or to revisiting prevalent paradigms.

This is why area studies as a strategy to integrate research from around the world in specific regional categories in a given discipline or field does not solve the main challenges of de-Westernization in media studies. During the Cold War years, the social sciences and humanities in the West engaged with the non-Western world under the rubric of area studies. Areas studies have been organized around geographical labels ("South Asian," "Middle Eastern") that assume commonalities among neighboring countries. So, "Latin American studies" tacitly assumes that countries south of the United States can be analyzed as a group under the assumption that they share common characteristics, such as political history, economics, and culture.[1]

The organization of knowledge about the "non-West" in area studies is fraught with problems. The main problem is not the division between "soft" empirical research ("area studies") and "hard" theory ("American" studies) (Bates, 1997; Franco, 1988; Graham & Kantor, 2007). Although such conclusions point out an extended, and unfortunate, perception, such generalizations unfairly portray the richness and diversity of such studies, and leave out several shortcomings. The crystallization of "international research" in "area studies" presents several problems. It replicates forms of conceptualizing academic knowledge through Western, geopolitical categories (Kratoska, Raben, & Schulte Nordholt, 2005; Nugent, 2010; Simpson, 1998; Szanton, 2004; Yudice, 2003). Area divisions perpetuate Western constructions of world regions ("Latin America," "Southeast Asia") that are linked for geopolitical, strategic reasons unrelated to analytical justifications. By building compartmentalized analytical categories, "area studies" also discourage dialogue and collaboration across regions. They tacitly relegate regional studies to the production of knowledge that informs and builds on models developed in the West. Finally, "area studies" reinforce the construction of the "non-West" as "the Other" (Harbeson, 1997; Rafael, 1994).

These criticisms point out to the problem of academic insularity and splintering—the construction of separate geographically bounded limits. Area studies produce findings that, even if they are of interest to regional specialists, may not be necessarily relevant to the field. Boxing up scholarship in clear-cut geographical categories is supported neither on theoretical

nor methodological distinctions. Typically, studies ask questions to understand the causes, characteristics, and consequences of specific national and
regional media systems, journalistic practices, news coverage, and other
subjects. As important as these issues are, they may not be directly relevant to the field at large if questions aren't linked to broad debates. "Thick
descriptions" (Geertz, 1973) of individual case studies are of interest primarily to area specialists. They reinforce analytical compartmentalization
grounded on geographical, and political, social, and cultural boundaries.
Such an approach has limited impact on the field at large.

These limitations are found in works about non-Western cases that,
although they discuss interesting questions, fail short of making theoretical
arguments that are relevant to the field at large. Because they are framed
as area studies, primarily concerned with local phenomena, they are dis-
engaged from broad theoretical discussions. The result is a rich body of
international literature with little impact on theoretical and conceptual debates that remain focused on "Western" issues. Area specialists primarily
talk to fellow area specialists. They live in separate academic worlds even
when, paradoxically, they may be interested in similar theoretical questions
(e.g., the power of news frames, various types of agenda-setting effects,
the impact of commercial media on political knowledge). Consequently,
geographical divisions are not conducive to metatheoretical debates and
intellectual cross-pollination.

This problem is manifested, for example, in edited volumes that show-
case a diversity of world cases, but are not sufficiently engaged with common themes and questions. They contribute to internationalizing the field
by making a wealth of cases available in English, yet they do not necessarily
probe theoretical arguments or advance conclusions that build on Western
scholarship. For Pippa Norris (2009), this is the problem of studies and
books that offer a "grand tour" of the world, but fail to make theoretical
contributions if they are not organized around broad and common questions. The problem is not the study of country cases per se; rather, it is a
matter of how questions and findings are linked to large theoretical and
empirical debates. The division of area studies leads to focusing on questions and arguments that, albeit relevant to specific regions, may not add to
the body of knowledge in the field at large.

"Area studies" presents other challenges, too. It clusters research on
presumed similarities among countries whereas those similarities actually
need to be critically examined. It assumes essentialist visions that ascribe
immanent similarities to geographical regions. Such regions are political

and academic constructions that ignore profound differences and similarities inside and across regions. In fact, this is what numerous country/regional studies show: the existence of important differences within geographical areas that make regional clusters questionable. Should South Africa be included with the rest of Africa? How about Mozambique, Kenya, and Senegal given different media legacies largely shaped by different colonial powers? Should China, Vietnam, and Cambodia be grouped together given their common communist history? Or should China be compared to the other BRIC economic powers of Brazil, Russia, and India? Should contemporary Russia be compared to other countries that feature "hybrid" political regimes between authoritarianism and democracy (e.g., Venezuela)? Should Lebanon, a country with the most open media system in the Middle East, be compared to monarchical media regimes in Morocco and Saudi Arabia? Should Indonesia be grouped with other countries with Muslim majorities? Should Brazil, a country with a strong tradition of market-driven media and journalistic practices inspired by the U.S. model of professionalism, be grouped with Latin American countries where those conditions are absent?

Asking questions about the logic of geographical groupings are also relevant to interrogate the binary division between "Western" and "non-Western" studies. Do we run the risk of essentializing countries, regions, and scholarship by continuing to establish differences between the West and the non-West (Godrej, 2009)? What is the non-West anyway? Arguably, the rationale for clustering dozens of countries together as the "non-West" is their geographical position as well as their presumably common relation to the West. Yet the justification for maintaining such a division is not obvious. Certainly, this dichotomy is found among defenders of "Western" traditions and geopolitics as well as among critics of "Western civilization." At a time when analytical and ideological categories (e.g., first/third worlds, core/periphery) that have dominated the social sciences during the past half a century are thrown into question, shouldn't we cautiously approach, or simply refrain from using, the "Western/non-Western" dyad?

How we answer these questions depends on what theoretical challenges are considered to be a priority in media studies. Even if regional groupings may be justified on the basis of common media history, language, colonial past, and political regimes, the problem is maintaining strong geo-analytical boundaries. Neat geographical divisions lose sight of the fact that theoretical questions should drive research agendas. Local and regional developments, inevitably, generate empirical questions. To name a few, the relation between media and regime transition, the role of media in the rise of right-wing populism, and the impact of new media on political identities are questions that stem from concrete developments in particular countries and, unsurprisingly, are more relevant to some media/political systems. The problem lies in approaching questions solely in terms of empirical relevance without considering their significance for the field of media studies. Area divisions constrain scholars to maintaining conversations with other area specialists instead of making research relevant to scholars beyond geographical borders.

Another problem of area studies is the preservation of "methodological nationalism" (Beck, 2007; Beck & Sznaider, 2010), that is, the focus on "national" questions within the boundaries of modern states. Such questions, Beck argues, are not the most urgent or important at a time of planetary challenges and global consciousness and actions. "Methodological nationalism" ignores the fact that problems need to be reconceptualized amid globalization. The shift from local/national to global requires researchers to ask questions beyond political-geographical boundaries.

Beck unnecessarily downplays the persistent significance of nations and states as analytical units. The rise of planetary problems doesn't invalidate the significance of a host of issues that remain relevant at the local/domestic level. For example, despite increased globalization, media politics as well as models of media and politics (Hallin & Mancini, 2004) remain largely anchored in local and national dynamics. It's not a question of "either/or," but rather the need to remain attentive to questions at multiple levels. Yet Beck's call to think "globally" rightly raises questions about the need to expand analytical perspectives in media studies. Implicitly, it offers a much-needed corrective to the geographical narrowness of area studies. A perspective grounded in area studies does not tend to formulate questions in terms of global developments and trends. Rather, it tilts the analysis in favor of questions that are primarily relevant to local and national media politics.

In summary, area studies as a path to "de-Westernize" media studies runs the risk of reinforcing scholarly insularity and fragmentation. It assumes commonalities instead of examining the basis for geographical-analytical divisions. It maintains and encourages parallel debates. Case studies are necessary to foreground how theoretical questions and arguments play out in various contexts. Yet the fragmentation and solidification of "case expertise" in geographical differences is a deterrent to cross-regional, global debates.

Finally, "de-Westernizing" media studies in the direction of area studies is particularly wrongheaded at the present juncture of the field. It fails to address a basic challenge in both media studies and political communication: the lack of robust empirical generalizations and theoretical arguments based on a range of cases. Foundational and contemporary theories and arguments in the literature overwhelmingly draw from case studies on the United States and Britain. Broadening the analytical base is necessary to determine the strengths of propositions across media and political systems. In summary, besides the problems of essentialist and geopolitical premises, area studies reinforce academic insularity and parallel debates.

Cosmopolitan Media Studies

To avoid the limitations of area studies, I propose to embrace a cosmopolitan outlook to further "de-Westernize" media studies. Here cosmopolitanism is understood as an analytical attitude open to multiple perspectives and developments beyond geography.

The idea of academic cosmopolitanism builds on the recent "cosmopolitan" turn in the social sciences and humanities (Caney, 2005; Dallmayr, 2003; Held, 1995; Nussbaum, 1996). Cosmopolitanism is generally associated with contemporary normative theories that, drawing from classic and modern philosophy, outline the need for a moral commitment to justice, law, human rights, and politics that transcends conventional state borders. It champions cosmopolitan governance premised on the notion of world citizens and equal members of the global community. At a time of unprecedented mobility of people, ideas, and goods as well as the porosity of political, economic, and cultural borders, world citizenship offers responses to critical issues and urgent needs. Along these lines, media scholars (Chouliaraki, 2006; Silverstone, 2006) have made persuasive arguments for why the media play critical roles in nurturing cosmopolitan consciousness and citizenship.

Cosmopolitan media studies demands studying the world to enrich and challenge intellectual premises, categories, and conclusions. It starts from the present condition of a globalized, interconnected world as the basis for stimulating a cosmopolitan outlook (Fine, 2007). It is not synonymous with the aggregation of "case studies" from around the world. It is contrary to clear-cut geographical separations that reify "otherness" in the categories of "international" or "global." Cosmopolitan scholarship is not reduced to being hospitable to "international" research. Instead, it is a globalized perspective that critically considers world differences to probe theoretical arguments and define empirical questions (also see Miller, 2009).

A cosmopolitan approach raises awareness about global differences and similarities (Ong, 2009). In a world characterized by interconnectedness and multiple flows (Appadurai, 2001; Giddens, 1990), it invites scholars to expand analytical horizons beyond the "comfort zone" of country borders. It promotes a global sensitivity guided by analytical questions and informed by research from around the world. It pushes for the globalization of knowledge and dialogue. It encourages country specialists to make broad theoretical and conceptual contributions.

Cosmopolitan media studies doesn't assume that borders, grounded in political, social, economic, and cultural differences, are irrelevant. Indeed, it assumes that they need to be taken into account to expand research agendas and produce arguments that examine differences and similarities. Contrasts across media and political systems, as well as their interactions, provide evidence to test conclusions. In doing so, cosmopolitan scholarship overcomes the limitations of theory-building based largely on Anglo-American scholarship. Because these countries have quite unique traditions of media and politics, casting a wider geographical net is indispensable to refine theories and arguments.

Cosmopolitan scholarship also contributes to a shift in the direction of knowledge flows. Like other social sciences (McFarlane, 2006), media studies has long been dominated by a one-way flow of "knowledge transfer" from the West (particularly U.S. and British scholarship) to the Rest. Such patterns are not only problematic for maintaining the primacy of theories and concepts produced in a few countries. They are also incongruous with the reality of multiple centers for academic production. Therefore, cosmopolitan scholarship seeks to rectify a lopsided flow of ideas by promoting more egalitarian global exchanges and debates.

I'm not proposing "cosmopolitan media studies" as a desirable academic identity, the equivalent of cosmopolitan citizenship in a world of increased mobility and fluidity. Nor I am suggesting that national borders are irrelevant to the study of media and politics on the assumption that they have been superseded by globalization and remain remnants of the old order. My argument is neither about normative citizenship ("a way of being in the academic world") nor the absolute preeminence of global questions. Rather, I propose cosmopolitan scholarship as an analytical perspective that prioritizes theoretical and critical thinking informed by international research and globalized dialogue. This approach is not simply consistent with a globalized academic world and the current challenges of global-ization. It is also necessary to overcome geographical divisions and bring together strands of research around common questions and arguments.

How to De-Westernize and Promote Cosmopolitanism

Just like philosophical and political arguments for cosmopolitanism, cos-mopolitan scholarship raises questions about strategies. How is cosmopoli-tanism possible? What strategies may stimulate a globalized perspective in the field?

Fundamentally, cosmopolitan media studies is about placing local re-search in the context of global debates and developments, and engaging with conversations that transcend local interests and phenomena. It is not only about prioritizing research questions that transcend borders. More importantly, it is about shifting the way questions are asked and answers are formulated.

Here I propose three research strategies to pursue the "de-Westernization" of media studies along the lines of cosmopolitanism: address questions that are absent in the literature in the West, conduct comparative studies featuring non-Western cases, and analyze global phe-nomena that transcend geographical and regional boundaries.

Analyze Neglected Issues

The first option is to approach the global South as a rich trove of cases that have been generally ignored in the West. Given the West-centric na-ture of research agendas, important questions in the global South have not been at the forefront or even discussed in the West. The research agenda has remained largely, and expectedly, local or national. Consequently, the literature has empirical and theoretical blindspots that reflect the powerful influence of Western concerns and categories.

Here, I'll mention just a few examples. Press performance amid condi-tions of statelessness is not uncommon in large swaths of the world given the chronic problems of state instability and the power of para-state actors (Waisbord, 2007). The links between media and various forms of media populism (Mazzoleni, Stewart, & Horsfield, 2003) also takes on particu-lar characteristics around the world. In countries dominated by authori-tarian regimes or where governments exert powerful influence on media economics and access to information, journalists' strategies to navigate government restrictions are different from the West (Lee & Chan, 2008). Worldwide, the role of religious values in the professional identity of journalists is different from the situation in secular Europe and the conventional norms of professional journalism in the United States. The impact of commercialism on state-controlled media systems is not identical to the much-discussed effects in Western countries (Porto, 2008; Sakr, 2007; Zhao, 1998). Media pluralism in societies with a long history of ethnic and religious conflicts may not be conducive to more democratic expression, but, instead, it deepens divisions and violence (Ismail & Deane, 2008). Different historical and philosophical traditions of civil society suggest that opportunities for citizens' participation in media policies and performance are different from the West (Rodríguez, 2001; Waisbord, 2010).

Because these issues aren't common either in the United States or Britain, or for that matter in the West, they are notoriously understudied in the English-language literature. The significance of such questions is not simply that they address key issues and dynamics in the global South. Also, they reveal questions that are theoretically important to understand the intersection between media and politics. They raise important questions about arguments at the core of the field such as freedom of expression and democratic communication; the interaction between media, states, and markets; the professional identity of journalists; and media models.

The purpose of studying these issues is not simply to demonstrate that "things are different" outside the West. Rather, the goal is to put the spotlight on issues that, because they are not common in the West, help us rethink arguments and broaden analytical horizons. To return to the previously mentioned examples: How to think about press freedom in situations where the state does not function? Does media tabloidization nurture populist attitudes and movements across political regimes and countries? Does commercialization have positive effects on media systems tightly controlled by governments? Does media pluralism necessarily contribute to more democratic expression or feed sectarianism and polarization? Is there a single model of professional journalism? Are the prospects for civic actors to promote media reforms widely different around the world? If so, why?

Conduct Comparative Research

Comparative research is another strategy to de-Westernize media studies in the spirit of cosmopolitan scholarship. In recent decades, interest in comparative research in media and politics has grown considerably since Blumler and Gurevitch's (1975) seminal article. In an updated version of their original call for comparative research, Gurevitch and Blumler (2004, p. 327) argue that the importance of systematic comparison lies on the need "to understand how varying contexts (such as those generated by different types of state regimes and political institutions, cultural regions, levels of development, or media systems) shape processes of political communications." Recent studies (Esser & Pfetsch, 2004; Hallin & Mancini, 2004; Voltmer, 2008) have renewed interest in comparative research, and contributed to breaking away from past approaches that categorized media/press models in ideological terms (Siebert, Peterson & Schramm, 1956; for a critique, see Nerone, 1995). These studies shared the premise that conceptual and theoretical rigor requires conclusions informed by comparative analysis (also see Norris, 2009). Also, comparative research has been motivated by the need to break away from the "U.S.-centrism" of the literature. Because central arguments and theories in the literature reflect the singular characteristics of U.S. media and politics, it is necessary to probe the generalizability of those arguments and theories.

The main contribution of cross-national, comparative research is not just to make the field less parochial. As has been discussed in other disciplines, the comparative method yields stronger propositions and general theories that are relevant beyond particular contexts (Skocpol & Somers, 1980). Its main virtue is not to open up attention to different settings or to stimulate curiosity, but rather to provide more solid and nuanced theoretical conclusions.

Two types of comparative studies can be distinguished in the recent literature on media and politics. One type is implicitly comparative: studies examine the applicability of conclusions from one country (or media/ political systems) to another without conducting country-to-country comparison. The other type is explicitly comparative: studies compare certain phenomena (e.g., news content, election campaigning, media impact on political knowledge) in two or more countries. Implicit comparisons mainly test the applicability of U.S.-based conclusions in other settings. Examples of such an approach are studies of the impact of news frames on political attitudes and participation (Aarts & Semetko, 2003; de Vreese & Semetko, 2002); the influence of political elites on news content (Archetti, 2008; Sheafer & Wolfsfeld, 2009); the impact of the nature of media systems on citizen information (Curran et al., 2010); the consequence of political communication systems on voter turnout (Baek, 2009), and the dynamics of agenda setting and policy making (Baumgartner, Green-Pedersen, & Jones, 2006; Walgrave & Van Aelst, 2006). In contrast, explicit comparisons examine media and politics across two or more countries and explain differences and similarities. Recent examples are studies about news coverage of war and peace (Dimitrova & Stromback, 2005; Peng, 2008), immigration (Benson, 2010), media models (Hallin & Mancini, 2004), and presidential communication (Hallin & Mancini, 1984). The purpose of comparing news coverage, media systems, and the interaction between media and political systems and dynamics is to develop evidence-based, theoretical arguments that draw from more than one case.

These two types of comparative research have produced novel insights and refined previous arguments. For example, they have questioned the applicability of conclusions about a necessary link among news, cynicism, and participation that was originally developed in the United States. In the context of different media and elections, cynical frames do not necessarily suppress participation or fuel political cynicism (de Vreese & Semetko, 2002). Also, they have produced eloquent evidence showing that the public or commercial nature of media systems affects the quality of news and information levels among citizens (Curran et al., 2010). Similarly, cross-national analysis of news coverage of immigration, war, antiwar movements, and scandals (Canel & Sanders, 2006) suggests that the unique characteristics of media and political systems as well as the interaction between them do affect content (Dimitrova & Stromback, 2005; Peng, 2008). Since variation at the system level is most clearly seen via cross-national comparative studies, international research is best positioned to build more generalizable theory about the production of journalistically mediated political discourse.

The recent crop of comparative studies in political communication is overwhelmingly focused on the West. They typically test the applicability of arguments originally made in the U.S. context in European countries, or, alternately, compare developments and trends across Europe. This pattern is not surprising given the preeminent position of U.S.-based research in communication/media studies and political communication in particular. Also, geographical proximity coupled with regional academic networks and funding agencies has facilitated cross-national research in Europe. The fact that many European academics write fluently in English coupled with incentives in European universities (Lillis & Curry, 2010) to publish English-language journal articles and books has also stimulated comparative research.

Yet it would be mistaken to attribute this pattern only to the presence of pan-European academic networks and the global position of U.S. academia. One could reasonably suggest that the Western focus of recent comparative studies also reflects the fact that U.S./western European cases lend themselves better to comparative research. They seemingly meet key conditions for comparative cross-national studies, namely, to apply John Stuart Mill's) method of agreement and difference presented in *A System of Logic* (1843). The existence of "party-press" parallelism, public broadcasting systems, the tabloid press, and parliamentary systems make European countries fertile settings for cross-national comparisons. Also, the presence of common elements (e.g., stable democracies, common philosophical traditions) and important differences (media systems, political systems) on both sides of the North Atlantic facilitate comparisons between U.S. and European countries.

Comparing Western and non-Western cases presents more challenges. Not only do more variations have to be accounted for but significant similarities are harder to find. Comparative studies should select cases that are sufficiently similar yet different rather than focus on cases that are vastly different (Przeworski & Teune, 1970). Countries that are too different make it difficult to produce parsimonious arguments that control for possible variations and causal relations. This challenge is more difficult to address for explicit than for implicit comparisons. Comparisons between countries with substantially different media as well as political histories and dynamics have trouble accounting for multiple factors that explain differences or similarities. Instead, research designs that conduct implicit comparisons ("do conclusions based on country X apply to country Y?") can resolve that challenge more effectively.

Applied to non-Western contexts, implicit comparisons may provide fresh insights into questions and arguments that have dominated the study of media and politics in the West. Does the news media promote a "virtuous circle" (Norris, 2000) by stimulating political interest and participation across democracies? Do political elites consistently exercise similar power in indexing news (Bennett, 2005) across issues and countries? Does elite-dominated news consistently reduce the range of public issues and citizens' voices? Does soft news stimulate political interest among young citizens? Do new media (from cable television to "social media") exacerbate political polarization? What factors influence news coverage of terrorism? How do new social movements use new information technologies to voice demands and advance political goals? Do different media promote or suppress political participation? Do "post-broadcast" media (Prior, 2007) reinforce in-equalities in access to political information? Why is the apparent crisis of newspapers and journalism in the United States less pronounced in many countries in the South? How do civic associations make news? How does civil society shape processes of media reform?

In summary, recent case studies that test the applicability of propositions produced in other political-media settings as well as comparative research conducted in Europe show two fruitful strategies for de-Westernization. Both research designs share an interest in exploring whether and why "context matters" to explain similarities and differences in the interaction between media and politics. They show the usefulness of case studies and small-N comparisons to refine theoretical conclusions.

Analyze Trans-Border, Global Questions

A third approach to de-Westernizing is to analyze empirical questions that transcend national and regional boundaries. These are trans-border, global issues that are seldom foregrounded in local/national case studies. By studying a phenomenon or process at a global scale, research highlights commonalities and differences, and explores causes, characteristics, and consequences.

One possible line of research is to study "global media events" that either deliberately or unexpectedly transcend local borders. "Planned" global media events (Dayan & Katz, 1992)—for example, the Olympics, the World Cup, U.S. presidential inaugurations, coronations, state funerals—which are designed to be experienced by astonishingly large audiences, raise interesting questions about the dynamics of media globalization, audience interpretations, the nexus between the local and the global, and the politics of news coverage. In contrast, "unplanned" media events are news that transcend the political/media boundaries of one country and become the subject of coverage and discussion worldwide. The "Mohammed cartoon crisis" (Eide, Kunelius, & Phillips, 2008) is one recent example. What initially was a local news event quickly became global. Global press coverage, reaction, and the political aftermath brought up important questions about global journalistic ethics, international news, and public diplomacy. Given that any media content may "go viral" and global on the Internet, such news events are likely to become regular features of globalized media politics.

Another set of "global questions" refer to planetary developments, that is, trends and phenomena that are not limited to one country or region. Recent examples include the globalization of news practices and ideals (Cohen et al., 1996); the "modernization/Americanization" of politics (Scammell, 1998; Swanson & Mancini, 1996); the "mediatization of politics" (Canel & Sanders, 2006; Strömbäck, 2008); the personalization of politics (McAllister, 2007); the professionalization of politics (Esser, Reinemann, & Fan, 2001; Holtz-Bacha et al., 2007); media populism (Mazzoleni & Schulz, 1999); the adoption of similar communication strategies by insurrectionary groups across the world (Bob, 2005); and the use of mobile telephony and other new informational platforms for civic participation (Aday & Livingston, 2008). Because these developments transcend the national boundaries of political and media systems, they need to be examined across borders. If they are not unique to one national media-political system, then it is reasonable to presume that globalizing dynamics underlie those processes.

This line of research shows that both the forces of homogenization and heterogenization are at work. Similar developments across media and political systems may have comparable causes but they do not necessarily have identical consequences. Instead, they reflect how global events and trends, disseminated by transnational institutions and technologies, play into local and national dynamics. Similar trends (e.g., media commercialization, the crisis of political parties, dumbed-down news) facilitate the rise of similar processes worldwide. Yet they are integrated within specific processes anchored in the logic of local media and political institutions.

In summary, the three lines of research presented in this section are possible strategies to "de-Westernize" media studies and promote cosmopolitan scholarship.

Globalization and Cosmopolitan Media Studies

Academic politics, however, may not strongly favor cosmopolitan scholarship. Despite academic enthusiasm for cosmopolitanism and the globalization of scholarship, cosmopolitan perspectives do not easily fit the conventions of academic research. The turn to cosmopolitanism may not necessarily lead to significant epistemological shifts or serious questioning of the premises of media studies. Undoubtedly, globalization has facilitated communication and academic links from around the world. The global networks of academic knowledge, such as information technologies, professional institutions, and international meetings, ease up connectivity. Such processes, however, does not necessarily motivate the major analytical and research shifts envisioned by Beck. Such processes bring new impetus and add novel questions to academic agendas, yet this is far from causing scholars to reconsider research and theoretical approaches. Cosmopolitan media studies bump up against the realities of academic work, namely, the persistent pull of local/national studies.

Locality continues to provide strong incentives for selecting topics, adopting perspectives, and framing academic research. Geographical proximity, research opportunities, language, and existing professional networks tilt research toward local and national issues. The "case study" approach to analyzing questions within the confines of the "nation-state," the dominant analytical unit of modern social thought (Gerring, 2007), remains enormously attractive. It is questionable whether cosmopolitan scholarship supersedes "national" approaches or, instead, produces important yet limited changes in the conceptualization of research questions. A globalized academia, as an interconnected community of world scholars, is compatible with the preeminence of local and national questions.

The other challenge is that inequalities in the global production of academic knowledge continue to stack the deck in favor of scholarship about U.S., and to a lesser extent, European media politics. The primacy of English as the lingua franca of global academia, the staggering amount of research produced in the United States, and well-established North-to-South flows of knowledge foreground research about the U.S. media and politics. Specialists in media and politics in the West may not find it necessary to globalize research interests or interrogate analytical approaches as long as the examination of developments and evidence in the West is deemed sufficient to produce relevant knowledge. Notwithstanding academic globalization, research agendas may still have a strong Anglo-American flavor and limit the impact of cosmopolitan scholarship. Given the weight of local factors in determining research agendas and the continuous presence of preceding flows of academic knowledge, the call to "de-Westernization" may powerfully resonate with media scholars in the West and the rest of the world, yet it may lead to major renovation of research priorities.

These challenges make it necessary to stimulate cosmopolitan perspectives through platforms that shape academic production and research agendas. Professional associations, funding agencies, academic curricula, journals, and book series need to stimulate globalized debates and research in ways that contribute to strengthening media theory. To be clear, I am not suggesting that only global questions push analytical horizons and produce better theory. Geographical scope neither determines the quality nor the theoretical relevance of the contributions. "Case expertise" remains critical to probe and flesh out theoretical propositions, and determine whether and how "context matters" in mediated politics. At the present juncture, however, a cosmopolitan outlook is necessary to "de-Westernize" media studies. Studying cases engaged with broad theoretical discussions, conducting comparative, cross-national research, and analyzing global developments and trends may, hopefully, make the field more inclusive and produce more nuanced propositions.

Conclusions

Unquestionably, the field of media studies has become less U.S.-centric in the last two decades. Renewed interest among European researchers has largely helped to probe conclusions originally developed in the United States. Ongoing collaboration among professional and individual networks and support from European Union agencies and foundations continue to drive this trend in promising directions (e.g., Koopmans and Statham, 2010). Simultaneously, the steady publication of "international studies" in books and journals has expanded the availability of "non-Western" cases in English.

Further cross-regional dialogue and collaboration is necessary. In a globalized world, "area studies" is not conducive to multiple-way conversations, but rather it solidifies inward-looking debates. Cosmopolitan scholarship, instead, offers an alternative that will further decentralize the field and facilitate collaboration around common theoretical and empirical questions. Yet cosmopolitan media studies requires institutional conditions that are not strongly developed yet. Moreover, funding sources, language barriers, and geographical distance limit the potential of globalized research. It is imperative to discuss ways to make media studies not only more receptive but also more engaged with arguments and perspectives from around the world.

REFERENCES

Aarts, K., & Semetko, H. A. (2003). The divided electorate: Media use and political involvement. *Journal of Politics* 65 (3): 759–84.

Aday, S., & Livingston, S. (2008). Taking the state out of state-media relations theory: How transnational advocacy networks are changing the press-state dynamic. *Media, War & Conflict* 1 (1): 99–107.

Appadurai, A. (2001). *Globalization*. Durham, NC: Duke University Press.

Appiah, A. (2007). *Cosmopolitanism: Ethics in a world of strangers*. New York: W. W. Norton.

Archetti, C. (2008). News coverage of 9/11 and the demise of the media flows, globalization and localization hypotheses. *International Communication Gazette* 70 (6): 463–85.

Baek, M. (2009). A comparative analysis of political communication systems and voter turnout. *American Journal of Political Science* 53 (2): 376–93.

Bates, R. H. (1997). Area studies and the discipline: A useful controversy? *PS: Political Science and Politics* 30 (2): 166–69.

Baumgartner, F. R., Green-Pedersen, C., & Jones, B. D. (2006). Comparative studies of policy agendas. *Journal of European Public Policy* 13 (7): 959–74.

Beck, U. (2007). The cosmopolitan condition: Why methodological nationalism fails. *Theory, Culture & Society* 24 (7–8): 286–90.

Beck, U., & Sznaider, N. (2010). Unpacking cosmopolitanism for the social sciences: A research agenda. *British Journal of Sociology* 61:381–403.

Bennett, W. L. (2005). *News: The politics of illusion*. New York: Longman.

Benson, R. (2010). What makes for a critical press? A case study of French and U.S. immigration news coverage. *International Journal of Press/Politics* 15 (1): 3–24.

Binderkrantz, A. S., & Green-Pedersen, C. (2009). Policy or processes in focus? *International Journal of Press/Politics* 14 (2): 166–85.

Blumler, J. G., & Gurevitch, M. (1975). Towards a comparative framework for political communication research. In S. H. Chaffe, ed., *Political communication: Issues and strategies for research* (pp. 165–95). London: Sage.

Bob, C. (2005). *The marketing of rebellion*. New York: Cambridge University Press.

Bourdieu, P. (1988). *Homo academicus. Trans.* P. Collier. Cambridge: Polity Press.

Canel, M. J., & Sanders, K. (2006). *Morality tales: Political scandals and journalism in Britain and Spain in the 1990s*. Creskill, NJ: Hampton Press.

Caney, S. (2005). *Justice beyond borders: A global political theory*. New York: Oxford University Press.

Chouliaraki, L. (2006). *The spectatorship of suffering*. London: Sage Publications.

Cohen, A. A., Levy, M., Roeh, I., & Gurevitch, M. (1996). *Global newsrooms, local audiences: A study of the Eurovision news exchange*. London: Libbey.

Curran, J., & Park, M.-J., eds. (2000). *De-Westernizing media studies*. London: Routledge.

Curran, J., Salovaara-Moring, I., Coen, S., & Iyengar, S. (2010). Crime, foreigners and hard news: A cross-national comparison of reporting and public perception. *Journalism* 11 (1): 3–19.

Dallmayr, F. (2003). Cosmopolitanism: Moral and political. *Political Theory* 31 (3): 421–42.

Dayan, D., & Katz, E. (1992). *Media events: The live broadcasting of history*. Cambridge, MA: Harvard University Press.

de Burgh, H., ed. (2005). *Making journalists: Diverse models, global issues*. New York: Routledge.

de Vreese, C. H., & Semetko, H. A. (2002). Cynical and engaged: Strategic campaign coverage, public opinion, and mobilization in a referendum. *Communication Research* 29 (6): 615–41.

Dimitrova, D. V., & Stromback, J. (2005). Mission accomplished? Framing of the Iraq War in the elite newspapers in Sweden and the United States. *International Communication Gazette* 67 (5): 399–417.

Eide, E., Kunelius, R., & Phillips, A. (2008). *Transnational media events: The Mohammed cartoons and the imagined clash of civilizations*. Göteborg: Nordicom.

Elenbaas, M., & De Vreese, C. H. (2008). The effects of strategic news on political cynicism and vote choice among young voters. *Journal of Communication* 58 (3): 550–67.

Epstein, D., Boden, R., Deem, R., Rizvi, F., & Wright, S., eds. (2007). *Geographies of knowledge, geometries of power: Framing the future of higher education*. New York: Routledge.

Esser, F., & Pfetsch, B. (2004). *Comparing political communication: Theories, cases, and challenges*. New York: Cambridge University Press.

Esser, F., Reinemann, C., & Fan, D. (2001). Spin doctors in the United States, Great Britain, and Germany: Metacommunication about media manipulation. *Harvard International Journal of Press/Politics* 6 (1): 16–45.

Fine, R. (2007). *Cosmopolitanism*. London: Routledge.

Fox, E., & Waisbord, S. R. (2002). *Latin politics, global media*. Austin: University of Texas Press.

Franco, J. (1988). Beyond ethnocentrism: Gender, power, and the third-world intelligentsia. In C. Nelson & L. Grossberg, eds., *Marxism and the interpretation of culture* (pp. 503–15). Urbana: University of Illinois Press.

Geertz, C. (1973). *The interpretation of cultures*. New York: Basic Books.

Gerring, J. (2007). The case study: What it is and what it does. In C. Boix & S. Stokes, eds., *The Oxford handbook of comparative politics* (pp. 90–122). Oxford: Oxford University Press.

Giddens, A. (1990). *The consequences of modernity*. Stanford, CA: Stanford University Press.

Godrej, F. (2009). Response to "what is comparative political theory?" *Review of Politics* 71 (4): 567–82.

Graham, L., & Kantor, J.-M. (2007). "Soft" area studies versus "hard" social science: A false opposition. *Slavic Review* 66 (1): 1–19.

Gurevitch, M., & Blumler, J. G. (2004). State of the art of comparative political communication research: Poised for maturity? In F. Esser & B. Pfetsch, eds., *Comparing political communication: Theories, cases, and challenges*. New York: Cambridge University Press.

Hallin, D. C., & Mancini, P. (1984). Speaking of the president: Political structure and representational form in U.S. and Italian television news. *Theory and Society* 13 (6): 829–50.

Hallin, D. C., & Mancini, P. (2004). *Comparing media systems: Three models of media and politics*. New York: Cambridge University Press.

Hansen, D. T. (2008). Curriculum and the idea of a cosmopolitan inheritance. *Journal of Curriculum Studies* 40 (3): 289–312.

Harbeson, J. W. (1997). Area studies and the disciplines: A rejoinder. *Issue: A Journal of Opinion* 25 (1): 29–31.

Held, D. (1995). *Democracy and the global order: From the modern state to cosmopolitan governance*. Stanford, CA: Stanford University Press.

Holtz-Bacha, C., Mancini, P., Negrine, R., & Papathanassopoulos, S. (2007). *The professionalization of political communication.* Bristol, UK: Intellect.

Ismail, J. A., & Deane, J. (2008). The 2007 general election in Kenya and its aftermath: The role of local language media. *International Journal of Press/Politics* 13 (3): 319–27.

Katz, E., Peters, J. D., Liebes, T., & Orloff, A., eds. (2003). *Canonic texts in media research: Are there any? Should there be? How about these?* Malden, MA: Polity Press.

Koopmans, R., & Statham, P., eds. (2010). *The making of a European public sphere: Media discourse and political contention.* New York: Cambridge University Press.

Kratoska, P. H., Raben, R., & Schulte Nordholt, H., eds. (2005). *Locating Southeast Asia: Geographies of knowledge and politics of space.* Athens: Ohio University Press.

Lee, F. L. F., & Chan, J. M. (2008). Professionalism, political orientation, and perceived self-censorship: A survey study of Hong Kong journalists. *Issues and Studies* 44 (1): 205–38.

Lilleker, D. G., & Lees-Marshment, J. (2005). *Political marketing: A comparative perspective.* New York: Palgrave.

Lillis, T., & Curry, M. J. (2010). *Academic writing in a global context: The politics and practices of publishing in English.* London: Routledge.

Mazzoleni, G., & Schulz, W. (1999). "Mediatization" of politics: A challenge for democracy? *Political Communication* 16 (3): 247–61.

Mazzoleni, G., Stewart, J., & Horsfield, B. (2003). *The media and neo-populism: A contemporary comparative analysis.* Westport, CA: Praeger.

McAllister, I. (2007). The personalization of politics. In R. J. Dalton & H. D. Klingemann, eds., *The Oxford handbook of political behavior* (pp. 571–88). Oxford: Oxford University Press.

McCargo, D. (2008). *Tearing apart the land: Islam and legitimacy in southern Thailand.* Ithaca, NY: Cornell University Press.

McFarlane, C. (2006). Knowledge, learning and development: A post-rationalist approach. *Progress in Development Studies* 6 (4): 287–305.

Mill, J. S. (1843/1956). *A system of logic.* New York: Longmans, Green.

Miller, T. (2009). Media studies 3.0. *Television and New Media* 10 (1): 5–6.

Mills, C. W. (1959). *The sociological imagination.* New York: Oxford University Press.

Nerone, J. C., ed. (1995). *Last rights: Revisiting four theories of the press.* Urbana: University of Illinois Press.

Norris, P. (2000). *A virtuous circle: Political communications in postindustrial societies.* New York: Cambridge University Press.

Norris, P. (2009). Comparative political communications: Common frameworks or Babelian confusion? *Government and Opposition* 44 (3): 321–40.

Nugent, D. (2010). Knowledge and empire: The social sciences and United States imperial expansion. *Identities* 17 (1): 2–44.

Nussbaum, M. (1996). Patriotism and cosmopolitanism. In J. Cohen, ed., *For love of country?* (pp. 3–18). Boston: Beacon Press.

Ong, J. C. (2009). The cosmopolitan continuum: Locating cosmopolitanism in media and cultural studies. *Media, Culture & Society* 31 (3): 449–66.

Peng, Z. (2008). Framing the anti-war protests in the global village: A comparative study of newspaper coverage in three countries. *International Communication Gazette* 70 (5): 361–77.

Porto, M. P. (2008). Democratization and election news coverage in Brazil. In J. Strömbäck & L. L. Kaid, eds., *The handbook of election news coverage around the world.* New York: Routledge.

Prior, M. (2007). *Post-broadcast democracy: How media choice increases inequality in political involvement and polarizes elections.* New York: Cambridge University Press.

Przeworski, A., & Teune, H. (1970). *The logic of comparative social inquiry.* New York: Wiley-Interscience.

Rafael, V. L. (1994). The cultures of area studies in the United States. *Social Text* 41:91–111.

Rodríguez, C. (2001). *Fissures in the mediascape: An international study of citizens' media.* Cresskill, NJ: Hampton Press.

Romano, A. R., & Bromley, M. (2005). *Journalism and democracy in Asia.* New York: Routledge.

Rudolph, S. H. (2005). The imperialism of categories: Situating knowledge in a globalizing world. *Perspectives on Politics* 3 (1): 5–14.

Sakr, N. (2007). *Arab television today.* New York: I. B. Tauris.

Scammell, M. (1998). The wisdom of the war room: US campaigning and Americanization. *Media, Culture & Society* 20 (2): 251–75.

Sheafer, T., & Wolfsfeld, G. (2009). Party systems and oppositional voices in the news media: A study of the contest over political waves in the United States and Israel. *International Journal of Press/Politics* 14 (2): 146–65.

Siebert, F. S., Peterson, T., & Schramm, W. (1956). *Four theories of the press: The authoritarian, libertarian, social responsibility and Soviet communist concepts of what the press should be and do.* Urbana: University of Illinois Press.

Silverstone, R. (2006). *Media and morality: On the rise of the mediapolis.* Cambridge: Polity Press.

Simpson, C. (1998). *Universities and empire: Money and politics in the social sciences during the Cold War.* New York: New Press.

Skocpol, T., & Somers, M. (1980). The uses of comparative history in macrosocial inquiry. *Comparative Studies in Society and History* 22 (2): 174–97.

Sparks, C. (2008). Media systems in transition: Poland, Russia, China. *Chinese Journal of Communication* 1 (1): 7–24.

Strömbäck, J. (2008). Four phases of mediatization: An analysis of the mediatization of politics. *International Journal of Press/Politics* 13 (3): 228–46.

Strömbäck, J., & Kaid, L. L. (2008). *The handbook of election news coverage around the world.* New York: Routledge.

Swanson, D. L., & Mancini, P. (1996). *Politics, media, and modern democracy: An international study of innovations in electoral campaigning and their consequences.* Westport, CT: Praeger.

Szanton, D. L. (2004). *The politics of knowledge: Area studies and the disciplines.* Berkeley: University of California Press.

Thussu, D. K. (2009). Why internationalize media studies and how? In D. K. Thussu, ed., *Internationalizing media studies.* London: Routledge.

Vliegenthart, R., Schuck, A. R. T., Boomgaarden, H. G., & De Vreese, C. H. (2008). News coverage and support for European integration, 1990–2006. *International Journal of Public Opinion Research* 20 (4): 415–39.

Voltmer, K. (2006). *Mass media and political communication in new democracies*. New York: Routledge.

Voltmer, K. (2008). Comparing media systems in new democracies: East meets South meets West. *Central European Journal of Communication* 1 (1): 23–40.

Waisbord, S. (2007). Democratic journalism and "statelessness." *Political Communication* 24 (2): 115–29.

Waisbord, S. (2010). The pragmatic politics of media reform: Media movements and coalition-building in Latin America. *Global Media and Communication* 6 (2): 133–53.

Walgrave, S., & Van Aelst, P. (2006). The contingency of the mass media's political agenda setting power: Toward a preliminary theory. *Journal of Communication* 56 (1): 88–109.

Ward, S. J. A., & Wasserman, H. (2010). *Media ethics beyond borders: A global perspective*. New York: Routledge.

Yudice, G. (2003). Rethinking area and ethnic studies in the context of economic and political restructuring. In J. Poblete, ed., *Critical Latin American and Latino studies* (pp. 76–102). Minneapolis: University of Minnesota Press.

Yusha'u, M. J. (2009). Investigative journalism and scandal reporting in the Nigerian press. *Ecquid Novi: African Journalism Studies* 30 (2): 155–74.

Zhao, Y. (1998). *Media, market, and democracy in China: Between the party line and the bottom line*. Urbana: University of Illinois Press.

NOTE

1. Arguably, area studies never achieved the same level of institutionalization in media studies as in other disciplines such as political science, history, and literature in the United States during the past half century. The analysis of this issue falls outside the scope of this paper, and needs further attention. Three reasons should be explored: the "late" development of communication/media studies compared to other disciplines and fields in the social sciences and humanities, the different power of various disciplines in leading universities, and the amount of public and private funding received from foundations and government agencies channeled to the development of areas studies after World War II.

CHAPTER TEN

Local Experiences, Cosmopolitan Theories

On Cultural Relevance in International Communication Research

Chin-Chuan Lee

Today's world is in fact a world of mixtures, of migrations, of cross-ings over.
—Edward W. Said (2000, p. 287)

From the particular, you may ascend to the general; but from the general theory there is no way back to the intuitive understanding of the particular.
—Leopold von Ranke (1795–1886), as quoted in Ringer (1997, p. 11)

When a British colleague asked me for a take on my experience as a teacher of international communication at a midwestern U.S. university, I quipped half-jokingly, "American students tend to define their country as an opposite rather than as a part of the international system." Hence "international" students are "foreign" students whereas "international" communication is defined, reductively and by default, as "non-U.S." communication. Just as baseball's pinnacle event in North America is called the "World Series," the International Communication Association (ICA) has been "international" primarily in the sense of holding an annual conference at a Hilton or Sheraton hotel in an overseas metropolis once every four years.[1]

Citing his survey of curriculum and introductory texts in major U.S. universities, Downing (2009, p. 274) observes that the trend in international media studies is "strongly in the direction of insularity rather than internationalism." If the Western-cum-global model symbolizes "the imperialism of the universal" (Bourdieu, 2001), then this "globalized" model in fact originated from "the parochialism of the particular" (the term coined after Pierre Bourdieu) writ universal.

The need to internationalize media studies has increasingly been recognized, with the impetus coming from scholars who do not conform strictly to the U.S. mainstream orbit and especially from those who have cross-cultural or multicultural experiences. Downing (1996) questioned the representativeness of media studies based on a few affluent, stable democracies with Protestant histories and imperial entanglements with the rest of the world. Curran and Park (2000, p. 3) took the first initiative to "de-Westernize media studies," editing a volume as "part of a growing reaction against the self-absorption and parochialism of much western media theory." Curran (2005, p. xiii) further criticized two forms of myopia: "the inward orientation of American journalism research" and "the spurious universality of European media and cultural theory." More recent albeit uneven attempts at de-Westernizing media studies have been made by Thussu (2009) and Wang (2011). It is fair to say that these sober voices have been murmured from a position of relative marginality; only those on the margin are more inclined to cross over and intersect various modes of knowledge.

The foreground of today's calls for "internationalizing" international communication research is set against the larger post–Cold War background that gave the United States an added sense of political triumphalism and cultural complacency. The United States proclaimed itself "bound to lead" (Nye, 1990) in the "new world order," oriented toward the neoliberal regime of the "Washington consensus." Instead of broadening international or cross-cultural dialogue, the rhetoric of globalization is often honed to promote strategic policy vantage points of the United States—to the point that we can legitimately ask if globalization is a thinly veiled disguise of the "manifest destiny" ideology. Fukuyama's "end of history" thesis (Fukuyama, 1992) posits, in a self-congratulatory way, liberalism's victory over fascism and communism as a final answer to history. Huntington (1993), a former advocate of the by-now bankrupt modernization theory, advances a bewilderingly reductive, fundamentalist, and exaggerated scenario of conflicts between Western, Confucian, and Islamic civilizations. His focal concern was not so much with the resolution of civilization-based clashes as it was with the potential threats of such clashes to dominant U.S. interests and Western values. International communication studies have not made much progress despite the marching trumpet of globalization.

In this chapter, I shall first argue that the extreme form of positivistic methodology, with its bent for subsuming cultural specificity to abstract generality, has reinforced the Western-cum-universal epistemology and practices. By way of making my point, I shall take the liberty of drawing on my own intellectual biography to reflect on what I consider to be the pitfalls of the once dominant paradigm of international communication in the United States. Seeing this methodological flaw as deriving in part from cultural vacuousness, I shall plead that we give the Weberian-phenomenological methodology its due attention, and take cultural meaning more seriously instead of treating it as an antecedent, a consequence, or a residual category of sociological or psychological variables.

Several preliminary remarks are in order. First, we must reject both the dominant view and the nativistic view. As Said (1978, p. 247) argues eloquently, cultures and civilizations are hybrid, heterogeneous, and "so interrelated and interdependent as to beggar any unitary or simply delineated description of their individuality." Such hegemonic views as Fukuyama (1992) and Huntington (1993) foreclose alternative thought and equal dialogue. On the opposite side, the nativistic reactions of Lee Kuan Yew's "Asian values" or Beijing-defined "Confucian ethos" represent self-righteous, arrogant, and anti-liberal backlashes against democracy (Lee, 2001). Second, social sciences are an art of managing the creative tension between generality and specificity. Universality that obliterates specificity is both hegemonic and colonial, while specificity without general implications is self-defeating. Cultural interpretation gives life to rich specificity that is dialectically interactive with generality; it also enlivens the meanings of generality by giving specificity a pride of place. Third, social sciences have a relatively brief history in the West and were not introduced into China until the late nineteenth century. Media studies are not yet fully institutionalized in today's China, where a nation of eager teachers and students have been groping for directions in the way of language, paradigms, epistemology, and methodology. Mutual borrowing is both necessary and healthy only if it is done as a critical choice and without losing one's firm cultural grips.

Pitfalls of the (Once) Dominant Paradigm

I was attracted to the emerging field of international communication in the early 1970s by way of exposure to several seminal works in "development communication." Daniel Lerner, Wilbur Schramm, and Everett M. Rogers were the leading proponents of this paradigm. They sought to explain the role and functions of the media in the process of national development, which was part of modernization theory, as conceived by American social scientists with the active encouragement of the U.S. government, on the assumption that economic growth held a key to democracy (Diamond, 1992). The newly emerging nations pursued national development projects with a vengeance from the 1950s to 1970s, at a time when the United States was at the peak of its global expansion and meanwhile pushing forward its Cold War agendas to prevent Communist encroachment.[2]

Lerner: The Passing of Traditional Society

Of the trio, both Schramm and Rogers acknowledged their intellectual debt to Lerner. Since Schramm (1964) was not based on primary research, I shall focus on the other two but start with Lerner's (1958) pioneering *The Passing of Traditional Society.* Lerner (1958) was a work of central importance to international communication research but curiously peripheral to the sociology of modernization. My point of concern in this chapter will focus on how Lerner went about mustering "evidence" both epistemologically and methodologically to make his theoretical case.

Based on a reanalysis of survey data originally conducted to test the effectiveness of U.S. propaganda vis-à-vis Soviet propaganda in the Middle East, Lerner proposed this model of modernization:

> Increasing industrialization has raised urbanization; rising urbanization has tended to raise literacy; rising literacy has tended to raise media exposure; increasing exposure has tended to increase political participation in economic and political life. (p. 46)

Lerner argues that the key to the *passing* of traditional society is to rid people of their fatalism. Individuals must collectively develop what he calls "empathy" or "psychic mobility," a modernizing personality that enabled people to discard fatalism and, further, to imagine beyond the narrow confines of their immediate roles and contexts. Mass media were conceived of as the "magic multiplier" of empathy and a crucial catalyst for social change. As more and more people acquire empathic capacity, the whole nation (as if it were a linear aggregate of individuals) would break off from the yoke of tradition and enter the threshold of modernization.

Various criticisms made of Lerner should be by now familiar, such as (see Lee, 1980, pp. 17–24): (a) rigidly segregating tradition from modernity instead of fostering a creative synthesis; (b) using a psychological variable (empathy) to explain the macro-societal transformation to the exclusion of acute structural constraints, global domination, imperialism, and post-colonial conditions; (c) imposing the Western pathway to modernization as a universal process, and thus contradicting the historical evidence showing a multiplicity of modernization routes in the West itself; and, also, (4) ignoring the differences in structural conditions between late development (the Third World) and early development (the European nations).

Lerner declared (1958, p. 79) that "what America is—to condense a rule more powerful than its numerous exceptions—the modernizing Middle East seeks to become." In his view, the Middle East would have to walk through the same linear path that the United States had trodden. The American experience was not only relevant to the geographical region called "the West" but was projected as a "globally" valid model. He rejected the calls made by the emerging nations for alternative models as "ethnocentric predicament" and "a formidable obstacle to modernization" (p. ix). Lerner's logically circular claim on a linear model of modernization, however, flies in the face of historical evidence presented by Moore (1967) and Tilly (1975). Moore showed that there were multiple pathways to modernization among the Western nations. Tilly argued that the Western model was an unintended consequence of an extractive, repressive, and coercive process; it was indeed considered a "lucky shot" that could not be reproduced.

Committed to a teleological vision, Lerner argued that the whole theoretical landscape required "some principle of unity in diversity" (p. 77). What does this mean? "By making explicit the regularities we document the process; by noting the deviations we locate each country in its proper phase" (p. 89). Generality subsumes exceptions. He thus postulated Turkey and Lebanon at the top of modernism (read: Westernization), Egypt and Syria in the middle, with Jordan and Iran at the bottom. Methodologically, Lerner set out to craft a series of six single-country narratives, which Harold D. Lasswell praised as "brilliantly arresting" (cited on the book cover). Each country narrative was a mix of historical facts, anecdotes, and secondary data geared toward constructing "a theory of modernization that articulates the common compulsion to which all Middle Eastern peoples are subject." Three comments should be made. First, these country narratives, however vivid or arresting, are only "illustrative" of his committed position at best; they do not offer a strong "proof" or fair test of his theoretical model. Second, it is critical to pay close attention to the "considerable latitude" he had admittedly taken to treat "specific topics that varied from one country to another," in order to discuss the "salient connections between communication, economic, and political behavior" (pp. 103–4). Each country story, by itself, is telling enough. But *selective* use of facts, topical emphases, and interpretations might have rendered these narratives not consistently comparable with reference to posited "salient connections" across six countries. As a whole, the theoretical edifice may thus sit on a shaky empirical ground. Third, given his penchant for pursuing "unity in diversity," Lerner tended to cast aside "deviant" cases that did not fit into his explanatory system as countries "not yet modernized" instead of treating such counter-evidence as an invitation for rethinking his model. It did not occur to Lerner that his model might be limited, one-sided, or wrong (as many of his critics later pointed out).

Rogers: Diffusion of Innovations

The diffusion of innovation was regarded as one of the "invisible colleges" (Crane, 1972) for scholarly investigation. *Diffusion of Innovations*, a popular text that Everett M. Rogers spent his entire career updating, was reissued in five editions over a span of four decades. Rogers tried to establish a propositional inventory as a middle-range meeting ground to bridge theoretical concepts and empirical findings. The first edition of this text (Rogers, 1962) sifted through 405 studies, mostly conducted in the United States and Europe. The second edition listed 103 propositions that were digested from 1,500 studies; the sharp takeoff in the number of studies conducted in the developing world in the 1960s gave Rogers much confidence to subtitle this edition "a cross-cultural approach" (Rogers & Shoemaker, 1971). Claiming to be even "less culture-bound," Rogers (1983) distilled 91 propositions out of 3,085 studies, 30 percent of which originated from the developing nations. Rogers (1995) estimated the total number of diffusion publications at 4,000, which was rising to 5,200 articles shortly before his death (Rogers, 2003).

The structure of propositional inventory was retained in all five editions, but only the second edition (Rogers & Shoemaker, 1971) offered a "scoreboard" to track the "popularity" of each proposition, for example:

5–29   Earlier adopters (of innovation) have a higher degree of opinion leadership than late adopters (42 studies, or 76 percent, support; 13 studies do not support).

5–30   Earlier adopters are more likely to belong to systems with modern rather than traditional norms than are later adopters (32 studies, or 70 percent, support; 14 studies do not support). (pp. 375–76)

In retrospect, it must have been this kind of prima facie scientific cogency that enticed this beginning graduate student to stake his career on the emerging field of communication. It was much later before I became well aware of the harsh criticisms made of Rogers. Downs and Mohr (1976) faulted Rogers's propositions as empirically too inconsistent to be interpreted. Rogers (1983, p. 132) was probably legitimate in his defense that the diffusion research compared favorably with other branches of social sciences in terms of consistency, but I suspect as a synthesizer he might have (inevitably) smoothed out the rough edges of empirical findings from the disparate literature to make them seem less conflicting. More serious was McAnany's (1984) criticism that Rogers's propositions were too crude for theory-building. For me, it is even more pertinent to ask another question in this context: How should anomalous findings be treated? Should they be dismissed purely as "nuisances" and "exceptions" to the "general rule," or should they prompt a critical reflection on the validity of the postulated model?

Even though many diffusion studies had originated from the developing countries, these studies were neither comparative nor "cross-cultural," but seemed to directly replicate or reproduce the deeply embedded middle-class American assumptions, frameworks, and worldviews in overseas outposts.[3] Over the life span of his text, Rogers did a few rounds of revision. He first took the "dominant paradigm" to task for displaying pro-innovation and pro-individualism biases (Rogers, 1983), then proposed a convergence model in place of the liner diffusion model (Rogers, 1995, p. xvi), and finally added new topics (the Internet, the AIDS epidemic, and world terrorism) to the diffusion process (Rogers, 2003). But none of these attempts have come close to addressing the fundamental criticisms of modernization theory that informed the diffusion research.

Methodologically, the diffusionists have skirted around, if not bypassed, three major issues in comparative research (Smelser, 1976, p. 166): (a) Are the social units comparable with one another? (b) Are the abstract variables applicable to the dissimilar units that have been selected for study? (c) Are the indicators of the independent and dependent variables comparable from one sociocultural context to another? It goes without saying that comparative analysts must grapple with the issues of conceptual and empirical equivalences across different systems. What's more, according to Smelser, sociocultural contexts might exert pressure on the articulation of the theory-data connections. Rogers seems to assume the diffusion process as unitary, universal, and invariant with respect to sociocultural contexts. Rogers (2003) collected many story tidbits from various cultures, as intriguing as Lerner's individual country narratives, but these stories only served to exemplify a stated position rather than to reflect on theoretical or methodological premises.

The diffusion of knowledge has in general been flowing from center to periphery, from developed to developing countries, and from the West to the East. Academic hegemony is exercised not through coercion but via the conditioning of certain beliefs and assumptions which, if internalized or codified, may lead to an entrenched system of intellectual dependency without conscious reflection, resistance, or challenge. Despite its waning popularity in international communication, the diffusion research is still going strong in such applied fields as marketing, health, or agricultural extension. As we witness a weakening influence of this paradigm in the global center, it has continued to exert considerable authority in the world periphery. This lack of self-consciousness and self-confidence in the Third World shows the obstinacy of the underlying structure of academic hegemony. If we can take something positive from the postmodern turn, it would be the possibility of decentering and multipolar centers, such that the periphery can someday become a center. That makes maintaining scholarly vigilance and cultural self-consciousness particularly crucial. What is the value of "cross-cultural" studies if they simply serve to endorse the propositions of middle-class American worldviews?

The Weberian-Phenomenological Approach

Lerner tailored different Middle East countries to his theoretical model, and Rogers ended up with rather ad hoc and "on the one hand, on the other hand" sort of findings. Both of them were in conformity with the dominant U.S. ideology. What seems seriously absent from the established frameworks is the much-needed sensitivity to the Weberian-phenomenological interpretations of cross-cultural meanings *by* and *of* social actors, thick description of deep motives and complex consequences, and ample allowance for multiple realities to be constructed by different cross-cultural interpretive communities (Berger & Kellner, 1981; Ringer, 1997).[4]

"Web of Significance": Causality and Meaning

Patterned after the natural sciences, positivistic social sciences aim to reduce the complex web of social phenomena to a parsimonious structure consisting of a handful of dominant variables and thus to establish causation between them—best of all, to express such causal relationships formally in mathematical terms (Luckmann, 1978). Interpretative social sciences, informed by humanistic studies, seek to elucidate and give order to layers of complex meanings in the "structure of feelings" (Williams, 1977) by means of "thick description" (Geertz, 1973). Whitehead used to say this about positivism: "Seek simplicity, and distrust it." Carey (1992) twisted it to describe the culturalist approach: "Seek complexity, but order it." The Weberian-phenomenological approach is the most important interpretive epistemology and methodology that tries to strike a middle ground between science and the humanities. What can we learn from it to enrich international communication research?

Weber's methodology obviously cannot be divorced from his substantive work,[5] but I shall focus on his methodological implications in this chapter. As Shils (1949) notes, social sciences have developed a whole series of accurate, concrete techniques of observation and analysis that even optimists could not have expected in Weber's time. But he laments, "Random curiosity has caused a vast sprawl of interest over a multitude of subjects that could not be coordinated into a unified body of knowledge." Shils calls for social scientists to heighten their consciousness of Weber's discussion of "value-relevance" that would guide the criteria of problem selection and bring order into the agenda and program of social sciences. What this means is that we should do well by starting our analysis with an account of significant "local knowledge" (Geertz, 1983), "relevance structure" (Berger & Kellner, 1981), and "lived and living experiences" (Williams, 1977) of social and cultural inhabitants. On this basis, scholars try to help social actors reinterpret (objectify or typify) their subjective interpretations of the lifeworld in larger contexts. In phenomenological terms, what we do in our scholarly investigation is attempt to transform first-order meanings "within" the lifeworld of social actors to second-order meanings "outside" it. Doing so requires establishing a greater distance from existential concerns by relating local experiences to a systematic body of theoretical knowledge (Berger & Kellner, 1981).

The Weberian approach strives to balance "causal adequacy" with "meaning adequacy." It provides empathetic understanding of social action with an explanation of its causes and consequences, while at the same time elucidating the layers of rich and complex meaning of this social action. Weberians make claims on causality in more fluid, more contingent, and less sweeping terms than do positivists; Weber did not wish to pursue abstract "general laws" but attempted to attribute concrete effects to concrete causes with general significance or historical interest (Ringer, 1997; Weber, 1978b). Two general implications can be highlighted. First, beware of "the imperialism of the universal" (Bourdieu, 2001). Let's not accept any externally imposed universal models—be they modernization theory, the development of underdevelopment, technological determinism, or economic determinism—as preordained assumptions or conclusions. In this regard, for example, I (Lee, 2011b) have taken exception to the tendency of the Heidelberg sinologists (Wagner, 2007) to view the early Shanghai press in China through contemporary and post-hoc lenses of Jürgen Habermas instead of contextualizing the press at its historical moments, thus resulting in overinterpreting the scope of the "public sphere" thought to have existed. Second, our selection of problem is best guided by "relevance structure" emanating from *within* our culturally and historically specific yet vital experiences. I echo Mills's plea (1959, p. 8) that our "sociological imagination" should start with reflecting on "the personal troubles of milieu," then relating such troubles to the "public issues of social structure," and ultimately integrating local problems into comparative and historical contexts.

By no means am I proposing an insular or parochial approach. The "local" is not synonymous with the "parochial," for the "local" must maintain a dynamic interaction with the "global." At a certain point we are bound to tie the specific to the general when we meet, consult, and confront a larger body of the literature, take advantage of cosmopolitan concepts, and reconstruct more cosmopolitan arguments. But as a matter of priority, we had better begin with the specific and move to the general through critical assessment, modification, and absorption of the relevant literature to reflect on our experiences. Specificity and generality exist as a dialectical pair: the more we understand ourselves, the more likely we are to understand others; on this basis, a meaningful cultural dialogue may occur, and it always occurs within a context. Leopold von Ranke (1795–1886), the dean of the nineteenth-century German historians, maintains: "From the particular you may ascend to the general; but from general theory there is no way back to the intuitive understanding of the particular" (quoted in Ringer, 1997, p. 11). International communication is a creative fusion of local perspectives and global visions, but using theories to explain our experiences should take primacy over appropriating our experiences to fit the theories. Cultural experiences are the horse and general theories the cart; we do not put the cart in front of the horse.[6] Why should we abandon our cultural bearings, only to provide foreign if not exotic "validation" of the Western "truth," often dressed up in the name of "scientific laws"?

Contrasting Two Dependency Perspectives

In the 1970s two major versions of dependency perspectives grew out of Latin America to rebel against modernization theory. The radical theory of the "development of underdevelopment" (Frank, 1972) was a positivistic mirror image and yet ideological antithesis of modernization theory. Frank claimed that the development of First World countries was achieved historically at the price of Third World underdevelopment through colonial exploitation, external conditioning of economies, and military conquest. Contrasting Frank's *formal theory* of underdevelopment was a far more sophisticated perspective of "dependent development" by Cardoso and Faletto (1979) that treated dependency as a *methodology* for analyzing concrete situations of underdevelopment. While Frank (1972) takes the sweeping, general-to-specific framework, Cardoso and Faletto (1979) takes the more contingent, specific-to-general route. Cardoso (1977) criticized U.S. sociologists for interpreting dependency perspectives through Frank's positivistic lenses.

By "dependent development," Cardoso and Faletto (1979) maintained that some economies in Latin America were capable of experiencing industrial development amid continuing dependence. Methodologically, they take a structural-historical approach to elaborate the key concepts that related "opposing forces that drag history ahead" and "*situations* of dependency" in a global way. "History becomes understandable when interpretations propose categories strong enough to render clear the fundamental relations (of domination) that sustain those that oppose a given structural situation in its globality" (p. xiii). Instead of focusing exclusively on the dimension of external exploitation, they try to account painstakingly for the intricate interplay between the strong state, the internal class structure, and their interaction with the international capitalist system. This line of structural-historical analysis has inspired a series of sophisticated studies on Brazil (Evans, 1979), South Korea, and Taiwan; a rare study of media "dependent development" was attempted by Salinas and Palden (1979). Dependency perspectives seem to have gone out of vogue in the past two decades, but not because they have exhausted their intellectual mileage or relevance. As the neoliberal regime and ideology prevailed in the post–Cold War era, it seems that academic hounds have moved on to hunt for newer and tastier targets in postmodernism and globalization.

Cross-Cultural Research

The trajectory of international communication research has not been fully internationalized or cross-culturalized. International research does not imply one-sided imposition of dominant Western perspectives on peripheral corners of the global frontier. In criticizing the literature on development communication and the diffusion of innovations, I do not mean to show disrespect for our intellectual forebears posthumously, but the hard and valuable lesson I learned as a young student has constantly forced me to reassess my own academic path. Equally important is that we must reject any reverse tendency toward nativistic claims on cultural exclusivity. Zhang (2004, 2010), a cultural scholar, warns against close-minded cultural nationalism as well as the East-West bipolarity, while urging sinologists to move out of their isolated cocoon and engage in a healthy dialogue with members of the larger intellectual community. Likewise, we should come out of the closed circle of "area studies" in favor of the empirically rich and theoretically sensitive "area-based studies" (to borrow a term from Prewitt, 2002, p. 8) to integrate the rich area knowledge into a theoretical framework.

Merton (1972), in a seminal essay, calls for mutual learning of the insider's and outsider's views. Borrowing from Williams James, he delineates two kinds of knowledge: "acquaintance with" and "knowledge about."[7] The insider may have the advantage of obtaining the "acquaintance with" type of knowledge, referring to direct familiarity and personal, firsthand experiences with the world. However, familiarity breeds inattention, and the insider cannot claim monopolistic or privileged access to other kinds of knowledge just because of his or her ascribed status (e.g., race, nation, culture). The "knowledge about"—that is, more abstract formulations of knowledge acquired through systematic investigation—requires certain academic detachment and trained capacity to know how to ask what kind of questions, and how to assemble and assess the relevant evidence. "Knowledge about" is not exclusively owned by the insider or the outsider, but accessible to those who have engaged in long-term patient cultivation and systematic inquiry. The insider's and outsider's views are cross-fertilizing. Moreover, there are two implications for the distinction made between two types of knowledge. First, as social scientists we are professionally trained to be "multiple persons" who traverse between the two zones of experience, holding the insider's intuitive insights on some topics and the outsider's detached analysis and systematic knowledge on other topics. There is always a vibrant flow of exchange between these two overlapping modes of knowledge, such that we trust our intuition on the one hand and distrust it on the other. Also we habitually attempt to turn "acquaintance with" into "knowledge about" as part of our professional activities. Second, in relating to the Weberian-phenomenological approach, the scholar's role is to help transform social actors' "acquaintance with" into a more systematic body of "knowledge about."

Newton's Apple: In Defense of Case Study and Comparative Study

Smelser (1976) starts his sophisticated text on comparative methodology with Tocqueville's single case-study treatise on American democracy, and proceeds to compare Weber's phenomenological method with Durkheim's positivistic method. He finally privileged Durkheim over Tocqueville and Weber, for he was in favor of the positivistic method capable of rigorous statistical control to tease out spurious variables. Multivariate statistical analysis requires a large number of cases—a condition that international and cross-cultural investigators often find difficult to meet, especially if the comparison is to be *contextually rich and culturally meaningful.* International communication studies, devoid of cultural meanings, tend to generate rather bland, reductive, and generally dubious conclusions.

What's more, Smelser's evaluative criteria could be severely challenged if our primary cognitive interest is to acquire intellectual insight through what Geertz (1973) calls "thick description" of patterns, structures, processes, motives, and interaction. Even today, any serious discourse on democracy has little recourse but to return to Alexis de Tocqueville's classic *Democracy in America* (first published in two volumes in 1835 and 1840, reissued in 1945) as a baseline. Closer to media studies is Lippmann's (1922) cogent analysis of public opinion in the United States, which can be disputed but not bypassed. I am arguing that social scientists may look up to the "scientific" tradition but do not have to model their work solely, much less blindly, on the "hard" scientific laws. We may indeed look for ways to profit from the enduring concerns, rich insights, and the interpretive methodology of various humanistic disciplines. Weber's methodology (Weber, 1978b) is a fruitful and practical middle-way position between objectivism (causal adequacy) and subjectivism (meaning adequacy). His substantive work (Weber, 1978a) is a guiding light that shows us the way.

As a leading proponent of the culturalist approach to media studies, Carey's profound work (Carey, 1992; Munson & Warren, 1997) was quintessentially American. Even though he did not excurse into the international terrain, many of his domestic analyses should stimulate comparative work. Silvio Waisbord argues in his otherwise eloquent chapter that "thick description" (Geertz, 1973) of individual case studies primarily holds the narrow interest of "area specialists," but not of cosmopolitan scholars. Ironically, Carey's "thick description" of the historical, cultural, and technological formation of the U.S. media possesses far greater appeal to theoretically informed, interdisciplinary humanists and social scientists than to specific circles of area specialists. The same remark can be made of the seminal work by Cardoso and Faletto (1979), who follow a Weberian tack. The real strength of a case study (better yet, a comparative case study) lies not in *empirical* generality, but in its ability to generate *conceptual* generality. Metaphorically, a seminal case study can be likened to Newton's apple with the ultimate aim to reveal the law of gravity. Articulation of robust concepts in relation to larger comparative, historical, or global terrains has unusual power to illuminate and open up ways of seeing the structure of the world anew—not only enabling us to understand the tree but also unlocking a side yet critical window on the wood.

To illustrate, Clifford Geertz (1963) developed the concept of "involution" to account for the social-ecological history of agricultural transformation on the Indonesian islands of Java and Bali. The superimposed demands of the Dutch rulers and rising population pressures forced the agricultural system in Java to take a self-defeating route of intensification rather than change. In other words, Java tried to absorb increased numbers of cultivators on a unit of cultivated land. This practice did not result in improving the per-capita output but, on the contrary, produced disastrous social and ecological consequences. The concept of "involution" was further extended to mean the introversive tendency toward internal elaboration of details and the dazzling display of technical virtuosity at the expense of conceptual innovation, bold experiment, and open change. Clement So (1988) aptly invoked this concept to interpret the increasing trend of core communication journals toward self-referencing instead of cross-referencing the larger social science literature. Instead of equating the supposed "self-sufficiency" in journal citation with disciplinary maturity, I too regard it as a classic case of academic involution characterized by self-absorption and conceptual inbreeding, particularly detrimental to the development of an emerging field like ours (see more discussion in chapter 1 of this volume). Technical hair-splitting on trifling problems serves to fortify the false security of various fragmented, inward-looking interest groups and erect academic walls against fresh and bold ideas; consequently, the field is insulated from active engagement with and open contestation over big issues. What I am trying to argue is that the concept of "involution," derived from a case study by a renowned U.S. anthropologist in the faraway islands of Indonesia, has exerted far-reaching influences that cut across, and reach beyond, disciplinary and cultural borders. Therefore, it is not case study itself that is at fault, but the real challenge is how to offer *conceptual* power in a case analysis. Given this, shouldn't we be inspired to revisit some of the more important interpretive media concepts derived from various case studies—such as "stereotype" (Lippmann, 1922); "strategic ritual of objectivity" or "news net" (Tuchman, 1978); "sphere of legitimate controversy" (Hallin, 1986); "incorporation" (Williams, 1977)—in order to draw out their international ramifications?

Generalizing Cross-Cultural Implications

If historians quarrel over whether to generalize their analysis, most media sociologists are unquestionably inclined to generalize their findings. International communication is at once comparative and generalizing, and the comparative horizons can arise within and between cultural communities. Through arduously administered focus-group discussion, Liebes and Katz (1993) linked the multifaceted and thick-meaning interpretations of an imported U.S. cultural text (a TV series, *Dallas*) to Israeli social contexts (i.e., multiple subcultural immigrant groups, each with different interests and perspectives that made up a cultural mosaic). By tapping into how subcultural assumptions may influence different groups in their decoding of a foreign cultural product, they contribute to the continuing debate on "cultural imperialism." They take exception to some political economists who tend to equate capitalist ownership and control of media institutions with the presumed ideological effect of capitalism, but between these two points there is little effort to investigate how the audience interprets media genre and content (Tomlinson, 1991). By no means is this big debate settled, but Liebes and Katz have reopened it in a fruitful way by showing the "polysemy" in cultural readings of media genre.

Their cross-cultural study can be extended from intranational to international contexts, but it would be a more difficult undertaking especially if language expertise and substantive cultural knowledge are to be expected. That is why, despite the rhetoric, comparative media studies of international scope have been so rare.[8] An exemplary project came from Hallin and Mancini (2004) who first compared the "most similar design" of media systems across 18 countries in western Europe and North America, and then fostered an interesting comparison with the "most dissimilar design" of some non-Western countries (Hallin & Mancini, 2012).

I hope to be pardoned for drawing on our work (Lee, He, & Huang, 2006, 2007) to make a further point, not because of its outstanding merits but because of my own familiarity with it. In this project, our problem selection was geared toward deciphering the mysterious myopia of China's media system that is being cross-pressured by a mix of Communist control and quasi-capitalistic market operation. Instead of beginning with any "universal" model, we set out to listen to the voices (i.e., meaning system) of media executives, editors, and journalists we interviewed, and then interpreted their insights in relation to our own long-term grasp of the situation and also to the larger literature. We reconstructed the concept of "corporatism" from Latin Americanists, but added to it critical elements of party-market collusion and collision that were unique to what I characterized as "Communist-capitalist media" in China (Lee, 2005). Finally, we propose three prototypes of "party-market corporatism" to account for the interlocking of the state, capital, and media in China. The first, as in Shanghai, is the pattern of clientelism in which media submission is exercised through the exchange of political silence for economic reward. The second prototype, as in Guangzhou, is "marketization of political management" where media corporatism is driven by fierce market competition within the party-state ideological limits. The third, as in Beijing, is a pattern of "political absorption of marketization," where "managed diversity" is maintained through a precarious balance of the emerging interest politics among counterbalancing power bases. It is hoped that we may contribute to comparative work on media-state-capital transition within *and* between former European Communist states and the right-wing dictatorships of Latin America and Asia.

For me, the most inspiring example has been Edward W. Said's work on Orientalism (1978). He read the same body of canonical Western literary texts and yet produced, in Williams's (1977) terms, a set of "alternative" and even "oppositional" interpretations vis-à-vis the "dominant" ideology. Said adopted the methodology of "contrapuntal reading" (in musical terminology) of the literary texts and linked them to the political, economic, and cultural contexts of European and American imperialism. Subsequently Said (1993) extended this analysis to show how Third World peoples sought to resist, subvert, and contest the cultural hegemony of the imperial center. By offering a formidable challenge to the dominant Western reading, he has sharply changed the interpretative contours and enriched the whole gamut of comparative discourse in culture, politics, and ideology. The post-colonial perspective, which Said's work has inspired, should constitute a starting point of analysis for many international communication studies. His method of "contrapuntal reading" should be systematically applied, so we can revise, develop, extend, or debunk the existing pool of concepts in international and cross-cultural media research.

Exemplary Cross-Cultural Encounter

Two masters in modern Chinese humanistic and social science studies— Wang Guowei and Chen Yinque—offer examples of most profound significance in terms of how they handled the interpenetration of Chinese and Western knowledge systems (based on Yu, 1998, pp. 331–51; Yu, 2007, pp. 279–90).[9] In his youth Wang Guowei (1877–1927) was intensively immersed in German philosophy (from Immanuel Kant, Arthur Schopenhauer, to Friedrich Nietzsche); as a figure so erudite in various branches of social sciences (ranging from psychology and sociology to law and logic) he also represented the highest level of understanding of Western knowledge in China. These early experiences formed part of his core intellectual nutrients that would continually provide a tacit reservoir of creative ideas for him throughout his career. When he turned to the study of medieval Chinese history and geography, he profited from a wealth of newly discovered archeological finds and also from the work of European and Japanese sinologists. But most important, he saw himself as an heir to the Qing tradition of Chinese textual research, surpassed it, and eventually established a new paradigm that exerted profound influences on the creative minds of his and the next generations. Although he hardly made any reference to Kant and others in his mature work, as if he was ignorant of them, Yu (2007) argues that Wang would not have been able to develop a paradigmatic program of scholarship tackling a series of original questions with such rigorous analysis had he not internalized his early Western training.

Chen Yinque (1890–1969), widely acknowledged as an encyclopedic historian who wrote a tablet inscription in honor of Wang at his death, was another exemplary figure. Chen was versed in a dozen languages critical to his study of cultural encounter and the economic interactions of the Tang dynasty, which marked the peak of China's glory, with the neighboring countries in Central Asia. In his youth Chen had studied at Tokyo, Berlin, Paris, and at Harvard, harboring the ambition to master world history with scientific methods. When Chen later returned to China and devoted himself to the study of Chinese historiography, he followed the example of Wang and went back to the classical Chinese textual tradition, raising culturally indigenous questions that were nonetheless of general implication. Owing to his broad range of Western learning in his early years, he was able to develop many key concepts that opened up new avenues to give old history renewed understanding. As Yu (1998) vividly illustrates, Chen forged a vital synthesis of Chinese and Western scholarly traditions; he preserved the best practices of Chinese historiography, modernized them, and took them to the new heights. Both Wang and Chen were the central figures whose creative transformation and integration of intellectual resources enhanced the scholarly dialogue across cultures to a level that few could match.

Coda

If international communication scholars are truly serious about achieving the goals of mutual understanding through cultural dialogue, it is imperative that we listen humbly to symphonic music whose harmonious unity has themes and variations and is made up of a cacophony of instrumental sounds. Mindful of the cultural trend toward crossings over, Said (2000, p. 583) urged conflict managers like Samuel Huntington and Henry Kissinger, of whom he was critical, to pay more attention to and "understand the meaning of the mingling of different musics, for example, in the work of Oliver Messiaen or Toru Takemitsu."

It is fitting to quote a deliciously moving poem, "Married Love," written some seven centuries ago by Guan Daosheng (1262–1319) in dedication to her husband:[10]

> You and I
> Have so much love,
> That it
> Burns like a fire,
> In which we bake a lump of clay
> Molded into a figure of you
> And a figure of me.
> Then we take both of them,
> And break them into pieces,
> And mix the pieces with water,
> And mold again a figure of you,
> And a figure of me.
> I am in your clay.
> You are in my clay.
> In life we share a single quilt.
> In death we will share one coffin.

To give this poem's rich images and metaphors a slight twist: if international communication is remolded as a lump of clay, we stand in need of building a figure of "me" and a figure of "you," so ultimately I can be in your clay and you in mine. This means interpenetration, mutual learning, and cross-fertilization. A figure of "you" without "me" as a partner is a futile attempt at communication. However, the current state of affairs in the field of international communication research is that the figure of "me" has been overshadowed by a figure of "you." We must strengthen a figure of "me" by producing an abundance of quality case-study, comparative, or cross-cultural accounts of cultural institutions, media representation, and everyday ways of life, on which a meaningful dialogue with others is predicated. There is a very long way to go toward building such an edifice. As a modest step, we should encourage the laying down of more bricks that comprise theoretically informed, culturally enriching case studies and comparative analyses. To understand "me" in relation to "you" so we can have a conversation is, to me, the essence of international communication studies that can be aided by the Weberian-phenomenological methodology.

To close this chapter, I would like to turn specifically to Chinese media studies. We abhor the Western-cum-universal hegemony, but we are not interested in creating any essentialized theories of Asian or Chinese media. We have nothing to do with any concept of "Chinese exceptionalism." We study Chinese media partly but not only because we are culturally Chinese. Nor because we are culturally Chinese can we only study Chinese media. The study of Chinese media is by no means intellectually self-sufficient or isolated; it should interpenetrate with the theoretical and methodological advances in the field of international communication and, more important, in the larger currents of the humanities and social sciences. What we aspire to establish is, in sum, certain general theoretical perspectives with Chinese characteristics that arise from and highlight cultural specificity in our problematic consciousness and interpretations, but ultimately emerge from this cultural reflection to develop a broader view of how the world works. If we succeed in establishing such general perspectives that allow for internal differences, speak with a distinctive cultural accent, and yet transcend theoretical parochialism, we will be in a strengthened position to maintain an open-minded and mutually enriching dialogue on an equal footing with the Western literature.[11] This is the cosmopolitan spirit that I believe should be the guiding light of international communication research.

REFERENCES

Berger, P., & Kellner, H. (1981). *Sociology reinterpreted*. New York: Anchor.

Bourdieu, P. (2001). Uniting to better dominate? *Issues and Items* 2 (3–4): 1–6.

Cardoso, F. H. (1977). The consumption of dependency theory in the United States. *Latin American Research Review* 12 (3): 7–24.

Cardoso, F. H., & Faletto, E. (1979). *Dependency and development in Latin America*. Berkeley: University of California Press.

Carey, J. (1992). *Communication as culture: Essays on media and society*. New York: Routledge.

Crane, D. (1972). *Invisible colleges*. Chicago: University of Chicago Press.

Curran, J. (2005). Introduction. In H. DeBurgh, ed., *Making journalists* (pp. xi–xv). London: Routledge.

Curran, J., & Park, M.-J., eds. (2000). *De-Westernizing media studies*. London: Routledge.

Diamond, L. (1992). Economic development and democracy reconsidered. *American Behavioral Scientist* 35 (4–5): 450–99.

Downing, J. D. H. (1996). *Internationalizing media theory*. London: Sage.

Downing, J. D. H. (2009). International media studies in the U.S. academy. In D. Thussu, ed., *Internationalizing media studies* (pp. 267–76). London: Routledge.

Downs, G. W., Jr., & Mohr, L. B. (1976). Conceptual issues in the study of innovation. *Administrative Science Quarterly* 21 (4): 700–714.

Evans, P. B. (1979). *Dependent development: The alliance of multinational, state, and local capital in Brazil.* Princeton, NJ: Princeton University Press.

Evenden, M., & Sandstrom, G. (2011). Calling for scientific revolution in psychology: K. K. Hwang on indigenous psychologies. *Social Epistemology* 25 (2): 153–66.

Frank, A. G. (1972). *Lumpenbourgeoisie, lumpendevelopment: Dependence, class, and politics in Latin America.* New York: Monthly Review Press.

Fukuyama, F. (1992). *The end of history and the last man.* New York: Free Press.

Geertz, C. (1963). *Agricultural involution: The process of ecological change in Indonesia.* Berkeley: University of California Press.

Geertz, C. (1973). *The interpretation of cultures: Selected essays.* New York: Basic Books.

Geertz, C. (1983). *Local knowledge: Further essays in interpretive anthropology.* New York: Basic Books.

Hallin, D. C. (1986). *The "uncensored war": The media and Vietnam.* New York: Oxford University Press.

Hallin, D. C., & Mancini, P. (2004). *Comparing media systems: Three models of media and politics.* New York: Cambridge University Press.

Hallin, D. C., & Mancini, P., eds. (2012). *Comparing media systems beyond the Western world.* New York: Cambridge University Press.

Huff, T. E. (1984). *Max Weber and the methodology of the social sciences.* New Brunswick, NJ: Transaction Books.

Huntington, S. (1993). The clash of civilizations. *Foreign Affairs* 71 (3): 22–49.

Lee, C.-C. (1980). *Media imperialism reconsidered: The homogenizing of television culture.* Beverly Hills, CA: Sage.

Lee, C.-C. (2001). Beyond orientalist discourses: Media and democracy in Asia. *Javnost–The Public* 8 (2): 7–20.

Lee, C.-C. (2005). The conception of Chinese journalists: Ideological convergence and contestation. In H. de Burgh, ed., *Making journalists* (pp. 107–26). London: Routledge.

Lee, C.-C. (2010). Bound to rise: Chinese media discourses on the new global order. In M. Curtin & H. Shah, eds., *Reorienting global communication* (pp. 260–83). Urbana: University of Illinois Press.

Lee, C.-C. (2011a). Voices from Asia and beyond: Centre for Communication Research, City University of Hong Kong. *Journalism Studies* 12 (6): 826–36.

Lee, C.-C. (2011b). Overinterpreting the "public sphere." *International Journal of Communication* 5:1009–13.

Lee, C.-C., He, Z., & Huang, Y. (2006). "Chinese party publicity inc." conglomerated: The case of the Shenzhen Press Group. *Media, Culture & Society* 28 (4): 581–602.

Lee, C.-C., He, Z., & Huang, Y. (2007). Party-market corporatism, clientelism, and media in Shanghai. *Harvard International Journal of Press/Politics* 12 (3): 21–42.

Lerner, D. (1958). *The passing of traditional society: Modernizing the Middle East.* New York: Free Press.

Liebes, T., & Katz, E. (1993). *The export of meaning: Cross-cultural readings of Dallas.* Cambridge: Polity.

Lippmann, W. (1922). *Public opinion.* New York: Harcourt Brace.

Luckmann, T. (1978). Philosophy, social sciences and everyday life. In T. Luckmann, ed., *Phenomenology and sociology* (pp. 217–56). London: Penguin.

McAnany, E. G. (1984). The diffusion of innovation: Why does it endure? *Critical Studies in Mass Communication* 1 (4): 439–42.

Merton, R. K. (1972). Insiders and outsiders: A chapter in the sociology of knowledge. *American Journal of Sociology* 78 (1): 9–47.

Mills, C. W. (1959). *The sociological imagination.* New York: Oxford University Press.

Moore, B. (1967). *Social origins of dictatorship and democracy.* Boston: Beacon.

Munson, E. S., & Warren, C. A., eds. (1997). *James Carey: A critical reader.* Minneapolis: University of Minnesota Press.

Nye, J. S. (1990). *Bound to lead: The changing nature of American power.* New York: Basic Books.

Park, R. E. (1940). News as a form of knowledge: A chapter in the sociology of knowledge. *American Journal of Sociology* 45 (5): 669–86.

Prewitt, K. (2002). The social science project: Then, now and next. *Items and Issues* 3 (1–2): 5–9.

Rexroth, K., & Chung, L., eds. (1982). *Women poets of the world.* New York: New Directions.

Ringer, F. K. (1997). *Max Weber's methodology: The unification of the cultural and social sciences.* Cambridge, MA: Harvard University Press.

Rogers, E. M. ([1962, 1983, 1995], 2003). *Diffusion of innovations.* New York: Free Press.

Rogers, E. M., & Shoemaker, F. F. (1971). *Communication of innovations: A cross-cultural approach.* New York: Free Press.

Rogers, E. M., & Svenning, L. (1969). *Modernization among peasants: The impact of communication.* New York: Holt, Rinehart and Winston.

Said, E. W. (1978). *Orientalism.* New York: Vintage Books.

Said, E. W. (1993). *Culture and imperialism.* New York: Knopf.

Said, E. W. (2000). *Reflections on exile and other essays.* Cambridge, MA: Harvard University Press.

Salinas, R., & Palden, L. (1979). Culture in the process of dependent development: Theoretical perspectives. In K. Nordenstreng & H. I. Schiller, eds., *National sovereignty and international communication* (pp. 82–98). Norwood, NJ: Ablex.

Schramm, W. (1964). *Mass media and national development.* Stanford, CA: Stanford University Press.

Shils, E. A. (1949). Foreword. In M. Weber, *The methodology of the social sciences* (trans. E. A. Shils & H. A. Finch). New York: Free Press.

Smelser, N. J. (1976). *Comparative methods in the social sciences.* Englewood Cliffs, NJ: Prentice-Hall.

So, C. Y. K. (1988). Citation patterns of core communication journals: An assessment of the developmental status of communication. *Human Communication Research* 15 (2): 236–55.

Thussu, D. K., ed.. (2009). *Internationalizing media studies.* London: Routledge.

Tilly, C. (1975). Western state-making and theories of political transformation. In

C. Tilly, ed., *The formation of national states in Western Europe* (pp. 3–83). Princeton, NJ: Princeton University Press.

Tocqueville, A. de. (1945). *Democracy in America.* New York: Knopf.

Tomlinson, J. (1991). *Cultural imperialism.* Baltimore: Johns Hopkins University Press.

Tuchman, G. (1978). *Making news.* New York: Free Press.

Wagner, R. G., ed. (2007). *Joining the global public: Word, image, and city in early Chinese newspapers, 1870–1910.* Albany: State University of New York Press.

Wang, G., ed. (2011). *De-Westernizing communication research: Altering questions and changing frameworks.* London: Routledge.

Weber, M. (1930). *The Protestant ethic and the spirit of capitalism.* London: Harper-Collins.

Weber, M. (1951). *The religion of China: Confucianism and Taoism.* Trans. H. H. Gerth. New York: Free Press.

Weber, M. (1978a). *Economy and society.* Berkeley: University of California Press.

Weber, M. (1978b). The logic of historical explanation (trans. E. Matthews). In W. G. Runciman, ed., *Weber: Selections in translation* (pp. 111–31). Cambridge: Cambridge University Press.

Williams, R. (1977). *Marxism and literature.* Oxford: Oxford University Press.

Yu, Y.-S. (1987). *Zhongguo jinshi zongjiao lunli yu shangren jingsheng* [*Modern Chinese religious ethos and the spirit of merchants*]. Taipei: Lianjing.

Yu, Y.-S. (1998). *Chen Yinque wannian shiwen shizheng* [*Interpretation of Chen Yinque's late poetry and articles*]. Taipei: Sanmin.

Yu, Y.-S. (2007). *Zhishiren yu zhongguo wenhua de jiazhi* [*Intellectuals and the value of Chinese culture*]. Taipei: China Times Press.

Zhang, L. (2004). *Zouchu wenhua de fengbiquan* [*Walking out of the cultural cocoon*]. Beijing: Sanlian.

Zhang, L. (2010). The true face of Mount Lu: On the significance of perspectives and paradigms. *History and Theory* 49 (1): 58–70.

NOTES

1. Most ICA members had been U.S. residents until recently. Now that its non-U.S. members have risen to 42 percent, it would be more interesting to observe the extent to which ICA's range of epistemological and methodological interests will change with its membership composition.

2. While modernization theory has been discredited, we witness that China has reversed its ideological course to pursue single-mindedly a program of economically driven modernization agendas in the context of globalization (Lee, 2010). Whether it is desirable to pursue modernization goals (of what kind?) is one thing, but whether different versions of modernization theory are robust enough is another. China is a dubious test case for modernization theory.

3. Rogers with Svenning (1969), for example, reported the results of a USAID-sponsored project to study the impact of communication on peasants in Brazil,

Nigeria, India, and Colombia, but the findings were based on translated versions of the same questionnaire. Rogers presented statistical correlations between such variables as empathy, literacy, innovativeness, achievement motivation, cosmopolitanness, opinion leadership, and media exposure, all pooled at the individual level regardless of national contexts.

4. I am referring to the Weber-Schultz line of methodology; see Luckmann (1978) for a sophisticated exposition. For Weber's relationship with positivism and phenomenology, see Huff (1984, pp. 1–26).

5. Weber's work on the rise of capitalism and the Protestant ethic (Weber, 1930) is a landmark achievement of lasting influence, but his extension to comparative religions of China and India has been controversial. Weber (1951) relied on translated texts to argue that Chinese religion, especially Confucianism, did not cultivate the ethos of "innerworldly asceticism" as did Calvinism, and was hence antithetical to the rise of capitalism. Yu (1987) refuted this theme; based on evidence from textual research he maintained that "innerworldly asceticism" was part of the Chinese religious ethos. Capitalism did not rise in China for a different reason: that its political and legal systems had not undergone the process of rationalization. This shows how difficult it is to do comparative research by making use of Weber's "ideal type" design.

6. Professor Zhang Longxi told a moving story about his "lived experience" of being sent to the countryside for hard labor during China's Cultural Revolution that had a real impact on his life, only to see some literary theorists abstractly romancing the beauty and nostalgia of that country life.

7. Chicago sociologist Robert Park (1940) also used this pair of concepts to analyze news as a form of "acquaintance with" knowledge.

8. Over the years I have been asked, or asked to recommend someone, to develop a comparative text on East Asian media systems (generally considered as the Confucian cultural area), but I really know of no one equipped with the requisite linguistic and substantive competence to do it. When East Asian scholars get together, English is the lingua franca, but English writings on these media systems are in short supply.

9. The account of Wang and Chen is based on Yu Yingshi, a distinguished historian at Princeton University, many of whose important works (for example, Yu, 1987) ask the Weberian questions.

10. Translated by Rexroth and Chung (1982, p. 53). Zhao Mengfu, a very prominent Yuan official, scholar, and calligrapher, was so moved by his wife's poem as to abandon the thought of picking up a concubine.

11. This paragraph is taken from Lee (2011a). Interestingly, Kuang-kuo Hwang expressed a similar vision for the movement of indigenous psychologies when he urged the development of a universal theoretical model to account for "one mind, many manifestations" (Evenden & Sandstrom, 2011). Instead of striving for balkanized indigenous theories, he argued, the goal should be to integrate various cultural manifestations into a higher-order theory.

CHAPTER ELEVEN

Theorizing Media Production as a Quasi-Autonomous Field

A Reassessment of China News Studies

Judy Polumbaum

A quarter century ago, Charles Berger and Steven Chaffee sought to delineate the contours of their preferred academic domain with the publication of the *Handbook of Communication Science* (Berger & Chaffee, 1987c). In an introductory chapter, they identified the coalescence of studies concerning communication into dedicated academic departments, scholarly journals, and schools of research as evidence that a formerly diffuse field was "acquiring the trappings of a discipline" (Berger & Chaffee, 1987a, p. 15). They contrasted this situation with Wilbur Schramm's observation, another quarter century earlier, that communication fell considerably short of disciplinary status, being rather "an academic crossroad where many have passed, but few have tarried" (Schramm, 1963, p. 2). Yet this increasingly self-conscious and institutionalized realm of knowledge remained immature, according to Berger and Chaffee. It was time, they proposed, to attempt to impose some theoretical coherence on the terrain.

Pairing the term "communication" with the term "science" was their admittedly limiting way of drawing boundaries that excluded some forms of research while valorizing others. What distinguishes science from non-science, they explained, with obvious allusion to the natural science model, is the development of "testable theories" in pursuit of generalizable explanations. Their definition explicitly rejected research conducted in the cause of media criticism or activism, as well as the study of "individual communication events" for their own sake rather than in furtherance of larger theoretical principles (Berger & Chaffee, 1987a, p. 17). The fundamental goals of science, they wrote, included "explanation, . . . prediction and control"—meaning control not of social outcomes, but in a narrow methodological sense of having a handle on the conditions under study; any "positive" or "negative" implications, while of legitimate concern for anyone as citizens, were beyond the ken of the scientist (Berger & Chaffee, 1987b, p. 100).

The *Handbook* should not be undervalued; its synthesizing essays offer both historical markers and enduring insights, and some of the entries are indisputably masterful. The custodians of the volume are unquestionably giants in the field—Steve Chaffee was already a legend when he died prematurely. The collection is particularly lucid about levels of analysis, and examines a wide range of communication modes and contexts whose exploration continues to give vigor to the field. Nevertheless, from the vantage point of the twenty-first century, the editors' circumscription of the field looks oddly stingy and self-defeating.

"Positivism" has become the popular epithet to describe adoption of the natural science model for use in the social sciences, but this oversimplifies the issue—not to mention needlessly promoting academic antagonisms. Theoretical assumptions, guiding questions, and methodological choices will always constrain research results; however, assuming transparent collection, data should be useful to anyone caring to examine it, and subject to reconsideration even in analyses that may have nothing to do with the original research intent. Doubts about the idealized scientific method exist even among the natural sciences, but that does not preclude advocates of different approaches from making mutual use of each other's empirical findings.

In the field of communication, however, it could be argued that the natural science model constrains the scope of research in ways that are ever more outmoded. From the rigidly scientific perspective, for instance, what we have long called "international" or "comparative" communication research becomes merely a source of sites of replication. The *Handbook*'s reduction of international communication to a single essay, relegated to the end, on "Cross-cultural Comparisons" (Gudykunst, 1987) is perhaps symptomatic of this rejection of particularistic study. The meager attention also highlights an inhibiting lack of curiosity about the world. By now, even among scholars of disparate persuasions, it is widely recognized that diversity and commonality are equally important constituents of human existence. This does not obviate the quest for transportable explanations, which emerge in part from identifying differences that make a difference. But variation may matter in other ways entirely.

At bottom, this chapter is a plea for generosity in the construction of what "counts" as progress in the study of communication, and for a correspondingly more expansive view of international communication. In such a spirit, I outline an approach that seems promising for advancing the international study of media production with reference to the body of research I know best, concerning the production of news in contemporary China. Drawing on a considerable accumulation of studies of Chinese journalism and news media in the post-Mao reform period, I try to integrate some of the most recent empirical findings into a coherent analysis in a manner that respects both ambitions of generalizability and the integrity of the particular.

As with other contributions to this volume, my discussion takes inspiration from the movement to "de-Westernize" media studies (Curran & Park, 2000), including the criticism of research conventions that deem Western/U.S. contexts the norm or template against which findings from other settings are measured. Of course, the critique does not dictate spurning everything that originates with Western thinkers. Along with fellow contributors, I find in Western social theory much useful guidance for international communication research, and in Western research practice many helpful exemplars. I am especially grateful to Rodney Benson for his explication, here and elsewhere (e.g., 1999, 2006), of Pierre Bourdieu's concept of "fields of cultural production," and to C.C. Lee for his argument for grounded, culturally nuanced studies that dignify rather than elide diversity; indeed, this chapter is intended as complement (as well as compliment) to theirs.

Fields as Arenas for Action

If my discussion begins as a rejoinder to conventional definitions and goals of social science as represented by Berger and Chafee, these reservations are by no means original. The fine tradition in this vein reached a kind of fervor in the early 1970s with the turn toward interpretive sociology, reflexive anthropology, and other alternatives to the mainstream canon, and continues in what arguably has become a more pluralistic, if less combative, academic climate today. The communication literature likewise is full of caveats arising from the "ferment in the field" of the 1970s, the transcontinental influence of cultural studies and, more recently, the interest in alternatives to Anglo-American constructions of media and journalism. Yet the fact that, even today, these trends typically are framed as critiques is indicative of how entrenched the natural sciences model remains.

In his best-known treatise, Giddens (1984) provides one of the strongest rejections of the natural science template, arguing for dispensing with a search for stable laws and even generalizations in the human realm. For him, social theory should refer to a mode of analysis that revolves around "conceptions of human being and human doing, social reproduction and social transformation" (p. xx). His substitute for the aim of establishing and validating generalizations is what he calls structuration, or analysis that hinges on the interactions of human agency and social structure. This is theory in the sense of conceptual assumptions about how the world works, rather than propositions to be tested. It is theory as starting point rather than outcome. It begs the question of why or whether we should call it theory at all, as opposed to, say, approach or framework or guiding premise. By whatever name, Giddens's interest in how social actors assert autonomy of action within the mechanics of power, as well as his emphasis on empirical study in particular spheres of meaning and action, are of direct relevance to those of us who study media production.

Bourdieu (1993) developed the idea of fields of production with reference to social spaces within which cultural producers operate. A field is a "space of possibles" (p. 176) where specialized agents and institutions interact to preserve or transform the established order. And while external configurations exert influence upon fields, these spaces in themselves allow for degrees of autonomy. Externally, economic or political forces, historical events or technological developments may contribute to expanding or circumscribing the elastic range of possibilities; while within a field, actors operating from various positions with variably distributed interests and resources interact in ways that may fortify established possibilities, promote emerging innovations, or yield new creations.

It seems to me that Giddens and Bourdieu have, if different languages, similar understandings of social actors at the individual level. Giddens sees "lay" people, meaning non-scholars who are the subjects as opposed to the conductors of research, as skilled and knowledgeable about their own behavior; Bourdieu sees the specialized producers he studies as strategic and purposive. Their formulations rest on sophisticated interpretations of agency that consider conscious action as well as the unconscious, intent as well as unintended consequences.

Fields are oriented around particular stakes and a structured set of positions; occupants holding those positions have varying resources and inclinations, and engage in strategic struggles to define and redefine the stakes. Fields have varying degrees of autonomy, a field's boundaries are fluid, and any field is interdependent with other fields (Warde, 2004). Bourdieu's concept of "habitus" resonates with Giddens's focus on "routine" as integral to day-to-day practices that go into the reproduction of social systems. They share the conviction that social systems structure possibilities for action, while action in turn creates and conditions social structures.

As Hesmondhalgh observes (2006, p. 216), Bourdieu provides an alternative to "naïve notions of creative freedom and innovation," and the same may be said for Giddens. Structuration is based on the conviction that the dynamics of human affairs entails give and take across levels of activity, from the workings of the individual mind to the most macroscopic of societal forces; and analysis of fields of production calls attention to articulation among the different levels as well as among different fields. As Ryfe notes (2006, p. 207, citing Benson), journalism is unique in playing a mediating role with respect to other social fields; for this reason, he argues, the field of news production is especially subject to influences from contiguous fields.

These ideas provide a fruitful framework for studying media production that is rooted in the particular, an approach consistent with the anthropological imperative of attending to context. To Geertz (1973), culture *is* context; his admonition to focus the microscope ever more closely on the phenomena under scrutiny underscores the importance of precision in deciphering meaning within an enveloping culture. The objective is not causal attribution, but rather grounded explanation. This mode of inquiry lends itself to pursuit of questions of "how" and "why" with respect to particular constellations of actors within particular institutional configurations at particular confluences of space and time—suggesting the interdisciplinary importance of geography, history, and biography. It also invites study of patterns of change within bounded yet permeable social systems—the attempt to track how and why things that used to work that way came to work this way, and what changed within and among the moving parts to reconfigure outcomes and consequences.

Such a framework has helpful implications for research questions and study design (e.g., Kunelius & Ruusunoksa, 2008) and is no less useful as a guide for re-analysis of completed studies. The recognition of degrees of autonomy within fields, with attention to enabling mechanisms working at multiple levels and in multiple directions, calls for examination of how social spaces for doing media work may expand or contract; and much of the empirical research on Chinese media production from recent years casts light on this very issue.

Surveying the Field of Chinese News

The once exceedingly small window on mass media in the People's Republic of China has expanded steadily with increased scholarly access from the 1980s on, and the literature continues to grow in volume, ambition, and sophistication (see Polumbaum, 2010). This essay revisits empirical studies of newswork in China published in English during the first, quite productive, decade of this century.

Regardless of stated theoretical approaches or objectives, most authors of this scholarship share an interest in social change and generally agree on its potential sources: state, market, media occupations, and audience influences. Methodologies vary, with field studies yielding the most productive findings about journalists and their practices, while content analysis continues to be used (not always wisely, sometimes well) as a basis for inference about practice. Fieldwork consistently identifies negotiation, improvisation, and even guile as important dynamics of the news production process. Scholars differ, however, on which actors exercise agency in ways that make a difference, and which benefit from the results, in both short and long terms. Traversing this literature with these discrepancies in mind helps identify the range of the possible and provides markers for further research.

Among the work that explicitly considers interactions of structure and agency, Pan (2000) views journalists as "entrepreneurial actors" who avail themselves of tensions between political controls and market freedoms to improvise and innovate in a manner that is reconfiguring institutional space differentially in different regions. Akhavan-Majid (2004) suggests that official and unofficial agents have collaborative interests in state policy initiatives that have enabled non-state agents to engage in "creative renegotiation and expansion," contributing to mass media reform. She identifies the replacement of ideology by pragmatism, the shift in authorities' operational emphasis from "ideological supervision" to "entrepreneurial collaboration," and common interests in media profitability in an increasingly commercial system as beneficial to these diverse categories of actors.

Hu (2003) discerns an intertwining of political and economic forces in the restructuring of media, with the establishment of media conglomerates fortifying the alliance between sources of capital and sources of political power. Lee, He, and Huang (2006, 2007) have gone the furthest in documenting the complicity of state and media agents and institutions, finding accommodation at many levels that ultimately serves both political and economic power.

Tilt and Xiao (2010), in a content analysis of coverage of the 2005 Songhua River chemical spill, supply further evidence that Chinese media are not homogeneous. "We were quite surprised to find CCTV, a huge news organization that is technically still owned and operated by the central government, airing news segments that exposed and condemned a major government cover-up," they write. They attribute CCTV's evident ability to control coverage of this story to greater financial independence—and suggest that increasingly even state-run news organizations inhabit a growing social sphere of collective interest between the state and informal society. Sullivan and Xie (2009) find preliminary evidence that communication about environmental activism on the Internet draws in diverse actors, including both unofficial and state, interrelating both informally and formally around various objectives in complex online social networks.

Such findings dovetail with some of the political science literature on China, such as the work of Mertha (2009), who argues that a system he characterizes as "fragmented authoritarianism" is becoming surprisingly pluralized, with what he calls "policy entrepreneurs"—including from the media—gaining access to policy processes. In the field of hydropower development, he gives examples of how interests among various agents can converge in a serendipitous manner, with media outlets and individual media producers playing an important role in the forging and recognition of shared interests.

While absolutist constructions of totalistic state control over media have been largely abandoned, some studies suggest that China's media succumb to direct political pressure on certain subjects and at certain times (Chen, 2005; E. Zhang & Fleming, 2005). Pugsley (2006) adds the twist of narrative analysis, finding that in times of controversy or crisis the Chinese news media give voice to officially constructed stories in culturally familiar ways. Zhang (2006) likewise concludes that political power governs the construction of current affairs programs to a greater extent during crisis. However, Tong (2007) suggests somewhat the opposite: that controversial events can provide openings for assertive journalistic practice. Tong (2009) also argues that journalists' strategic editing of reports on politically sensitive topics helps further the prospects for publication of controversial news.

More commonly, scholars see a chronic tug-of-war between media and the state that spawns various configurations of benefits for opposing parties. Huang (2003, 2007) emphasizes the idea of adaptation within fairly strong structural determinants, and discerns that the pragmatic requisites of absorbing private, including foreign, capital as well as managerial needs have spurred transition to a "capitalist corporation" model of media that is still politically and financially state-controlled. Yet he maintains that greater structural diversity and openness in the media market also will promote journalistic professionalism and deter corruption. Wang (2010) finds that local journalists, while respecting explicit boundaries, actively employ a variety of "strategies for mild resistance" vis-à-vis government pressures.

Lin Jie (2004), offering a Chinese media producer's perspective while a Neiman fellow on leave from her producer job at CCTV, characterizes state and profession as pitted against each other in trying to leverage advantages through the market. "As a special force functioning in an overlapping area of political and economic realms, China's media now seem to stand at a critical point," she writes; "the more the government allows or even encourages the media to perform as a commercial unit, the more certain will it raise unavoidable and crucial challenges to the current political structure." Meanwhile, she suggests, a kind of accommodation has emerged in which the Chinese government's "optimistic" belief that media content can be separated from media management is working out quite well.

Chan (2002, 2007) suggests the state is the more agile agent in these times; he sees media organizations as compliant in the service of exercising ideological hegemony by using ever more subtle and flexible methods. Stockmann (2010), studying Beijing residents' views on anti-Japanese protests in the spring of 2005, identifies a kind of "outsourcing" of media control to the market—as long as the commercialized press is reflecting government views. Her view is that commercialization actually promotes the state's ability to influence public opinion through the mass media.

In her empirically rich thesis on China's television industry, Xu (2010) finds that new central government policies and practices have shifted production risks to independent TV producers, who engage in a variety of cautious negotiating strategies that result in ideologically safe content. She concludes that commercialization, channel specialization, and other reforms promoted by the state since China's admission to the World Trade

Organization have not attenuated state control, and in some respects have strengthened it.

Hassid (2008) cautions against regarding Chinese journalists as either an arm of the party-state institutional structure or as advocates for citizens' interests, calling them "contentious actors in their own right." He, too, however, identifies the push for journalistic independence from the state as a primary dynamic, working against political and economic externalities. His study is problematic in that it relies for evidence mainly on high-profile episodes of journalistic resistance, not on original fieldwork; his examples do, however, lead him to conclude that "purely structural approaches" to understanding politics are insufficient.

The difficulty of disentangling state forces from market forces emerges in Xin's (2006) examination of the Xinhua News Agency. This study finds that competition from other outlets has forced what was once an exclusive state-sponsored content provider into a strategy of diversification, and thus the ostensibly official news service has transformed itself from an apparatus of the propaganda system into a client-oriented operation in which newspapers and other entities using its services have gained leverage. In such a struggle within the field of news production, political and economic interests simultaneously are in cahoots and at odds not only among organizational actors but also within these very organizations.

Zhao (2000) envisions a multifaceted strategic alliance represented by "watchdog journalism" that ultimately, and most importantly, strengthens the power of the state. In her analysis, investigative reporting has emerged primarily from party and state imperatives to "reassert control over a dysfunctional bureaucracy" and reinforce the central leadership's legitimacy, while also serving journalists' professional interests and media organization's commercial interests.

Huang Dan (2011) similarly sees the policy of "supervision by public opinion" (*yulun jiandu*) as an instrument extended by the party-state to facilitate administrative effectiveness and promote legitimacy. Huang's analysis of the ostensibly hard-hitting TV news program, China Central Television's *Focus*, finds its content aligned with party and government interests. The watchdog mission does provide some space for criticism as well as for promoting technical aspects of journalistic professionalism; but at bottom, what seems to favor journalistic autonomy and independence is merely "strategic rhetoric," Huang writes. In sum, "the media's ability to serve as a check on power is a mechanism for self-adjustment and self-improvement within the established power structure" (p. 110).

In contrast, Tong and Sparks (2009) see institutionalized practices of journalistic investigation as primarily market-driven, and secondarily undergirded by a developing professional ideology among journalists. Tong (2010), further qualifying premises of centralized media control and confluence of interest between political and economic power, casts central authorities in a curiously progressive role versus elites at the local level who collude to counteract central policies.

Sun's (2006) case study of contention over supervision of a town TV station offers more nuanced distinctions for understanding state actors, finding a loss of central authority as local governments at different levels prove capable of manipulating the media market in their own interests. Dispersal of control and juggling of interests emerge again in Sun's (2010) examination of "public opinion supervision," in which government, commercial media, and journalists form strategic relationships premised on assessments of risks and gains.

Pugsley (2010), reviewing the succession of high-profile news stories emerging from China during 2008—the Olympics (a "celebratory media event"), the Tibet disturbances and torch relay demonstrations ("conflicted" media events), the Sichuan earthquake (disaster), and tainted milk (scandal)—asserts that international news flows have attenuated CCTV's role as "central gatekeeper" for news coverage, making it harder for the Chinese state to control the broadcast of media events. However, he maintains that the state still defines and regulates "cultural forms and practices" shaping national culture as reflected in domestic media.

These statements may seem self-evident, but they find considerable qualification in Chin's (2011) study of central government efforts to facilitate the entry of overseas TV programming into China from 2000 to 2008. The empirical evidence reveals complex and subtle interactions between provincial-level authorities, national policymakers, and other actors, with different parties exploiting their own points of leverage. Policy is initiated from the top, Chin observes, whereupon the central authorities face a delicate balancing act, relying on lower levels for management and sanctions while also trying to prevent abuse of this ceded administrative flexibility. Provincial officials and broadcasters, meanwhile, intervene during policy implementation and revision in ways that may stymie central government objectives. In Guangdong, Chin finds, provincial interests countered central policy by promoting stricter barriers to access, more extensive regulation, and other measures, including blocking signals, with the aim of fending off domination of the local media market by overseas TV.

Mass communication research typically distinguishes reception from production for purposes of both theorizing and empirical study. Conceptualizing media production as a field, however, requires integral consideration of the audience dimension. Ryfe (2006, p. 206) makes the case well: "Because it sits between social actors, the news is especially sensitive to the shared, constitutive commitments of its community of readers. More simply, the news takes it shape in large part from the public it serves."

Among China scholars who underscore the role of audiences in shaping news production and product, Zhang (2000) proposes that changes in the official ideological positioning of media audiences, coupled with commercialization, have created new institutional space for the flexing of journalistic muscles as well as new managerial methods. Sun, Chang, and Yu (2001) suggest the importance of audience in the marketplace helps explain why market-oriented media are on the rise as official party organs flounder. Although these examples incorporate audience into the analysis, empirical studies probing the audience-producer interrelationship in the Chinese context have yet to be devised.

As a side note, the desirability of research designs that gauge actual practices (as opposed to self-reports) is reinforced by a number of cautionary studies revealing disjunctures between attitudes and action. De Burgh (2003) found that Hangzhou TV reporters' beliefs about journalists' social responsibilities were not manifested in actual news reports. On the basis of a survey of Guangzhou journalists, Lin Fen (2010) identifies both changing demographics and new "complexity" in journalists' attitudes and behavior arising from the combination of party values and professional values. In general, she says, journalists tend to be "inactively liberal"—in particular, despite liberal beliefs, professional agency seldom emerges in actual coverage of political, cultural, or moral issues.

Cumulatively, such empirical studies can further the larger project of explaining how the journalistic field interacts with other fields, including political, economic, legal, and technological fields; and elucidate how changes in adjoining fields might impinge upon, interpenetrate, alter, compete with, or otherwise disturb the field of journalistic production in ways that modify news practices and products and realign public constructions of meaning (Benson, 1999; Peterson & Anand, 2004). Unsurprisingly, as Internet penetration advances and electronic modes of communication grow in volume, variety, and salience, researchers have turned increasing attention to media technologies. To date, however, few studies from the Chinese context shed light on how technology might figure in the news production mix.

He and Zhu (2002), employing "ecology" and "virtual community" as organizing concepts in an early study of online editions of Chinese news-papers, provide a start with their attempt to forecast the prospects for on-line papers in light of social factors interacting with telecommunications infrastructure and formal characteristics of new communication technolo-gies. At the time, they judge online editions not yet viable in light of weak and primitive infrastructure, uneven distribution, and excessive cost to consumers in conjunction with political and social constraints; and attri-bute the content homogeneity of print and online editions to similar fac-tors. The study sets a good example in its endeavor to integrate technology into a larger picture, even if the pace of Internet development in China has superseded the findings.

Xin's (2010) study of interactions between conventional news media and "citizen journalism" from blogs and other informal channels yields fairly predictable findings—that netizen accounts are an increasingly important news source for mainstream outlets in China as well as constituting an alternative conduit for information, while party controls still shape public use of the Web. More noteworthy is attention to the element of interactiv-ity, which is certainly vital to understanding how technology alters the in-teractions of audiences and producers in the new media environment, and thus germane to studying restructuring of the field of news production.

An additional caveat against ascribing too much potency to grassroots media activity comes from Pugsley (2010), whose study of Chinese cover-age of major domestic news events during 2008 suggests the state main-tains overall hegemony over media culture even as global influences erode aspects of state control. In this context, he cautions that the role of citizen journalists should not be over-estimated given their limited "ability to cre-ate ongoing networks of dependable news-gathering."

Examining joint ventures in China's Internet industry, Weber and Jia (2007) do not address news media per se, but their findings nevertheless are suggestive for understanding changes in fields of media production, espe-cially the element of self-restraint. Their focus is the fast-growing online entertainment sector, in the service of which state media employ what they call "strategic commercialization," an approach intended to elicit maximum returns through appeals to consumer audiences. The strategy includes co-production arrangements and importation of cultural content, encourag-ing domestic Internet portals to make cooperative deals with global media firms for developing online services and products. Case studies of several such joint ventures suggest that the most successful hinge on "targeted" entertainment provision, with technology coordinated with content needs.

The authors highlight that local partners almost invariably have signed an official "pledge" that includes the promise to conform to government content restrictions. Such self-regulation, they say, insulates foreign operators from content control issues and puts the onus on domestic service providers. In other words, self-regulatory provisions limit foreign investors' perceived risks and make partnerships more attractive, while enlisting the complicity of domestic firms in facilitating state influence and control, thus promoting state interests in both economic and political realms.

Weber and Jia, in identifying points of articulation between domestic and global agents along with related interactions among domestic entities, link the local with the global in a way that illuminates process as well as product. Studies such as this help point the way for scholars trying to make connections between the local and the global in an accessible and measurable manner. It is tempting to seek explanations for local-global interactions at high levels of abstraction. Yet, along with C.C. Lee in this volume, I would argue that closely focused local studies remain essential for understanding the workings of the global system.

A primary concern of globalization studies has been the question of cultural integrity—that is, the ability of national cultures to resist the onslaught of American or Western culture. Knight (2006), in an insightful essay on globalization's implications for China, calls for much greater precision regarding sources of cultural authority, and his reasoning further accents the importance of localized study: "So-called 'national' cultures are very likely to be constructed and maintained by national governments in the attempt to instil in their often culturally diverse populations a unified national consciousness that will deliver political unity and loyalty to the state. Consequently, these fragile politically constructed national cultures may well be more subject to the erosive effects of globalisation than cultures attached to particular locations and communities, where the linkage of place and culture remains strong. The impact of globalisation is likely to be different at these different levels" (p. 4).

Zhu (2001) distinguishes "theorizing" and "indigenizing" approaches to research on Chinese mass communication, defined respectively by their pursuit of the universal versus the unique, and favors research strategies that integrate both. Lee (2004) has called for developing theoretical visions from China's cultural specifics. Both are eloquent calls for knitting local study with attempts to fathom the workings of human society more broadly. And the inescapable recognition that China is ever more entwined with transnational movements of goods, people, ideas, information, money, and all the other elements propelling globalization means that China can never be considered in isolation; this applies to rural interior China as much as to the metropolises. Making empirical linkages between fields of media production with this larger set of externalities is surely one of the greatest challenges facing international communication scholars.

On Staying Grounded, Flexible, and Good-Humored

I have attempted to show how an approach inspired by Giddens's concept of structuration and Bourdieu's notion of fields of media production can help us sort out the wide range of empirical findings emerging from the Chinese newswork context as well as contributing to formulation of future studies. I have also expressed common cause with scholars who emphasize closely focused grounded study. In furtherance of this project, and by way of conclusion, I would offer two additional guiding concepts for international communication research: *circumstances* and *serendipity*. Finally I propose a third, optional but highly recommended, principle: *whimsy*.

The literature spurring this tripartite formulation comes not from the field of communication, nor from social theory, but rather from management and organization studies. It is nearly four decades since organizational theorists Cohen, March, and Olsen (1972) introduced what has become a classic, if still-debated, rejoinder to scholarship premised on assumptions of regularity and rationality in human systems with their article "A Garbage Can Model of Organizational Choice." Their purpose was to explain decision making in organizations characterized by fluid participation, shifting technologies, and changing objectives, which are "characteristic of any organization in part—part of the time" but "particularly conspicuous in public, educational, and illegitimate organizations," they explained (p. 1).

Within organizations, they proposed, decisions arise from interplay among numerous factors that combine in unpredictable ways. These factors, furthermore, consist of "streams" of ingredients—specifically, flows of choices, problems, solutions, and participants with varying degrees of involvement. "From this point of view," they wrote, "an organization is a collection of choices looking for problems, issues and feelings looking for decision situations in which they might be aired, solutions looking for issues to which they might be the answer, and decision makers looking for work" (p. 2).

The garbage can analogy was not meant to be pejorative; rather, it supplied an easily grasped metaphor for a messy conjuncture of phenomena.

The authors concluded that, while their garbage can process was not particularly successful in resolving problems, it did enable choices to be made and problems to be addressed in ambiguous and variable environments. The model, as Olsen later summarized (2001, p. 193), "views organizational life as highly contextual, driven primarily by timing and coincidence."

These scholars have since extended their work (e.g., March & Olsen, 1989, 1995) into larger institutional realms of governance, democracy, the military, and the nature of national, regional, and international political orders, promoting an approach known as the "new institutionalism." A handful of media scholars have applied the new institutionalism to news production to explain phenomena such as content homogeneity across news organizations (Cook, 2006) and the sometimes surprising counterpoint, content variability (Ryfe, 2006).

Concerns at the institutional level may eclipse quixotic explanations of decision making within single organizations, but the fundamental posture expressed in the garbage can model endures: human affairs are best understood not as outcomes of rational calculations and orderly processes but rather as historically contingent and socially emergent. From this perspective, distinctive socio-cultural understandings govern action, while socially constructed rules and practices themselves are continually molded through interactions and experience, and institutional structures are created, maintained, and transformed in interplay with multiple interests, changing resources, and twists of history.

With circumstances and serendipity as operative concepts, the garbage can model and its institutional augmentations are suggestive for the study of media, including comparative and transnational media research. The scheme originates from a certain kind of setting (fluid) with the presence of certain factors (choices, problems, solutions, participants), presenting identifiable, describable circumstances. And interactions among the key factors, producing not particularly efficient or sensible outcomes, are animated by serendipity—not pure chance or luck, but rather a mix that creates opportunity for those opportunely positioned (see Golin, 1957; also Zilber, Tuval-Mashiach, & Lieblich, 2008).

Circumstances are "facts on the ground," practices and routines, behaviors and actions, comportment and relationships, by and among agencies of human society, from individual actors to encompassing structures. They are the stuff of description, but also the basic ingredients of any social configuration. Serendipity, a term often found in accounts of scientific discovery, refers to how circumstances combine and interact in ways that agents who don't control this confluence may nonetheless avail themselves of opportunities thus created. It is the stuff of explanation and analysis. These terms in themselves do not suggest theories or models; rather, they offer organizing principles for how to approach the challenges of social research. They also should help call attention to culturally revealing anomalies, exceptions, and outliers, which conventional social science is apt to discard. For the most vivid exaggerations or egregious departures from "normality" may be significant cultural markers in their own way, no less important than the common patterns and prevailing standards that fill the bell of the normal curve.

For scholars whose pride does not prevent playfulness, the garbage can model also suggests a third principle—that of *whimsy*. In their original 1972 article, evidently in anticipation of those who might question the seriousness of their intent, Cohen, March, and Olsen translated the model into quantitative form for computer simulation (employing the programming language current at the time, Fortran), a touch that seemed to offer assurances of rigor and sobriety. But in the main narrative, the authors clearly were happy to sound a bit silly by using an everyday object as theoretical terminology—betraying, I would hope, a general commitment to levity as a stimulus for discussion and discovery.

Responding to a dissection of the garbage can model long after the original article's publication (Bendor, 2001), we find reaffirmation of this propensity from Olsen (2001, p. 192), who likens what he viewed as the critics' lack of imagination to "the grumbling of humorless people who accidentally wander into the lively part of town." Ultimately, whimsy is a property of the scholar's disposition, and might be seen as a call for modesty in the purported understandings we assert for our work.

REFERENCES

Akhavan-Majid, R. (2004). Mass media reform in China. *Gazette* 66 (6): 553–65.
Bendor, J. (2001). Recycling the garbage can: An assessment of the research program. *American Political Science Review* 95 (1): 169–90.
Benson, R. (1999). Field theory in comparative context: A new paradigm for media studies. *Theory and Society* 28 (3): 463–98.
Benson, R. (2006). News media as a "journalistic field": What Bourdieu adds to new institutionalism, and vice versa. *Political Communication* 23 (2): 187–202.
Berger, C. R., & Chaffee, S. H. (1987a). The study of communication as a science. In C. R. Berger & S. H. Chaffee, eds., *Handbook of communication science* (pp. 15–19). Newbury Park, CA: Sage.
Berger, C. R., & Chaffee, S. H. (1987b). What communication scientists do. In C.

R. Berger & S. H. Chaffee, eds., *Handbook of communication science* (pp. 99–122). Newbury Park, CA: Sage.

Berger, C. R., & Chaffee, S. H., eds. (1987c). *Handbook of communication science.* Beverly Hills, CA: Sage.

Bourdieu, P. (1993). Principles for a sociology of cultural works. In R. Johnson, ed., *The field of cultural production: Essays on art and literature* (pp. 176–91). New York: Columbia University Press.

Chan, A. (2002). From propaganda to hegemony: Jiaodian Fangtan and China's media policy. *Journal of Contemporary China* 11 (30): 35–51.

Chan, A. (2007). Guiding public opinion through social agenda-setting: China's media policy since the 1990s. *Journal of Contemporary China* 16 (53): 547–59.

Chen, C. H. (2005). Framing Falun Gong: Xinhua news agency's coverage of the new religious movement in China. *Asian Journal of Communication* 15 (1): 16–36.

Chin, Y. C. (2011). Policy process, policy learning, and the role of the provincial media in China. *Media, Culture & Society* 33 (2): 193–210.

Cohen, M. D., March, J. G., & Olsen, J. P. (1972). A garbage can model of organizational choice. *Administrative Science Quarterly* 17 (1): 1–25.

Cook, T. E. (2006). The news media as a political institution: Looking backward and looking forward. *Political Communication* 23 (2): 159–71.

Curran, J., & Park, M.-J., eds. (2000). *De-Westernizing media studies.* London: Routledge.

de Burgh, H. (2003). Great aspirations and conventional repertoires: Chinese regional television journalists and their work. *Journalism Studies* 4 (2): 225–38.

Dickinson, R. (2007). Accomplishing journalism: Towards a revived sociology of a media occupation. *Cultural Sociology* 1 (2): 189–208.

Geertz, C. (1973). *The interpretation of cultures.* New York: Basic Books.

Giddens, A. (1984). *The constitution of society: Outline of the theory of structuration.* Berkeley: University of California Press.

Golin, M. (1957). Serendipity-bit word in medical progress: Does "pure luck" deserve all the credit? *Journal of the American Medical Association* 165 (16): 2084–87.

Gudykunst, W. B. (1987). Cross-cultural comparisons. In C. R. Berger & S. H. Chaffee, eds., *Handbook of communication science* (pp. 847–89). Newbury Park, CA: Sage.

Hassid, J. (2008). China's contentious journalists: Reconceptualizing the media. *Problems of Post-Communism* 55 (4): 52–61.

He, Z., & Zhu, J. J. H. (2002). The ecology of online newspapers: The case of China. *Media, Culture & Society* 24 (1): 121–37.

Hesmondhalgh, D. (2006). Bourdieu, the media and cultural production. *Media, Culture & Society* 28 (2): 211–31.

Hu, Z. (2003). The post-WTO restructuring of the Chinese media industries and the consequences of capitalisation. *Javnost–The Public* 10 (4): 19–36.

Huang, C. (2003). Transitional media vs. normative theories: Schramm, Altschull, and China. *Journal of Communication* 53 (3): 444–59.

Huang, C. (2007). Trace the stones in crossing the river: Media structural changes in post-WTO China. *International Communication Gazette* 69 (5): 413–30.

Huang, D. (2011). Power and right: "Yu lun jian du" as a practice of Chinese media from an institutionalism perspective. *Journalism Studies* 12 (1): 106–18.

Knight, N. (2006). Reflecting on the paradox of globalisation: China's search for cultural identity and coherence. *China: An International Journal* 4 (1): 1–31.

Kunelius, R., & Ruusunoksa, L. (2008). Mapping professional imagination. *Journalism Studies* 9 (5): 662–78.

Lee, C.-C. (2004). *Chaoyue xifang baoquan: Chuanmei yu wenhua zhongguo de xiandaixing* [Beyond Western hegemony: Media and Chinese modernity]. Hong Kong: Oxford University Press.

Lee, C.-C., He, Z., & Huang, Y. (2006). "Chinese party publicity inc." conglomerated: The case of the Shenzhen Press Group. *Media, Culture & Society* 28 (4): 581–602.

Lee, C.-C., He, Z., & Huang, Y. (2007). Party-market corporatism, clientelism, and media in Shanghai. *Harvard International Journal of Press/Politics* 12 (3): 21–42.

Lin, F. (2010). A survey report on Chinese journalists in China. *China Quarterly* 202:421–34.

Lin, J. (2004). China's media reform: Where to go? *Harvard China Review* 5:116.

March, J. G., & Olsen, J. P. (1989). *Rediscovering institutions: The organizational basis of politics*. New York: Free Press.

March, J. G., & Olsen, J. P. (1995). *Democratic governance*. New York: Free Press.

Mertha, A. (2009). "Fragmented authoritarianism 2.0": Political pluralization in the Chinese policy process. *China Quarterly* 200:995–1012.

Olsen, J. P. (2001). Garbage cans, new institutionalism, and the study of politics. *American Political Science Review* 95 (1):191–98.

Pan, Z. (2000). Spatial configuration in institutional change. *Journalism* 1 (3): 253–81.

Peterson, R. A., & Anand, N. (2004). The production of culture perspective. *Annual Review of Sociology* 30:311–34.

Polumbaum, J. (2010). Looking back, looking forward: The ecumenical imperative in Chinese mass communication scholarship. *International Journal of Communication* 4:567–72.

Pugsley, P. C. (2006). Constructing the hero: Nationalistic news narratives in contemporary China. *Westminster Papers in Communication & Culture* 3 (1): 77–92.

Pugsley, P. C. (2010). *Transnational media showdowns in China's Olympic year. In E. Morrell & M. D. Barr (eds.), Crises and opportunities: Proceedings of the 18th biennial conference of the Asian Studies Association of Australia*, Adelaide, Australia. Canberra: ASAA & University of Adelaide (published online at http://asaa.asn.au/ASAA2010/reviewed_papers/).

Ryfe, D. M. (2006). The nature of news rules. *Political Communication* 23 (2): 203–14.

Schramm, W. (1963). *The science of human communication*. New York: Basic Books.

Stockmann, D. (2010). Who believes propaganda? Media effects during the anti-Japanese protests in Beijing. *China Quarterly* 202:269–89.

Sullivan, J., & Xie, L. (2009). Environmental activism, social networks and the Internet. *China Quarterly* 198:422–32.

Sun, T., Chang, T.-K., & Yu, G. (2001). Social structure, media system, and audiences in China: Testing the uses and dependency model. *Mass Communication and Society* 4 (2): 199–217.

Sun, W. (2006). A small Chinese town television station's struggle for survival: How a new institutional arrangement came into being. *Westminster Papers in Communication & Culture* 3 (1): 42–56.

Sun, W. (2010). Alliance and tactics among government, media organizations and journalists: A description of public opinion supervision in China. *Westminster Papers in Communication & Culture* 7 (1): 43–55.

Tilt, B., & Xiao, Q. (2010). Media coverage of environmental pollution in the People's Republic of China: Responsibility, cover-up and state control. *Media, Culture & Society* 32 (2): 225–45.

Tong, J. (2007). Guerrilla tactics of investigative journalists in China. *Journalism* 8 (5): 530–35.

Tong, J. (2009). Press self-censorship in China: A case study in the transformation of discourse. *Discourse & Society* 20 (5): 593–612.

Tong, J. (2010). The crisis of the centralized media control theory: How local power controls media in China. *Media, Culture & Society* 32 (6): 925–42.

Tong, J., & Sparks, C. (2009). Investigative journalism in China today. *Journalism Studies* 10 (3): 337–52.

Wang, H. (2010). How big is the cage? An examination of press autonomy in China. *Westminster Papers in Communication & Culture* 7 (1): 56–72.

Warde, A. (2004). *Practice and field: Revising Bourdieusian concepts.* Manchester: Centre for Research on Innovation & Competition, University of Manchester.

Weber, I., & Jia, L. (2007). Internet and self-regulation in China: The cultural logic of controlled commodification. *Media, Culture & Society* 29 (5): 772–89.

Xin, X. (2006). A developing market in news: Xinhua News Agency and Chinese newspapers. *Media, Culture & Society* 28 (1): 45–66.

Xin, X. (2010). The impact of "citizen journalism" on Chinese media and society. *Journalism Practice* 4 (3): 333–44.

Xu, M. (2010). *Globalization, cultural security and television regulation in the post-WTO China.* PhD diss., National University of Singapore.

Zhang, E., & Fleming, K. (2005). Examination of characteristics of news media under censorship: A content analysis of selected Chinese newspapers' SARS coverage. *Asian Journal of Communication* 15 (3): 319–39.

Zhang, X. (2006). Reading between the headlines: SARS, *Focus* and TV current affairs programmes in China. *Media, Culture & Society* 28 (5): 715–37.

Zhang, Y. (2000). From masses to audience: Changing media ideologies and practices in reform China. *Journalism Studies* 1 (4): 617–35.

Zhao, Y. (2000). Watchdogs on party leashes? Contexts and implications of investigative journalism in post-Deng China. *Journalism Studies* 1 (4): 577–97.

Zhu, J. J. H. (2001). Zhongwen chuanbo zhi lilunhua yu bentuhua: Yi shouzhong ji meijie xiaoguo de zhenghe lilun weili [Theorization versus indigenization in Chinese communication research: The integrated theory of audiences and media effects as a case study]. *Mass Communication Research* 68 (1): 1–22.

Zilber, T. B., Tuval-Mashiach, R., & Lieblich, A. (2008). The embedded narrative: Navigating through multiple contexts. *Qualitative Inquiry* 14 (6): 1047–69.

CHAPTER TWELVE

Translation, Communication, and East-West Understanding

Zhang Longxi

As human beings, we are all born in medias res, that is, in a particular social, historical, and political environment with a particular language and a culture already in place before and after us. That pre-given environment and our upbringing determine the native language we speak, our social customs and cultural values, our basic points of view, our horizon of understanding, and our sense of belonging or identity. Such predetermined elements obtain in individual lives as well as in social fabrics, in the positions taken and choices made by individuals, groups, communities, and nations. That is to say, all human beings start out to be terribly parochial. The wonderful thing about being human, however, lies precisely in the capability to transcend our self-enclosures on the individual level and to go beyond the social enclaves on the level of communities and nations. Parochialism and cosmopolitanism, nationalist tendencies and cross-cultural openness are forces that contend constantly, and human life is always a process of negotiation that tries to keep a delicate balance.

It is almost "natural" to tip the balance toward the parochial, while the cultivation of a cosmopolitan spirit and openness of the mind requires a lot of effort. Border-crossing in languages and cultures is indeed a distinctly human act, an indication of a person's level of education and ability, and therefore of his or her social standing. This is true not only of a person in our time, but has been true almost since time immemorial. Those who can translate different languages and thereby help others get out of their linguistic and cultural cocoons are endowed with a special talent, and were even thought of in earlier times as in possession of some sort of a magic power. Translation has always served to make communication possible. If we consider the Greek assimilation of elements of Egyptian culture, the Greek and Roman interrelations, the contribution of Arabic scholarship to the Latin Middle Ages and the Renaissance, and the introduction of Buddhist texts from India to China and East Asia, we realize that translation was happening very early in human history, and that it has always played a significant role in the expansion of knowledge, the conceptualization of the world, and the development of human civilization.

The notion of the world has developed gradually as human knowledge increases. In ancient times, the idea of the world was limited geographically, linguistically, and culturally. In the part of the world we now call East Asia, the concept of *tian xia* or "all under heaven" was a Sinocentric world with the Chinese language and culture as major sources of reference, which hardly had any knowledge of or contact with Europe. The early European concept of the world, on the other hand, was largely influenced by the biblical understanding of how Noah and his descendants populated the different parts of the postdiluvian earth. The medieval European *mappa mundi* or the T-O map had only a very rough idea of the world with Europe on the left side, Africa on the right, and Asia on top of the T. What was thought of as Asia was a vague idea of India. It was Marco Polo (1254?–1325?) in the late thirteenth century with his famous travelogue that expanded European knowledge of the world and provided information for many of the place names and their locations in the East. For example, the well-known Catalan map (1375) evidently used Marco Polo's book as a major source of information. As John Larner (1999, p. 105) remarks, Marco Polo gave Europe "an amazing gift, a geographical treatise of a vast extent and complexity, an unparalleled opening of horizons." Marco Polo left Venice as a young man, following his father and uncle to China as merchants. The China he came to know was under the rule of Kublai Khan as emperor of the Yuan dynasty, namely a Mongolian empire that provided him with very little opportunity to get in contact with the majority Han Chinese and their culture. That may explain why there are so many things that modern readers identify as typically Chinese—for example, Confucianism, writing brush and calligraphy, tea drinking, chopsticks, women's bound feet, the Great Wall of China—are hardly observed and commented on by Marco Polo, or not mentioned at all in his book. Some have thus questioned the veracity of his account (Wood, 1995; Yang, 1999). For Europe, then, as Larner argues, Marco Polo's significant contribution lies in the discovery of the world, the increase of geographical knowledge to include East Asia.

For cultural encounters between the East and the West, it took another three hundred years to start in earnest when Matteo Ricci (1552–1610), another Italian, went to China as a Christian missionary in the late sixteenth century. When Ricci and the other Jesuit missionaries arrived in China of the late Ming dynasty, they found a country with a long history, a thriving economy, a sophisticated culture, and a rich intellectual tradition. The Jesuits realized that they could not simply declare that the Chinese had no culture, offer to teach them the spiritual truth of the revealed religion, and convert tens of millions of them into Christians overnight. So they adopted the so-called accommodation approach in their missionary work: they learned the Chinese language and tried to find concepts and terms in ancient Chinese writings that might be used to translate Christian ideas, and presented themselves as learned scholars from the West, trying to impress the Chinese emperor and the literati-officials with the latest European science and technology. Ricci wrote his Christian doctrine in Chinese, *Tianzhu shiyi* or the *True Meaning of the Lord of Heaven*, and translated the first six books of Euclid's *Elements* into Chinese in collaboration with Xu Guangqi (1562–1633), a high-ranking official at the Ming court and one of the most important Christian converts. The Jesuit "accommodation approach" and the translation activities they engaged in certainly had a religious agenda and ultimately aimed to convert the Chinese to Christianity; at the same time, however, these were also significant efforts at cross-cultural understanding at a time when the East and the West first came into contact and tried to find some common ground for understanding and communication.

The Jesuit fathers also introduced Chinese culture, particularly Confucianism, to Europe. In numerous letters, treatises, and pamphlets, China became quite well known among European intellectuals through the mediation of Jesuit missionaries, whose interpretation of Confucian moral and political philosophy made a strong impact in Europe, drawing attention from such leading philosophers as Gottfried Wilhelm Leibniz and Voltaire. If Marco Polo initiated an "unparalleled opening of horizons" in medieval Europe, Matteo Ricci and his followers certainly further opened those horizons and deepened European understanding of China and the East. In material culture, imported Chinese goods such as porcelain, silk, wallpaper, furniture, and the art of gardening already created a craze for things Chinese in Europe during the seventeenth and the eighteenth centuries, an infatuation with what was thought to be Chinese in European imagination, or what is known as chinoiserie, which, as Hugh Honour (1961, pp. 7–8) argues, "may be defined as the expression of the European vision of Cathay."

The significant presence of China in Europe, however, was not limited just in material culture and popular imagination, but also, and perhaps more important, in the area of cultural influence and social implications. The Jesuits' positive representation of China as a well-governed country, based on natural theology, helped many European thinkers of the Enlightenment to reflect on secular culture, meritocracy, and civil service based on a system of civil examination. The secular orientation of Confucianism suggested to Enlightenment philosophers the separation of church and the state, an important concept for the modern nation-state. The examination system through which learned scholars were recruited and assigned government offices was extremely attractive to intellectuals in Europe, where social mobility was severely limited under the hereditary system of aristocratic lineage. As Adolf Reichwein (1925, p. 26) argued many years ago, the eighteenth century was the time of the first "metaphysical contact" between China and the West, and philosophers such as Leibniz and Voltaire found in China and Confucian philosophy "a vision of happy living such as their own optimism had already dreamed of." Indeed, Reichwein (1925, p. 77) declares, "Confucius became the patron saint of eighteenth-century Enlightenment. Only through him could it find a connection link with China." The enthusiasm about China and Confucianism can be seen in Leibniz's (1994, p. 51) spirited proposal that the Europeans "need missionaries from the Chinese who might teach us the use and practice of natural religion, just as we have sent them teachers of revealed theology." For Leibniz (1994, p. 45), it was almost a divine plan that China and Europe should have developed such different but equally great civilizations at the opposite ends of the world "so that as the most civilized and distant peoples stretch out their arms to each other, those in between may gradually be brought to a better way of life." Thus, with very different agendas and ideological orientations, the Jesuit missionaries and the Enlightenment philosophers all believed in, and promoted, mutual understanding between the East and the West.

That cosmopolitan spirit, the idea that different peoples at great distance from one another with very different cultures and histories can understand each other and be brought together to form a common humanity, had a major influence in eighteenth-century European thinking. For the Enlightenment philosophers, the positive image of China as a country built on reason rather than religious faith had important implications for the secularization of European life. The Catholic Church, however, saw the secularizing tendency as a threat and did not appreciate the Jesuit presentation of a pagan country and a pagan culture in such a positive light. Shortly after Ricci's death, a heated debate known as the "Chinese rites controversy" flared up within the Catholic Church in the seventeenth and the early eighteenth centuries, in which the doctrinaire purists condemned the Jesuit "accommodation approach" for giving too many concessions to the language and culture of a pagan people. Whether Chinese converts to Christianity should be allowed to continue performing the rites of "ancestor worship," or paying homage to Confucius in the Confucian temples, became hotly contended issues. There was also the terminology debate, namely, whether the Chinese language could have terms to translate the Christian concepts of God, angels, and the other spiritual truths. In his study of that rites controversy, the French sinologist Jacques Gernet presents the purist argument that the Christian spiritual concepts and terms are indeed untranslatable into a pagan language like Chinese and, more fundamentally, they are not even conceivable in the Chinese mind. The Chinese converts had no real understanding of the truth of Christianity, and "where they appear to speak of our God and his Angels," as Gernet (1985, p. 33) quotes the Franciscan father Antonio de Caballero saying, "they are merely aping the Truth." Niccolò Longobardi, another purist opposed to Ricci's views, claimed that "the Chinese have never known any spiritual substance distinct from matter" (Gernet, 1985, p. 203). Eventually, the Jesuit "accommodation approach" was considered unacceptable, and the use of Chinese terms for translating God and other such concepts was forbidden; "the terms Heaven (*tian*) and Sovereign on High had to be condemned," as Gernet (1985, pp. 31–32) observes, "by Pope Clement XI in 1704 and 1715." What comes out of the Chinese rites controversy is thus a dichotomous view of China and Europe that sees the East and the West in a set of opposite concepts, terms, categories, and values.

Such a dichotomous view created in "the missionary beginnings of European sinology," as Haun Saussy (1993, p. 36) argues, still influences modern Western views of China. For example, seeing the Chinese rites controversy as a cultural conflict, Jacques Gernet (1985, p. 3) basically agrees with the Catholic purists and traces all the difficulties the missionaries encountered in China to a fundamental difference—"not only of different intellectual traditions but also of different mental categories and modes of thought." In his idea of the distinct "modes of thought," Gernet was probably influenced by Marcel Granet's (1884–1940) *Pensée chinoise* (1934), which described the "Chinese way of thinking" as fundamentally different from that of the Europeans and was in turn influenced by Lucien Lévy-Bruhl's (1857–1939) concept of the collective *mentalité*, which, according to Lévy-Bruhl, each people of the world had as a distinct "way of thinking." Gernet not only agrees with the purist view of the East-West dichotomy, but he gives that dichotomy a metaphysical foundation on the level of thinking and language, for he emphasizes the fundamental difference between China and the West as a sharp contrast between the Chinese and the Indo-European languages. "Now, a model of a language more different from that of Greek, Latin or Sanskrit cannot be imagined," says Gernet. He describes Chinese as a language without proper grammatical distinctions and therefore without the capability to express abstract notions, for "there was no word to denote existence in Chinese, nothing to convey the concept of being or essence, which in Greek is so conveniently expressed by the noun *ousia* or the neuter *to on*. Consequently, the notion of being, in the sense of an eternal and constant reality, above and beyond that which is phenomenal, was perhaps more difficult to conceive, for a Chinese" (Gernet, 1985, p. 241). For Gernet (1985, p. 244), language and the mode of thinking are interconnected, and the sharp contrast with Chinese "confirms Benveniste's analysis: the structure of Indo-European languages seems to have helped the Greek world—and thereafter the Christian one—to conceive the idea of realities that are transcendental and immutable as opposed to realities which are perceived by the senses and which are transitory."

Here we find a number of themes that are later picked up by other Western scholars, notably François Jullien, who in his many works reiterated in different ways the same dichotomy between Greece and China. He argues that "China presents a case study through which to contemplate Western thought from the outside" (Jullien, 2000, p. 9). This is his invariably repeated argument, which comes out rather clearly in the title of his book *Penser d'un Dehors (la Chine)*, in which he declares that the only way for an European to "go beyond the Greek framework" is to take a voyage that is "China-bound," because Chinese is the "only civilization that is recorded in substantial texts and whose linguistic and historical genealogy is radically non-European" (Jullien & Marchaisse, 2000, p. 39). Jonathan Spence (1998, p. 145) once remarked that to set up "mutually reinforcing images and perceptions" of an exotic China "seems to have been a particularly

French genius." That kind of exoticism, however, is certainly not limited to the French. Developing further the ideas of mentalities and modes of thinking, the American scholar Richard Nisbett (2003, pp. xvi–xvii) sets up a sharp contrast between all Westerners with all Asians: "Human cognition is not everywhere the same. First, that members of different cultures differ in their 'metaphysics,' or fundamental beliefs about the nature of the world. Second, that the characteristic thought processes of different groups differ greatly. Third, that the thought processes are of a piece with beliefs about the nature of the world: People use the cognitive tools that seem to make sense—given the sense they make of the world." In such a dichotomous view, all "Westerners" and all "Asians" think differently between them, but within the West or Asia, people think uniformly in one particular way. That is indeed another feature of the East-West dichotomy, namely, differences between cultures are overemphasized, while differences within the same culture are minimized. The absurdity of this particular view lies in the incredibly large concept of homogenous "Westerners" and "Asians," who are neatly set up as opposites without internal differences. Even more influential theoretically is the general tendency in contemporary Western scholarship toward an overemphasis on cultural differences and distinct identities. We may think of Jacques Derrida's (1976, p. 90) idea of *différance* and his claim that logocentrism is exclusively Western, or Michel Foucault's (1973, p. xv) image of China as an incomprehensible *heterotopia*.[1] All these constitute an intellectual environment that makes East-West comparative studies difficult, if not impossible, and if there is any effort at comparison at all, the emphasis is likely to fall on their differences much more than on any kind of similarities, shared values, or affinities.

Like the doctrinaire purists in the "Chinese rites controversy," some modern scholars view the Chinese as materialist without spiritual understanding, their mode of thinking concrete rather than abstract, and their outlook immanent rather than transcendental. Of course, not every sinologist subscribes to such a dichotomous view, but some do and they have exerted a noticeable influence on the way China and the Chinese are understood in the modern West. Again, like the doctrinaire purists in the "Chinese rites controversy," those who see the East and the West as opposites emphasize the untranslatability of concepts and terms, and the incommensurability of cultural values and ideas. "Oh, East is East, and West is West, and never the twain shall meet." These lines by Rudyard Kipling, the poet of the British Empire, are sometimes cited out of context to articulate the idea of cultural incommensurability between the East and the West. To quote Gernet (1985, p. 239) again, in the Chinese language it is "so difficult to express how the abstract and the general differ fundamentally, and not just occasionally, from the concrete and the particular" that it became, he declares, "an embarrassment for all those who had, in the course of history, attempted to translate into Chinese concepts formed in inflected languages such as Greek, Latin or Sanskrit. Thus, linguistic structures inevitably pose the question of modes of thought." Gernet made this claim despite the fact that Buddhist sutras in Sanskrit were translated into Chinese many centuries ago, but probably he would regard all Chinese translations of Sanskrit as nothing but distortions and corruptions, in which the pure essence of Buddhism was forever lost. This is a clear example of how those who see East and West as opposites would deny the possibility of translation in spite of historical and textual evidence, and how the dichotomous view powerfully influences their self-imposed "mode of thinking." Typically, the concept of untranslatability is a denial of communication that flies in the face of historical facts and textual evidence, for the purist insistence on an unadulterated essence is not concerned with the actual translation of texts, not even the actual cases of untranslatable words or terms, but the impossibility of understanding and communication on the level of conceptualization, the incommensurability of mentalities or mental categories.

Among modern critical theories, Thomas Kuhn is probably the most famous in proposing the incommensurability of different paradigms, which made a great impact on the study of philosophy, social sciences, and the humanities in general far beyond his original purpose of discussing the historical changes in science, or what he calls scientific revolutions. Kuhn argues that scientific revolution is a rupture, a complete breakthrough, the rise of a new paradigm that displaces the old, and that different paradigms are totally incommensurate. Scientists operating under different paradigms do not speak the same language; indeed, the paradigmatic change is so great that "after a revolution," says Kuhn (1970, p. 135), "scientists work in a different world." For quite some time in the 1970s and after, Kuhn's concept of radical incommensurability was borrowed to discuss cultures and traditions and became highly influential. Such borrowing had certain consequences that were not all that positive, because it fed the dichotomous view and, as Lindsay Waters (2001, p. 144) puts it, offered the "justification for a resurgent tribalism." In the humanities and social sciences, Kuhn's widely circulated idea became "a perversion of incommensurability," "the key idea that legitimates an identity politics that insists on the impossibility of thinking across groups." In its most militant form, "incommensurability legitimates a blinkered, absolutist, nonpluralist relativism" (Waters, 2001, p. 145). Such social consequences are certainly unintended, but even for the history of science, the concept of incommensurability is surely an exaggeration, because scientists working under different paradigms, for example, the Ptolemaic geocentric view and the Copernican heliocentric view, could quarrel over and debate important issues precisely because they understood what the other side was proposing as the center of the universe. Debate is also communication, and it certainly presupposes a language in which different views and their very difference can be expressed.

In his later years, Kuhn retreated from his concept of radical incommensurability famously proposed in his book, *The Structure of Scientific Revolution*, but he still insisted on the concept of untranslatability. He admits that when scientists working under different paradigms meet, they may indeed share most terms and much of the same language, but they understand certain terms they use very differently. On the one hand, Kuhn (2000, p. 36) allows a common language, and the problem of understanding is thus reduced and limited. "Only for a small subgroup of (usually inter-defined) terms and for sentences containing them do problems of translatability arise." Thus, incommensurability is localized as a linguistic problem, "a claim about language, about meaning change." On the other hand, however, the semantic change of terms can be so drastic that Kuhn (2000, p. 93) considers old and new terms to be untranslatable. "Incommensurability thus becomes a sort of untranslatability," he says, "localized to one or another area in which two lexical taxonomies differ." But the difficulty of translation, as Hilary Putnam (1990, p. 127) argues, "does *not* mean that there is no 'common language' in which one can say what the theoretical terms of both theories refer to." As a concept, untranslatability is a pure construct, for in reality translation, however difficult, partial, or imperfect it may be, has always worked to make human communication possible.

Translation does not have to engage two languages, because even understanding in the same language, as George Steiner (1975, p. 47) argues, is already translation, while inter-lingual translation is just a "special case of the arc of communication which every successful speech-act closes within a given language." Steiner uses the term "translation" in a broad sense to mean any cognitive or communicative act. "Any model of communication is at the same time a model of trans-lation, of a vertical or horizontal transfer of significance" (Steiner, 1975, p. 45). Translation across languages can provide a model because it most clearly poses questions of communication. "On the inter-lingual level, translation will pose concentrated, visibly intractable problems; but these same problems abound, at a more covert or conventionally neglected level, intra-lingually . . . *inside or between languages, human communication equals translation*" (Steiner, 1975, p. 47). Thus the purist concept of untranslatability is a denial of communication, a concept that pulls back toward parochialism, that is, toward the "natural" tendencies of inertia and ethnocentrism. "The very aim of translation—to open up in writing a certain relation with the Other, to fertilize what is one's Own through the mediation of what is Foreign," as Antoine Berman (1992, p. 4) argues, "is diametrically opposed to the ethnocentric structure of every culture, that species of narcissism by which every society wants to be a pure and unadulterated Whole." Indeed, the concept of untranslatability is based on nothing but that narcissistic desire of cultural and linguistic purity, the ethnocentric illusion that one's own language and culture are unique, superior to, and incomparable with any other.

In a narrow and restricted sense, we all know that certain words and expressions may indeed be untranslatable because what exists in one language may not exist or may not have a close equivalent in another. Many idioms, puns, set phrases, jokes, and technical terms are in this sense untranslatable, but that technical problem often finds solution in transliterations and loan words. This is in fact not the unique problem with translation, for the growth of language itself has always been a case of catachresis, that is, a process of borrowing from the existing vocabulary to signify what is new and unnamed, what Steiner calls "transfer of significance." This is true especially of abstract notions and concepts. As Giambattista Vico (1999, p. 76) observes, the "property of the human mind is that, when people can form no idea of distant and unfamiliar things, they judge them by what is present and familiar." He further points out "the fact that in all languages most expressions for inanimate objects employ metaphors derived from the human body and its parts, or from human senses and emotions" (Vico, 1999, p. 159). This seems to be the common principle of etymology and semantic growth in all languages, that is, to use a familiar term to signify something unfamiliar, based on some kind of a relation between the two, the known and the unknown, the familiar and the unfamiliar. In an ancient Chinese text, the appended words to the *Book of Changes*, we find a remarkably similar formulation of the same principle, where it is said that the ancient king Pao Xi invented hexagrams by observing the configurations of heaven and earth and by imitating the pattern of traces left by birds and animals on the ground. "By taking hints near at hand from his body and farther away from external things, he created hexagrams to make the virtue of gods comprehensible and the nature of all things known in signs" ("Zhouyi zhengyi" [The correct meaning of the Book of Changes], 1980, p. 86). This is later understood as the way in which Chinese scripts are created as well. That is to say, language and its vocabulary are largely metaphorical; they grow by borrowing from their own stock, as it were, by transferring the meaning of one word to another. Words are taken out on loan not only between languages, as in translation, but within the same language as well. That is the reason why George Steiner, as we have seen above, emphatically asserts that "*inside or between languages, human communication equals translation*" (emphasis in original). Understanding, translation, communication—all these acts of cognition are efforts to make sense of an original at a remove, to interpret something from the past in our present moment, and therefore acts of using one expression to signify another, but not the purist fantasy of reproduction of the original.

In a famous essay on translation, Walter Benjamin (1973, p. 70) emphatically states that "the translatability of linguistic creations ought to be considered even if men should prove unable to translate them." Benjamin is speaking on a metaphysical level rather than the level of technical considerations of translation as practice. Deeply rooted in Jewish mysticism as well as German philosophical idealism, Benjamin conceives of translation not as a mere rendering of an original foreign work, but as the attempt to articulate what no work in the original can articulate, what he calls the intention of all languages or the "pure language." As Berman (1992, p. 7) comments, Benjamin's idea of the task of the translator "would consist of a search, beyond the buzz of empirical languages, for the 'pure language' which each language carries within itself as its messianic echo. Such an aim, which has nothing to do with the ethical aim, is rigorously metaphysical in the sense that it platonically searches a 'truth' beyond natural languages." In Benjamin's own words, it is this "pure language" that links all languages together. "Languages are not strangers to one another," he remarks, "but are, a priori and apart from all historical relationships, interrelated in what they want to express" (Benjamin, 1973, p. 72). What all languages want to express is a deep intention, "the intention underlying each language as a whole—an intention, however, which no single language can attain by itself but which is realized only by the totality of their intentions supplementing each other: pure language. While all individual elements of foreign languages—words, sentences, structure—are mutually exclusive, these languages supplement one another in their intentions" (Benjamin, 1973, p. 74). To put it in a clear way, Benjamin insists on the translatability of languages because human communication is rooted in the very nature of all languages and their shared intentionality. To affirm translatability is thus to affirm that things, values, and ideas in different individuals, social groups and cultural traditions are essentially commensurable, that it is possible to have understanding and communication across barriers of languages and cultures. In making comparisons and finding equivalents between what is alien and what is familiar, and in bringing what is foreign to our own range of knowledge, translation expands our minds and bridges linguistic and cultural differences.

But when the differences are between the East and the West, is translation still possible? My argument so far has of course tried to give a definitely positive answer, but as long as the dichotomous view of cultural incommensurability and the overemphasis on cultural difference exert a considerable influence on scholarly discourses, East-West studies still face great challenges. As we move into an increasingly globalized world in the twenty-first century, however, things are changing rapidly, the physical as well as the psychological distance between the East and the West is diminishing, and East-West studies are emerging as a burgeoning new field of study in social sciences and the humanities. The critique of Eurocentrism and any other kind of ethnocentrism has prepared the way for a truly open horizon and the possibility, as Kwame Anthony Appiah (2006, p. xvi) argues, of a new kind of cosmopolitanism, a strongly committed moral sense "that each human being has responsibilities to every other." The social and intellectual climate now seems to have changed favorably for East-West studies. Translation, as I said earlier, has always worked in various degrees to make human communication possible, and in our world today with East Asian economy and culture on the rise, East-West studies are drawing more attention in scholarship internationally, and may finally have a chance to gain better cross-cultural understanding and communication. The challenge of acquiring adequate linguistic skills and in-depth knowledge of both Eastern and Western traditions is quite daunting, and it constitutes another challenge for engaging in East-West studies. Given such challenges, it is certainly no easy task for any scholar to acquire sufficient linguistic skills and cultural knowledge to engage in serious work in East-West studies, but that is definitely a task worthy of our effort, a new area of study to which we shall feel proud to make significant contributions.

REFERENCES

Appiah, A. (2006). *Cosmopolitanism: Ethics in a world of strangers.* New York: W. W. Norton.

Benjamin, W. (1973). The task of the translator (trans., H. Zohn). In H. Arendt, ed., *Illuminations* (pp. 69–82). Glasgow: Fontana.

Berman, A. (1992). *The experience of the foreign: Culture and translation in romantic Germany* (trans., S. Heyvaert). Albany: State University of New York Press.

Derrida, J. (1976). *Of grammatology* (trans., G. C. Spivak). Baltimore: Johns Hopkins University Press.

Foucault, M. (1973). *The order of things: An archaeology of the human sciences.* New York: Vintage Books.

Gernet, J. (1985). *China and the Christian impact: A conflict of cultures* (trans., J. Lloyd). Cambridge: Cambridge University Press

Honour, H. (1961). *Chinoiserie: The vision of Cathay.* New York: E. P. Dutton.

Jullien, F. (2000). *Detour and access: Strategies of meaning in China and Greece* (trans., S. Hawkes). New York: Zone Books.

Jullien, F., & Marchaisse, T. (2000). *Penser d'un dehors, la Chine: Entretiens d'Extrême-Occident.* Paris: Éditions du Seuil.

Kuhn, T. S. (1970). *The structure of scientific revolutions.* Chicago: University of Chicago Press.

Kuhn, T. S. (2000). Commensurability, comparability, communicability. In J. Conant & J. Haugeland, eds., *The road since* Structure: *Philosophical essays, 1970–1993, with an autobiographical interview.* Chicago: University of Chicago Press.

Larner, J. (1999). *Marco Polo and the discovery of the world.* New Haven, CT: Yale University Press.

Leibniz, G. W. (1994). Preface to the *Novissima Sinica* (trans., D. J. Cook & H. Rosemont). In *Writings on China.* Chicago: Open Court.

Nisbett, R. E. (2003). *The geography of thought: How Asians and Westerners think differently—and why.* New York: Free Press.

Putnam, H. (1990). The Craving for objectivity. In J. Conant, ed., *Realism with a human face.* Cambridge, MA: Harvard University Press.

Reichwein, A. (1925). *China and Europe: Intellectual and artistic contacts in the eighteenth century* (trans., J. C. Powell). New York: Knopf.

Saussy, H. (1993). *The problem of a Chinese aesthetic.* Stanford, CA: Stanford University Press.

Spence, J. D. (1998). *The Chan's great continent: China in Western minds.* New York: W. W. Norton.

Steiner, G. (1975). *After Babel: Aspects of language and translation.* New York: Oxford University Press.

Vico, G. (1999). *New science* (trans., D. Marsh). Harmondsworth, UK: Penguin.

Waters, L. (2001). The age of incommensurability. *Boundary 2,* 28 (2): 133–72.

Wood, F. (1995). *Did Marco Polo go to China?* London: Secker & Warburg.

Yang, Z. (1999). *Make Boluo zai Zhongguo* [Marco Polo in China]. Tianjin: Nankai University Press.

Zhang, L.-X. (1992). *The tao and the logos: Literary hermeneutics, East and West.* Durham, NC: Duke University Press.

Zhang L.-X. (1998). *Mighty opposites: From dichotomies to differences in the comparative study of China.* Stanford, CA: Stanford University Press.

Zhouyi zhengyi [The correct meaning of the Book of Changes]. (1980). In Y. Ruan, ed., *Shisan jing zhushu* [Thirteen classics with annotations] (vol. 1). Beijing: Zhonghua.

NOTE

1. I have argued against such exoticization of China and East-West dichotomies in my works: see Zhang (1992) for a discussion on Derrida's critique of logocentrism; Zhang (1998, chapter 1) for a discussion on Foucault's idea of China as *heterotopia*.

CHAPTER THIRTEEN

Public Spheres, Fields, Networks

Western Concepts for a De-Westernizing World?

Rodney Benson

Media research is finally internationalizing in its geopolitical ambitions, but what does or should this mean for how scholars theorize, analyze, and evaluate data? At least three distinct claims are being made about the challenges of truly international media research. The first is that moving beyond Anglo-American and continental European contexts introduces a new level of empirical variation and complexity, requiring new theoretical models (Appadurai, 1990; Thussu, 2009). The second is that as research begins to flow in multiple directions—the West studying the non-West, the non-West studying the West, the non-West studying the non-West (with "West" and "non-West" of course always encompassing multiple standpoints)—questions of epistemology, of the limits and biases of forms of knowledge, come to the fore (Smith, 1999). And the third is that baseline Western attitudes of what constitutes the good and just and "democratic" society—indeed whether democracy is the only worthy goal—can no longer be presumed (Latour, 2005a; Silverstone, 2006).

One could argue that the challenge is so far-reaching and fundamental that entirely new non-Western theories and models are needed, or more radically, that the "North," however we define it, is simply not epistemologically or morally equipped to study or critique what is happening in the "South," and thus we need new researchers and new institutions of research too. Without accepting such critiques in their entirety, we can certainly agree that new theories and new research communities are more than welcome. But the reality is that global research is being conducted for the most part by the usual suspects using the usual theories. My question, then, is how well are some of these Western-originated theories meeting the ontological, epistemological, and normative challenges that emerge in diverse non-Western settings?

I focus my attention on three master concepts—public spheres, fields, and networks—that increasingly are being used to map the world's complex and inter-connected media environments. In this chapter, I analyze each of the terms based on how they are actually defined by their primary theoretical proponents (Jürgen Habermas and Bernhard Peters for public sphere, Pierre Bourdieu for field, and Manuel Castells and Bruno Latour for network) and deployed by international media scholars. Broadly speaking, I argue that as one moves from Habermas/Peters and Bourdieu, on the one hand, to Castells and especially Latour, on the other hand, the ontological accounts become more fluid, the epistemological accounts (to the extent they are elaborated) become more relativist, and the politics become more open-ended. I will conclude with a discussion of what is at stake in these different approaches and to what extent the various theories are mutually complementary, antagonistic, or simply represent distinct alternatives.

Public Sphere

The term "public sphere" is most closely associated with the work of Jürgen Habermas, and in general refers to the social space or spaces through which citizens debate and attempt to influence their government. There has long been criticism of the initial public sphere concept (Habermas, 1989) for being institutionally underspecified (Benson, 2004; Calhoun, 1992; Peters, 2008). Drawing extensively on the work of his late student and colleague Bernhard Peters (translated into English and collected in Wessler, 2008), Habermas now acknowledges the multi-layered complexity of the contemporary public sphere, in an effort to develop a model with "empirical relevance" (Habermas, 1996, p. 373; 2006).

In the essay that laid the foundation for this approach, Peters (2008) argues that democratic societies are organized according to principles of "center" and "periphery." The "institutional core of the system of government" has four departments: "the parliamentary complex, the judiciary, government ['the political leadership'] and administration ['non-political' or civil service]" (Peters, 2008, p. 23). The outer periphery consists of the informal associations of the lifeworld's various "private" social spheres (p. 20). Mass media, along with other public sphere organizations, play a crucial role as an intermediary "sluice" to bring progressive and emancipatory ideas from this outer periphery into the center. The public sphere is at the inner periphery of the political system, consisting of "mass media, opinion research, numerous and diverse communicative networks and 'publics' crystallized around current topics or around publications, professional contacts and contexts for discussion specific to particular milieus." While the center or core is where "debates or processes linked to the resolution of problems are condensed and formed into decisions," the "legitimacy of (these) decisions depends on the formation of opinions and political will in the periphery" (Peters, 2008, p. 25).

How well does this new model work in practice to describe communication practices at least partially outside of Europe and North America and transcending a single nation-state? Sonia Serra (2000) uses a case study of activism, media coverage, and policy making around the issue of "the killing of street children" in Brazil to try to demonstrate this (new) Habermasian "international public sphere" in action. For many years, Brazilian religious, left-wing, and human rights activists from the "periphery" challenged national government policies that encouraged or at least permitted the police killings of poor youths, many of whom were engaged in petty or even violent crime (see, e.g., the film *City of God*). They made no progress until their activities were able to attract the attention of such international NGOs as Amnesty International and the Catholic Church, and through them well-respected media outlets such as *Le Monde*, the *Guardian*, the *New York Times*, and CNN, which acted as "sluices" to move the issue from the Brazilian periphery simultaneously to the Brazilian governmental center and to Western/international centers of power such as the United Nations (and linked organizations UNICEF and Defense for Children International) and the Organization of American States. As a result of this international (U.S./European) attention, the Brazilian government created a national commission to deal with the problem and ultimately enacted a new law restricting police killings, over the objections of "powerful groups in the judiciary, the army, the police and business associations" (Serra, 2000, p. 162).

On one level, this is a story about peripheral associations "outside the structure of power" in a developing country allying themselves with (Western) international civil society groups and mainstream media organizations in order to "influence national policy-making" (Serra, 2000, p. 169). It complicates Habermas's center-periphery model: in effect, the periphery challenges one national center of power (Brazil) by mobilizing support from international bodies (UN-related) whose power in turn ultimately rests on linkages to the globally dominant national centers of power (such as the United States, United Kingdom, France). But it is precisely in this linkage to U.S. and European power that we see the democratic and critical limits of this international public sphere, at least in this particular case. It's not so surprising that Western media were willing to cover a dramatic, heartrending story that also reaffirmed "cultural images of Third World countries as places of barbarism" (Serra, 2000, p. 166). The killing must stop, the NGOs and Western media pronounced. But what of the social conditions that helped produce the petty crime and the police brutality, what of the role of Western governments and corporations and international monetary bodies in encouraging and facilitating economic policies that contributed to Brazil's extremes of wealth and poverty? The "progressive" NGOs and media had almost nothing to say about these problems: in effect, the real "center" in this account—the Western and international centers of power—were challenged not in the slightest and even allowed to revel in their sense of moral superiority and beneficence.

Serra acknowledges these complexities and ironies. In the end, her account demonstrates the utility and flexibility of Habermas's new public sphere theory for transnational and non-Western research, even as it exposes the sharp limitations of Habermasian deliberative democratic politics to move Western powers toward substantial self-critique and progressive economic reform.

As for its epistemological and normative aspects, Habermas's model was initially based on his historical research on the emergence of the western European bourgeois public sphere as a counterpoint to state power, and Habermas has been a vocal defender of the Western Enlightenment project. However, his concept of "communicative action"—in which knowledge is supposed to be produced through a process of mutual understanding—by definition seems quite epistemologically open. Research guided by communicative action, whose forms would by necessity change in any given cultural setting, would seem to be the absolutely necessary precondition for any attempt to engage with the "Other," even if it remains vague (by necessity) how this engagement, let alone comprehension, is to be achieved.

More problematic perhaps is Habermas's normative stance in favor of a particular kind of democracy—deliberative democracy—which may not be appropriate for all societies. In his recent work (1996; see also his essay in Calhoun, 1992), Habermas acknowledges the need to make room for a wider variety of communication styles to ensure that a narrowly defined "rational" public deliberation does not end up reinforcing privileges rooted in education, wealth, and patriarchy. Nevertheless, the continued focus on open-ended deliberation may be neither politically realistic nor resonate with long-standing cultural practices in some non-Western societies.

Whether the public sphere ideal is used narrowly (to emphasize the need for reasoned, critical debate) or broadly (to emphasize inclusion, and make room for diverse communicative styles) does not necessarily correlate with the national origin or location of the scholar. United Arab Emirates media scholar Muhammad Ayish (2006) is sharply critical of Al Jazeera's *The Opposite Direction* for its extreme sensationalism—what he terms "brinkmanship"—and he offers a careful quantitative parsing of the show's techniques aimed at bringing guests to the verge of fisticuffs. While acknowledging the show's importance as a forum for "robust debate," Ayish concludes in high Habermasian fashion that "talk shows need to promote real dialogue rather than sensational shouting matches among participants" (p. 125). On the other hand, American media scholar Marc Lynch, while acknowledging similar problems of sensationalism, tends to emphasize the positive aspects of Arab media. According to Lynch (2006, pp. 247–48), "the new Arab public sphere is a genuine public sphere, characterized by self-conscious, open, and contentious political argument . . . reform has been a consistent obsession of this new public, a constant topic of intense public argument in the op-ed pages and on the talk shows."

Field

The concept of field is most often associated with the French sociologist Pierre Bourdieu, though in fact it is also widely used by "new institutionalist" theorists and researchers (e.g., Powell & Dimaggio, 1991; Fligstein 2001; in media studies, see Cook, 1998) and the term itself owes its origins to the social psychologist Kurt Lewin (see Martin, 2003). The "fields" in field theory refer to the contemporary differentiation of society into multiple, competing, hierarchically organized, partially autonomous, and increasingly specialized spaces of professional and creative endeavor. Within and among these fields, relations of power fundamentally structure human action. Bourdieu brings Ferdinand de Saussure to Max Weber, Karl Marx and Émile Durkheim, insisting that the "real is relational" at both the social and discursive levels: the fundamental opposition is between economic and various forms of cultural power, which at the same time are inter-convertible and can thus be allied.

Empirically, field theory offers a flexible model that nonetheless aspires to universal validity. As a comparativist, Bourdieu rejects in principle any claim that there are "transhistorical laws of the relations between fields," insisting that "we must investigate each historical case separately" (Bourdieu & Wacquant, 1992, p. 109). Yet, in a speech delivered at the University of Todai, Japan, in 1989, Bourdieu (1998c) insists that the deep structural, relational analysis of culture and power that he developed from his research in Algeria and France is not limited to those settings, but has wider, even universal applicability:

> I think that if I were Japanese I would dislike most of the things that non-Japanese people write about Japan. . . . Does this mean that I shall confine myself to the particularity of a single society and shall not talk in any way about Japan? I do not think so. I think, on the contrary, that by presenting the model of social space and symbolic space that I constructed for the particular case of France, I shall still be speaking to you about Japan (just as, in other contexts, I would be speaking about Germany or the United States). (p. 1)

Bourdieu (1998c) continues, and it is worth quoting at length, particularly since this viewpoint will be so roundly condemned by another theorist we are about to consider:

> I am convinced that, although it has all the appearance of ethno-centrism, an approach consisting of applying a model constructed according to this [relational] logic to another social world is without doubt more respectful of historic realities (and of people) and above all more fruitful in scientific terms than the interest in superficial features of the lover of exoticism who gives priority to picturesque differences . . . The researcher . . . seeks to apprehend the structures and mechanisms that are overlooked—although for different reasons—by the native and the foreigner alike, such as the principles of construction of social space or the mechanisms of reproduction of that space, and that the researcher seeks to represent in a model aspiring to *universal validity*. (pp. 2–3, italics in original)

What is potentially universal then is a basic structural, relational model of social relations.[1] The concrete forms that it takes in any given social context are expected to vary. As a working hypothesis, across the industrialized world at this particular moment, one would certainly predict the economic field to be dominant. But contra Marx, this is not the result of any historical necessity; it is just, in Weberian fashion, the contingent result of a path-dependent historical process. How dominant the economic field will be, how autonomous the opposing fields of cultural production will be, and how the realms of the economic and cultural are understood would certainly be expected to vary cross-nationally. In the industrialized West, especially in western Europe, the artistic and scientific "cultural" fields will constitute the primary opposition to the economic field; however, in many countries the religious field may be the major opposing field or even the dominant field. In some countries, the military or command-economy political fields may be dominant. Thus, in Bourdieu's field theory, a basic structural framework posited to have universal validity is balanced, at least partially, by an open-ended investigation of the particular empirical forms that these structures will take in any given social realm.

Indeed, field theory is already being put to use in fruitful ways for a variety of studies beyond the Anglo-American or French orbits (e.g., Kjær & Slaatta, 2007; Hovden, 2008; Hallin & Mancini, 2004), as well as comparative studies that demonstrate the persistence of national field logics against the supposed homogenizing force of Americanization (e.g., Benson & Hallin, 2007; Benson, Blach-Ørsten, Powers, Willig, & Vera Zambrano, 2012; Benson, 2013). In recent years, field theory also has been adopted usefully for scholarship of the global South.[2]

Orayb Najjar (2007) draws on field theory for a study of the rise of transnational news media outlets like Al Jazeera (Arabic and International) in Qatar and TeleSur in Venezuela. Najjar goes beyond a straight political economy account to emphasize, in Bourdieuian fashion, distinctions between funding (economic capital) and legitimacy (symbolic capital), and the relational basis of all symbolic claims to legitimacy. Najjar takes seriously field theory's insistence that field relations extend beyond national boundaries, as when Bourdieu (1998b, p. 41) remarks that for a journalistic field analysis to be complete "the position of the national media field within the global media field would have to be taken into account."

In Najjar's study of Al Jazeera and TeleSur, field structure and dynamics are shown to be a product of history, which in the case of global media must take into account the global South's long-simmering dissatisfaction with the ethnocentrism of the dominant Western news agencies counter-balanced by admiration of U.S. journalistic professional ideals, which emphasize "independence" from the state. This pre-existing state of the field helps explain why Al Jazeera and TeleSur, in their effort to expand their audience, revenues, and professional legitimacy, have been constrained to simultaneously emphasize their links to UNESCO's challenge to U.S. media hegemony during the 1970s *and* their autonomy from their sponsoring states (Qatar in the case of the former; primarily Venezuela, but also Argentina, Uruguay, Cuba, and Brazil in the case of the latter) (Najjar, 2007, pp. 7–8).

Najjar thus nicely captures how the drive for symbolic capital shapes action in the global journalistic field:

> TeleSur, even while introducing a revolutionary project, could not move away from the tenets of global journalism and from the negative perception of media owned by government. Because the idea for TeleSur was initially proposed by Cuba's President Castro and because the station's critics were already calling it "Telechavez" even before it went on air, the station had to work to "unbrand" itself by moving away from a political field funded by the president of Venezuela, to [a relatively more autonomous position] similar to Al-Jazeera, i.e., funded by the ruler but whose board of directors is independent. (p. 10)

In a world in which U.S. political, economic, and cultural hegemony are arguably diminishing, Al Jazeera's efforts to professionalize and diversify journalistic staff (as Al Jazeera International is well known for doing), to provide a wide diversity of perspectives, and to cover in a sustained and non-sensationalistic manner areas of the world ignored by the Western media are likely to reap real dividends in the accumulation of symbolic capital; indeed, they already have, if a glowing appraisal of Al Jazeera English in the *Columbia Journalism Review* is any indicator (Editors, 2011). Ironically, the U.S. government has failed to recognize how influence is contingent on symbolic capital in its openly government-funded and controlled "public diplomacy" efforts to counter Al Jazeera; as Najjar (2007, p. 17) notes, these efforts are "viewed as illegitimate because they fall in the political, rather than in the journalistic field."

In contrast to Habermas, epistemological questions are front and center in field theory, at least in Bourdieu's version of it. Attitudes, tastes, physical bearing—what Bourdieu terms "habitus"—are all indelibly shaped by one's position in this complex system of stratification and the partially contingent circumstances through which one arrived at this position: "To speak of habitus is to assert that the individual, and even the personal, the subjective, is social, collective. Habitus is socialized subjectivity" (Bourdieu & Wacquant, 1992, p. 126). Of course, this goes for the social researcher as much as for anyone else. How then does field theory escape an empirically paralyzing relativity, the kind that marks Niklas Luhmann's systems theory? In a word: reflexivity.

For Bourdieu, what makes scientific research "scientific" is less the systematic testing of hypotheses and gathering of facts than it is the adequacy of one's epistemological break with naturalized, common sense categories of knowledge. Heavily influenced by the French epistemologist Gaston Bachelard, Bourdieu succinctly describes his research process: "Facts are conquered [through rupture with common sense], constructed, confirmed" (Bourdieu et al., 1991, p. 24). Before one can adequately "objectivize" a given social world, one must also engage in self-objectivation, meaning not only taking into account class trajectory and position, ethnicity, and gender, but also the privileged position of the "scholarly gaze" that produces knowledge "from afar and from above": "What must be objectivized is not (only) the individual who does the research in her biographical idiosyncrasy but the position she occupies in academic space and the biases implicated in the view she takes by virtue of being 'off-sides' or 'out of the game'" (Bourdieu & Wacquant, 1992, pp. 70–72).

If Bourdieuian reflexivity conceptually solves the epistemological problem of producing objective knowledge transcending the biases of the observer, in both his or her individual specificity and institutional location, it is a little more mysterious about how this process works in practice. From my observations and readings of many Bourdieu-inspired studies, as well as my own research, reflexivity means never accepting without skepticism the categories offered up by official agencies or previous scholarly research, treating one's own categories as provisional subject to ongoing critical reflection (e.g., what presumptions are built into terms, whose interests do they implicitly support, who or what is excluded by use of such terms), and spending just as much time listening to the individuals acting in a field and learning about their practice-based "subjective" categories of action as in gathering data about the "objective" social factors that supposedly constrain their action. Bourdieu's injunction to interrogate naturalized categories is not so far from Blumler, McLeod, and Rosengren's (1992, pp. 3–18) defense of comparative research that "cosmopolitanizes, opening our eyes to communication patterns and problems unnoticeable in our own spatial and temporal milieux."

What are field theory's implicit normative stances, its politics? For Bourdieu, economic injustice furthered through the "symbolic violence" of the state and the mass media is a significant problem and one that he denounced as an "activist" in his later years (see, e.g., Bourdieu, 1998c). Seemingly separate from this project is Bourdieu's spirited defense of artistic and especially scientific autonomy (Bourdieu, 1996), though Bourdieu has argued that a science understood as a critique of received categories of knowledge and as the uncovering of relations of power is inherently allied to projects of social justice. While Bourdieu has written eloquently and critically about patriarchy (2002) and his long-time collaborator Abdelmalek Sayad was a leading French scholar of immigration, "social justice" is conceptualized almost entirely in terms of economic justice and worker rights. He has been critical of U.S.-style identity and ethnic politics, not only their culturally imperialistic pretensions to be applicable to the rest of the world, but also, implicitly, the uses to which they have been put to suppress attention to what he would see as more pressing problems of economic justice (Bourdieu & Wacquant, 1999).

These political stances, however, are not inherent to field theory, that is, a relational-structural model of social relations acknowledging the existence of multiple, if limited, forms of power (capital) that extend beyond just economic power. In "new institutionalist" field theory, the stance is often relatively conservative, or at least conventionally "liberal pluralist": in these approaches, there is no presumption of the overwhelming power of the economic field, and there is little or no attention paid to deep culturally patterned class stratification (see, e.g., some chapters in Powell & DiMaggio, 1991).

Network

Analysis of social networks has diverse intellectual sources and long precedes the current fascination with the worldwide digital network commonly called the Internet.[3] I focus on two strains of network theory that seem to me to have particular relevance for global media studies: the "network society" model of Manuel Castells (1996, 1997, 2000, 2007), and the actor-network theory most often associated with Bruno Latour (2005a; but see also Callon, 1986, and Law, 2007).

Although Castells is now widely associated with network analysis, in his 19 February 2010 introductory speech at a USC-Annenberg conference (see endnote 3), he conceded that his initial preferred title of his book *The Network Society* was actually "flows" and it was only the publisher who suggested "network society" as a more exciting title and an apt description of Castells's account of the rise of the Internet. In contrast, Latour and others developed the concept of actor-networks long before the Internet as a means of avoiding the individual-society opposition and as a methodological blueprint for research in the sociology of science; only in recent years has Latour turned his attention to digital networks and have media researchers turned to Latour (see, e.g., Turner, 2005; Hemmingway, 2008). I begin with Castells both because of his earlier link to media studies and because his framework lies somewhere between the macro-political economy models of Habermas and Bourdieu and the more micro-oriented, anti-structuralist, and epistemologically relativist approach of Latour.[4]

Castells's Network Society

Castells's admitted hesitation about the title of the first volume of his three-part, truly encyclopedic *The Information Age* is telling: his project is about a lot of things, and "network" per se is not necessarily at the center. In an analysis (similar to those of David Harvey and others) emphasizing an epochal economic change since the 1970s from a Fordist to a post-Fordist, "flexible accumulation" capitalist order, Castells (2000, p. 695) argues that alongside this "new economy" there has also emerged a "new society"—"a society where the key social structures and activities are organized around electronically processed information networks." For Castells, networks are "set[s] of interconnected nodes . . . flexible, adaptive structures that, powered by information technology, can perform any task that has been programmed in the network." Networks have long existed alongside "large, centralized apparatuses"; the rise of the Internet simply provides a powerful technological boost for networks over other forms of social organization (p. 695). What thus sets Castells apart from geographers and critical political economists like David Harvey is his emphasis on technology, which at times approaches McLuhan-style technological determinism (though he rejects the label).

For Castells, media are increasingly central to the operation of power across the globe. This is so because of the convergence of previous forms of media (radio, television, print) into the single medium of the Internet. As Castells (2007) writes in one of his most compact and cogent essays:

> [T]he ongoing transformation of communication technology in the digital age extends the reach of communication media into all domains of social life in a network that is at the same time global and local, generic and customized in an ever-changing pattern. As a result, power relations, that is the relations that constitute the foundation of all societies, as well as the processes challenging institutionalized power relations are increasingly shaped and decided in the communication field. (p. 239)

Inside this communication field or "media space," Castells (1997, p. 312) suggests politics is "structured" by the "logic" of electronic media, a logic defined as involving "computerized political marketing, instant polling as an instrument of political navigation, [and] character assassination as political strategy."

Castells does an admirable job in documenting changes in political communication that are increasingly evident around the world, and despite his oft-stated view that states are losing power in relation to global capital, he cites and has helped publish a number of Western and non-Western national case studies that highlight cross-national variation in the functioning of the global "network society" (see Castells, 2004). Castells acknowledges exceptions to a fault. The problem is that he doesn't theorize them. Castells's broad concept of "media space" cannot help explain why some political debates are more or less simplified, personalized, dramatized, or contextualized than others (for instance, he notes in passing that trust in government has not declined in Scandinavia, but he doesn't ask why; see Castells, 2007, p. 244).

Partially counter-balancing this (mass) media logic, a "new kind of media space" of "mass self-communication" ("horizontal networks of interactive communication") has also emerged on the Web (Castells, 2007). Blogs, social media websites, and a range of other kinds of user-created media sites, increasingly connected to mobile telephony, are changing the way the Internet is used and who uses it. While much of this horizontal network communication is apolitical, it is also linked to an increase in the number, range of types, and global reach of social movement activism. On the one hand, the Internet makes it easier for activists to directly challenge corporate power via "culture jamming . . . a strategy that turns corporate power against itself by co-opting, hacking, mocking, and re-contextualizing meanings" by creating and circulating negative, often humorous messages or images about corporate brands (Bennett, 2003). On the other hand, militant groups, such as the Zapatistas in Mexico, have used the Internet to create international support networks on behalf of battles against both national governments and (less effectively) global economic and political institutions (Castells, 1997; Russell, 2001).

Even as "mass self-communication" potentially aids resistance movements in developing countries, Castells (2007, p. 249) insightfully notes that "the development of the technology of self-communication is also the product of our culture, a culture that emphasizes individual autonomy and the self-construction of the project of the social actor," thus suggesting that it could also serve as a form of U.S./European modernizing stealth power. Castells also emphasizes the ways in which capitalist media corporations have attempted to co-opt and gain access for advertising and marketing research on various social networking websites, as evidenced by Google's ownership of YouTube, Yahoo Inc!'s purchase of Tumblr, and so on.

Castells's use of theory of whatever sort is flexible, eclectic, and pragmatic. If he has an explicit epistemology, he does not highlight it. His observations are tested in the crucible of continuous, often team-based empirical research that draws on diverse primary and secondary sources.

Politically, like both Habermas and Bourdieu, his work emphasizes the progressive potential of social movement action. Unlike Bourdieu, he acknowledges and seems to approve of "new" cultural and identity-based social movements as well as class-based activism. Castells (2007) differs from both Habermas and Bourdieu in his arguably more optimistic assessment of long-term political outcomes:

It is plausible to think that the capacity of social actors to set up autonomously their political agenda is greater in the networks of mass self-communication than in the corporate world of the mass media. While the old struggle for social domination and counter-domination continues in the new media space, the structural bias of this space toward the powers that be is being diminished every day by the new social practices of communication. (pp. 257–58) (see also Castells 2012)

Latour's Actor-Network Theory

In contrast to Castells, who places contemporary economic and technological transformations front and center in his work, Latour and other Actor-Network Theory (ANT) theorists claim that actor-networks are and have always been the fundamental building block of human societies: data collection enabled by the Internet simply make this aspect of human existence more "traceable" and visible (Latour, 2010).

While Latour's work originated in his studies of scientists, and originally had the most impact in the field of science and technology studies, in recent years he has linked his project to that of the nineteenth-century French sociologist Gabriel Tarde on behalf of a broader effort to challenge what he has called the "sociology of the social" (that is, any analysis that conceives of society as a sui generis unit of analysis, separate from and larger than the sum of its individual human parts). For Tarde, the representative of this "social" approach was Durkheim; for Latour, it is Pierre Bourdieu. In contrast to the sociology of the social, a Tardean/Latourian approach starts with the actor-network, that is an understanding of the human being (as well as non-human object) as constituted by its relations to other actors (both humans and non-human things) without any necessary link to a larger structure: "Every actor is a network, every network is made up of actors" (Latour, 2010; see also Latour, 2005b).

At first glance, ANT's relational approach would seem quite close to field theory. They are both forms of "constructivism," beginning from the premise that there is no unmediated knowledge of the real but rather that "principles of vision and division of the social world" (Bourdieu) or "objects of concern" (Latour) are socially and discursively produced. Both eschew abstract theorizing and are designed to be put to use in empirical research. Bourdieu's (1989) "structuralist constructivism," however, effectively privileges one construction over all others—that is, the reflexive sociologist's construction of the historically shaped structure within which others act. ANT's strict constructionism is neutral to an extreme, providing only a flat account of others' accounts without venturing any judgment on whose is closest to "reality." As Michel Callon (1986, p. 4) puts it, "Instead of imposing a pre-established grid of analysis . . . the observer follows the actors in order to identify the manner in which these define and associate the different elements by which they build and explain their world, whether it be social or natural."

No human, animal, or thing is privileged above another, thus ANT's famous, or infamous, equation of humans and non-humans. For this reason, some ANT theorists such as John Law (2007, p. 2) prefer the term "material semiotics" to describe their approach. While ANT theory would not deny that structures exist, it sees them as unstable, fragile, ephemeral, or, as philosopher Michel Serres has put it, "patches of order in a sea of disorder" (Law, 2007, p. 5). Law portrays ANT as "an empirical version of poststructuralism" with close affinities to Gilles Deleuze's nomadic philosophy. According to Law (2007, p. 6), both "actor-network" and "assemblage" (a Deleuzian term also used by Latour, Callon, and others) "refer to the provisional assembly of productive, heterogeneous and (this is quite crucial) quite limited forms of ordering located in no larger overall order."

The empirical relevance of such ANT theory to global media studies may not be obvious. But I would like to venture some possible connections. First, how stable are structures of global media and cultural power? ANT seems to lie at the extreme end of a range of theories that stress fluidity, uncertainty, impermanence. Castells moves in this direction, but does not let go of the notion of power as something that endures beyond the particular situation. At the February 2010 USC network theory conference (see endnote 3), Latour responded to Castells's (2010) remarks by suggesting that he abandon the notion of power and Castells "agreed to disagree completely." Similarly, Arjun Appadurai's (1990) conception of the global cultural economy as a "complex, overlapping, disjunctive order, which cannot any longer be understood in terms of existing center-periphery models (even those which might account for multiple centers and peripheries)" can be read as a rebuke, in advance, of Habermas's or Bourdieu's later writings on media power. Yet Appadurai's insistence that he does not want to completely "elide the social referent" (p. 6, n2) and his very use of the structural-sounding suffix "scapes" suggests he would not go as far as Latour and company in stressing contingency and chaos. Rather than decide the issue in advance, either in favor of fluidity/contingency or structure/constrained agency, it seems more reasonable to suggest that there is more agency and contingency in some social realms than others and this can only be confirmed through empirical research.

How do we simultaneously study the "global" and the "local" and their complex inter-relations? For Latour, there is no global and no local, just as there is no macro and no micro; there are only network sites (Wall Street trading rooms, scientific laboratories, legal offices, and so forth), with some being more "networky" than others, that is, approaching "a star-like shape with a center surrounded by many radiating lines with all sorts of tiny conduits leading to and fro" (2005b, p. 177). As Latour (2005b) argues:

> [A]s soon as the local sites that manufacture global structures are underlined, it is the entire topography of the social world that is being modified. Macro no longer describes a *wider* or a *larger* site in which the micro would be embedded like some Russian Matryoshka doll, but another equally local, equally micro place, which is *connected* to many others through some medium transporting specific types of traces. No place can be said to be bigger than any other place, but some can be said to benefit from far safer connections with many *more* places than others. (p. 176, italics in original)

A final potentially useful aspect of ANT is in the analysis of technology. As Tatnall and Gilding (1999, pp. 57–58, 63) argue, "ANT deals with the social-technical divide by denying that purely technical or purely social relations are possible" and thus seeks to avoid both technological and social determinisms. Fred Turner provides the example of Jim Romanesko's media news column for Poynter Online. The human being Jim Romanesko is only part of what makes his media site influential; the digital technology is also an actor, in the sense that "any *thing* that does modify a state of affairs by making a difference is an actor" (Latour, 2005b, p. 71). As Turner (2005, p. 323) writes, "From a traditional point of view, new media simply offer new channels for the distribution of information. From the point of view of ANT, however, they and their human partners collaborate in the creation of new socio-technical formations. Digital media do not just offer professionals like Romanesko a new voice; rather, they offer them the ability to build new linkages of institutions, individuals, and machines." Similarly, Emma Hemmingway's (2008) detailed ethnography of regional BBC television news highlights the way in which technologies (e.g., cameras and microphones, recording equipment) play an important role in shaping news production. She does so, however, not in a technological determinist vein, but rather in the ANT fashion of tracing what she sees as unstable, highly contingent collaborations between humans and machines.

Finally, ANT would seem to be the most epistemologically and politically open and non-judgmental of the theories examined here, making it especially appropriate for Western research in non-Western societies. The injunction to treat equivalently all actor accounts, including that of the researcher, provides assurance that both Western and non-Western perspectives, in all their diversity, will be presented and respected. And this extends to politics as well. If the good society is defined as what "assembles" people, then what works to assemble in one setting cannot be assumed to work in another. Against the deliberative democratic dreams of Habermas, Latour ventures "getting together might not be such a universal desire after all!" (2005a, p. 34). Latour argues (without documentation) that there are diverse worldwide attitudes toward basic Western notions such as "representation" (in the Japanese tradition, "the very word 'representation' strikes their ears as quaint and superficial"; ibid., p. 35) or "the idea of politics as speaking one's mind in the middle of an assembly" ("the Chinese tradition seems to ignore it entirely"; ibid.). "Can we enlarge our definition of politics to the point where it accepts its own suspension?" Latour asks. "But who can really be that open-minded? And yet, do we have another course of action?" (ibid., p. 36). Latour takes comfort in the fact that in spite of the lack of any success in conceptualizing a politics (democratic or otherwise) that could unite peoples across so many diverse cultures, the fact is that in myriad ways, through "those makeshift assemblages we call markets, technologies, science, ecological crises, wars and terrorist networks," we are already "connected"—"it's simply that our usual definitions of politics have not caught up yet with the masses of linkages already established" (ibid., p. 37).

Conclusion

Each of the terms (and their accompanying theoretical frameworks) discussed in this paper—public sphere, field, network (network society, actor-network)—has advantages and disadvantages for truly internationalized, de-Westernized, or trans-nationalized media research.

Public sphere is probably the most commonly used term for research extending beyond North America, western Europe, Australia, and New Zealand, but it is often used only descriptively rather than analytically. Habermas's "new" "core-periphery" public sphere model holds some promise as a framework for empirical research, especially if room is made for multiple cores and peripheries. Even so, it suffers from the shortcomings of Habermas's previous work in that it places too much weight on the periphery (or lifeworld) as the generator of emancipatory movements while simultaneously offering little guidance on how system components such as the media can effectively challenge concentrated political and economic power. A strict interpretation of Habermas's project in "deliberative" terms (civil, reasoned, inclusive debate) imposes a normative standard that is inappropriate or irrelevant (at least in the short term) for much of the globe; on the other hand, the notion of communicative action oriented toward mutual understanding provides both a normative and epistemological bridge between East and West, North and South.

Field theory is only beginning to be used in non-Western settings. As an empirical and epistemological model, it holds some promise. The basic framework points to social processes that are (potentially) at work in all societies, that is, relational processes of identity formation, unequal distribution of resources (capital), and especially the importance of symbolic as well as economic power. So far, the de-Westernizing and trans-nationalizing field-theory-inspired research I have encountered mostly ignores the issue of reflexivity (for the researcher) and only begins to tap the full potential of the empirical/conceptual toolkit.

Castells's "network society" has the virtue of offering a loose and flexible framework for empirical research related to the Internet in a variety of Western and non-Western settings. Network society theory highlights both technological and economic factors as well as the ongoing conflict between established power and new forms of counter-power. The virtue of the theory—its flexibility and comprehensiveness—can also be its weakness. However vaguely or flexibly defined, Castells retains an interest in power and democratic politics. The same cannot necessarily be said for actor-network theory. Does this make it the ideal theory for internationalizing media studies?

ANT theory is similar to field theory in that it begins with a series of basic guidelines to help orient research, though the guidelines themselves are quite different. In ANT, one should follow the actor, consider non-human objects and humans as equal partners in constituting networks, and look for nodes in the network that are mediators (which "transform, translate, distort, and modify the meaning or the elements they are supposed to carry") as opposed to intermediaries (transporting meaning "without transformation") (Latour, 2005b, p. 39). Moreover, rather than attempting to construct an objective portrait of the world with the help of reflexivity, and in so doing critically uncover relations of power, ANT does not privilege one account—epistemological, ontological, or normative-political—over another. Such extreme relativism seems antithetical to any truly critical project; behind the veneer of radical post-structuralism, ANT arguably ends up being a rather conventional form of pluralist theory (see Steven Lukes's [2005] "first face" of power). Even so, when Latour speaks

276 · INTERNATIONALIZING "INTERNATIONAL COMMUNICATION"

of re-assembling the social, he seems to be echoing Elihu Katz's important concern with community (see, e.g., Dayan & Katz, 1992). In an era of increasing ethnic, religious, and political strife, the virtues of such a community-mapping and building project should not be underestimated.

Despite such differences, there may be ways that the aforementioned theories are complementary as well as antagonistic. Public sphere theory, when it goes beyond a narrow defense of rational-critical deliberation, forces us to think and rethink the contours and limits of democracy. Even if a radical de-Westernizing in the spirit of Silverstone (2006) or various post-colonial theorists as noted by Thussu (2009) lies beyond the theory's grasp, at least the question of how to achieve domination-free politics has been raised. Field theory goes beyond the core-periphery model to show how power is structured relationally and involves both cultural as well as economic resources. Although Latour has insisted that his sociology of associations is the antithesis of Bourdieu's sociology of the social, some scholars have suggested that only the two models together can provide a complete portrait of the social world: as Bourdieu admits, the social space is not all fields, so perhaps actor-networks are the "spaces between" (Eyal, 2013). As for the network society, whether or not Castells is able to offer a fully coherent or consistent model, the synthesis of vast amounts of data is a significant contribution in its own right; through his voluminous books, articles, and edited volumes, and the output of his online journal *International Journal of Communication*, Castells has become the central node in an ever widening global network of empirical research with encyclopedic ambitions.

In sum, there is no reason why researchers can't fruitfully draw upon any or all of these approaches, and there is every indication that they are doing so, either in direct dialogue with one another (e.g., Volkmer's [2003] use of Castells to develop a model of the global public sphere); in respectful acknowledgment but limited engagement (e.g., Dahlgren's [2001] nod to Castells in an essay otherwise focused on Habermasian concerns); or in succession, as when researchers draw on Castells for one project, Bourdieu for the next, and so forth, depending on the case study and what it is that needs to be explained (e.g., Russell's [2001] network society analysis of the Zapatistas, followed by her [2007] field theory study of media coverage of the French urban riots).

Whether or not these theories have fully taken stock of their "Western" biases, they all have the virtue of moving beyond abstract philosophical quandaries to help facilitate systematic research. Habermas, Bourdieu,

Castells, and Latour certainly do not exhaust the possibilities for internationalizing media studies. They suggest only a range of possible approaches upon which or against which future theorizing—both Western and non-Western—might fruitfully build.

REFERENCES

Appadurai, A. (1990). Disjuncture and difference in the global cultural economy. *Public Culture* 2 (2): 1–24.
Ayish, M. I. (2006). Media brinkmanship in the Arab world: Al Jazeera's "the opposite direction" as a fighting arena. In M. Zayani, ed., *The Al Jazeera phenomenon: Critical perspectives on new Arab media* (pp. 106–26). Boulder, CO: Paradigm Publishers.
Bennett, W. L. (2003). New media power: The Internet and global activism. In N. Couldry & J. Curran, eds., *Contesting media power* (pp. 17–37). Lanham, MD: Rowman and Littlefield.
Benson, R. (2004). Bringing the sociology of media back in. *Political Communication* 21 (3): 275–92.
Benson, R. (2013). *Shaping immigration news: A French-American comparison.* Cambridge: Cambridge University Press.
Benson, R., Blach-Ørsten, M., Powers, M., Willig, I., & Vera Zambrano, S. (2012). Media systems online and off: Comparing the form of news in the U.S., Denmark, and France. *Journal of Communication* 62 (1): 21–38.
Benson, R., & Hallin, D. (2007). How states, markets and globalization shape the news. *European Journal of Communication* 22 (1): 27–48.
Benson, R., & Neveu, E., eds. (2005). *Bourdieu and the journalistic field.* Malden, MA: Polity.
Blumler, J. G., McLeod, J. M., & Rosengren, K. E. (1992). An introduction to comparative communication research. In J. G. Blumler, J. M. McLeod, & K. E. Rosengren, eds., *Comparatively speaking: Communication and culture across space and time.* Newbury Park, CA: Sage.
Bourdieu, P. (1989). Social space and symbolic power. *Sociological Theory* 7 (1): 14–25.
Bourdieu, P. (1996). *The rules of art: Genesis and structure of the literary field.* Stanford, CA: Stanford University Press.
Bourdieu, P. (1998a). *Acts of resistance: Against the tyranny of the market.* New York: New Press.
Bourdieu, P. (1998b). *On television.* New York: New Press.
Bourdieu, P. (1998c). Social space and symbolic space. *Practical reason* (pp. 1–13). Stanford, CA: Stanford University Press.
Bourdieu, P. (2002). *Masculine domination.* Stanford, CA: Stanford University Press.
Bourdieu, P., Chamboredon, J. C., Passeron, J. C., & Krais, B. (1991). *The craft of sociology.* New York: Walter de Gruyter.
Bourdieu, P., & Wacquant, L. (1992). *An invitation to reflexive sociology.* Chicago: University of Chicago Press.

Bourdieu, P., & Wacquant, L. (1999). On the cunning of imperialist reason. *Theory, Culture & Society* 16 (1): 41–58.

Calhoun, C. J., ed. (1992). *Habermas and the public sphere.* Cambridge, MA: MIT Press.

Callon, M. (1986). Some elements of a sociology of translation: Domestication of the scallops and the fishermen of St. Brieuc Bay. In J. Law, ed., *Power, action and belief: A new sociology of knowledge?* (pp. 196–223). London: Routledge.

Castells, M. (1996). *The rise of the network society.* Oxford: Blackwell.

Castells, M. (1997). *The power of identity.* Oxford: Blackwell.

Castells, M. (2000). Toward a sociology of the network society. *Contemporary Sociology* 29 (5): 693–99.

Castells, M., ed. (2004). *The network society: A cross-cultural perspective.* Cheltenham, UK: Edward Elgar.

Castells, M. (2007). Communication, power and counter-power in the network society. *International Journal of Communication* 1:238–66.

Castells, M. (2010). Remarks at USC-Annenberg conference on networks, 20 February. http://ascnetworksnetwork.org/ann-network-theory-seminar-report-manual-castells.

Castells, M. (2012). *Networks of outrage and hope: Social movements in the Internet age.* Malden, MA: Polity.

Cook, T. E. (1998). *Governing with the news.* Chicago: University of Chicago Press.

Dahlgren, P. (2001). The public sphere and the net: Structure, space, and communication. In W. L. Bennett & R. M. Entman, eds., *Mediated politics.* Cambridge: Cambridge University Press.

Dayan, D., & Katz, E. (1992). *Media events: The live broadcasting of history.* Cambridge, MA: Harvard University Press.

Editors. (2011). Lift the shroud: Why we need Al Jazeera English. *Columbia Journalism Review* 4 (4).

Eyal, G. (2013). Spaces between fields. In P. S. Gorski, ed., *Bourdieu and Historical Analysis* (pp. 158–82). Durham, NC: Duke University Press.

Fligstein, N. (2001). *The architecture of markets: An economic sociology of twenty-first-century capitalist societies.* Princeton, NJ: Princeton University Press.

Habermas, J. (1989). *The structural transformation of the public sphere: An inquiry into a category of bourgeois society.* Cambridge, MA: MIT Press.

Habermas, J. (1992). Further reflections on the public sphere. In C. Calhoun, ed., *Habermas and the public sphere* (pp. 421–61). Cambridge, MA: MIT Press.

Habermas, J. (1996). *Between facts and norms: Contributions to a discourse theory of law and democracy.* Cambridge, MA: MIT Press.

Habermas, J. (2006). Political communication in media society: Does democracy still enjoy an epistemic dimension? The impact of normative theory on empirical research. *Communication Theory* 16 (4): 411–26.

Hallin, D. C., & Mancini, P. (2004). *Comparing media systems: Three models of media and politics.* New York: Cambridge University Press.

Hemmingway, E. (2008). *Into the newsroom: Exploring the digital production of regional television news.* London: Routledge.

Hovden, J. F. (2008). Profane and sacred: A study of the Norwegian journalistic field. PhD diss., University of Bergen, Bergen, Norway.

Kjær, P., & Slaatta, T., eds. (2007). *Mediating business: The expansion of business journalism.* Copenhagen: Copenhagen Business School Press.
Latour, B. (2005a). From realpolitik to dingpolitik or how to make things public. In B. Latour & P. Weibel, eds., *Making things public: Atmospheres of democracy* (pp. 14–41). Cambridge, MA: MIT Press.
Latour, B. (2005b). *Reassembling the social: An introduction to actor-network-theory.* Oxford: Oxford University Press.
Latour, B. (2010). Remarks delivered to USC conference on networks, 19 February. Retrieved from http://ascnetworksnetwork.org/ann-network-theory-seminar-report-bruno-latour.
Law, J. (2007). Actor network theory and material semiotics. Available from John Law's STS webpage, retrieved 5 November 2010, http://www.heterogeneities.net/publications/Law2007ANTandMaterialSemiotics.pdf.
Lukes, S. (2005). *Power: A radical view.* 2nd ed. New York: Palgrave Macmillan.
Lynch, M. (2006). *Voices of the new Arab public: Iraq, Al-Jazeera, and Middle East politics today.* New York: Columbia University Press.
Martin, J. L. (2003). What is field theory? *American Journal of Sociology* 109 (1): 1–49.
Mellor, N. (2007). *Modern Arab journalism: Problems and prospects.* Edinburgh: Edinburgh University Press.
Monge, P. R., & Contractor, N. (2003). *Theories of communication networks.* New York: Oxford University Press.
Najjar, O. (2007). New trends in global broadcasting: "Nuestro Norte es el Sur" (Our North is the South). *Global Media Journal* 6 (10): 1–26.
Peters, B. (2008). Law, state and the political public sphere as forms of social self-organization. In H. Wessler, ed., *Public deliberation and public culture: The writings of Bernhard Peters, 1993–2005* (pp. 17–32). New York: Palgrave Macmillan.
Powell, W. W., & DiMaggio, P., eds. (1991). *The new institutionalism in organizational analysis.* Chicago: University of Chicago Press.
Russell, A. (2001). The Zapatistas online: Shifting the discourse of globalization. *Gazette* 63 (5): 399–413.
Russell, A. (2007). Digital communication networks and the journalistic field: The 2005 French riots. *Critical Studies in Media Communication* 24 (4): 285–302.
Serra, S. (2000). The killing of Brazilian street children and the rise of the international public sphere. In J. Curran, ed., *Media organisations in society* (pp. 151–72). London: Arnold.
Silverstone, R. (2006). *Media and morality: On the rise of the mediapolis.* Cambridge: Polity Press.
Smith, L. T. (1999). *Decolonizing methodologies: Research and indigenous peoples.* London: Zed Books.
Tatnall, A., & Gilding, A. (1999). Actor-network theory and information systems research. Paper presented at the Australasian Conference on Information Systems, Wellington, New Zealand.
Thussu, D. K. (2009). Why internationalize media studies and how? In D. K. Thussu, ed., *Internationalizing media studies.* London: Routledge.
Turner, F. (2005). Actor-networking the news. *Social Epistemology* 19 (4): 321–24.
van Loon, J. (2000). Organizational spaces and networks. *Space and Culture* 2 (4–5): 109–12.

Volkmer, I. (2003). The global network society and the global public sphere. *Development* 46 (1): 9–16.

Wessler, H., ed. (2008). *Public deliberation and public culture: The writings of Bernhard Peters, 1993–2005.* New York: Palgrave Macmillan.

NOTES

1. Neil Fligstein, in a fascinating interview with the *McGill Sociological Review* 1 (2010), pp. 59–65, published online at http://www.mcgill.ca/msr/volume1/interview/, speaks to field theory's ambitions: "I think field theory is a huge breakthrough. It cuts across the social sciences . . . . [sociologist and fellow field theorist] John Levi Martin and I have a standing joke that we're working on the theory of everything. So we call it the TOE when we're hanging out together. That is a joke! But I think with field theory, you come back to what do human beings do and how they make collective action happen. . . . how groups of people and groups of groups do these kinds of interactions and watch other people and reference other people and take positions, a very generic level of social process."

2. While for reasons of space I focus in this paper on Najjar's work (2007), Noha Mellor (2007) also makes extensive use of Bourdieu (and Habermas). Unlike Najjar, Mellor is explicit that "Western theories developed to account for changes in Western societies cannot be used uncritically to analyze non-Western societies . . . rather, field theory is meant to serve as a building block" (p. 4). Mellor suggests some interesting modifications to field theory based on characteristics of Arab media and their audiences. For instance, Al Jazeera (and many other Arab media) uses an elevated written variant of Arabic yet its audience is more likely to be composed of low-income/low-education viewers than high-income/high-education viewers. This challenges Bourdieu's argument that there will tend to be "homologies" between media production and consumption (ibid., 4; see also Benson & Neveu, 2005 for discussion of the possibility of such variations in the extent of homologies).

3. See Monge & Contractor (2003) for a comprehensive review of the social network literature. All of these strains of network theory are increasingly in dialogue with another, as evidenced by an International Network Theory Conference held 19–20 February 2010 by the USC-Annenberg School of Communication featuring presentations by Manuel Castells, Bruno Latour, Noshir Contractor, Peter Monge, Yochai Benkler, and others (see http://ascnetworksnetwork.org/ann-conference for summaries and videos of presentations).

4. Van Loon (2000, pp. 109–10) offers a similar analysis: "[W]ith the publication of Manuel Castells's *Rise of the Network Society* (1996), network-theory became firmly established as a mainstream force in contemporary political economy. However, Castells's almost uncompromising economism which is seductively intertwined with an ethos of technological determinism, made it difficult for those bending towards more cultural analytical orientations to engage productively with this concept. Instead, refuge was being sought in the more elusive and complex Deleuzoguattarian concept of assemblage. . . . Somewhere between the political-economic notion of 'network' and the differentialist notion of 'assemblage,' we can find 'actor networks.' Actor networks are more dynamic than network structures, but less elusive than assemblages."

CHAPTER FOURTEEN

Cosmopolitanism and International Communication

Understanding Civil Society Actors

Peter Dahlgren

Academic fields are (fortunately) never fully unified; there are always disparate voices and challenges to what is perceived as the dominant mainstream. This is intellectually healthy; internal contention in a field helps keep its participants alert. At this point in the history of international communication, however, it may be that we are seeing more than just the usual discussion and debate on the margins. There is a growing restlessness, a sense that the turbulent realities of the world over recent decades require some serious rethinking about what research in this field should be doing—and how it should be doing it. Proposing some new "paradigm" for international communication is far beyond the ambition of this chapter, however. What I wish to do instead, taking into account some of the common critiques of the field, is to explore one important trajectory that the study of international communication could incorporate, and to mobilize some of the key intellectual equipment that will facilitate that step. What I have in mind is the vast landscape of transnational civil society actors, and the alter-globalization movement in particular, with its use of online technologies. Moreover, I suggest that the analysis of these actors and their practices could be fruitfully analyzed through the lens of cosmopolitanism.

I build upon a number of central premises. First of all and on a very general level, though he may overstate the case at times, I share the basic sensibility that Zygmunt Bauman tries to capture in his use of the adjective "liquid," in regard to globalized late modernity (see, among his many works on this theme, the overview he offers in Bauman, 2007). This oft-cited term signifies the intensity of change and the seeming lack of permanence among structures and institutions at global and local levels, the fluidity of much of the cultural realm, as well as the growing challenges to maintaining stable life courses and identities. It is clearly not a measurable concept, but it signals a temperament that is willing to focus at least as much attention on impermanence as on that which still seems firmly entrenched in the world.

Further, I assume that among the key factors contributing to the rapid transformations we are seeing are the contemporary information and communication technologies (ICTs) and the uses to which they are put—by millions and millions of people all around the world. Yet another premise is the importance of taking into account the evolving political landscape of the world, both in the established democracies and in the newer, emerging ones. (The recent insurrections against several authoritarian regimes are of course also highly significant, but lie beyond the limits of this presentation.) These changing political landscapes are facilitating increased communication across national boundaries. The upshot here is that today we have a much wider range of actors who are engaged in various ways in politics in the global arena. Moreover, the character of politics and the modes of participation are taking newer forms as a result of the affordances of the ICTs.

I refer to these newer participants in politics in transnational contexts as civil society actors. While some of them and their activities may reinforce the older patterns of Western dominance of international communication, albeit in new ways, on other fronts we see new, non-Western actors and settings emerging. International communication research needs to seriously engage with these developments if it is to keep up with changing global realities. In particular adding civil society actors to the existing roster of nation-states, private corporations, official international bodies, and major media organizations would be an important step.

If we seek to understand such actors analytically, the recent and somewhat sprawling literature on cosmopolitanism—if carefully selected—can help us get theoretical handles on the contexts and the modes of agency involved, as well as the subjective horizons and normative visions of the actors. This literature derives from various currents in moral and political philosophy and from social scientific efforts at various levels of abstraction. While the social scientific efforts as yet remain in the minority, I would argue that we still have here a very fertile terrain that invites engagement from scholars in international communication. The theoretic horizon in turn needs to be complemented with empirical strategies, and if the current critiques about the limitations that the traditional quantitative methods can offer are to be taken seriously, I would suggest that the terrain I am pointing to offers ample opportunity for using expanded methodological toolkits.

In what follows, I will first offer an overview of this perspective, situating it within the current discussions about international communication. From there I introduce the horizons of cosmopolitanism, and endeavour to establish its conceptual utility. Then I take up the changing media landscape and look at some civil society actors—social movements engaged in alter-globalization campaigns—to exemplify my argument. I end with a few short reflections on research methodology.

Getting Our Bearings

The Force Fields of the Field

As in just about any field of inquiry, international communication has a number of tensions around what are suitable theories, concepts, methodologies, intellectual currents, in short: what the field is about. These discussions, in various versions, have been with us at least four decades and have in fact become quite "normal"—which we can take as a sign of health. Indeed, too much complacency may signal that a field has reached its twilight years.

One, admittedly oversimplified, way of rendering the current tensions is to see them at expressing the ambivalence between defining the field in a *narrow* and neat way, thus providing clarity and certainty of mission, reducing ambiguity. The other is to take an *expansive* approach, probing, exploratory, seeing what new intellectual elements can be incorporated—with the risk of contributing to fuzziness, too much heterogeneity, and fueling factionalism. This chapter lands firmly on the side of the expansive, and advocates engagement with phenomena and literature that have not seen as part of the field's mainstream.

As several of the authors in his volume discuss, international communication has found itself in the force field between several meta-theoretic horizons, or paradigms, over the past decades. From development and modernization, to cultural imperialism and globalization, there has been a quest for an integrative analytic vision. Even the most recent paradigm on offer, globalization, seems to fall short of delivering what is needed. Globalization theories encompass a very broad range of elements, issues, and debates; there is no unified theory to culled from all this. The term thus remains at an abstract level, and is not directly useful as a paradigm for the field. However, it offers concepts and perspectives that international communication studies can draw on. If globalization is theoretically too dispersed a concept, the various concrete historical—and empirical— developments that we associate with it remain of the utmost relevance.

The effort to establish an overarching paradigm should be abandoned since even its non-attainment serves a useful purpose of highlighting issues and clarifying positions. In the meantime, we also hear many calls, also in this volume, to continue with the de-Westernization of the field, opening it up to more scholars and perspectives beyond the United States and Europe. Few would argue against this goal, though most will acknowledge the array of difficulties involved. Yet it is a concrete aim that we all can share and strive for, and the perspective I offer here certainly points in that direction as well.

The Global Media Environment

Returning to the theme of the concrete manifestations of globalization, Tsan-Kuo Chang in his chapter underscores how the terrain of international communication began to change rapidly in the 1990s as other channels began to follow CNN's model from the 1980s of 24/7 TV news. With their national or regional bases, they began to seriously compete with the established channel such as the BBC and CNN, offering news and commentary from their particular view of the world. This heterogenization of what he calls the "global media environment" has had a major impact on the character of contemporary international communications, with new actors injecting new social and political angles into the transnational symbolic milieux. From our present historical location we can see that this global media environment is now undergoing yet another dramatic change in the face of the widely accessible ICTs and their affordances. This new era of digital communication allows actors all over the world to enter into international communication via a wide array of platforms and communicative modes on the Internet and its ancillary technologies, such as mobile telephony.

The sheer scale of this activity is altering the center of gravity of international communication, in the sense that the empirical realities of who is actually communicating what across national boundaries—and to whom, for what purpose, and with what effect—are undergoing profound transformation. The communicative spaces of transnational settings are now populated by millions of actors who previously had no position or role in these contexts. Even if we leave aside all the trans-border electronic communication that is essentially personal or private in character, we are still left with a huge range of individuals, groups, organizations, networks, and movements of many kinds whose communicative practices have to do with political, economic, social, or cultural realms and can in some way be described as "public." All these actors and their practices defy easy classification, but as a first analytic step, however, let us speak of civil society actors, signifying people and groups who operate beyond both formal nation-states and major economic entities.

Civil Society Actors and Alter-Globalization

Transnational civil society actors vary greatly in their fundamental raison d'être. Some are humanitarian in their orientation, and others are engaged in social or cultural networking, for example diasporic or religious groups. Many of these actors are involved in various genres of advocacy, for themselves or as representatives of larger causes or interest groups. A good number of these actors work in tandem with large established international organizations such as the United Nations or the European Union, which actively consult with civil society organizations. Many such actors have become a significant factor at the level of policy making. There is a large range of explicitly political actors; some give voice to long-standing, protracted conflicts, others air newly emerged ones, while yet others are working politically to alter the behavior of governments, regulatory bodies, or corporations based on normative visions of global change. For some political actors religion is a motivational force. Many civil society actors display healthy democratic profiles. Others may have goals or use practices that are questionable, even from within the wide range of definitions and interpretations of democracy that circulate in the world today. Hate groups, racists, and others with obviously anti-democratic and uncivil visions of the world (e.g., terrorist organizations) fall outside the definition of global civil society given that their ambitions run counter to the ideals of democracy. However, there will no doubt always be a definitional gray zone here about who are legitimate actors in global civil society, precisely because the concept of democracy itself remains contested.

In terms of organization we encounter here the broad terrain of non-governmental organizations (NGOs): non-profit organizations, activist networks, interest and advocacy groups of all kinds, including at times very amorphous social movements. Even alternative journalistic organizations figure here, the most well known being Indymedia. In short, there is an ever expanding domain of global civil society, where international communication is taking place in a myriad of crisscrossing patterns. One of the striking features about all this civic and political international communication is that the range of actors and the breadth of the ideological spectrum visible in global public spheres has become so much larger than it was prior to the spread of digital ITCs beginning in the mid-1990s. Thus, the rather unified and bounded view of international communication has become more heterogeneous, as the field begins to incorporate the perspective of global civil society. Some literature on these developments retains to a greater or lesser degree the framework of international communication, slotting global civil society into this tradition (e.g., Chandler, 2006; Eberly, 2008; Scholte, 2011), while other studies frame global civil society in terms of critical engagement with power relations on the transnational level. Such contributions often have little interface with the field as such, yet are obviously dealing with phenomena that have to do with international communication (e.g., Drache, 2008; Keane, 2003; Keck & Sikkink, 1998; Thörn, 2009; Walker & Thompson, 2008).

For my purposes, I want to identify a particular strand of global civil society analysis that derives from this latter, critical approach and focuses on what has come to be known as the alter-globalization movement, also sometimes called the global justice movement. It is comprised of a variety of movements, networks, and organizations that focus on a set of themes or issues, such as economic fairness, especially for countries in the global South, the environment, human rights, gender issues, labor issues, protection of indigenous cultures, and so on. The alter-globalization movement is thus also large and diverse in itself, but within this corner of global civil society there is a basic conceptual unity. It has to do with the struggles to find counter-hegemonic alternatives to the present trajectory of neoliberal societal development.

These activists are politically on the left, but it is largely a reformist movement, seeking to mobilize public opinion and to influence both lawmakers at different levels and corporate actors who are perceived to be doing societal harm in transnational contexts. Another unifying aspect is that almost all of these actors have some kind of presence on the Internet; in fact, it could be argued that without these ICT affordances the movement would not be as developed as it has become. Even the media themselves can become the focus of such activities, especially the attempts to develop alternative media practices and more democratic public spheres. (Reports of such efforts, based on cooperation between activists and academics, are found in the two companion volumes by Rodriguez, Kidd, & Stein, 2010 and Stein, Kidd, & Rodriguez, 2009.)

A further element that pulls together much of the alter-globalization movement is that there is a loose, overarching organization that has been operating for the past decade, the World Social Forum (WSF)—which also has regional spinoffs, such as the European Social Forum.

With participants all over the world, and its roots in the global South, the WSF has a strong non-Western profile. It holds a major annual meeting, with tens of thousands participating; these began in Brazil as a counterpoint to the Davos meetings of global political and economic elites. The meetings seek to globally coordinate, build alliances, share knowledge and experiences, and develop strategies. The alter-globalization movement generally, and the WSF in particular, has been made academically visible in recent years; see, for example, Acosta (2009); Gills (2011); Hosseini (2010); Maeckelburgh (2009); Pleyers (2011); Sen & Waterman (2007); de Sousa Santos & Rodriguez-Garavito (2005); Smith, Della Porta, & Mosca (2007).

Just in passing, it should be mentioned that while the WSF and global civil society generally have benefited enormously from the affordances of ICTs and the networking they make possible (Castells, 2010), the impacts of technologies are always shaped by their interplay with social factors. The contingencies that make possible and delimit phenomena can never just be reduced to ICT's. Thus, analyses of international communication in this regard—and in fact more generally—must take into account the larger societal contingencies that come into play.

Cosmopolitanism and International Civic Communication

In another chapter in this volume, Silvio Waisbord argues forcefully for an increased cosmopolitan character of media studies generally and international communication more specifically. By this he means "an analytic attitude open to multiple perspectives and developments beyond geography. . . . At a time of unprecedented mobility of people, ideas, and goods, as well as the porosity of political, economic, and cultural borders, world citizenship offers responses to critical issues and urgent needs." I certainly concur, and would further assert that the theme of cosmopolitanism pertains not just to the character of the research and the researchers but also to the actors themselves and their practices, to those who are engaged in global civil society and alter-globalization, and what they do with their media. We find within the literature on cosmopolitanism a strong normative strain that offers an inspirational vision that "another world is possible" (to cite WSF's slogan).

But there is more: ethical ideals and value commitments are also an important foundation for civic transnational practices. Modes of personal and group identity that extend beyond one's own nationality, ethnic, or religious group, have shown be crucial in such forms of international communication. Thus, in the contemporary circumstances of globalization, many actors are motivated by thought that has its roots in versions of cosmopolitanism. This is definitely not about "moralizing"; rather, this horizon suggests that if we are interested in exploring the motivational grounds for international communication with global civil society and the alter-globalization movement, cosmopolitanism offers us a potentially useful analytic toolkit.

The Horizons of Cosmopolitanism

The notion of cosmopolitanism is of course quite old; even Socrates famously claimed that he was not an Athenian, nor a Greek, but a citizen of the world. Immanuel Kant gave the concept a strong ethical dimension in his modern version of the world citizen; this element remains prominent even today, as the concept is being reinvented. Cosmopolitanism has in recent years become somewhat of a buzzword, but this does not per se make it useless or misleading. With the continuing integration of the world via the processes of globalization—albeit often in very uneven, unequal, and contested ways—the other, or rather the many others, come all the closer to us in our everyday lives. On one level we can see cosmopolitanism as an expression of concern for the other, transferred to global contexts. More specifically—and more useful for research—cosmopolitanism offers an analytic frame for approaching issues about social perceptions of and relations with distant others in the world. Morality, as the fundamental conceptions of right and wrong in human affairs—and ethics, as the application, or codification of morality into concrete norms of behaviour—constitute, at bottom, the foundation of most human action, even if only implicitly. It thereby remains an important analytic angle of vision for understanding the social world, not least in the context of international communication.

It could be said that the actual status of cosmopolitanism in today's world gets at best mixed reviews. Yes, in the wake of globalization, many people across the globe have developed new horizons about themselves and the world they live in. We can note with enthusiasm that there is plenty of evidence that indicates a growth in engagement in transnational social realities and empathy for concrete human situations beyond one's own national contexts. And yet . . . many contemporary circumstances make the picture more sombre; the inventory of global ills that contest the growth of cosmopolitanism is woefully long. Not least, the media's role in these contexts is often discouraging, if familiar: they serve all too often to cement the mental boundaries between "us and them."

However, the enormous transnational difficulties that we face challenge us all the more to understand, to analyze, and this is evidenced in the extensive literature that has recently merged on cosmopolitanism. Much of it ranges over moral theory and political philosophy (Breckenridge et al., 2002; Brock & Brighouse, 2005; Nussbaum, 2006), addressing the vision of a better, more democratic global political order (Archibugi, 2008; Gould, 2004; Held, 2010) or ethical order (e.g., Sullivan & Kymlicka, 2007; Vernon, 2010); the notion of citizenship, and the issues of rights and inclusion in the contemporary global situation, not least in regard to the EU (e.g., Benhabib, 2006; Habermas, 2006). Other interventions address the socio-cultural preconditions for cosmopolitanism or its subjective dimensions (e.g., Appiah, 2007; Beck & Cronin, 2006; Hannerz, 1996; Kendall, Woodward, & Skrbis, 2009; Robertson, 2010). A few authors engage with cosmopolitanism in a critical way, framing it in terms of a critique of neoliberalism (Cheah, 2006; Dallmayr, 2003; Delanty, 2009; Harvey, 2009).

One or Many Cosmopolitanisms?

Not surprisingly, all this diverse literature on cosmopolitanism encompasses a certain conceptual looseness. Kendall, Woodward, and Skrbis (2009), in their extensive review, insist that the notion lacks clarity and risks becoming all things to all people. Given that cosmopolitanism is framed in varying ways, the points of tension need to be made visible, even if they cannot always be resolved. These authors also note a certain degree of political naïveté in some of the literature, and in their view there is often an implicit utopian drive to construct a new world of tolerant and responsible citizens, with little analytic insight on how to get there. Not least some of the literature tends to ignore major global divides, a point also made by David Harvey's (2009) critical evaluation of several key authors. Discussions of cosmopolitanism would probabaly be more fruitful if the moral dimension were a bit more modest and if the concept could be developed more in an empirical manner.

In a recent publication, Corpus Ong (2009) discusses how theorists in various disciplines view cosmopolitanism, which he takes to be an "openness to the world." He derives four basic categories, under which major authors are placed: *closed* (i.e., un- or anti-cosmopolitan), *prestige* (where status and privilege are closely associated with it), *banal* (an everyday, "ordinary" openness to otherness as an expression of one's own identity), and *ecstatic*, a kind of visionary enthusiasm. Such a map can no doubt help one navigate through the literature—and one will likely find that quite a few authors end up in the "ecstatic" category.

A more specific issue that abounds in the literature has to do with the basic tension between universalism and the particular (or local, or national). Is there one set of cosmopolitan values and perceptions, a "one-size-fits-all"? The answers have political implications. In their introduction, Breckenridge et al. (2002) propose that the concept be used in the plural, and not be associated with the unitary, privileged position of the European tradition, since the motivation and capacity to reflect on those beyond one's own culture is to be found in all regions of the world. The chapters of the book explore modes of cosmopolitanism in different regions of the non-Western world.

On the other hand, Bryan S. Turner (2002) draws on the sixteenth-century writer Michel Montaigne to develop a sense of universal cosmopolitan virtue. Turner sees Montaigne as espousing what he calls the softer (feminine) values of mercy, compassion, and tenderness—in response to the horrors of the wars of his time. Cosmopolitan virtue basically encompasses pacifist values that preclude violence and promote human agency and dignity. Turner argues that cosmopolitan virtue involves an opposition to suffering and "constitutes a standpoint that both transcends and unites different cultures and historical epochs" (p. xx). Indeed, he asserts that the vulnerability of the human body provides a starting point for an account of human commonality and compassion as the basis for a cosmopolitan ethic. For him, the UN Declaration of Human Rights is obviously a very cosmopolitan document, which he builds into his argument.

Thus, we can sense an unresolved ambivalence between cosmopolitanism as an expression of multiple empirical realities around the world and as a unitary global ideal, with universalist virtues. Turner takes a clear stand against moral relativism: cosmopolitan virtue is not compatible with indifference. However, one could respond that Turner's position is "easy": to reduce physical suffering is perhaps not so controversial. In situations that, for example, have to do with expressions of minority community membership in majoritarian cultural settings (e.g., apparel of religious expression), it may not always be so easy to identify an operable cosmopolitan ethic. And the espousal of universalism has not seldom stumbled into the terrain of ethnocentrism and cultural power.

The Power Dimension

Thus, even if we cannot readily resolve this tension, in treating cosmopolitanism as a dimension of culture we at some point have to touch base with the themes of history and power, as Harvey (2009) argues. Culture in today's world is of course not some simple mirroring of the flow of economic and political power from centres to peripheries, yet the history of colonialism makes it difficult to deny the importance of these mechanisms (and here of course the structures of the media and the patterns of their representation loom especially large). In short, if globalization constitutes the key contemporary condition for the actualization of cosmopolitanism, then the prevailing power relations (and their historical origins) in the global arena would seemingly have importance for understanding the character and possibilities of cosmopolitanism.

Yet, the horizon of power does not always appear in the literature on cosmopolitanism; as with the literature on globalization, most versions avoid this topic. Global power can of course be approached from a number of angles, not least through the political economy of the world system, but the perspective of post-colonialism offers a significant cultural prism through which to view cosmopolitanism. Post-colonialism, in ways similar to cultural studies (with which it at times blends together), is sensitive to how culture and the production of meaning are always bound up in some way or other with relations of power.

It is interesting to note that in the past two decades or so that two key theoretic traditions—globalization (with its home largely in the social sciences) and post-colonialism (hovering more in the humanities)—have had relatively little encounter with each other. They seemingly exist in parallel universes, when in fact they should be very much entwined—even if this lack of interaction is beginning to be addressed (for example, see the collection by Krishnaswamy & Hawley, 2008). For cosmopolitanism, post-colonialism can serve to help alert us to the historical antecedents of a vast array of aspects where power, especially cultural power, has relevance: patterns of cultural influences, images of the other, identity processes, integration/assimilation, language use, institution-building, and so on. Conceptually and empirically cosmopolitanism cannot be reduced to a mere function of power, yet neither can power be ignored. If it is not obviously manifest, then it is always hovering there—in both micro- and macro- circumstances. Power evokes counter-power, so it is not simply a case of unidirectional and deterministic mechanisms, even though hegemonic positions are usually prevalent.

Media and Civic Cosmopolitanism

The Media Connection

Oddly enough, the media have not figured extensively in the literature on cosmopolitanism. One major empirical effort to establish the contours of links between media use and cosmopolitan mind-sets is found in Norris and Inglehart (2009). Generally, it seems that exposure to global media will promote cosmopolitanism. However, the authors underscore the research complexity of establishing causal relationships, and make the point that there also many non-media variables at work. More focused efforts are found in Boltanski (1999), who addresses in a theoretic manner the theme of recognizing and identifying with distant others via news coverage of suffering; Chouliaraki (2006), who addresses this theme but in a more rigorously empirical manner; and Robertson (2010), who takes a broader look at television news, its journalists/editors, and viewers around the world to elucidate the role of the media in fostering cosmopolitan horizons. Lai (2008) probes these themes from the horizons of the Internet. This literature underscores the media's importance for cosmopolitanism, while at the same time reminding us of the limits of our knowledge in these matters.

Another angle on the media's connection to cosmopolitanism is found in Roger Silverstone's (2006) last major work. The book's style is more essayistic than empirical, and has more of the normative character of the dominant literature on cosmopolitanism. However, it assumes that the media play a decisive role in the constitution of late modernity and its forms of globalization. It provides a useful starting point for some reflections on international communication and cosmopolitanism, with a focus on their relationship to democracy. More specifically, I want to highlight his basic ideas with an eye toward cosmopolitanism as a necessary element for civic agency in the modern globalized world, and the character of the media as a precondition for such agency.

Silverstone navigates carefully between optimism and pessimism, yet he clearly is conveying an ambitious vision. He also adroitly balances the tension between one or many cosmopolitanisms: he pushes strongly for a generalized shared ethics of responsibility for the other, but adamantly acknowledges that people's actions and moral frameworks must be contingent on their circumstances if they are to be meaningful and effective. He argues that media today have imposed conditions of cosmopolitanism on us: we can—and must—respond accordingly from the standpoint of our own lives. Not least, he is very much aware of the significance of power relations, especially in regard to the institutions and functioning of the media. This ushers us into the realm of democracy and civil society actors. However, I will first backtrack a bit and summarize his main points.

The Mediapolis

In brief, Silverstone observes that the media are becoming what he calls "environmental": they no longer can be seen as simply discrete flows of messages or information, but rather take on the character of dense symbolic ecologies that penetrate just about every corner of our existence. What he terms the mediapolis is composed of the vast communicative space of mediated global appearances. It is via the media that the world appears to us and where appearance constitutes the world. It is through the media that we learn who we are—and who we are different from, and where relations between self and other are conducted in a global public arena. The media establish connections and relationships; they position us in the world.

The mediapolis is both a normative and an empirical term. Empirically, it is something other than a rational Habermasian public sphere; it is cacophonic, with multiple voices, inflections, images, and rhetoric—it resides beyond logic and rationality, and it cannot offer any expectation of fully effective communication. The communications dynamic that Silverstone sees here he calls *contrapunctual*: each communicative thread gains significance at best only in relationship to others—together, the ensemble of tension-ridden, contradictory communicative interventions comprise the tumultuous whole.

Normatively, however, despite differences in communicative and other forms of power, the mediapolis demands mutual responsibility between producers and audiences/users, as well as a capacity for reflexivity on the part of all involved, including recognition of cultural differences. This moral response is expressed in our responsibility for thinking, speaking, listening, and acting. It of course raises issues of the kinds of reality created by the mediapolis, the kinds of publicness, who appears—and how—as well as who does not appear. There is clearly an element of media power here: definitional control lies most immediately with the media organizations, but Silverstone emphasizes that there is still responsibility on all sides. Journalists, editors, and producers have a responsibility for the representations they offer, while audiences/users have an obligation to reflect on what they encounter and to respond in an ethical manner—both to the world portrayed and toward the media.

The notion of mediapolis is a thus a challenge, a challenge to inequities of representation, mechanisms of exclusion, the imbalances of media power (via both state and capital), and "the ideological and prejudicial frames of unreflexive reporting and storytelling" (Silverstone, 2006, p. 37). The media, in their representations of the world, inevitably engage in what he calls boundary work: boundaries are constantly being drawn, reinforced, and altered between various constellations of "us and them." In underscoring the significance of morality and ethics, Silverstone means that moral dimensions should become a focus of analytic concern, just as social, political, and cultural perspectives are part of our analytic approach to the processes of communication.

From Morality to Global Civic Engagement

In all this Silverstone admits that we have an enormous difficulty to deal with. The public, as the aggregate of the audiences of mediapolis, is hardly an efficacious agent. Thought, speech, and action are disconnected and compromised by absence of context, memory, and analytic rigour, and increasingly, by the absence of trust, and we witness patterns of withdrawal from the public realm into the private—in fact, precisely the major dilemmas confronting democracy. Though he does not have much to say in concrete terms about political agency, Silverstone's political sensibility indicates that the mediapolis is not only a site for moral response, but, potentially, for practices. The cosmopolitan moral agent must move beyond the state of merely thinking about his or her responsibility; it must be enacted, embodied via some kind of action (which, in the context of the political, will often take some form of communication).

Such a proactive social ethics, which demands engagement with and responsibility for global others, points us toward cosmopolitan citizenship, which engages with the world not least via the mediapolis, in a manner that is strongly tied to some version of democracy. This link between cosmopolitanism and democratic civic agency—I call it civic cosmopolitanism—involves translating the cosmopolitan moral stance into concrete political contexts that benefit not just our own interests but those of globalized others. Cosmopolitanism becomes thus an inexorable dimension of contemporary global civic virtue and agency.

It is here, in a sense at the outer edges of his work, where I would like to pick up his baton and run with it. I have previously grappled with how to understand civic agency, that is, to comprehend the subjective realities that can promote people's engagement in politics and the role of the media in this regard (Dahlgren, 2009). I sketched such themes as the globalization of citizenship, civil society, and political activism, as well as the relevant media circumstances. However, the transnational dimension remained underdeveloped. There was really no conceptual connection between such agency and global moral responsibility. I find that Silverstone's book, with its promotion of cosmopolitanism and its normative anchoring, invites us, in a compelling manner, to better conceptualize those links.

In talking about the mediapolis, Silverstone tends to foreground the mass media, but underscores how the Internet and ancillary technologies are altering its basic parameters. He rightly points out that, in terms of publicness, the Internet requires the mass media as a referent, a context, to avoid spiraling away into small isolated islands. (The Internet itself has of course the character of mass mediated communication.) If we thus connect his framework of the mediapolis with the realm of net-based global civil society in general, and the alter-globalization movement and WSF in particular, we bring into focus a relatively specific and delimited group of actors who engage in international communication. We of course lose from sight the vast majority of people in online mediapolis who are not thus engaged, but in the interests of keeping an eye on possible research it is important to narrow our focus.

Researching the Civic Cosmopolitanism of Alter-Globalization

Over the past decade and a half, a new generation of international communicators has been emerging across the globe, using ICTs in new and imaginative ways. Among these civil society actors is the alter-globalization movement, with the WSF. These actors are motivated in strongly normative terms; they have a variety of goals, all aimed at transforming the current direction of global development. They meet live, face to face, on many occasions, but also make extensive use of the digital media. They are operating in a mediapolis where they constitute counter-hegemonic voices to the dominant representations that support neoliberal mechanisms for driving society forward.

Empirical and Comparative Angles

There are two obvious and complementary lines of empirical research open here. One has to do with the nature of the international communication that flows from these groups. Here we can distinguish that which is intended as internal communication—within and between groups, even across national borders. The other is communication directed to the outside world, to global publics, but even to decision makers, to power holders. I find the latter the more relevant one. A good starting place is the official website, www.forumsocialmundial.org.br/, which is available in Portuguese, English, French, and Spanish. There are different kinds of information available, including journalistic news, organizational and mobilizational information, including developments in preparation for the next annual World Social Forum meeting. One can follow links and pursue topics, debates, and continue to the information made available by the vast number of specific participating networks, groups, and movements.

The other line of research has to do with the actors themselves, as individuals and members of collectivities. Their backgrounds, motivations, perceptions, organizational strategies, media use, and so on open up many avenues of possible research. The grounds for their civic identities and practices in particular, coupled not least to the cosmopolitan themes of global others, their moral horizons, offer fertile research possibilities.

Such research is very much in its infancy. Lai (2008) offers some conceptual starts in regard to online activism; the work of de Sousa Santos (2005) offers a number of important concrete insights on the horizons of WSF activists. Uldam (2010) takes some important steps in such explorations in studying the identities, commitments, and strategies of two groups engaged in global justice issues in London. A general line of questioning can be built upon the extensive work already done in national contexts, exploring what factors promote and inhibit civic engagement and participation in social movement and political groups, and also how the media may (or may not) help generate civic cultures (see Dahlgren, 2009 for an overview).

In such research efforts directed towards the actor and their media practices, the comparative dimension should be a strong guide: one could study comparable groups and their communication practices in different geographical locations, or the interface between such alternative political communication and mainstream versions. How do such communications "travel" in the global mediapolis, what impact does it have, how does it relate to mainstream forms of communication on such topics, and what does all this mean for the character of international communication? Western and non-Western dimensions could figure prominently here. Also, the online world is in rapid transition, and alter-globalization efforts are increasingly making use of popular platforms such as YouTube to gain access to larger audiences (see Askanius & Gustafsson, 2010). How does this alter their communicative strategies and their identities? What are the implications of inserting politics into a media environment that is so strongly tilted toward popular culture and entertainment? Comparisons of strategies in various sectors of the mediapolis and their political efficacy can be seen as a research theme of growing relevance. Possible data include the media productions of various groups, their coverage of events, and the discussions and comments that ensure.

There is of course an ethical dimension to such research: what motivates it, what knowledge will it generate, for whom will it be useful, and in particular what relationship and responsibility will one have to those one studies. Such issues need to be clarified in advance of any such undertaking—for oneself as a researcher and for those that one wants to research. Research on these actors and their practices can and should be incorporated into the broader development of the field of international communication, helping us to understand exactly in what ways it is evolving as a result of these developments.

Negotiating Methodology

Chin-Chuan Lee argues in his chapter that cultural meanings need to be taken more into account in the research of international communication. And Jan Servaes, also in this volume, takes up the methodological issue of moving beyond the strict quantitative approaches that have characterized the field and underscores, among other things, the need for focusing increased research attention on the power of culture. We need to understand agency from the point of view of the agents, from the meaning such action has for them. From my vantage point, these appeals direct us precisely toward the importance of the normative and cultural frameworks of civic international communication actors, and these can be refracted at least in part through the prism of cosmopolitanism.

I find it unproductive to get locked into trench warfare over methodologies, since no one method is inherently privileged, no one approach a priori better or worse than any other. Rather, it is the kinds of knowledge we are looking for, the research questions posed, and the kinds of materials we have at hand that are ultimately decisive. Having said that, it would seem that any effort to probe the self-perceptions, motivations, and identity of social actors will at some point have to mobilize qualitative methods. Through depth interviews and onsite observations, processes of sense-making and reality construction can be illuminated. Likewise, in analyzing media products, the elucidation of meaning, the illumination of discourses mobilized, and not least the multi-media dimensions of much of the materials (visuals, sound, and text) suggest that qualitative methods are needed.

However, such approaches most definitely need not stand in opposition to quantitative procedures; the two have often been productively combined. For example, a quantitative overview of specific media materials can often provide an important profile, and will function very well together with deeper qualitative analyses of selected portions. The two strategies become complementary. Similarly, larger survey interviews of actors can serve well in relation to depth interviews with a more limited number. Over the past decades we have seen "cultural turns" in the social sciences, and the growth of qualitative approaches aimed at analyzing the processes of social construction, by which people produce meaning and define the social world and their place in it. We have seen this not least in the area of media and communication research, with an increase of cultural theories and methods. It is hardly controversial, and it would be puzzling if international communication were for some reason to define itself as off limits for such procedures.

Quantitative methods per se should not be automatically equated with "positivism," nor are qualitative approaches an automatic guarantee of research quality. Rather, positivism has to do with what Habermas once called "a refusal to reflect." As researchers, we always have to be alert not only about what we are studying, we must also periodically question our own assumptions and pre-understandings. That way we develop not just our field of inquiry but also ourselves. The study of mediated civic cosmopolitanism offers an opportunity to do both.[1]

References

Acosta, R. (2009). *NGO and social movement networking in the World Social Forum: An anthropological approach.* Saarbrücken: VDM Verl.

Appiah, A. (2007). *Cosmopolitanism: Ethics in a world of strangers.* New York: W. W. Norton.

Archibugi, D. (2008). *The global commonwealth of citizens: Toward cosmopolitan democracy.* Princeton, NJ: Princeton University Press.

Askanius, T., & Gustafsson, N. (2010). Mainstreaming the alternative: The changing media practices of protest movements. *Interface: A Journal for and about Social Movements* 2 (2): 23–41.

Bauman, Z. (2007). *Liquid times: Living in an age of uncertainty.* Cambridge: Polity Press.

Beck, U., & Cronin, C. (2006). *The cosmopolitan vision.* Malden, MA: Polity.

Benhabib, S. (2006). *Another cosmopolitanism.* New York: Oxford University Press.

Boltanski, L. (1999). *Distant suffering: Morality, media, and politics.* Cambridge: Cambridge University Press.

Breckenridge, C. A., Pollock, S., Bhabha, H. K., & Chakrabarty, D., eds. (2002). *Cosmopolitanism.* Durham, NC: Duke University Press.

Brock, G., & Brighouse, H. (2005). *The political philosophy of cosmopolitanism.* Cambridge: Cambridge University Press.

Calhoun, C. J. (2010). *Cosmopolitanism and belonging: From European integration to global hopes and fears.* London: Routledge.

Castells, M. (2010). *Communication power.* Oxford: Oxford University Press.

Chandler, D. (2006). *Constructing global civil society: Morality and power in international relations.* Houndmills, Basingstoke, Hampshire: Palgrave Macmillan.

Cheah, P. (2006). *Inhuman conditions: On cosmopolitanism and human rights.* Cambridge, MA: Harvard University Press.

Chouliaraki, L. (2006). *The spectatorship of suffering.* London: Sage Publications.

Dahlgren, P. (2009). *Media and political engagement: Citizens, communication, and democracy.* Cambridge: Cambridge University Press.

Dallmayr, F. (2003). Cosmopolitanism: Moral and political. *Political Theory* 31 (3): 421–42.

Delanty, G. (2009). *The cosmopolitan imagination: The renewal of critical social theory.* Cambridge: Cambridge University Press.

de Sousa Santos, B. (2005). Beyond neoliberal governance: The World Social Forum as subaltern cosmopolitan politics and legaity. In B. de Sousa Santos & C. A. Rodriguez-Varaviti, eds., *Law and globalization from below: Towards a cosmopolitan legality* (pp. 29–63). Cambridge: Cambridge University Press.

de Sousa Santos, B., & Rodriguez-Garavito, C. A., eds. (2005). *Law and globalization from below: Towards a cosmopolitan legality.* Cambridge: Cambridge University Press.

Drache, D. (2008). *Defiant publics: The unprecedented reach of the global citizen.* Cambridge: Polity.

Eberly, D. E. (2008). *The rise of global civil society: Building communities and nations from the bottom up.* New York: Encounter Books.

Gills, B. K., ed. (2011). *Globalization and the global politics of justice.* London: Routledge.

Gould, C. C. (2004). *Globalizing democracy and human rights.* New York: Cambridge University Press.

Habermas, J. (2006). *The divided West.* Cambridge: Polity.

Hannerz, U. (1996). *Transnational connections: Culture, people, places.* London: Routledge.

Harvey, D. (2009). *Cosmopolitanism and the geographies of freedom.* New York: Columbia University Press.

Held, D. (2010). *Cosmopolitanism: Ideals and realities.* Cambridge: Polity Press.

Hosseini, S. A. H. (2010). *Alternative globalizations: An integrative approach to studying dissident knowledge in the global justice movement.* London: Routledge.

Keane, J. (2003). *Global civil society?* Cambridge: Cambridge University Press.

Keck, M. E., & Sikkink, K. (1998). *Activists beyond borders: Advocacy networks in international politics.* Ithaca, NY: Cornell University Press.

Kendall, G., Woodward, I., & Skrbis, Z. (2009). *The sociology of cosmopolitanism: Globalization, identity, culture and government.* Basingstoke: Palgrave Macmillan.

Krishnaswamy, R., & Hawley, J. C. (2008). *The postcolonial and the global.* Minneapolis: University of Minnesota Press.

Lai, O.-K. (2008). Rediscovering kosmopolis in the cyber-information age? Social agencies and activism in their geo-historical place. In R. Lettevall & M. K. Linder, eds., *The idea of kosmopolis* (vol. 37, pp. 121–42). Huddinge: Södertörns Högskola.

Maeckelbergh, M. (2009). *The will of the many: How the alterglobalisation movement is changing the face of democracy.* London: Pluto Press.

Norris, P., & Inglehart, R. (2009). *Cosmopolitan communications: Cultural diversity in a globalized world.* New York: Cambridge University Press.

Nussbaum, M. C. (2006). *Frontiers of justice: Disability, nationality, species membership.* Cambridge, MA: Belknap Press.

Ong, J. C. (2009). The cosmopolitan continuum: Locating cosmopolitanism in media and cultural studies. *Media, Culture and Society* 31 (3): 449–66.

Pleyers, G. (2011). *Alter-globalization: Becoming actors in the global age.* Cambridge: Polity.

Robertson, A. (2010). *Mediated cosmopolitanism: The world of television news.* Cambridge: Polity.

Rodriguez, C., Kidd, D., & Stein, L., eds. (2010). *Creating new communication spaces* (vol. 1). Cresskill, NJ: Hampton Press.

Scholte, J. A. (2011). *Building global democracy? Civil society and accountable global governance.* Cambridge: Cambridge University Press.

Sen, J., & Waterman, P. (2007). *World social forum: Challenging empires.* Montreal: Black Rose Books.

Silverstone, R. (2006). *Media and morality: On the rise of the mediapolis.* Cambridge: Polity Press.

Smith, J., Della Porta, D., & Mosca, L. (2007). *Global democracy and the World Social Forums*. Boulder, CO: Paradigm Publishers.

Stein, L., Kidd, D., & Rodriguez, C. (2009). *National and global movements for democratic communication* (vol. 2). Cresskill, NJ: Hampton Press.

Sullivan, W. M., & Kymlicka, W. (2007). *The globalization of ethics: Religious and secular perspectives*. New York: Cambridge University Press.

Thörn, H. (2009). *Anti-apartheid and the emergence of a global civil society*. Basingstoke: Palgrave Macmillan.

Turner, B. S. (2002). Cosmopolitan virtue, globalization and patriotism. *Theory, Culture & Society* 19 (1–2): 45–63.

Uldam, J. (2010). Fickle commitment: Fostering political engagement in the "fighty world of online activism." PhD diss., Copenhagen Business School, Copenhaegn.

Vernon, R. (2010). *Cosmopolitan regard: Political membership and global justice*. New York: Cambridge University Press.

Walker, J. W. S. G., & Thompson, A. S., eds. (2008). *Critical mass: The emergence of global civil society*. Waterloo, ONT: Wilfrid Laurier University Press.

NOTE

1. I am greatly indebted to my colleague Fredrik Miegel at Lund University for inspiration for this text; the master's course on Media and Cosmopolitanism that he initiated and that I joined provided the starting point for many of the thoughts expressed here.

CHAPTER FIFTEEN

Postcolonial Visual Culture

Arguments from India

Arvind Rajagopal

Analysts of visual culture have only recently begun to reckon with the complexity of postcolonial visual culture in those regions where a history of semi-colonial or colonial rule remains important in understanding the period of national development thereafter. "Postcolonial" is a historical marker, therefore, and a reminder that where efforts at modernization were accompanied or preceded by struggles against foreign rule, a distinct set of conditions apply that need to be specified in any adequate attempt at historical analysis. For example, some or more aspects of modernization are usually perceived as a foreign import in postcolonial countries. Given that nation-centered development is the modal political form of modernization, the nation-state has to negotiate the differences between the forms of knowledge that existed previously and more modern forms of knowledge. The authority of these new and more "modern" forms of knowledge seldom acquire the same status they have in the West, where two or more centuries span a similar process. Images, as a privileged mode of communicating knowledge in modernity, become a key site for negotiating and contesting authority. How this happens, and what we can learn from analyzing the visual culture arising in the process, is worth considering. Certainly it is clear that "international communications" as a field of study did not anticipate the new forms of visual communication that would arise across the world, or the effects such communication would have.

Recent work by scholars acknowledges that postcolonial media culture presents discontinuous temporalities and complex aesthetic forms that challenge routine ways of relating the history of media form to conventional historical processes (Curtin, 2007; Fox & Waisbord, 2002; Jain, 2007; Lee, 2003; Pinney, 2004; Ramaswamy, 2010; Servaes, 2008). For example, visual realism appears as only one among a range of options utilized by cultural producers in South, Southeast, or East Asia, to mention a few regional examples, despite extensive and sophisticated communications industries in those regions. Technological sophistication does not always lead to the annihilation of older aesthetic forms, but may instead provoke their renewal, whether martial arts film and their link to Beijing opera traditions or mythological epic traditions and their transformation in India and elsewhere.

For scholarship on earlier periods, by comparison, arguably a greater scholarly consensus prevails about the protocols of research and argument, and there exist more accessible archives. Or else scholars have focused on specific crafts and technologies of visual culture such as painting, print, or film, deferring broader questions about the institutionalization of visual practices across media that socialize audiences into new habits of perception. Image making in postcolonial society is now so extensive and multifarious however, and the questions they pose are so unpredictable, that the guidelines for inquiry available from nationalist historiography, art, and cultural criticism or from postcolonial social sciences are manifestly inadequate.

With the proliferation of media technology and of mediatic forms across print, cinema, television, mobile telephones, and the Internet, South Asia seems to have arrived at a communicative modernity in the space of barely two decades, or from the first Gulf War onwards, when satellite television was launched in the region. Globally, South Asia's communicative modernity signaled a post–Cold War period defined by intensification of securocratic regimes of visual surveillance, and geopolitical alignments organized around Islamic "terror" instead of the specter of communism.[1] In India alone, the past two decades have witnessed a compressed series of developments. The long-delayed market prominence of indigenous language media in relation to English was closely followed by the ascendancy of an aggressive strain of Hindu nationalism that has taken on a new intensity with the growth of privately owned media. On the other hand, the dense spread of television news coverage provides greater visibility to a host of actors and events, with diverse political agenda, from terrorists in Mumbai who use the media as surveillance aids to a growing Maoist campaign in defense of tribal land rights that is gaining public sympathy.[2] Hence to simply associate increasing media density with growing support for any specific postcolonial ideology would be misleading. However, the larger context of India's new economy within which both of the above problems have emerged suggests the need to historically situate questions of media visibility and density, and explore ways to produce multi-causal, or contingent, models of explanation.

In South Asia, greater communication has neither seen the reduction of violence nor an increase in political transparency in any simple sense. Since the 1937 provincial elections in India, the authorities have tended to overlook mass violence, while the culprits and their sponsors have tended to derive electoral capital from targeted acts of violence. Investigative journalism, including the release of "sting" videos, confirms the existence of institutionalized corruption and secrecy without altering them. Hindu militant groups can paralyze the entire country, such as around the anticipation of violence over a court ruling on the demolition of a historic mosque. When the culprits are rewarded rather than punished, sober media commentators celebrate the verdict for having thwarted further violence.

Clearly, visuality does not always work in the ways Enlightenment thinkers assumed.[3] Greater visibility in public does not ensure more rationality, nor does a greater density of information flow assure less violence or more democratization. On the one hand there are those who assert the demystifying gaze of the modern imagination, according to which "seeing is believing." On the other hand we can observe the enchantment or glamour in what millions behold, for which the opposite may be true, that is, "believing is seeing." Analysts of postcolonial visual culture would need to acknowledge both of these possibilities, while specifying what happens to each term in this reversible proposition, in this age of digital reproduction. South Asia provides a useful site for such discussion given its manifestly heterogeneous visual practices alongside a growing homogenization of screen culture that introduces new regimes of surveillance and regulation.[4] The specific question this chapter will pose is whether postcolonial visual culture itself displays regularities over time that can illuminate the modes of political performance, while avoiding historicism, that is, the presumption that historical context determines both media and meaning, as well as technological determinism.

Media as/and a History of the Senses

I take it for granted that the senses are interconnected, and that their separation occurs through technological means. Technologically mediated forms of sense perception recombine and acquire a prosthetic character with the growth of the apparatuses of communication. For instance, when sound and light from audio-visual media impinge on the observer, they convey or imply the sense of touch at the same time. Here I draw on Marshall McLuhan (1994), who theorized the media as the interface between the body and technology, correlating communication technologies with changing ratios of sense perception. McLuhan argued that audio-visual media require to be read not so much on the register of visual and auditory perceptions as on that of tactility. Hence the immediate apperception from mass media, McLuhan argued, was one of intimacy rather than remoteness. The result was that rules of social distance reflecting understandings of hierarchy or potency, that is, vis-à-vis class and gender differences, appeared to shift or erode due to media impact.

McLuhan provided an ingenious argument about the power of media, linking concerns about social order and the fear of the crowd to latent apprehensions about the power of Communist ideology, with the possibility of utopian transcendence. If the medium was the message, it implied that propaganda, the feared weapon of the East Bloc, would be neutralized by the character of modern media, which might in fact serve as silent allies of the West in the Cold War. The "global village" fashioned from the expansion of communications could be a friendly and intimate space, he suggested, in a distinctly North American conception of community.

McLuhan also provided a genealogy of the West that defined backwardness in terms of media literacy, but without overt condescension. Electric media, McLuhan argued, "re-tribalized" Western man, and allowed him to overcome inherited, print-dominated forms of rationality. Modern media, he claimed, enabled forms of communication that were both more individualized and more communal, both "hot" and "cool." The argument was difficult to follow, and perhaps ultimately incoherent, but it served an important purpose. It insisted that technology was not other to human beings, but altered their capacities in ways that quickly "became" them, although human beings might fail to recognize it. And technology could be used to order world history in a cumulative sequence of developments while acknowledging then-prevalent trends of cultural auto-critique. If mass media were the problem, more media, intelligently applied, could be the cure. The dominance of the West was thus simultaneously acknowledged, criticized, and offered again as a possible overcoming of its previous limitations, provided the appropriate steps were taken.

McLuhan's broad schema provided little room for sensory histories that were discrepant with his teleological argument, except to relegate them as "old media." New media, in this view, provide the form of all media; they defined the sense ratio of older media, until supplanted by newer media. He did not consider how uneven technological impact might result in highly contingent forms of individual and collective action that were not predicted by his schema. Despite the global ambition of his theories, McLuhan's imagination was itself more parochial, and showed the limits of its Western origins.

Media as Totality?

The assumption that the media could create a level playing field where society can effectively be unified gained enormous prestige, and was promoted by U.S.-based think tanks and philanthropic foundations during the Cold War. A version of this assumption can be seen in Daniel Lerner's *The Passing of Traditional Society* (1958), where mass media, from print to radio, are believed to stimulate empathy for modernization, in an account that anticipates some elements of McLuhan. Such assumptions align media with a normative conception of state power, hence their importance for projects of planned development across the world.

Yet in contexts where the link between development and modernization was understood variously, the spread of technological communication was known to have unpredictable outcomes. Modern apparatuses of communication are argued to have transformed social interaction and its conception, from the hierarchical cosmologies of the medieval age to the anonymous, horizontal sodalities of print capitalism, in a rationalizing effect that is tacitly presumed to be ongoing. The underlying modernist conceit is that social interactions can be redrawn through the intervention of communications technology, and that there is, for all practical purposes, no "outside": the media and society, it is held, map congruently onto one another. The deeper underlying supposition is that of knowability, or predictability. The growth of mass media can in this understanding be likened to the spread of light across a terrain, leading to the ability to cognitively apprehend and potentially control what occurs within it.

And yet the growth of mass media in postcolonial societies has manifestly not had such an effect. The joint presence of older and more recent forms of fetishistic thinking, such as the alliance between devotional and ritualistic forms of worship with commodity culture, for example, or the ideals of modernization as initially embodied in the racial difference of colonial rulers and subsequently in postcolonial technocrats, points to the creation of new and more complex communicational environments. If the practice of vision in South Asia enfolded a tension between sight as a privileged access to divine truth and everyday life as profane, unimportant, or unreal, such understandings were consecrated in a visual culture that sharply distinguished between what was good to see and what ought not to be revealed.[5]

As a result, visibility does not always equate with acceptance or popularity, while invisibility may signal secrecy rather than irrelevance in such contexts.[6] Hence, I suggest, the decades-long silence in India attending the large-scale killings accompanying the partition of the subcontinent after 1947 (into India and Pakistan), and the unexpected rupture of this silence with the emergence in politics of the so-called angry Hindu in the late 1980s, or for that matter the 1984 massacre and rape of many hundreds of Sikhs (to name only one such episode) that still awaits its moment of public reckoning and redress. In these contexts of violence the notion that the truth will set you free, or that power can be transparent, do not have much traction. Such silences point to a complex and agonistic polity, the majority of whose members are excluded from the privileges of a civil society where their concerns can be aired and addressed.[7]

Some of the mediatic underpinnings of this complexity are indicated by the continued growth of the press even as television expands, and the relegation of the English language media to a minority share of the market even while it commands the highest advertising revenues. Vernacular media, meanwhile, increase their audiences at historically high rates. There exists here a multilingual market both at regional and national levels. English language media never question their status as the more global segment, however, thereby confirming their insularity vis-à-vis vernacular media, though the latter is the site where affective orders and social relations are being changed most rapidly and powerfully.[8]

New mass media are invariably accompanied by the utopian expectation that they can help re-imagine the world as unfettered and inclusive (Rajagopal, 2005). Radio, television, and digital media have each been accompanied by similar, heady expectations that are unlikely to be realized. After all, each medium enters a space already dense with pre-existing media forms and sedimented communicational practices that seek to define or domesticate new media rather than succumb to them. As a result, new media reactivate earlier media forms in unexpected ways, rather than erase or supplant them. The greater visibility of epic and mythological imagery successively with print, cinema, and television provides a convenient example of the way in which older image repertoires and symbol systems have been the vehicle for new communication technologies. For example, Indian cinema and television gave the appearance, temporarily, of bringing audiences together across a public that the state split into more and less modern parts, for the purpose of development. However, the same division could appear with its polarity reversed due to the experience of nationalist mobilization, in terms of less versus more culturally authentic parts. This reversible formation, which indicates both the dynamism and instability of cultural formation in postcolonial contexts such as South Asia, can be explained by the concept of a *split public*, wherein the provisions for the unification of the different components of the public are variously understood across its divisions. That is to say, *the expansion of the media did not result in greater social unity so much as in greater visibility for existing social divisions.*[9]

A postcolonial analytic of these emergent communication circuits and the synthetic forms they take can also make visible how such differences work across different domains in society. Such an argument challenges the Habermasian model of the public sphere where ideals of equality are realized in a model of communication based on the contract, while power differences are bracketed by the exercise of tact.[10] Such a model of communication is inadequate for addressing the deep divisions in postcolonial societies. Any adequate account of the postcolonial public sphere must accommodate not only rational-critical discourse but also contentious counter-discourse and political silences, acknowledging that *the protocols of agreement are not in fact shared.* In other words, publicity has to be understood as a site for asserting power, and for power to be visualized.

Postcolonial Visuality

Now, in the conventional account of modern society, power is invisible, contained in capabilities and in modes of discipline, in rules and institutions such as the bureaucracy and the market, rather than in persons, classes, or things. Such an account was made possible by making invisible those acts that in their very operation demonstrated power, for example, the punishment of criminals. One of the ways in which the present age understands itself as modern, we now know, is by relegating such activities out of sight to the public, and by making them secret.[11]

At the same time, however, modern modes of seeing presuppose a disembodied gaze, a view "from nowhere" that produces data whose validity does not depend on the person who sees. This is because the mechanisms of sight can be technologically reproduced in the absence of a physical observer. Seeing in modernity therefore has a distinct socio-technical character. It implies knowing what to see and what not to see, and absorbing the rules by which the prevailing threshold of visibility operates, that is, how they are socially prescribed and technically reproduced.

Where such rules of vision cannot be assumed to operate, the prevailing forms of power tend to be signaled more explicitly by concrete symbols, objects, persons, and rituals. They exist to be seen, and in the case of Hindu religious objects and persons, they are also, conventionally, bestowed with the capacity to see. Forms of vision in this context confirm who is seeing and who is seen, in what has been called an "embodied gaze" (Pinney, 2004). Rather than providing a view from nowhere, the embodied gaze validates existing rules of social space rather than disrupts them, because the sense of space is not empty, homogeneous, or infinite; rather, it corresponds to the presumption of a bounded, known universe.[12]

The contrast between these two ways of seeing could be read as the difference between, say, science and popular culture, or between secular and religious life. And the meeting of these different modes of perception could be described as an encounter of knowledgeable and naïve ways of seeing, but since this also reflects a social hierarchy, a more complete description should include the so-called naïve view of the powerful. I do not have the space to explore this problem in detail here, but clearly anticolonial nationalism sought to incorporate this difference through charismatic and culturalist forms of mobilization, while also offering a program for modern economic development.

Communication associated with the former became relegated in nationalist history to the popular level, or was accorded the status of a vanishing mediator, while the latter were understood to belong to official nationalism.[13] And in postcolonial society, while communicational circuits are initially largely top-down, for developmental policy implementation, for example, the growth of media, especially Indian language print and electronic media, introduces the possibility of bottom-up forms of communication on a hitherto unprecedented scale.

What postcolonial society brings to collective awareness is the existence of plural ways of seeing and a form of sovereignty that is not singular but divided. With the emergence of a visual regime that cuts across different media platforms, the battle for hegemony between different modes of perception is itself a public one, and any attempt to erect one form of seeing as dominant cannot be tacit, rendered invisible, or relegated to the corridors of power. The persistence of such contestations over both the content and the form of common knowledge, I suggest, ensure that the outcomes of postcolonial politics are unpredictable.

The Postcolonial Split Public

The category of the postcolonial remains relevant to mark the agonistic relationship with Western media forms, whose developmental narrative operates as the standard of measure against which the specificity of postcolonial media must be situated. The former are typically ordered on the model of technological developments of Euro-American provenance, such as print, radio, cinema, and television. The result is to relegate theory-generative phenomena outside the West to so many varieties of socio-technical imaginings, or iterations of media modularity, or as phenomena of interest to area specialists and intelligence experts at best. However, postcolonial modernity is inaugurated not only by submitting to the West but also, and crucially, by selectively resisting modernization (Rajagopal, 2009).

A well-known argument has it that, to forge unity across their internal divisions against colonial power, anticolonial nationalists established their claim to sovereignty in the cultural domain, and demarcated it as a distinct arena from that of the external world, where the superiority of colonial power was undeniable at least for the moment. This result of a nationalist compromise arrived at toward the end of the nineteenth century, we are told, endures into the postcolonial period.[14]

The great insight in this argument is the development of a bipartite rather than a unitary model of sovereignty in anticolonial nationalism. Such a model has effectively relegated religion and spirituality to the private realm and matters of political economy to the public realm. But each of these spaces is characterized by communicative acts that both reify and challenge a structural dichotomy between private and public life. As such, we could think of each of these realms as, in fact, a "public." And a communicative public is by definition something that is in a process of *becoming*, rather than a static element in a model.

The rules in these different publics ("religious" and "political") diverge, but presume each other. For example, colonial power claimed to be a modernizing influence but relied on force. Meanwhile indigenous society, with the growth of nationalism, claimed cultural authenticity as the real seat of legitimacy. This split public, held together by coercion as well as by consent, was one in which neither segment of the public was transparent to the other. Each believed that its claims trumped those of the other's, but the contest was not one that could be adjudicated in rational terms. Postcolonial development extended this dynamic, by virtue of the demands of modernization, with the difference that voters could now elect who would govern them. The idea of a split public grasps this process of productive misrecognition as a key dialectic shaping and reshaping these agonistic spaces (Rajagopal, 2001).

Spectacle, Commodity, and the Labor of Seeing

We have seen that the teleological thrust of most varieties of media studies order themselves by technology (e.g., print, radio, cinema, television). Below, I speculate on what media, both as perceptual ensemble, and as furthering market logics, that is, as both technology and commodity, might reveal about emergent postcolonial political forms.

A noteworthy critical argument that theorized the shift in the character of visuality in late capitalism is Guy Debord's *Society of the Spectacle*, a text that continues to resonate more than a half century after it was written. Debord argued that everyday life had dissolved into a series of spectacles that claimed to unify the world through their representation of it. The spectacle was an extension of the commodity, he wrote, and as such was an expression of the alienation of expressive from productive life and of capital's domination over living labor. However, the distinguishing feature of the society of the spectacle, as Debord defined it, was that the commodity had succeeded in completely colonizing social life, so that commodification was coterminous with the known world (Debord, 1995).

Debord's argument linked knowledge and power as they manifested in the domain of perception. The spectacle claimed a fullness of representation, offering a transparent window onto the world. What the spectacle made visible was real, and what was invisible in the spectacle was neither real nor salient. The power of the spectacle was in fact that of regulating perception, of distinguishing between what was worth seeing and what could be ignored. Where the logic of commodification had extended to every sphere of life, what was excluded from the spectacle becomes insignificant, in this argument.

Debord's argument embedded visual perception (which in the Renaissance conception of seeing, presumed agency as a component) with a fairly durable epistemic regime where the scope for anyone to intervene was limited at best.[15] This was because, according to Debord, extensive socio-technical apparatuses of communication already encoded the place of individual observers within them, and anticipated their response. Truth or accuracy of depiction were less relevant criteria of perception than the extent to which existing circuits of communication "recognized" what was sought to be circulated, and assisted in the propagation of those elements that enhanced capital accumulation and reinforced "the spectacle."

The Society of the Spectacle is a polemical rather than a dispassionate text. It presents an analysis whose totalizing force is more provocative than it is precise. It responded to a context, namely post–World War II Europe, which Debord saw as pacified by Americanization following the Allied victory and the ensuing Marshall Plan. In this sense it was an early critical response to media globalization from within the West.[16]

A significant portion of the world's population, however, lives outside a fully commoditized market economy, and relies for its sustenance on other sources such as land, or on non-market relations of charity, servitude, welfare, and so forth. This is not to say that they are therefore altogether insulated from the modern world, and from what Debord calls the spectacle. The extensive reach of government agencies through a range of service and surveillance functions (including welfare), and the profusion of both state and non-state communicational programs, for example in a country like India, from religious festivals and election propaganda to marketing campaigns, leave few if any untouched. In such contexts, images reproduced by various technological means have become familiar now, although more so in urban areas, from cell phones to the cinema, television and video, to say nothing of billboards, periodicals, and posters (Rajagopal, 2010, pp. 209–28).

The spectacle in such contexts is not so much an extension of commodity logic as it is a site where heterogeneous factors are brought together to enhance the marketability of the commodity. Here, the spectacle itself cannot adjudicate the contest between its constituent elements. The power of these elements vis-à-vis each other is decided externally, for example by frames of perception inculcated over time that separate what requires notice from what can be ignored, and through contingencies attending the image's passage across society. Just as the circulation of commodities emphasizes exchange value over use value, and abstract labor over real labor, the circulation of the commodity image appears to absorb the real labor of seeing into the abstraction of consumers whose viewing time generates value.[17] As we know, however, the reproduction of capital can be assumed, but that does not insulate it from the contingencies of history and politics, which in fact provide no guaranteed outcome.

It is helpful here to disarticulate issues of perception and its effects from the political economic context, which for Debord is the relatively undifferentiated milieu of late capitalism. These topics are conflated in Debord's expansive use of his concept of the spectacle.

Wolfgang Haug's concept of the commodity image suits the purpose, signaling the interconnections between perception and political economy, but allowing them to be considered separately. In his argument, the commodity image is designed to enhance the commodity in an expressive space that is contiguous with the economic but not reducible to it. While Haug posits a relation between commodity and image that is functional to capitalism, his concept of "commodity aesthetics" points to a cultural domain in which the rules of the economy apply, but not exclusively. Debord's argument about the spectacle aims to provide an account of late capitalism's dynamics as secured through its governing mode of perception. As such, the term serves not only to index this theory but also works as a concept that applies to different levels of abstraction, such as, specific images or scenes and ideological frames sutured together by visuality.[18] However, where images form an aspect of a still-emergent public sphere, where the meaning of "publicness" is uncertain, they may provide a domain where the rules about what it is to see, and what there is to see, are worked out.[19] In Marxian terms, the labor of seeing and the value placed on visuality in an emergent market economy are not apparent at the start, but are negotiated over time, in ways that it would be necessary to trace.

In that sense it is worth asking precisely what is foreclosed by Marx's understanding of commodity fetishism as the resignification of religious aura or affect. Marx argued, it will be recalled, that with the commodity taking on a life of its own, akin to a celestial being, human beings failed to realize that the economy was subject to human control, but instead granted it power over themselves.[20] Let us look, however, to a different context, where religious imagery and the commodity form together secure value for the product, as the commodity-image is itself interpellated into places of commerce and worship both. This is important because, in the subcontinent, religious imagery, commodity form, and public performance have long been allied.

The first images to be circulated on a large scale in South Asia were god pictures, in advertisements for goods and services such as in calendar art.[21] When there were protests against the use of religious imagery, these were dismissed on the grounds that trade would suffer without the use of such representations.[22] Such portraits did not document the external world, nor in themselves depict goods and services being sold. Rather, they appeared as religious fetishes with an auratic power that helped sell products. Such aura added value to the commodity but also served to mystify it and, by so doing, *visualized the commodity fetish.* The spread of the commodity economy might have been eroding communal forms of production, but the commodity image was at the same time able to call up its prehistory, and in the process media technologies themselves acquired a magical aspect.

What this meant was that these technologies might have been seen as modernizing, but they were also imagined as providing access to the past, and to valorize a history that, if not already gone, was being erased as its idea was summoned and broadcast anew. The rapid growth of television in India following the telecast of Hindu epics on Doordarshan is perhaps the most dramatic recent example of this tendency, followed as we know by widespread attacks on Muslims and the ascendancy of overt Hindu majoritarianism, albeit with internal contradictions (Rajagopal, 2001). Something very different from the Foucauldian account of the modern optical regime occurs here. Communicative modernity is announced in the South Asian context not by the withdrawal of violence but by its greater visibility.

In contrast to the kind of arguments Jonathan Crary has made about the emergence of both expert and popular practices that helped socialize the destabilization of visual perception, and the way professional and managerial discussions sought to contain the effects of this crisis, elsewhere such destabilization tends to reverberate upward and downward, yoking the existential together with the national-political (Crary, 2001). The most crucial distinction to be marked here is that the context Crary focuses on, the consolidation of Western nation-states and the governmentalization of their populations, is accomplished by the early twentieth century, at least in relation to the rest of the world, which remained under colonial rule during the period he focuses on (mid-nineteenth to early twentieth centuries). Elsewhere, changes in perception and in politics tend more directly to be read through each other. As a result, the crisis of the perceiving subject, in the different ways it is experienced outside the West, telescopes into more generalized crises of self-making and nation-building, that reverberate with and compound each other. It is in the partial depiction and propulsion of this turbulence that any regularities of postcolonial visual culture must be found.

REFERENCES

Appadurai, A. (2006). *Fear of small numbers: An essay on the geography of anger.* Durham, NC: Duke University Press.

Benson, R. (2009). Shaping the public sphere: Habermas and beyond. *American Sociologist* 40 (3): 175–97.

Brosius, C., Ramaswamy, S., & Saeed, Y., eds. (forthcoming). *Houseful? Image essays on South Asian popular culture from Tasveer Ghar.* New Delhi: Yoda Press.

Calhoun, C. J. (2007). *Nations matter: Culture, history, and the cosmopolitan dream.* London: Routledge.

Chakrabarty, D. (2007). The two histories of capital. *Provincializing Europe: Postcolonial thought and historical difference* (pp. 47–71). Princeton, NJ: Princeton University Press.

Chatterjee, P. (1986). *Nationalist thought and the colonial world: A derivative discourse.* Minneapolis: University of Minnesota Press.

Chatterjee, P. (2004). *The politics of the governed: Reflections on popular politics in most of the world.* New York: Columbia University Press.

Crary, J. (2001). *Suspensions of perception: Attention, spectacle, and modern culture.* Cambridge, MA: MIT Press.

Curtin, M. (2007). *Playing to the world's biggest audience: The globalization of Chinese film and TV.* Berkeley: University of California Press.

Dandekar, A., & Choudhury, C. (2010). *PESA, left-wing extremism and governance: Concerns and challenges in India's tribal districts.* Anand: Institute of Rural Management.

Debord, G. (1995). *The society of the spectacle.* New York: Zone Books.

Elias, N. (1978). *The civilizing process: Sociogenetic and psychogenetic investigations.* Oxford: Blackwell.

Foster, H. (1988). *Vision and visuality.* Seattle, WA: Bay Press.

Fox, E., & Waisbord, S. R. (2002). *Latin politics, global media.* Austin: University of Texas Press.

Freitag, S. B. (2007). South Asian ways of seeing, Muslim ways of knowing. *Indian Economic & Social History Review* 44 (3): 297–331.

Habermas, J. (1991). *The Structural transformation of the public sphere: An inquiry into a category of bourgeois society* (trans., T. Burger). Cambridge, MA: MIT Press.

Haug, W. F. (1986). *Critique of commodity aesthetics: Appearance, sexuality, and advertising in capitalist society.* Minneapolis: University of Minnesota Press.

Jain, K. (2007). *Gods in the bazaar: The economies of Indian calendar art.* Durham, NC: Duke University Press.

Latour, B. (1986). Visualization and cognition: Drawing things together. *Knowledge and Society: Studies in the Sociology of Culture, Past and Present* 6:1–40.

Lee, C.-C., ed. (2003). *Chinese media, global contexts.* London: Routledge.

Lerner, Daniel. (1958). *The passing of traditional society: Modernizing the Middle East.* Glencoe, IL: Free Press.

Masselos, J. (2006). A goddess for everyone: The mass production of divine images. In J. Menzies, ed., *Goddess divine energy* (pp. 147–87). Sydney: Art Gallery of New South Wales.

McLuhan, M. (1994). *Understanding media: The extensions of man.* Cambridge, MA: MIT Press.

Nelson, R. S. (2000). Descartes's cow and other domestications of the visual. In R. S. Nelson, ed., *Visuality before and beyond the Renaissance: Seeing as others saw* (pp. 1–21). New York: Cambridge University Press.

Pinney, C. (2004). *Photos of the gods: The printed image and political struggle in India.* London: Reaktion.

Rajagopal, A. (2001). *Politics after television: Hindu nationalism and the reshaping of the public in India.* Cambridge: Cambridge University Press.

Rajagopal, A. (2005). Imperceptible perceptions in our technological modernity. In C. Wendy & K. Thomas, eds., *Old media, new media* (pp. 275–85). New York: Routledge.

Rajagopal, A. (2008). Violence, publicity, and sovereignty. Retrieved from http://blogs.ssrc.org/tif/2008/12/15/violence-publicity-and-sovereignty.

Rajagopal, A. (2009). Beyond media therapy. *Television & New Media* 10 (1): 130–32.

Rajagopal, A. (2010). The strange light of postcolonial enlightenment: Mediatic form and publicity in India. In C. Siskin & W. Warner, eds., *This is enlightenment: An invitation in the form of an argument* (pp. 209–28). Chicago: University of Chicago Press.

Ramaswamy, S. (2010). *The goddess and the nation: Mapping Mother India.* Durham, NC: Duke University Press.

Ramnarayan, G. (2004). No easy answers, *The Hindu,* 5 September.

Report of the Bombay Chamber of Commerce for the year 1915. (1916). Bombay: Bombay Chamber of Commerce.

Servaes, J., ed. (2008). *Communication for development and social change.* Thousand Oaks, CA: Sage Publications.

Siegel, J. T. (1998). *A new criminal type in Jakarta: Counter-revolution today.* Durham, NC: Duke University Press.

van der Veer, P. (2010). The visible and the invisible in South Asia. In Meerten B. ter Borg & Jan Willem van Henten, eds., *Powers: Religion as a social and spiritual force* (pp. 103–15). New York: Fordham University Press.

Vasudevan, R. S. (2010). *The melodramatic public: Film form and spectatorship in Indian cinema.* Basingstoke: Palgrave Macmillan.

Vasudevan, R. S., Thomas, R., Majumdar, N., & Biswas, M. (2010). A vision for screen studies in South Asia. *BioScope: South Asian Screen Studies* 1 (1): 5–9.

Vieira, S., Martin, W. G., & Wallerstein, I. M. (1992). *How fast the wind? Southern Africa, 1975–2000.* Trenton, NJ: Africa World Press.

NOTES

1. The term "securocratic regime" is from Vieira, Martin, & Wallerstein (1992), p. 205. For a discussion of some of the cultural dynamics attendant on such a context, see Appadurai (2006).

2. On the Mumbai terror attacks, see Rajagopal (2008). For the most authoritative recent survey of the Maoist issue, see Dandekar & Choudhury (2010).

3. Hal Foster distinguishes vision from visuality: the former refers to the mechanism of sight and the datum of vision, the latter refers to its historical techniques and discursive determinations. See Foster (1988), p. ix.

4. On the most significant visual surveillance initiative in recent times, see "UIDAI Strategy Overview," Unique Identification Authority of India (UIDAI), Planning Commission, Government of India, April 2010.

5. The internal variety within and among South Asian ways of seeing is not as yet something about which a great deal has been written. For one of the few recent essays addressing the subject, exploring the question in relation to Muslims, see Freitag (2007).

6. For an argument about the pervasiveness of secrecy at the heart of publicity in relation to state-sponsored violence in Indonesia, see Siegel (1998).

7. See Chatterjee (2004). Chatterjee does not explore the relationship between civil and political society, and thus ignores the existence of the many forms of connection, including media circuits, that cut across the divide he argues for.

8. See in this connection the interview with the poet Arun Kolatkar in Ramnarayan (2004).

9. I have made this argument vis-à-vis television in Rajagopal (2001). For a relevant critical discussion, see Benson (2009).

10. Whereas the contractual agent engages in exchange out of interest, and is not personally modified by the act of exchange, the communicative act transforms the person engaging in discourse over time. Habermas responds to this problem by arguing that personally transforming communication is intimate and remains in the private sphere, unlike rational-critical communication (Habermas, 1991).

11. In this context, see van der Veer (2010). For a shift in the domain of etiquette corresponding to the new secrecy of punishment, see Norbert Elias on the growth of shame attending the display of hitherto "public" practices that began to be considered private in the early modern era (Elias, 1978).

12. Note that the difference between the claims of modernist vision and its uneven instantiation in the colonies is the outcome of the culturalization of colonial polities as well as of the resulting politicization of the culture concept. What I am describing here are practices that willy-nilly created the effect of a temporal and developmental divide between a society organized around a particular politics of vision and one that was fractured by diverse visual practices.

13. See Calhoun (2007) for an incisive analysis of the failures of nationalist universalism.

14. I refer to Partha Chatterjee's seminal argument, outlined in its initial version in Chatterjee (1986).

15. For an argument about the relevance of the Renaissance in making the conditions of modern visuality possible, see Nelson (2000), pp. 1–21.

16. For an important discussion of critical perspectives on media globalization and the question of development, see Servaes (2008).

17. See in this context Dipesh Chakrabarty's distinction between real and abstract labor in Chakrabarty (2007), pp. 47–71.

18. On the commodity image and commodity aesthetics, see Haug (1986), for example, p. 8.

19. Bruno Latour defines a new visual culture in terms of understanding "what it is to see, and what there is to see" (Latour, 1986).

20. Karl Marx, *Capital*, vol. 1, chap. 1, section 4, "The Fetishism of Commodities and the Secret Thereof." http://www.marxists.org/archive/marx/works/1867-c1/ch01.htm#S4. Accessed 6 October 2010.

21. See my essay, "The Commodity Image in the (Post) Colony," published in

2010 in tasveerghar.net, in Brosius, Ramaswamy, and Saeed (forthcoming). The appearance of religious imagery appears to be prior to that of non-religious imagery in advertising and packaging. See Masselos (2006), pp. 146–51.

22. See, e.g., "Use of Hindu Mythological Pictures as Designs for Trademarks," *Report of the Bombay Chamber of Commerce for the year 1915*, pp. 67–68. Also Masselos (2006), pp. 148–49.

Contributors

Editor

Chin-Chuan Lee is Chair Professor of Communication at the City University of Hong Kong, where he founded the Center for Communication Research (2005) and the Department of Media and Communication (2008). During his tenure at the University of Minnesota, he also established the China Times Center for Media and Social Studies (1989) and the U.S.-based Chinese Communication Association (1990). He won the B. Audrey Fisher Mentorship Award of the International Communication Association (ICA) in 2014. His books include *Media Imperialism Reconsidered: The Homogenizing of Television Culture* (1980); *Mass Media and Political Transition: Hong Kong's Press in China's Orbit* (1991; with Joseph Man Chan); *Global Media Spectacle: News War over Hong Kong* (2002; with Joseph Man Chan, Zhongdang Pan, and Clement So); *Communication, Public Opinion, and Globalization in Urban China* (with Francis Lap-fung Lee et al., 2013); *Chaoyue xifang baoquan* (Beyond Western Hegemony: Media and Chinese Modernity, 2004); *Wenren lunzheng* (Literati and the Press in Modern China, 2008); and *Baoren baoguo* (To Serve the Nation: Journalists as Prisms of Chinese Press History, 2013). The four volumes under his editorship have become part of the basic literature on Chinese media studies: *Voices of China: The Interplay of Politics and Journalism* (1990); *China's Media, Media's China* (1994); *Power, Money, and Media: Communication Patterns and Bureaucratic Control in Cultural China* (2000); *Chinese Media, Global Contexts* (2003).

Contributors

Rodney Benson is Associate Professor in the Department of Media, Culture, and Communication and an affiliated faculty member in the Department of Sociology at New York University. He has also been a visiting professor at universities in Denmark, Finland, France, Germany, and Norway. Benson is the author of *Shaping Immigration News: A French-American Comparison* (Cambridge, 2013) and of numerous articles on comparative media systems and field theory. He is the coauthor with Matthew Powers of *Public Media and Political Independence* (Free Press/Open Society, 2011) and co-editor with Erik Neveu of *Bourdieu and the Journalistic Field* (Polity, 2005; Chinese translation forthcoming 2015). His current research examines the logics of commercial, public, and civil society media ownership. Benson holds a PhD in sociology from the University of California–Berkeley.

Tsan-Kuo Chang is Professor in the Department of Media and Communication at the City University of Hong Kong. He earned his PhD from the University of Texas at Austin. He received the Outstanding Contributions Award from the International Communication Division of the Association for Education in Journalism and Mass Communication (AEJMC) in 2005. In addition to three books, his articles have appeared in such journals as *Communication Research, International Communication Gazette, International Journal of Press/Politics, International Journal of Public Opinion Research, Journal of Broadcasting & Electronic Media, Journal of Communication, Journal of Health Communication, Journalism & Mass Communication Quarterly, New Media & Society, Political Communication,* and *Public Opinion Quarterly.*

Michael Curtin is the Mellichamp Professor of Global Studies in the Department of Film and Media Studies at the University of California, Santa Barbara. He is also director of the Media Industries Project at the Carsey-Wolf Center. Curtin's books include *The American Television Industry* (2009); *Reorienting Global Communication: Indian and Chinese Media beyond Borders* (2010); and *Playing to the World's Biggest Audience: The Globalization of Chinese Film and TV* (2007). He is currently at work on *Media Capital: The Cultural Geography of Globalization.* With Paul McDonald, he is coeditor of the International Screen Industries book series for the British Film Institute and, with Louis Leung, he is coeditor of the *Chinese Journal of Communication.*

Peter Dahlgren is professor emeritus at the Department of Communication and Media, Lund University, Sweden. His work focuses on media and democracy, from the horizons of late modern social and cultural theory. More specifically, he often addresses the theme of democratic participation, in particular in relation to the digital media. Active in European academic networks, he has also been a visiting scholar at several universities in Europe and the United States. Along with journal articles and book chapters, his recent publications include *The Political Web* (Palgrave, 2013), *Media and Political Engagement* (Cambridge University Press, 2009), and the coedited volume *Young People, ICTs and Democracy* (Nordicom, 2010).

Elihu Katz is Trustee Professor of Communication at the Annenberg School for Communication at the University of Pennsylvania and emeritus professor of the Hebrew University of Jerusalem. His books include *The End of Television?* (with Paddy Scannell), *Media Events* (with Daniel Dayan), *The Export of Meaning* (with Tamar Liebes), and a fiftieth-anniversary edition of *Personal Influence* (with Paul Lazarsfeld). He holds honorary degrees from the Universities of Ghent, Haifa, Montreal, Paris, Rome (La Sapienza), Bucharest, Quebec, and Northwestern.

Paolo Mancini is Professor in the Department of Institution and Society at the University of Perugia, Italy, where he chairs the undergraduate program in Communication Sciences and the PhD program in Social and Political Theory and Research. He was a fellow at Harvard and Oxford. His major publications in English include *Politics, Media and Modern Democracy* (with David Swanson); *Comparing Media Systems: Three Models of Media and Politics* (with Daniel Hallin); and *Comparing Media Systems beyond the Western World* (coedited with Daniel Hallin).

Judy Polumbaum is Professor of Journalism and Mass Communication at the University of Iowa in Iowa City, and was a visiting professor at the City University of Hong Kong during 2012 and 2013. Her research interests include journalism and mass media in contemporary China, freedom of expression, and the interactions of media, sport, and culture. She has a background in newspaper reporting, magazine journalism, and photojournalism.

Arvind Rajagopal is Professor in the Department of Media, Culture and Communication, and affiliate faculty in the Departments of Sociology and Social and Cultural Analysis at NYU. He has published articles in scholarly journals. He is editor of *The Indian Public Sphere* (Oxford, 2009) and *Politics after Television* (monograph, Cambridge, 2001), and has three other volumes to his credit. *Politics after Television* won the Ananda Kentish

Coomaraswamy Prize from the Association of Asian Studies in 2003. He has won awards from the MacArthur and Rockefeller Foundations, and has also been a member of the Center for Advanced Study in the Behavioral Sciences at Stanford University. He is currently completing a book under contract with Duke University Press titled *After Decolonization: The Cultural Politics of Globalization in India.*

Jan Servaes is Chair Professor and head of the Department of Media and Communication at the City University of Hong Kong. He was UNESCO Chair in Communication for Sustainable Social Change at the University of Massachusetts at Amherst. He is the editor-in-chief of *Telematics and Informatics* (Elsevier), and editor of book series on "Communication for Development and Social Change" and "Communication, Globalization and Cultural Identity." He has undertaken research, development, and advisory work around the world and is known as the author of journal articles and books on such topics as international and development communication; ICT and media policies; intercultural communication and language; participation and social change; and human rights and conflict management. His latest book is *Sustainability, Participation, and Culture in Communication. Theory and Praxis* (Bristol: Intellect; Chicago: University of Chicago Press, 2012).

Colin Sparks is Chair Professor of Media Studies in the School of Communication at Hong Kong Baptist University. He is one of the founding editors of *Media, Culture and Society.* He has written widely on different aspects of the mass media. His most recent work is on the comparative study of media systems in societies undergoing rapid political and economic change. He holds a doctoral degree in Cultural Studies from the Centre for Contemporary Cultural Studies at the University of Birmingham, but his subsequent work is more easily located within the tradition of political economy.

Jaap van Ginneken was a longtime associate professor at the International School and Communication Science Department of the University of Amsterdam in The Netherlands. On the one hand, he published several studies on media images of other cultures, such as *Understanding Global News* (1998), about current events, and *Screening Difference* (2007), about Hollywood blockbusters. On the other hand, he wrote about rapid shifts in large groups, with *Crowds, Psychology and Politics* (1992), *Collective Behavior and Public Opinion* (2003), and *Mass Movements* (2007), *Mood Contagion* (2013), and *Political Hubris in Western Leaders* (2014). He is currently an independent speaker and writer based near Nice in southern France.

Silvio Waisbord is Professor in the School of Media and Public Affairs at George Washington University. He is the editor-in-chief of the *International Journal of Press/Politics*. His last book is *Reinventing Professionalism: News and Journalism in Global Perspective* (Polity, 2013).

Zhang Longxi is Chair Professor of Comparative Literature and Translation at the City University of Hong Kong. He is an elected foreign member of the Royal Swedish Academy of Letters, History and Antiquities, and also of Academia Europaea. He is an advisory editor of *New Literary History*. His books in English include *The Tao and the Logos: Literary Hermeneutics, East and West* (Duke, 1992); *Mighty Opposites: From Dichotomies to Differences in the Comparative Study of China* (Stanford, 1998); *Allegoresis: Reading Canonical Literature East and West* (Cornell, 2005); *Unexpected Affinities: Reading across Cultures* (Toronto, 2007); an edited volume, *The Concept of Humanity in an Age of Globalization* (V&R Unipress, 2012); and *From Comparison to World Literature* (forthcoming from SUNY Press, 2015).

Index

Actor-network theory, 267, 271–74, 275
  Cf. network-society theory (Castells), 271–72
  See also Latour, Bruno
Afghanistan, 11, 16, 162, 163
Africa, 12, 46, 56, 76, 136, 138, 142, 143, 146, 171, 183, 245
Al Jazeera, 44, 50, 172, 173, 262, 264–65
Appadurai, Arjun, 111, 272
Arab, Arabic, 12, 30, 31, 33, 36, 117, 139, 144, 172, 245, 262, 264
Area studies, 16, 195, 212
  Area-based studies, 16, 212
  And de-Westernization, 180–85
Asia, 4, 76, 78, 79, 80, 81, 96, 123, 124, 128, 136, 138, 143, 144, 147, 173, 203, 217, 220, 245, 246, 303
  East Asia, 38, 96, 100, 126, 128, 139, 143, 149, 245, 246, 255, 303
  South Asia, 19, 119, 120, 122, 149, 181, 303, 304, 307, 308, 313, 314
  Southeast Asia, 79, 94, 112, 120, 123, 149, 181, 303
Asian values, 203
Avatar, 23, 140–41
  Cultural reception, 151–52
  Themes, 141–50

BBC, 32, 36, 44, 129, 168, 172, 273, 284
Beijing, 61, 113, 124, 125, 127, 128, 129, 203, 216, 232, 303
Benjamin, Walter, 254
Benson, Rodney, 11, 17, 190, 227, 255, 259, 264
Berelson, Bernard, 7
Berger, Charles, 2, 225, 227
Blockbuster, 23, 33, 126, 129, 135, 136, 137, 138, 140, 141, 144, 150, 151, 152
  See also Hollywood films
Blumer, Herbert, 6
Bourdieu, Pierre, 16, 17, 69, 202, 210, 227, 228, 229, 238, 259, 262, 263, 264, 265, 266–67, 268, 270, 271, 272, 276
  See also Field theory; Imperialism of the universal
Brazil, 9, 18, 134, 160, 162, 167, 183, 212, 260, 261, 265, 287

Cameron, James, 140, 144, 145, 150, 151, 152
Canada, 76, 135, 168
Capitalism, 111, 114, 152, 306, 313
  And imperialism, 19, 21, 22–23, 216
  Late capitalism, 311, 313

Cardoso, F. H., 9, 211, 214
Carey, James, 209, 214
Case study, 79, 113, 138, 182, 185, 192, 194, 213–15, 219, 234, 236, 249, 260, 276
Castells, Manuel, 17, 112, 259, 267, 268–70, 271, 272, 275, 276, 277, 287
  See also Network society theory
Chaffee, Steven H., 2, 225, 226, 227
Chen, Yinque, 217–18
China, 12, 13, 14, 16, 17, 18, 21, 23, 50, 111, 124, 126, 129, 134, 150, 165, 166, 172, 183, 203, 217, 218, 227, 230, 231, 234, 237, 238
  China's media, 8, 127, 135, 139, 162, 210, 216, 231, 232, 235, 236, 245, 246, 247
  See also China Central Television; Xinhua News Agency
China Central Television (CCTV), 44, 125, 127, 172, 231, 232, 234
Chinese media/news studies, 220, 230–38
Civic cosmopolitanism
  Global civic engagement, 294–95
  Media connection, 292–93
  Mediapolis, 293–96, 297
  See also Cosmopolitanism
Civil society, 47, 78, 80, 188, 192, 260, 285–87, 288, 295, 307
  See also Global civil society
Civil society actors, 281, 282, 283, 285. 293, 295
Clash of civilizations, 11
Clientelism, 19, 76, 94, 102, 119, 216
CNN, 44, 92, 172, 260, 284
Cold War, 2, 3, 6, 7, 10, 11, 18, 30, 47, 70, 161, 181, 202, 204, 212, 305, 306
Colonialism, 32, 139, 146, 291
Communism, 9, 47, 98, 162, 202, 303
Comparative methodology, 4, 208, 213, 296–97
Comparative research (studies), 3, 4, 16, 17, 18, 38, 41, 60, 61, 67, 71,

75, 76, 77, 104, 188–92, 195, 207, 208, 210, 213, 214–17, 219, 226, 239, 250, 267, 297–97
  See also Hallin, Daniel, & Mancini, Paolo
Comparing Media Systems, 90, 91, 92, 93, 95, 106
Contrapuntal reading, 217
Cosmopolitan citizenship, 16, 68, 185, 186, 295
Cosmopolitan media studies, 185–87, 193–95
Cosmopolitan scholarship, 179, 185, 186, 188, 194, 195
Cosmopolitan spirit (outlook, ethic), 17, 24, 180, 220, 244, 247, 290
Cosmopolitanism, 17, 24, 180, 185, 197, 193, 244, 255, 281, 282, 283, 298
  De-Westernize media studies, 187–93
  Horizons, 288–89
  And international civic communication, 287–88
  One or many? 289–91
  Power dimension, 291–92
  See also Civic cosmopolitanism
Cross-cultural approach, 212–15
Cross-cultural comparison (experiences, meaning, dialogue, interpretation), 2, 4, 6, 7, 32, 36, 202, 206, 207, 208, 209, 216, 217, 219, 244, 246, 255
Cross-cultural encounter, 217–18
Cultural border-crossing, 4, 17, 218, 244
Cultural imperialism, 9, 11, 12, 19–20, 21–22, 25, 32, 33, 46, 47, 48–49, 51, 52, 53, 54, 57, 58, 61, 101, 157–61, 162–63, 169–70, 171, 174, 215, 284
  See also Imperialism; media imperialism; Schiller, Herbert I.
Cultural nationalism, 25, 212
Cultural studies, 10, 117, 160, 228, 291

Cultural values, 14, 18, 102, 244, 250
Curran, James, 45, 101, 178, 179, 202

Dallas, 32, 33, 44, 137, 138, 215
Deliberative democracy, 261, 274
Democracy, 1, 16, 17, 37, 61, 68, 76, 77,
    79, 80, 82, 95, 100, 102, 169, 183,
    203, 204, 213, 239, 258, 261, 276,
    285–86, 293, 294, 295
Democratization, 19, 61, 100, 102,
    304
Dependency perspectives, development
    of underdevelopment, dependent
    development, 8–10, 46, 54, 55, 56,
    211–12
    See also Keying of concepts
"Determination," Marxist theory of,
    21–22
Development communication, 7, 8, 66,
    67, 68, 70, 71–72, 204, 212
    See also Diffusion of innovations,
    Lerner, Daniel; Modernization
    theory, Rogers, Everett M.; Sch-
    ramm, Wilbur
De-westernize (or de-Westernization
    of) media/communication studies,
    1, 178, 179, 180, 181, 184, 185,
    187, 188, 192, 193, 194, 195, 202,
    227, 294
    See also Area studies
Diffusion of innovations, 4, 8, 30–31,
    34, 35, 72, 212
    Methodological critique of, 206–8
Disney, 22, 51, 136, 138, 141, 142, 143,
    146, 149, 151, 168

East-West conflict, 8–9
East-West dichotomy, 3, 183, 212,
    248–49, 250, 251, 255
Eastern Europe, 33, 38, 47, 75, 76, 94,
    96, 98, 99, 134
Egypt, 33, 119, 205
Empathy, 14, 30, 36, 38, 47, 71, 204–5,
    289, 306
    See also Lerner, Daniel
"End of history," 11, 202

Epistemology, 15, 80, 203, 209, 258,
    270
Ethnocentrism, 74, 253, 255, 265, 291
European representation of China,
    246–48
    Chinese rites controversy, 18, 248,
    250
    Jesuits vs. Catholics, 247–48
European Union (EU), 91, 169, 195,
    285
Export of meaning, 101
Export of meaning, 33, 44

Field theory, 17, 263–67, 275, 271, 275,
    276
    Field, 16, 227, 228, 238, 262,
    Fields of production, 16, 227, 264
    Habitus, 229, 266
    Symbolic capital, 264, 265
    See also Bourdieu, Pierre
Four Theories of the Press, 18, 66, 75–77,
    103
Fox News, 92
France, 44, 76, 158, 261, 263
Frank, A. G., 9, 20, 211
"Free market," 79, 99, 134, 172
Fukuyama, Francis, 11, 202, 203

Galtung, Johan, 42, 45, 48, 60
Gans, Herbert J., 104
Geertz, Clifford, 2, 4, 14, 80, 182, 209,
    213, 214, 229
Germany, 76, 135, 165, 171, 263
Giddens, Anthony, 228–29, 238
Global civil society, 285–86, 287, 288,
    295
Global communication, 1
Global studies, 110, 111, 117
Globalization, 10, 11, 22, 24, 35, 52, 53,
    54, 67, 68, 78, 79, 80, 82, 105, 111,
    134, 156, 161, 162, 178, 184, 186,
    193, 202, 203, 212, 237, 238, 284,
    288, 291, 295
    Alter-globalization, 281, 283, 285–
    88, 295, 297
    Anti-globalization, 11

Globalization (*continued*)
And cosmopolitan media studies,
192–95
Internet, 52, 192, 292, 295
Media globalization, 22, 110, 192,
312
See also Keying of concepts
Goffman, Erving, 42, 43, 52, 53
Great Britain. *See* United Kingdom
Grounded research (theory), 16, 238–
40
Gulf War, 34, 303

Habermas, Jürgen, 17, 101, 210, 259,
261, 262, 265, 268, 270, 272, 274,
276, 289, 293, 298, 308
See also Public sphere
Hall, Stuart, 3, 10, 20, 21–22
Hallin, Daniel, & Mancini, Paolo, 18,
37, 38, 75, 76, 77, 80, 90, 94, 184,
189, 190, 216, 264
Handbook of Communication, 2
Handbook of Communication Science, 2,
225
Harvey, David, 114, 165, 268, 290, 291
Hegemony, 5, 6, 12–14, 24, 47, 208,
217, 220, 232, 236, 265, 309
Hollywood films, 23, 32, 35, 109, 112,
116, 122, 124, 125, 126, 127, 129,
136, 140, 141, 147, 148, 150, 151,
152, 161, 162
Genres and stereotypes, 137–40,
141–50
Portrayal of Native Americans and
Africans, 143–44
See also *Avatar*; Blockbuster; Cam-
eron, James
Hong Kong, 19, 25, 112, 113, 116, 129
Media capital, 122–28
Huntington, Samuel, 102, 202, 203,
218
Hybridization, 95, 105, 106

Ideological, 5, 7, 14, 19, 20, 21, 74, 96,
97, 105, 126, 136, 140, 151, 183,
189, 211, 230

Ideological frame, 294, 313
Ideological hegemony (effects, con-
ditioning), 5, 20, 216, 232, 235
Ideological orientations, 139, 247
Ideological parameters (limits, spectrum), 75, 216, 286
Ideology, 10, 172, 202, 208, 212, 217,
230, 304, 305
Imperialism, 10, 32, 53, 54, 55, 56, 59,
102, 156–57, 161, 163–65, 167,
168, 171, 217
See also Cultural imperialism;
Keying of concepts; Media
imperialism
Imperialism of the universal (Bour-
dieu), 202, 210
India, 12, 21, 119, 120, 121, 122, 134,
135, 136, 162, 167, 170, 171, 183,
245, 302, 303, 304, 307, 312, 314
Indonesia, 183, 214, 215
Information and communication
technologies (ICTs), 68, 69, 77, 82,
282, 284, 287, 295
Innis, Harold, 18, 109
Instrumentalization, 93–95, 96, 106
Intercultural communication, 1, 2, 31,
80
International communication research
And cosmopolitanism, 281–98
Cultural relevance in, 201–20, 227–
29
Vs. domestic U.S. communication,
6–7
Imperial dimension of, 156–74
And life cycle of theories, 45–57
And nation-state, 1, 6, 24
New point of departure, 14–19
Origin and paradigm shift, 6–8
Paradigm testing, 57–59
And sociology of knowledge, 43–45
See also Keying of concepts; "West-
ern bias"
International public sphere, 260, 261
International Telecommunications
Union (ITU), 35
Internationalize (or internationalizing)

international communication, 1,
18, 24, 81, 110, 202, 212, 274, 275,
277
Justification, 1–6, 201–4, 218–20,
281–83
New point of departure, 14–19
Internet, 17, 37, 45, 47, 49, 51–52, 77,
92–93, 112, 114, 128, 135, 145,
173, 192, 207, 213, 235, 236, 267,
268, 269, 270, 271, 275, 284, 287,
292, 295, 303
Internet Corporation for Assigned
Names and Numbers (ICANN),
173
Invisible college, 206
Involution (Geertz), 2, 214–15
Iraq, 11, 146, 163
Ireland, 76, 135, 167
Israel, 5, 31, 32, 33, 152

Japan, 12, 21, 33, 44, 50, 127, 135, 160,
162, 167, 173, 263
Journalism, 23, 24, 77, 78, 81, 82, 95,
101, 102, 135, 172, 192, 202, 227,
228, 229, 233, 236, 265
See also Professional journalism, professionalization of journalism
Journalism culture, 103–6
See also Instrumentalization

Katz, Elihu, 23, 25, 44, 92, 215, 216,
276
Keying of concepts (modernization/
imperialism/dependency/global-
ization), 10, 56–59
Korea, 4, 38, 127, 160, 167, 212
Kuhn, Thomas, 42, 52, 57–58, 67,
251–52

Lasswell, Harold, 3, 6, 205
Latin America, 8, 9, 10, 20, 46, 70, 76,
78, 181, 211, 216, 217
Latour, Bruno, 17, 258, 259, 267, 268,
271, 272, 273, 274, 275, 276, 277
See also Actor-network theory
Law, John, 272

Lazarsfeld, Paul F., 3, 6, 7, 30, 37, 38,
41, 42, 43, 44, 54, 61
Lerner, Daniel, 2, 3, 7–8, 30, 36, 67–68
70, 71, 72–73, 208, 306
Methodological critique of, 204–6
See also Empathy
Liberalism, 11, 92, 202, 289
See also Neoliberalism, neoliberal
Life cycle of theories (Galtung), 42,
45–46
Limited effects of the media, 7, 37,
38
Lippmann, Walter, 3, 213
Local contexts, 109
Local experiences, 201
Local knowledge (Geertz), 4, 14, 80,
209

Marco Polo, 245–46
Market, 51, 61, 76, 91, 114, 116,
118, 119, 129, 156, 167, 216,
230, 232, 233, 247, 308, 311, 312,
313
See also "Free market"; Hollywood
films; Media market
Marketing (campaign, research), 70, 74,
91, 114, 118, 150, 152, 208, 269,
270, 312
Marketization, 61, 216
Marketplace of ideas, 44, 105
"Marxism without final guarantees,"
21–22
Mead, George Herbert, 6
Media capital, 19
Defined, 113–14
Hong Kong, 122–28
Key principles, 113–17
Mumbai, 119–22
Vs. political capital, 19, 21, 96,
119
Media education, 81–82
Media events, 33, 36, 37, 192, 234
Media imperialism, 29, 44, 50, 110,
117, 158
See also Cultural imperialism; Impe-
rialism

Media market, 18, 22, 23, 58, 74, 78,
    92, 105, 112, 121–28, 150, 157,
    160, 168, 169, 171, 234, 303, 307
    See also Hollywood films; Market
Media production, 116, 161, 225, 227,
    235, 236, 238, 297
    Theorized, 228–30
Media studies, 6, 16, 24, 36, 60, 102,
    104, 109, 178, 181, 183, 184, 185,
    193, 202, 203, 213, 267, 272, 275,
    284, 287
    U.S. dominance and de-
    Westernization, 1, 3, 4, 54, 76, 93,
    179, 180
    See also Cosmopolitan media
    studies
Media systems, 8, 18, 38, 47, 50, 75, 77,
    80, 82, 91, 92, 110, 178, 180, 182,
    184, 185, 186, 188, 189, 190, 191,
    193, 216
Mediation (Williams), 21
Merton, Robert K., 6, 7, 38, 43, 212
Methodology, 4, 9, 203, 209, 211, 213,
    214, 217, 219, 283
Mexico, 160, 167, 270
Middle East, 30, 44, 67, 76, 136, 138,
    146, 172, 181, 183, 204, 205, 206,
    208
Mills, C. Wright, 3, 210
MIT, 7, 8, 30, 31
Modernization, 8, 9, 11, 47, 55, 56, 69,
    71, 72, 284, 310
Modernization theory, 7, 8, 9, 11, 14,
    46, 47, 68, 69, 202, 204, 206, 210,
    211
    Critical assessment, 72–75
    See also Cold War; Development
    communication; Diffusion of
    innovations; Keying of concepts;
    Lerner, Daniel; Rogers, Everett
    M.; Schramm, Wilbur
Murdoch, Rupert, 92, 152

Narcotizing dysfunction, 38
National culture, 114, 116, 159, 160,
    162, 170, 234, 237

Nationalism, 25, 44, 49, 50, 51, 184,
    212, 303, 309, 310
Nation-state, 35, 44, 50, 52, 109, 113,
    194, 247, 260, 282, 285, 302, 314
    Nature of, 98–101
    Relevance to international commu-
    nication, 1, 6, 24
Neoliberal, neoliberalism, 10, 11, 212,
    286, 296
    See also Liberalism
Network, 17, 24, 30, 36, 49, 92, 115,
    119, 120, 124, 145, 236, 259, 260,
    268, 269, 270, 272, 274, 275, 285,
    286, 296
    Academic/professional network, 190,
    191, 193, 194, 195
    Global/transnational network, 19,
    52, 57, 276
    See also Social networks
Network society theory, 11, 52, 57, 61,
    268–70, 274, 275, 276
    Cf. Actor-network theory (Latour),
    271–72
    See also Castells, Manuel
New institutionalism, 239
New media, 19, 36, 132, 184, 191, 236,
    270, 273, 306, 307
New World Information and Commu-
    nication Order (NWICO), 9, 47,
    161, 171
New York Times, 51, 145, 146, 150, 151,
    152, 260
News Corporation, 22, 152, 168
Normative theory (standard, vision,
    stance), 16, 17, 75, 76, 77–78, 91,
    178, 185, 261, 267, 275, 282, 285,
    288, 292, 293, 295, 298, 306

Orientalism, 138, 217

Paradigm, 10, 13, 46, 67, 68, 69, 77,
    181, 203
    Dominant paradigm, 46, 204–8
    Paradigm shift, 6–12
    Paradigm testing, 57–59, 217, 251–
    52, 281, 284

Park, Robert, 6
Parochialism, 2, 18, 24, 178, 202, 220, 244, 253
Party-market corporatism, 216
Party-press parallelism, 85, 191
Passing of Traditional Society, 7, 30, 104, 306
Pax Americana, 4, 69, 162
Peters, Bernhard, 17, 259, 260
Phenomenology, 14
  And local knowledge, thick description, 209
  Phenomenological methodology (approach, etc.), 203, 208–11, 213, 219
  Vs. positivism, 209, 213–15
Polarized-pluralist model, 98, 106
  And instrumentalization, 93–95
  Case of Thailand, 79–80
Political economy, 24, 117, 159, 165, 264, 268, 291, 310
  Vs. audience decoding, audience reception, 22–23, 151–52, 216, 313
  Vs. cultural studies, 21–22, 117
Political parallelism, 18, 95–98, 99
Pool, Ithiel de sola, 2, 7, 8
Populism, 184, 187, 193
Positivism, 73, 209, 226, 298
Positivistic methodology (perspective, approach), 4, 8, 16, 67, 73, 203, 209, 211, 213
Post–Cold War, 10, 202, 303
Post-colonial perspective, 19, 217, 276, 291, 292
Post-colonial split public, 310–11
Post-colonial visuality, 308–10
Post-colonialism, 291–92
Post-Communist, 1, 76
Pragmatism, 6, 230
Production of knowledge, 42, 53, 57, 60, 180, 181
Professional journalism, professionalization of journalism (news, media), 15, 18, 19, 76, 77, 90, 91, 93, 94, 95, 103, 105–6, 188, 232, 233
  Education, 81, 93, 101, 188

Ideals, culture, identity, 101, 188
Models, 90, 93, 106
Standards, rules, and conduct, 82, 105, 172
Values, ideology, 234, 235
Public opinion, 30, 100, 214, 232, 233, 234, 286
Public sphere, 17, 24, 36, 82, 92, 101, 210, 259–62, 274, 276, 286, 287, 293, 308, 313
  Center-periphery model, 261, 272
  Communicative action, 261, 275
  See also Habermas, Jürgen
Pye, Lucian W., 7, 8

Ranke, Leopold von, 211
Reflexivity, 14, 17, 266, 275, 294
Relativism, 252, 275, 291
Replication, 8, 226
  Vs. cross-cultural comparison, 207–8
Ricci, Matteo, 246, 248
Riesman, David, 30, 36, 38
Rogers, Everett M., 8, 72, 204, 206–8
Russia, 18, 21, 44, 50, 94, 165, 183

Said, Edward W., 10, 11, 20, 24, 203, 217, 218
  See also Contrapuntal reading; Orientalism
Schiller, Herbert I., 9, 20, 30, 47–50, 101, 157, 158–59, 161, 163, 166, 171
  See also Cultural imperialism
Schramm, Wilbur, 2–3, 8, 18, 70–71, 75, 103, 204, 225
Serra, Sonia, 260, 261
Shanghai, 113, 123, 126, 210, 216
Silverstone, Roger, 276, 292–95
Singapore, 4, 113, 123, 125, 128
Smelser, Neil J., 208, 213
Social change, 68, 94, 205, 230
Social movement, 31, 191, 269, 270, 283, 286, 296
Social networks, 78, 93, 116, 231, 267, 270
Sociological imagination, 3, 24, 210

Sociology of knowledge, 7, 42, 43, 60
Soft power, 11, 113, 128, 129, 157
Sony, 22, 136
South Africa, 18, 183
Soviet Union, 8, 47, 76, 134, 165, 171
Star Wars, 139, 140, 146, 151
Structural-functionalism, 6
Structuration (Giddens), 16, 228, 229, 238
Structure of feelings (Williams), 209
Structure of Scientific Revolution, 57, 252
Symbolic interactionism, 6

Taiwan, 94, 123, 125, 127, 135, 166, 173, 212
Terror, terrorist, terrorism, 16, 191, 207, 274, 285, 303
Thatcherism, 10, 22
Thick description (Geertz), 182, 209, 213, 214
Third World, 2, 3, 7, 8, 9, 10, 13, 20, 25, 32, 67, 68, 74, 205, 208, 211, 217, 261
Time Warner, 22, 136
Tocqueville, Alexis de, 213
Translation and cross-cultural understanding, 17, 35, 38, 135, 245, 251–55
Tunstall, Jeremy, 3, 44, 48–51, 157, 160
Turner, Fred, 268, 273

UNESCO, 8, 9, 134, 159, 161, 265
United Kingdom, Great Britain, 10, 32, 76, 90, 135, 158, 160, 164, 170, 185, 211
United Nations, 69, 134, 260, 285
United States, 3, 13, 19, 38, 49, 61, 136, 144, 152, 159, 169, 172, 173, 179, 181, 185, 190, 214, 261, 263
Cold War, 2, 6, 9, 11, 70, 165, 204
Media exports, 22, 48, 127, 135, 136, 150, 157, 162
Media studies, 179, 185, 190, 194, 195, 203, 205, 206, 284
U.S. media, 19, 20, 22, 48, 76, 90, 95, 167–68, 188, 192
World hegemon, imperial power, 6, 11, 158, 162, 163, 164, 165, 166, 170, 171, 202
U.S. foreign policy, 6, 70

Viacom, 22, 16

Wang, Guowei, 217–18
Washington Consensus, 61, 202
Weber, Max, 9, 163, 203, 209, 210, 213–14, 262, 264
Weberian-phenomenological approach, 208–11
West vs. non-West dichotomy. *See* East-West dichotomy
Western bias, 2, 7–8, 66, 67, 102, 276
Historical context, 69–75
"Journalism culture" as shortcut to avoid, 103–6
See Lerner, Daniel; Modernization theory; Rogers, Everett M.; Schramm, Wilbur
Williams, Raymond, 10, 21, 209, 215, 217
"Window Shopping," 30, 36, 38

Xinhua News Agency, 44, 172, 233

Printed and bound by CPI Group (UK) Ltd, Croydon, CR0 4YY

09/06/2025

14686091-0003